Guyana

Public Sector Review

The World Bank
Washington, D.C.

Copyright © 1993
The International Bank for Reconstruction
and Development/THE WORLD BANK
1818 H Street, N.W.
Washington, D.C. 20433, U.S.A.

World Bank Country Studies are among the many reports originally prepared for internal use as part of the continuing analysis by the Bank of the economic and related conditions of its developing member countries and of its dialogues with the governments. Some of the reports are published in this series with the least possible delay for the use of governments and the academic, business and financial, and development communities. The typescript of this paper therefore has not been prepared in accordance with the procedures appropriate to formal printed texts, and the World Bank accepts no responsibility for errors.

The World Bank does not guarantee the accuracy of the data included in this publication and accepts no responsibility whatsoever for any consequence of their use. Any maps that accompany the text have been prepared solely for the convenience of readers; the designations and presentation of material in them do not imply the expression of any opinion whatsoever on the part of the World Bank, its affiliates, or its Board or member countries concerning the legal status of any country, territory, city, or area or of the authorities thereof or concerning the delimitation of its boundaries or its national affiliation.

The material in this publication is copyrighted. Requests for permission to reproduce portions of it should be sent to the Office of the Publisher at the address shown in the copyright notice above. The World Bank encourages dissemination of its work and will normally give permission promptly and, when the reproduction is for noncommercial purposes, without asking a fee. Permission to copy portions for classroom use is granted through the Copyright Clearance Center, 27 Congress Street, Salem, Massachusetts 01970, U.S.A.

The complete backlist of publications from the World Bank is shown in the annual *Index of Publications*, which contains an alphabetical title list (with full ordering information) and indexes of subjects, authors, and countries and regions. The latest edition is available free of charge from the Distribution Unit, Office of the Publisher, The World Bank, 1818 H Street, N.W., Washington, D.C. 20433, U.S.A., or from Publications, The World Bank, 66, avenue d'Iéna, 75116 Paris, France.

ISSN: 0253-2123

Library of Congress Cataloging-in-Publication Data

Guyana : public sector review / [produced under the general direction
    of Jose Sokol.].
        p.   cm. — (World Bank country study)
    ISBN 0-8213-2645-7
    1. Privatization—Guyana. 2. Guyana—Economic policy.
3. Structural adjustment (Economic policy)—Guyana. 4. Finance,
Public—Guyana.   I. Sokol, José B.   II. International Bank for
Reconstruction and Development.   III. Series.
HD4115.3.G893   1993
338.9881—dc20   93-37862
                                                                CIP

ACRONYMS AND ABBREVIATIONS

ATC	Air Traffic Control
BERMINE	Berbice Mining Corporation
BIDCO	Bauxite Industry Development Company Ltd.
BoG	Bank of Guyana
CAD	Civil Aviation Directorate
CARICOM	Caribbean Community
CDB	Caribbean Development Bank
CET	Common External Tariff
CGCED	Caribbean Group for Cooperation in Economic Development
CIDA	Canadian International Development Agency
CFR	Crash Fire Rescue Services
CTPU	Central Transportation Planning Unit
COFA	Cooperative Financial Institutions Agency
D&I	Drainage and Irrigation
DIEC	Department of International Economic Cooperation
DME	Distance Measuring Equipment
dwt	deadweight
EC	European Community
ERP	Economic Recovery Program
FAA	US Federal Aviation Administration
GDP	Gross Domestic Product
GEC	Guyana Electric Corporation
GCE	General Certificate of Education
GNEC	Guyana National Engineering Corporation
GNFS	Goods and Non-factor Services
GNP	Gross National Product
GNSC	Guyana National Shipping Corporation
GOG	Government of Guyana
grt	gross registered tonnage
GS&WC	Georgetown Sewerage and Water Commissioner
GTT	Guyana Telephone and Telegraph
GUYMINE	Guyana National Bauxite Company
GUYSUCO	Guyana Sugar Cane Corporation
GUYWA	Guyana Water Authority
HF	High Frequency
IATA	International Air Transport Association
ICAO	International Civil Aviation Organization
IDA	International Development Agency
IDB	Inter-American Development Bank
ILS	Instrument Landing System
IMF	International Monetary Fund
IRP	Intra Regional Payment Arrangements
LINMINE	Linden Mining Corporation
MET	Meteorological Services
MIGD	Million Imperial Gallons Per Day
MOPWCRD	Ministry of Public Works, Communications and Regional Development
NDB	Non-Directional Beacon
NIS	National Insurance Scheme
PAP	Pulbic Administration Project
PCS	Public Corporations Secretariat
PFP	Policy Framework Paper

ACRONYMS AND ABBREVIATIONS
(continued)

PPF	Project Preparation Facility
PSIP	Public Sector Investment Program
PSM	Public Sector Management
RD	Roads Division
RDC	Regional Democratic Council
RV	Ratable Values
RWD	Regional Water Division
SILWFC	Sugar Industry Labor Welfare Committee
SIMAP	Social Impact Amelioration Program
SPS	State Planning Secretariat
teu	twenty foot equivalent units (containers)
THD	Transport and Harbors Department
UNDP	United Nations Development Program
USAID	US Agency for International Development
VHR	Very High Frequency
VOR	Very High Frequency Omni-directional Range
vpd	vehicles per day
WB	World Bank

This report is based on the work of a World Bank mission to Guyana in December, 1992, supported by BDD, CIDA and the EC. The mission benefited greatly from the extensive support provided by the State Planning Secretariat in Guyana. Mission participants were Axel Peuker (task manager), Rosaria Troia (PSIP), Jos Verbeek (RMSMX), Richard Moore (public administration), Monica Fidel (public administration), Nizar Jetha (resource mobilization), Henry de Greef (tax administration), Keith Herbert (customs administration), Prince Taylor-Lewis (resource allocation), Martin Greeley (agriculture), Olaf van Duin (sea defenses), Pauline Kehoe (transport), Tom Lauga (coastal and river transport), Emmanuel Njomo (water) and Carolyn Winter (social sectors). The report was produced under the general direction of Jose Sokol. Laura Bishop provided invaluable secretarial assistance.

CURRENCY EQUIVALENTS

Average exchange rates prevailing during recent
years, Guyanese dollars (G$) per US$1.00,
period average:

Year	Rate
1988	10.00
1989	27.16
1990	39.53
1991	111.80
1992	125.50

FISCAL YEAR

January 1 - December 31

TABLES

Totals in tables do not always equal the sum of their components because of
rounding.

GUYANA: PUBLIC SECTOR REVIEW

CONTENTS

MAPS

Summary and Policy Agenda

Guyana has abundant natural resources. Yet its per capita gross national product (GNP), $290 in 1991, is the lowest in the western hemisphere. This is in large part a direct consequence of the increasingly dominant role that the state played in the economy after independence. All major economic activities were subject to state intervention, either directly through state ownership, or indirectly through price, credit, and foreign exchange controls. Private initiative was discouraged. These policies resulted in a rapid decline in output in the 1980s, the exodus of many of the better-educated and more highly skilled workers, and severe deterioration in the economic and social infrastructure and the provision of public services.

In light of this experience, the previous Government embarked on a medium-term Economic Recovery Program (ERP) in mid-1988. The program consisted of a set of far-reaching adjustment measures and structural reforms to transform Guyana's state-dominated economy into a market-oriented one. Fiscal performance was improved considerably through expenditure restraint and tax reforms; the exchange rate and trade regimes were liberalized; and the incentive framework for the private sector was improved substantially.

The current Government has set out its policy agenda in the 1992-94 Policy Framework Paper. The paper expresses the Government's strong commitment to the fundamental principles of the ERP, including the pursuit of a sound macroeconomic framework and of market-oriented sectoral policies. At the same time, it attaches the highest priority to human resource development and poverty reduction efforts.

Despite the progress achieved under the ERP, however, the legacy of more than 20 years of economic mismanagement remains a heavy burden for Guyana. And the tasks facing the current Government may well be more difficult to accomplish than those of the first phase of the ERP. The Government not only needs to consolidate the macroeconomic and incentive framework in support of private-sector-led growth. It also needs to initiate a comprehensive public sector reform to reflect the changing role of the state under the ERP and to rehabilitate the country's basic economic and social infrastructure. Only if the Government succeeds in all these areas will Guyana experience the economic growth necessary to raise the population's living standards and substantially reduce poverty over the coming decade. In this context, the Government faces three major challenges:

▲ To reduce the scope of and reorient public sector activities, and sharply reduce the public sector's control over the country's economic resources. The public sector, still involved in direct productive activities and heavily dominating social services, is overextended. Its severe financial constraints prevent it from adequately fulfilling its core responsibilities in managing its affairs and providing a base for private sector and human resource development.

▲ To meet the country's immediate investment needs, which far exceed its financing and institutional absorptive capacity, after a long period of deterioration in the economic and social infrastructure. This implies that the country needs to both attract new commitments and use limited resources available more effectively.

▲ To service its huge debt overhang—about $1.8 billion (675 percent of Guyana's gross domestic product, or GDP) at end-1992—which is at the core of the country's financial constraints. Guyana will continue to require substantial inflows of foreign capital to finance its public sector investment program (PSIP), to meet its debt service obligations, and to provide the foreign exchange needed to sustain import levels consistent with the projected economic growth. A large part of these capital requirements will have to be met through additional donor assistance, including further debt relief.

In view of these challenges, the purpose of this report is to examine the role of the public sector and to identify priority areas where the Government should focus its limited resources to address Guyana's key development issues within the framework of the ERP. The report also assesses the need for further external assistance and debt relief to achieve external viability and sustainable growth. The organization of the report reflects the major tasks facing the Government:

▲ To maintain a sound macroeconomic framework.
▲ To improve public sector management and administration.
▲ To define sector strategies and expenditures.

The central importance of an increased role for the private sector in Guyana's development is a theme that runs throughout the report. A parallel report, *Guyana: Private Sector Development* (Report no. 11705, 1993), addresses the issue in greater detail and should be read in conjunction with the *Public Sector Review*.

Macroeconomic framework

Guyana's macroeconomic performance following independence was dismal: real GDP growth amounted to only 0.4 percent a year on average during 1966-89, the lowest growth rate in the Commonwealth Caribbean. The Government had borrowed excessively and was unable to meet its debt service obligations. By end-1988, the public sector (including the Bank of Guyana) had accumulated external arrears of $1,031 million on its external debt, which was $1,760 million. Following the introduction under the ERP

of far-reaching adjustment measures and structural reforms in incentive policies, fiscal and monetary policies, public sector policies, and sectoral policies, economic activity began to recover and real GDP increased by 6 percent in 1991. In 1992, the recovery continued, with real GDP increasing by 7.5 percent, and inflation declining drastically, from 82 percent in 1991 to 14 percent (table 1).

Guyana's resource balance improved significantly in recent years, from a deficit of 21 percent of GDP in 1990 to a surplus of 3 percent of GDP in 1992. This reflects mainly the recovery in Guyana's main traditional exports, sugar and rice, which benefit from preferential markets. In the future, export growth will have to come from more diversified sources. To diversity its exports, Guyana will need to further improve its international competitiveness. The depreciation of the real exchange rate following the exchange rate liberalization has already contributed to this end. But Guyana will also have to move quickly toward free trade to improve its competitiveness and its incentive framework for export-led growth. This is particularly important for Guyana because of the steps already taken by its Latin and Central American neighbors. Most have not only removed most quantitative restrictions, but narrowed their tariff range to 5 to 20 percent, with an average tariff of about 15 percent.

The key objectives of the current Government's macroeconomic policy agenda are described in the recently approved 1992-94 Policy Framework Paper and reiterated in the 1993 budget speech. The main reforms of incentive and financial sector policies to advance the adjustment process include the following:

▲ Deepening the cambio (private foreign exchange) market
▲ Continuing trade liberalization, including adopting the revised Common External Tariff (CET), with a range of 5 to 20 percent, on a "fast track" as agreed with the Caribbean Community (CARICOM)

▲ Improving monetary policies by strengthening the role of the central bank and shifting to more flexible monetary instruments

▲ Increasing efficiency in the financial sector by encouraging new private entrants into the financial sector, and by improving regulations and supervision.

Public sector finances and reform

Public sector finances continue to be under great stress. Greater control of noninterest expenditures and increases in revenues in the course of the adjustment process led to a substantial improvement in the primary current account balance, from 16 percent of GDP in 1988 to an estimated 32 percent of GDP in 1992. But the net domestic borrowing requirements of the public sector, including the Bank of Guyana, remained at about 26 percent of GDP in 1991 and 1992 (table 2). These domestic borrowing requirements reflect mainly the increase in the debt service burden in local currency to about 40 percent of GDP during 1991-92 on account of the depreciation of the nominal exchange rate.

Further improvement of public sector finances should be pursued in the context of a comprehensive public sector reform, including privatization, strengthening public sector administration, enhancing resource mobilization, and improving the efficiency of resource allocation.

The key constraint to efficient public administration is the deterioration in the quality of the public service. To address this issue, the Government will need to provide wage incentives to fill vacancies for higher-level technical positions while reducing labor redundancies, especially at lower levels. To enhance resource mobilization, the Government needs to strengthen tax and customs administration and to widen the tax base by eliminating exemptions. While the share of revenues in GDP appears high (50 percent of GDP in 1992, due in part to the underestimation of GDP), the revenue comes from a rather narrow tax base. For example, only 2,000 companies, 18,000 self-employed individuals, and 30,000 employees are assessed for income taxes. More important, most of the assessed firms are granted

Table 1. Selected macroeconomic indicators, 1980–92

(percent)

	1980-88	1989	1990	Est. 1991	Prel. 1992
Average growth rates					
Real GDP (factor cost)	–2.9	–3.3	–2.5	6.0	7.5
Real exports (goods and nonfactor services)	–5.7	–0.9	–8.8	17.5	28.0
Real imports (goods and nonfactor services)	–8.0	–5.5	2.8	–2.5	18.4
Urban consumer prices (end-period)	19.7	104.7	75.9	81.5	14.2
Shares in GDP					
Consumption	83.6	79.4	79.5	76.4	62.9
Gross domestic investment	29.5	29.5	41.6	41.6	31.7
Gross domestic savings	16.4	20.6	20.5	23.6	37.1
Resource Balance	–13.2	–9.7	–21.1	–18.0	2.6
Exports (goods and nonfactor services)	58.8	90.4	83.6	122.4	132.1
Imports (goods and nonfactor services)	72.0	100.2	104.6	140.4	129.5
External current account	–25.7	–43.2	–56.4	–56.1	–29.8
External debt (outstanding and disbursed)	147.9	806.2	743.9	856.9	675.5
Scheduled debt service	54.8	106.4	83.8	68.6	50.9

Source: Main report.

some form of concession for company taxes, consumption taxes, and import duties.

To help finance essential public services, such as water and electricity, cost-recovery measures need to be strengthened. In the medium term, enhanced user charges could yield an additional $28 million a year, equivalent to about 10 percent of 1992 GDP. Reductions in expenditures on goods and services, combined with a weak budget process, have been so severe as to impair the functioning of Government. The provision for operations and maintenance expenditures, in particular, is insufficient and needs to be reassessed. Nonetheless, the continuation of transfer payments to the Guyana Electricity Company (GEC) and significant contributions to a large number of organizations without assessment of their benefits indicate that the Government's limited resources need to be used more efficiently. To this end, the Government will also need to improve the budget and expenditure control processes, and establish financial management systems.

Privatization

The state continues to control a wide variety of economic activities through its 30 nonfinancial public enterprises and its financial holdings. Years of state ownership and inefficient management have left these entities in extremely poor condition. To rehabilitate them will require investments of hundreds of millions of dollars that are not at the Government's disposal. Without comprehensive privatization, these enterprises will increasingly become an impediment to the successful continuation of the ERP. The current Government has committed itself to continuing the process of privatization. It is essential that its privatization strategy be comprehensive to improve efficiency, generate savings, and further enhance the role of the private sector in the economy. It should also be rapidly implemented to avoid a deterioration of public enterprises' performance on account of their uncertain status and lack of capital, and to reduce uncertainty among interested private investors. At the same time, care should be taken to ensure that the procedures adopted generate confidence in the program.

The three most important public enterprises are GUYSUCO (sugar), LINMINE and BERMINE (bauxite), and GEC (power). Privatization of sugar and bauxite operations should begin within two years in the context of the donor-financed rehabilitation projects. The energy sector should be opened immediately to private investment. In particular, the GEC should be operated under a private management contract, competing private energy generation should be encouraged, and transmission and distribution functions should be handed over to the private sector. All other public enterprises should be offered for sale within a year. In addition to its nonfinancial public enterprises, the Government needs to divest its financial sector holdings. In both cases, however, privatization needs to be accompanied by the

Table 2. Summary of public sector operations, 1987–92

(percentage of GDP)

	1987	1988	1989	1990	Est. 1991	Prel. 1992
Primary account balance	27.1	15.5	18.1	16.9	27.9	32.2
Current account balance	−8.5	−15.7	−25.6	−28.7	−20.8	−10.9
Capital expenditure	−28.4	−18.2	−25.6	−36.8	−23.9	−23.1
Overall balance after grants	−34.0	−32.5	−47.9	−58.2	−32.8	−28.4
Net domestic borrowing requirements	−2.2	15.0	12.3	17.0	25.6	25.7

Note: Includes nonfinancial public sector and the Bank of Guyana.

Source: Main report.

establishment of an appropriate regulatory framework. Such a comprehensive privatization program is projected to yield about $10 million a year during 1993-2001.

Public sector investment program

To support the Government's development strategy, a medium-term public sector investment program (PSIP) is proposed in this report. The program would involve projected expenditures of $343 million for the period 1993-96 ($86 million a year), including transfers of $18 million from externally financed projects to provide foreign exchange to the private sector. The size of the PSIP is based on the central government's projected financial and institutional absorptive capacity.[1] Its composition largely reflects the Government's focus on the provision of basic economic and social infrastructure for private-

sector-led growth. It emphasizes, first, the rehabilitation of the economic infrastructure (53 percent of total expenditures) and, second, social sector investments (29 percent). Investments in economic support services are limited to the agriculture sector (13 percent). Other investments account for 5 percent of total expenditures (table 3). If implemented, this PSIP is projected to provide the base for private-sector-led growth of about 5 percent a year during 1993-96.

Of the total PSIP financing requirements of $343 million, $306 million comes from identified sources. Identified domestic financing is projected to amount to about $79 million, which is in line with the capacity to mobilize domestic resources. The remaining $227 million of identified project financing is projected to come from external sources. But a *project financing gap* of $37 million remains for proposed key projects in agriculture, transport, education, and health (see

Table 3. Public sector investment plan (PSIP), 1993-96

(millions of 1992 U.S. dollars)

	Budgeted 1993	1994	1995	1996	1993-96 Amount	Share (%)
Agriculture	12.2	11.4	10.8	9.0	43.3	12.6
Infrastructure	20.3	37.4	56.9	66.6	181.2	52.8
Power	5.3	8.8	11.0	5.5	30.6	8.9
Transportation	7.5	16.1	27.5	35.2	86.2	25.1
Water	2.9	3.8	6.5	9.1	22.3	6.5
Sea defenses	2.9	8.1	11.3	16.1	38.4	11.2
Urban	1.8	0.6	0.6	0.7	3.7	1.1
Social	22.0	20.1	28.3	29.5	99.8	29.1
Poverty	6.7	7.8	7.8	4.8	27.0	7.9
Education	6.0	5.6	9.1	11.5	32.2	9.4
Health	9.3	6.7	11.4	13.2	40.6	11.8
Other	6.7	4.0	3.9	4.0	18.6	5.4
Total gross PSIP	61.2	72.9	99.8	109.0	342.9	100.0
Unidentified	0.0	0.0	14.7	22.3	37.0	10.8
Transfers	7.0	6.9	4.1	0.0	18.0	5.3
Total net PSIP	54.2	66.0	95.7	109.0	324.9	94.7
Memorandum items						
Identified net PSIP/GDP (%)	17.6	19.0	20.9	20.2	19.5	
GDP growth (%)	5.5	5.0	4.5	4.5	4.9	

Source: Main report.

the section on sector strategies and expenditures), toward which new external project assistance of about $33 million (90 percent) should be directed on a priority basis.

Economic outlook, external financing requirements, and debt relief

Guyana's medium- and long-term economic prospects are promising, provided that the Government maintains a sound macroeconomic framework, drastically reduces the size of the public sector and its command over economic resources, pursues sector strategies supportive of private-sector-led growth, and improves public sector management and administration. In addition, Guyana will need further financial assistance, including enhanced concessions for debt rescheduling and debt forgiveness, to achieve external viability over the medium to long term.

Under these assumptions, Guyana's real GDP at *market prices* is projected to grow at 5 percent a year on average during 1993-96, and at 4 percent a year thereafter, compared with almost 8 percent

in 1992. This projected growth path is based on annual growth rates of about 3 percent in agriculture, 4 percent in manufacturing, 5 percent in mining, and 8 percent in services and is supported by moderate growth in public infrastructure and private investments of 2 percent a year on average. Real exports of goods and nonfactor services are projected to grow rapidly, at about 7 percent a year on average during 1993-2001, propelled mainly by strong rice, timber, and gold exports and a steady expansion in sugar production. Real imports are projected to grow faster than GDP during 1993-96, averaging 7 percent a year, to cover increasing private consumption and exports, and to follow the GDP growth trend of 4 percent during 1997-2001. At the same time, the resource balance is projected to deteriorate slightly, from a surplus of 3 percent of GDP in 1992 to a deficit of 5 percent during 1993-96 and only a small surplus of 0.1 percent during 1997-2001. Because of Guyana's large interest payments, the external current account balance is projected to continue to record substantial deficits, averaging 31 percent of GDP during 1993-96 and 19 percent of GDP during 1997-2001.

Guyana will continue to require substantial foreign capital inflows to finance the PSIP, to meet its debt service obligations, and to provide foreign exchange to sustain import levels that are consistent with the projected economic growth (table 5). The major sources of financing are projected to be private capital inflows, generated in large part through

Table 4. Actual and projected macroeconomic indicators, 1992-2001

(percent)

	Prel. 1992	Projected 1993-96	1997-2001
Average growth rates			
Real GDP (market prices)	7.9	4.9	4.1
Real exports of goods and nonfactor services	28.0	8.0	5.6
Real imports of goods and nonfactor services	18.4	7.4	4.2
Urban consumer prices (end-period)	14.2	9.3	8.4
Share of GDP			
Consumption	62.9	70.7	69.5
Gross domestic investment	34.5	34.3	30.4
Gross domestic savings	37.1	29.3	30.5
Resource balance	2.6	−5.0	0.1
Exports (goods and nonfactor services)	132.1	131.5	139.5
Imports (goods and nonfactor services)	129.5	136.5	139.4
External current account	−29.8	−31.4	−18.7
External debt (outstanding and disbursed)	675.5	623.7	501.0
Scheduled debt service	50.9	34.2	29.1

Source: Main report.

privatization; grants and concessional loans for balance of payments support and project assistance; and debt relief.

Foreign direct investment is projected to average about $40 million a year during 1993-2001. But these projected levels are contingent on the implementation of a comprehensive privatization program, accompanied by major private rehabilitation investments. Similarly, the projections also include privatization receipts of $10 million a year on average during 1993-2001. Guyana's total aid requirements *after* private capital flows during 1993-96 amount to $446 million. Of this amount, only $295 million have been identified in the form of concessional loans or grants. This leaves an *external financing gap* for 1993-96 of $151 million, of which $33 million represents proposed projects with unidentified external financing. The external financing gap increases to $92 million a year on average during 1997-2001. Further balance of payments support or debt relief beyond the assumed 1993-95 rescheduling on Enhanced Toronto Terms for Paris Club and Trinidad and Tobago debt would be required to fill this gap and avoid jeopardizing Guyana's growth prospects.

The recent (May 1993) 1993-95 rescheduling of Paris Club debt on Enhanced Toronto Terms is an important contribution to the alleviation of Guyana's debt burden. However, as the projections presented above imply, Guyana's tight external finances will require further debt relief in the near future. At a minimum, and consistent with the provisions under Enhanced Toronto Terms, such debt relief could take the form of 100 percent rescheduling of the principal by 1998. In addition, Guyana would need to apply these terms not only to its Paris Club debt but also to the debt it owes to Trinidad and Tobago. Under such a scenario, Guyana's debt service payments would be reduced by an additional $34 million per year during 1998-2001 and would amount to 25 percent of GDP by the year 20001, compared to 34 percent in the base case scenario. Similarly, its debt at the end of the projection period would amount to $2,299 million (439 percent of GDP), compared to $2,434 million (465 percent of GDP) in the base case scenario.

Table 5. Projected external financing requirements, 1993-2001

(millions of U.S. dollars)

	1993	1994	1995	1996	1997-2001
Financing requirement	−168	−179	−162	−153	−180
Financing sources	168	179	162	153	180
Foreign direct investment	34	24	23	35	48
Sale of assets	5	2	6	10	13
Rescheduling, debt relief a	15	43	20	0	0
Grants	34	34	33	32	30
Medium- and long-term loans	79	75	81	75	90
Memorandum item					
Total aid requirement	112.8	108.6	112.4	112.3	119.9
Identified	88.4	66.0	75.1	66.0	27.5
Loans	59.7	58.4	65.6	56.6	27.2
Grants	28.7	7.6	9.5	9.4	0.3
Unidentified	24.4	42.6	37.3	46.3	92.4
Loans	19.1	16.2	14.8	23.7	62.4
Grants	5.3	26.4	22.5	22.6	30.0

a. Assumes 1993-95 rescheduling on Enhanced Toronto Terms.

Source: Main report.

Public sector management and administration

The fundamental shift that has been taking place in economic policy and the macroeconomic framework requires a corresponding comprehensive public sector reform. This reform should reduce the scope of the public sector's activities, reorient its activities to focus on human resource development and support of the private sector, and sharply decrease the public sector's command over the country's economic resources. This involves reorganizing the public administration—reallocating tasks between the center and the regions, strengthening public service management, and improving the quality of public sector employment while eliminating redundancies.

Since 1970, the public sector has experienced dramatic expansion in both its functions and its size, as is evident in the growth of the central Government and in the spread of semi-autonomous agencies, constitutional agencies, public corporations, and public financial institutions. And the creation of regional administrations in 1980 added another layer of administration, resulting in an institutional apparatus that is unmanageable. Although a recent reorganization within the central Government, which reduced the number of ministries from 18 to 11, has reduced the complexity of the ministerial structure, there remains a need for reorganization within ministries, and between the central Government and other public entities to clarify functional responsibilities. This would include examining the rationale for semi-autonomous agencies, privatizing public corporations and financial holdings, and redefining the responsibilities of the regional administrations to ensure greater accountability.

The quality of Guyana's public service has deteriorated markedly. The principal cause of this deterioration has been the sharp decrease in real emoluments, which declined by about 40 percent on average during 1987-92. Moreover, regular salaries have decreased even more rap-

idly for higher-level staff. Consequently, vacancy rates are particularly high for technical positions, amounting to more than 40 percent of budgeted positions. At the same time, more than 70 percent of budgeted positions are for low-level positions, resulting in a bottom-heavy public service. Because of its shortage of technical staff, the Government is unable to adequately carry out such basic functions as data collection and analysis, accounting and cost control, and essential service delivery. Hence, the overriding concern for the Government in this area is to provide wage incentives to fill vacancies for higher-level technical positions while reducing labor redundancies, especially at lower levels. These actions will be taken within the framework proposed by the IDA's Public Administration Project.

Resource mobilization: institutional aspects

Recent years have seen major reforms of the tax system. The tax structure that has resulted is broadly satisfactory. The main priority now should be broadening the coverage and improving the administration of taxes. This applies in particular to the consumption tax and the import duty, where revenue forgone on account of remissions is estimated at G$2.9 billion, or 65 percent of revenues collected from these taxes. For the consumption tax, all remissions should be abolished to transform the tax into a pure revenue levy free of protective effects. And the consumption tax should be extended to cover services other than hotel accommodations. For import duties, a drastic reduction in remissions should be pursued, accompanied by measures to ensure that inputs embodied in exports are not taxed. These measures would also more than compensate for potential revenue losses due to the reduction in the CET. Further, fiscal concessions under income taxes are overly generous, and should be curtailed, taking into account the arrangements elsewhere in the region.

In 1993, the Government imposed a 10 percent development levy on "commercial" companies, effectively increasing their company taxes from 35 to 45 percent, as a short-term expedient to raise additional revenue. But this measure has only a limited revenue potential, and should not replace the efforts to broaden the tax base. In addition, it has increased the distortions arising from the gap between personal income and company taxes, and will discourage private investment. Hence, it is recommended that the Government discontinue this levy and subsequently unify the top income and company tax rates.

Tax and customs administrations are weak. Overall staffing levels appear adequate, but existing staff needs to be better trained and their remuneration needs to be increased to reduce staff turnover and the incentive for corruption. Computer facilities are outdated and ineffectively used. Procedures need to be streamlined to derive full benefit from the new equipment and software provided under the IDA's Public Administration Project and the IDB's tax administration project. A serious shortcoming of the inland revenue administration is the absence of verification in the field, which results in collections of income taxes which fall far short of their potential. Similarly, there is no mechanism to verify payments of motor vehicle licenses, and receipts from motor vehicles could most likely be doubled by introducing an annual sticker to be attached to the windscreen of each vehicle. In customs administration, the system for processing export and import documents is too complex, and the administration is not sufficiently supported by computerization. Also, too many resources are allocated to monitoring the low-value "barrel" traffic. These resources could be more effectively employed in assessing high-value commercial imports.

A source of revenue that has been neglected is user charges and other cost-recovery measures. Almost all public services are either totally or partially subsidized. As a result, the Government lacks the funds to maintain the quality of these services. While in some areas services may need to be improved before cost-recovery measures are implemented, their revenue potential in the medium term is large—they could yield an additional $28 million a year, equivalent to about 10 percent of 1992 GDP (table 6). To increase the incentive to pursue cost recovery, some form of earmarking of revenues for operations and maintenance should be considered. For example, private agencies could be entrusted to carry out operations and maintenance and to collect user fees in exchange for a share of the revenues collected.

Table 6. Current and target revenue from cost recovery

(millions of U.S. dollars)

Sector	Main source	Main use	Current	Target
Drainage and irrigation	User fees	O&M expenditure	<0.5	5.0
Power	Tariff	Operating expenses	19.0	27.0
Road transport	Fuel tax/vehicle license	Road O&M expenditure	1.3[a]	6.0
Water and sanitation	Tariff	Operating expenses	<0.1	2.0
Sea defenses	Levy	O&M expenditure	0.0	5.0
Education	Tuition	Recurrent expenditure	~0.0	1.0
Health	User fees	Recurrent expenditure	~0.0	3.0
Total amount			20.9	49.0
Total share (percentage of 1992 GDP)			7.9	18.2

~ means approximately.

Note: Based on full recovery (100 percent) of targeted expenditures, except for education (15 percent, 40 percent, and 60 percent for primary, secondary, and tertiary education, respectively) and health (30 percent) expenditures.

a. Budgeted for operation and maintenance.

Source: Main report.

Resource allocation: institutional aspects

The existing budgetary system and related public sector financial management practices in Guyana suffer from a number of deficiencies that need to be addressed. First, there are a number of key financial management practices that are inappropriate: there has been little or no attempt to relate each year's budget with an integrated program, accounting practices have been largely in the form of cash management, and treasury decisions are based neither on a cash flow program nor on portfolio options. Second, the accounting system broke down in 1981, and no official financial statements for the public sector have been produced since. Third, the audit of accounts has been severely hampered and inordinately delayed, and control is therefore ineffective. Fourth, although disbursements are authorized through the executive function of the Releases Committees, with no financial statements for audit examination, the public and the Parliament have had no means to monitor appropriated funds. All of these management shortcomings suggest urgent need for financial management reform.

The *de jure* budget process is complex and seems intricate in detail. But because of the lack of technical capacity, the use of the line item budget, and the diffusion of responsibilities, the process is neither timely nor transparent. Responsibility for preparing the budget is diffused among a number of agencies. And the budget review process involves a number of ad hoc arrangements and committees, but their membership, procedures, and guidelines have not been properly defined, or lack transparency. Most of the line ministries' and agencies' draft estimates are prepared by poorly qualified and inexperienced staff. Prior to the 1993 budget, the ministries and agencies had made only limited attempts to base their proposed expenditures in the draft estimates on any clearly defined objective or set of priorities. To address these issues, both the Office of the Budget and the budget functions in line agencies need significant strengthening in staffing and equipment. Further, the budget needs to be developed within a well-defined annual or medium-term economic framework and oriented toward programs and activities.

The PSIP process and donor coordination

PSIP planning, implementation, and monitoring have improved over the 1990-92 period, as reflected in the increase in the implementation ratio from 58 percent during 1990-91 to 88 percent in 1992. Nonetheless, addressing Guyana's extensive investment needs will strain its absorptive capacity, and will require further improvements in the PSIP process. Institutional strengthening is a key issue. Until recently, information and responsibilities regarding the PSIP process have been fragmented and scattered throughout the public sector. As a result, the PSIP has been of only limited use as an instrument to facilitate planning, implementation, and monitoring of projects.

A first step in reforming the institutional setup for the PSIP is currently being undertaken through the merger of the two major agencies involved in the PSIP process, the State Planning Secretariat (SPS) and the Department of International Economic Cooperation (DIEC), into the Ministry of Finance. Improvements in the information flow will depend, however, on the specific arrangements that would centralize project information in one sub-unit of the Ministry of Finance. For project identification, it should be the role of the SPS to provide a set of updated guidelines and basic macroeconomic indicators to inform the decisions of the line agencies. The selection of projects should feed back into the budget and planning process in the form of provisions for counterpart funding and future maintenance expenditures. This should make it possible to better incorporate the recurrent cost implications of capital expenditures into the budget and planning process.

To support project implementation, project execution units should be consolidated and given more autonomy. For a set of selected priority projects (core PSIP), a task force should be established within the Ministry of Finance and supported by higher-level officials to ensure speedy implementation. To address the lack of counterpart funds for projects that progress more quickly than expected, shifting resources from local projects, and pooling and *pari passu* disbursement of local counterpart funds should be considered. Further, the IDB project to develop a project cycle management system should be rapidly implemented. These actions would require additional technical assistance to enhance training. Further measures to strengthen the line agencies are needed to ensure the smooth implementation of the ambitious 1993-96 PSIP. But as long as the salary issue is not addressed, qualified staff will continue to leave the SPS or the line agencies, putting at risk the sustainability of these reform efforts.

Private sector and community participation

The scope of private sector involvement in the project cycle needs to be broadened. The private sector should be encouraged not only to substitute for or complement public investments, but also to support the implementation of public investments.

The Social Impact Amelioration Program (SIMAP) has been very successful in integrating communities and nongovernmental organizations into the PSIP process for small local projects, and it continues to be the most effective means for doing so. But over the medium term, community participation could be increased further by providing block grants at a local level—as has been done in other countries—so that communities and nongovernmental organizations can undertake rehabilitation works on their own (box 1).

Donor coordination and policies

With the implementation of Guyana's ERP and the resulting significant increase in external do-

nor support, the need for close donor coordination has assumed increasing importance.

▲ Enhanced donor coordination would contribute significantly to a more efficient use of scarce resources on the project level. Achieving better donor coordination requires, first, the establishment of joint project execution units; second, pooling and *pari passu* disbursement of local counterpart funds; and, third, consistent donor conditionality.

▲ Donors should agree to assume operations and maintenance expenditures on a declining basis over time, and to design cost-recovery mechanisms as an integral part of any project.

▲ There should be a more systematic exchange of information on programs of assistance and project implementation. This could be accomplished through a project list approach, providing details on all projects, including timetables for implementation and analysis of implementation problems. There is also a need for mechanisms to follow up on agreements reached in donor meetings, for example, in the form of progress reports.

▲ Donors could also facilitate Government planning by making multiyear commitments, at least on a planning basis, in particular for commodity assistance, and by assisting the Government in making more accurate estimates of expected disbursements in the context of the Government's budget process.

Sector strategies and expenditures

The following paragraphs define strategies for the main sectors of the economy: agriculture, the power sector, sea defense, transport, water and sewerage, and the social sectors.

Agriculture

Since the liberalization of the economy, there has been a rapid turnaround in the performance of agriculture, and there is real opportunity for further rapid and sustainable growth.[2] But this opportunity is heavily circumscribed by the macro-

Box 1. Community participation in public investment

The components of rural development are always the same—roads, electricity, water supply, small irrigation, markets, schools, health posts, and services. The projects are usually small, widely dispersed, and often quite simple. But experience has shown that central planning for hundreds of distinct localities cannot succeed because of the complexity problems arising from the location specificity of needs. Therefore, community participation in planning has been advocated and elaborate methodologies developed. A successful first step in a number of countries has been to establish Social Funds—the approach followed in Guyana with the establishment of SIMAP. In the short term, and in an environment in which community participation was not encouraged and Government agencies are weak, Social Funds can achieve impressive rates of execution and relatively successful targeting.

In the medium term, however, a more promising approach may be to take community participation a step further and overcome the complexity problems through fiscal decentralization with community-based project execution. As interventions lose their "emergency" character, Social Funds seem to be severely threatened by "improvements" of project design, selection, procurement, and disbursement rules, which are intended to reduce potential or real abuses, but in the end may well convert the management of the funds into giant project execution units, familiar from the traditional rural development experience. What is required instead is the systematic improvement of local decision-making mechanisms and rules so that they ensure real authority at the local level over the execution and the financial resources, as well as transparent decisions, and include innovative mechanisms for auditing by the communities themselves.

A good example of the benefits of a truly community-based approach is Mexico's Solidaridad program. Prior to the implementation of that program, rural municipalities and smaller communities had virtually no own-revenue sources and received only very limited financial support from the states. Virtually all local investment was executed by state or federal line agencies on whom local groups were completely dependent for funding. Under the "fiscal systems" approach of Solidaridad, the following measures were implemented or are under implementation:

- Revision of revenue-sharing formulas in favor of the poorer states and municipalities.
- Increases in own-revenue generation of municipalities and states combined with greater transfer of fiscal investment resources from the federal level to states and municipalities.
- Systematic lowering of the level at which investments are executed and money is controlled.
- Reform of money flows and systems for money release from the central government to states, municipalities, and other executing agencies, in which each subproject operates with a special account, and cumbersome ex ante controls are replaced by ex post auditing.
- Special allocation of investment resources to municipalities for small projects under community control, with donated community labor and materials, and extremely simple procurement procedures. These municipal funds operate according to a special manual that ensures a transparent project selection process at the community level.
- Reform of state auditing institutions and mechanisms, with much greater involvement of private sector.
- Clear rules ensuring that the line agencies maintain control for approving (not developing) technical designs for all but the simplest projects, for program quality standards, and for other regulatory functions.

The program built on many institutional features—including the requirement that communities contribute to costs, usually in the form of donated labor—that essentially give the poor veto power over projects.

The impact has been tremendous, with resources for poverty-alleviating investments in rural areas and urban slums more than doubling over three years. More than 12 million people were connected to electricity and potable water, and had their school improved in a period of about three years. Perhaps the most outstanding success was the municipal funds, which operate in 1,100 municipalities and execute 30,000 to 40,000 small projects annually at very low fiscal costs. In Guatemala the earmarking of 8 percent of national fiscal revenue for municipal investments (not payroll) has also had similar, but less well-documented impacts. The incredible impact of the municipal funds in Mexico is clearly due to the fact that, small as they are, they removed a critical constraint to action by communities—their complete lack of funds.

Source: Hans P. Binswanger, 1992, "Central Planning vs. Fiscal Systems Approaches to Rural Development." Unpublished note. World Bank, Washington, D.C.

economic constraints that limit public investment. Moreover, as in other sectors, the neglect of the productive infrastructure during the 1980s has created a need for substantial rehabilitation investment. This dictates a need for the most careful prioritization of public expenditure. But the fragmented and ad hoc approach to planning is a considerable barrier to this; it constrains the efficient allocation of public investment and the equally vital institutional reforms necessary to promote cost recovery and complementary private investment.

In developing an expenditure strategy, the Ministry of Agriculture must acknowledge its dependence on external sources of funding. There are very limited opportunities for further privatization in the nonsugar agricultural sector, and although there are opportunities for cost recovery, these are unlikely to generate significant resources in the short term. Access to donor funding, in turn, depends crucially on having a strategic approach to sector development with clearly identified roles for the public and private sectors, strategies for dealing with problems of absorptive capacity, and commitment to cost recovery where feasible. There must be clearly defined priorities and a vision of where the sector is going. Within the agricultural sector, the overwhelming importance of relaxing current production constraints to sectoral growth dictates the following hierarchy of priorities: first, sustainable rehabilitation of drainage and irrigation systems; second, support for short-term productive capacity; and, third, enhancement and diversification of the production base, including strengthening research and extension services.

Sustainable rehabilitation of the drainage and irrigation systems must have precedence over everything else. Such an effort involves, first, rehabilitating the drainage and irrigation infrastructure and, second, improving its operation and maintenance. This requires radical institutional reform to improve the complex and muddled system of joint responsibilities within

single systems that now prevails. Third, once drainage and irrigation systems are rehabilitated, cost recovery is imperative to ensure their sustainability.

The key elements in supporting the second priority—support for short-term productive capacity—are strengthening the planning capabilities within the Ministry of Agriculture, improving the data base on which planning can draw, and pursuing land reform and improving credit services to enhance rice production. The third priority—enhancing and diversifying the production base—should only be pursued once the first two priorities have been adequately addressed. There is significant potential for nontraditional agricultural products, including pineapples and heart of palm.

Projected disbursements in agriculture under the 1993-96 PSIP amount to $43 million, or 13 percent of total gross investment, including transfers of $18 million (5 percent) from externally financed projects to provide foreign exchange to the private sector. Other externally funded projects cover area development (IFAD), fishery facilities (CIDA), agricultural research (UNDP), and general sector support (IDB). The importance of drainage and irrigation rehabilitation, which promises considerable returns in productivity gains, is not adequately reflected in ongoing and new externally funded investments, and should be given priority by donors. Therefore, this PSIP includes a proposal for additional investments in drainage and irrigation rehabilitation with unidentified financing of $9 million (3 percent). These investments should, however, be contingent on the reforms in the drainage and irrigation subsector described above.

Power

The power sector,[3] of crucial importance for Guyana's economic recovery, is in a severe crisis. The existing generation, transmission, and distribution facilities are worn out, supply is unreliable, and capacity does not meet peak demand. The IDB continues to finance an institutional rehabilitation program for the Guyana Electric Corporation, but the improvements will not be sustained without a reform of the institutional setup in Guyana's power sector. The poor performance of the GEC suggests that it cannot be charged with the responsibility for the power sector. The GEC suffers from weak management compounded by a fragmentation of responsibilities among the board, the general manager, and a team of consultants financed by the IDB. Staff morale is extremely low. The GEC is heavily dependent on Government transfers, which amount to about $10 million, or 3.5 percent of GDP, in 1992. This is partly a result of its low tariffs, which are well below the estimated long-run marginal costs (LRMC), and partly a reflection of its inefficient operations, which result in short-term operational costs well above the LRMC.

In view of this situation, it is recommended that the Government seek immediate private sector participation in the power sector. As a first step, a private management contract allowing autonomous management of the GEC should be entered into. At the same time, the Government should invite short-term private power generation to supplement the GEC's limited capacity, for example, under a build, own, and operate (BOO) scheme. To finance energy purchases and to cover the GEC's cost of operations, electricity tariffs should be increased by about 50 percent on average. As a second step, the Government should privatize transmission and distribution systems and allow competition in energy generation, accompanied by the formulation of an adequate regulatory framework.

In the expectation that the Government will rigorously pursue private sector participation, the PSIP provides for only the most urgent investments needed to prevent the imminent collapse of the power sector. It includes disbursements of about $31 million (9 percent of PSIP disbursements), allocated to the ongoing power rehabilitation project and an emergency transmission project funded by the IDB. This amount is well below the estimated rehabilitation and expansion needs of about $100 million over the next four years.

Sea defenses

Budgetary constraints and the lack of qualified staff resulted in a severe deterioration of sea defenses and an increasing number of breaches, up to 49 in 1990. At present, the backlog in rehabilitation works is about 20 years. The maintenance requirements will remain high for the coming decades, because there is a severe backlog in the maintenance of all the sea defenses and because deteriorated sea defenses require more intensive maintenance.

For the next four years, some $50 million have been allocated to the rehabilitation and maintenance of the most critical sections in the old sea walls. This is a very ambitious program, and its successful implementation will require a concerted effort to address institutional and other issues that have already delayed disbursements. The proposed strategy for the sea defenses focuses on (1) supporting the early start of the rehabilitation efforts through the establishment of a joint project execution unit and measures to increase competition in the quarry sector; (2) improving the maintenance of the existing sea defenses, including through the involvement of local contractors; and (3) designing a comprehensive sea defense policy, including the identification of adequate design standards and priority locations of sea defense works.

Projected disbursements in sea defense rehabilitation amount to $38 million (11 percent of PSIP disbursements), financed by the EC, the CDB, the IDA, and the IDB. All investments included in the PSIP are funded, and the allocation for capital works is considered adequate in view of the country's competing investment needs. But the complete rehabilitation of the sea defenses is estimated to require some $300 million, and the country will continue to depend on donor support in this sector for some time to come.

Transport

The country's transportation infrastructure has deteriorated severely because of poor management and lack of maintenance. The management of transport facilities has been adversely affected by misguided policies and lack of resources. The main roads have not been maintained since the 1970s and need full rehabilitation. Feeder roads have deteriorated and do not allow adequate access to and from production areas. Similarly, airport and port facilities need immediate attention in some areas and will need to be upgraded before a serious effort at export development, particularly of nontraditional commodities, can be successful. No new facilities are warranted in the near future.

Problems in the Ministry of Public Works mirror those of the entire public sector: low salaries, a lack of qualified staff, insufficient recruitment, a need for training, lack of a budgeting process, lack of system information, lack of clear lines of responsibility and accountability, no national-level planning, and poor donor coordination. The lack of national planning in transport, in particular, is a critical bottleneck to the efficient allocation of resources, and there is need for a national transportation plan.

The planned rehabilitation of the main *road* sections by the IDB, the IDA, and the CDB over the next five years will effectively return Guyana's main road network to acceptable standards. But successful implementation will require strengthening the absorptive capacity of the Ministry of Public Works and of local contractors. Also, sea defense and road works need to be integrated. The main issue after reconstruction is effective maintenance, which would be facilitated if responsibilities were recentralized. The most significant issue with respect to financing is the proposed Government expenditure of about $14 million to complete the Mabura-Lethem (Guyana/Brazil) Road. This investment is not essential at this time and, because of its low priority, should be deferred to the extent possible.

In *aviation*, the main issues are the urgent need to upgrade airport security, the establishment of a self-financing airport authority, and enhanced private sector involvement. There is a case for privatizing Guyana Airways Corporation (GAC), as domestic services could be provided more efficiently by the private sector, and the GAC is not competitive internationally.

Finally, there are a number of problems in *water transportation*. Guyana's marine navigation services are inadequate and unsafe by international standards. A high proportion of navigation aids and radio beacons are out of service, even though harbor dues generate surpluses above the costs of navigation services. Investments in this area, facilitated by institutional reform to establish an autonomous port authority, would be highly cost-effective.

To address these issues, the Government should establish national-level planning, and pursue institutional reforms, including recentralization of road operations and maintenance and the creation of airport and port authorities. It should make some immediate interventions, in particular, to facilitate the implementation of the main road rehabilitation projects, to improve aviation facilities, and to improve port and river navigation. It should support an increased role for the private sector in transportation and increase transportation user charges. In the near term, the Government should rely on air access to the hinterland, and in the long term, it should consider new aviation and marine facilities and completion of the Guyana-Brazil road.

Projected disbursements in transportation amount to $86 million (25 percent of PSIP disbursements) to cover the basic needs in road, air, and water transport infrastructure. These investment needs reflect the severe deterioration of the transport infrastructure and services over the past decade, which is a severe impediment to private sector activities. Ongoing projects by the EC focus on the reconditioning of ferries and the rehabilitation of the essential Demerara harbor bridge, while new projects by the IDB and the

IDA provide mainly for the rehabilitation of the main roads in Guyana. In addition, investments of about $14 million with unidentified financing are proposed to cover, in particular, critical feeder roads and airport rehabilitation.

Water and sanitation

Although access to potable water through house connections and public standpipes is quite high, the water and sanitation sector suffers from grave deficiencies. Nearly the entire network faces incipient or actual failure. Back-siphonage of polluted water poses a significant health risk. Preventive maintenance is nonexistent, and there is chronic shortage of spare parts and supplies. Sector institutions have limited capabilities due to human resource constraints, and they are financially bankrupt. Their weakness is compounded by an inadequate institutional framework, with fragmented responsibilities between the center and the regions and a general lack of accountability. Budgetary practices are inappropriate, and cost recovery is extremely weak. For example, the annual water tariff charged to households outside Georgetown is less than $2.

The proposed strategy for the development of the water and sanitation sector in Guyana calls for (1) rehabilitating or replacing the existing facilities to improve service levels; (2) restructuring the sector's regulatory framework and strengthening the sectoral institutions; and (3) improving the sector's finances and financial management practices to enable it to eventually attain self-sufficiency. The last requires raising the water tariffs to levels that at least cover the operations and maintenance of the water and sewerage system. In the short term, the main instrument for implementing this strategy will be the Georgetown Water Supply and Sewerage project financed by the IDB and the regional Water Supply Technical Assistance and Rehabilitation project financed by the IDA and the U.K. It is recommended that the Government undertake any effort to support implementation

of these key projects, in particular because of the incipient cholera threat.

Projected disbursements in water supply and sanitation amount to $22 million (7 percent of PSIP disbursements), including an ongoing project to develop a master plan for the Georgetown water supply (IDB) and new projects for Georgetown emergency water supply, water improvement, and technical cooperation (IDB) and rural water supply and institutional reform (IDA). While the overall rehabilitation needs in the sector are estimated at $45 million to $50 million, the proposed investment should cover the key needs in this sector over the 1993-96 period, and further allocations to the water sector should be contingent on the improvement of its weak absorptive capacity. In view of the successful operation of the Eccles Plant facilities, further private sector involvement should be sought to complement or replace public investments.

Social sectors

Most social services in Guyana are public and at least partially subsidized. The exclusion of the private sector from social service delivery and the reluctance to institute cost recovery have led to a sharp decline in the quality of services provided. The infrastructure is severely dilapidated, and books and equipment are unavailable, broken, or obsolete. These poor working conditions, coupled with low salaries, have encouraged skilled and qualified personnel to move out of the sectors or seek work abroad. As a consequence, Guyana's education and health indicators today are among the lowest in the Caribbean.

The information necessary to obtain a clear picture of the nature and extent of *poverty* is not available in Guyana. More reliable information should become available in mid-1993, however, as data are issued from the 1990 National Census as well as from an Incomes and Expenditure and Living Standards Measurement Survey. Completion of these surveys should enable the IDA to prepare a *Poverty Assessment* focusing on human resource development and poverty reduction efforts in the context of policies for growth. For the time being, the existing efforts under SIMAP and the Basic Needs project continue to be the best mechanisms for alleviating poverty. SIMAP finances small-scale subprojects initiated and implemented at the community level. Financing is provided to the communities for a variety of project activities, including the rehabilitation and equipping of primary health care facilities, food distribution and nutritional surveillance activities targeted at children and pregnant and lactating mothers in primary health care facilities, the construction, rehabilitation, and equipping of daycare centers, and the installation and rehabilitation of basic water supply facilities and sanitation systems. Community and nongovernmental organizations may submit proposals for funding within these categories. The Basic Needs project basically follows the SIMAP approach.

The challenges facing the *education sector* are considerable. The sector's efficiency is low, teacher quality is poor, educational materials are lacking, and the infrastructure is dilapidated. The decline of the education system reflects, to a large extent, the decreasing resources available to the sector, which amounted to 2 percent of GDP in 1990, well below levels in other Caribbean countries. However, while additional resources will be essential, there is also a need to improve efficiencies in resource use and to develop institutional capacity.

During 1993-96, the most urgent needs of the education sector will be covered by ongoing IDB projects with projected disbursements of about $25 million. Hence, it is recommended that the Government's efforts, initially, focus on (1) developing a comprehensive strategy plan for the sector that develops medium-term objectives, prioritizes the activities to be undertaken, and assesses what can be achieved given anticipated revenue flows; (2) increasing the resources available to the sector through the introduction of selected user fees; and (3) strengthening the planning and management capacities of key personnel in the Ministry of Education and Regional Administrations. In parallel, sector reform would focus on (1) reallocating resources where social returns are highest and more equitably distributed, in particular in primary education; (2) strengthening teacher training and restructuring the salary schedule; and (3) improving teacher and student access to textbooks and teaching aids. Room should also be given to private education, and community-based initiatives and support from nongovernmental organizations should be strongly encouraged.

The quality of the services provided in the *health sector* has declined markedly over the 1980s. Although Government allocations to the sector dropped sharply over this period, amounting to 3 percent of GDP in 1990, high levels of inefficiency, the fragmented organization of the sector, an inability to identify and prioritize objectives, and the limited coordination between the relevant agencies have greatly contributed to this decline. The deterioration in care has been most severe in smaller urban and rural areas where health facilities are severely understaffed and lack even the most basic drugs and diagnostic equipment. In this context, projects to complement the IDB's Georgetown Hospital Rehabilitation project, or a diversion of funds from this project to support health facilities outside Georgetown, would be desirable.

Although investments in infrastructure are badly needed, substantial improvements in health service delivery are possible if recurrent funds are used more efficiently and resources augmented through the introduction of cost-recovery measures. The following initial steps should be taken by the Government: (1) identify priorities and establish a coherent set of medium-term objectives; (2) move to increase the resources available to the sector through the introduction of a carefully structured fee schedule; and (3) strengthen the management and budgeting capacity of administrative staff in the Ministry of Health, the regional administrations, and the hospitals. In parallel, the reforms should focus on (1) redirecting resources from curative to primary health care; (2) strengthening preventive health care services; and (3) improving the availability of pharmaceutical and medical supplies, particularly in the regions. Minor health projects should continue to be implemented through SIMAP and the Basic Needs project. At the same time, private delivery of health services should be seen as an integral part of the health sector strategy, and community-based initiatives and support from nongovernmental organizations should be strongly encouraged.

Projected disbursements in social sectors amount to $100 million (29 percent of PSIP disbursements), of which $27 million (8 percent) is allocated to SIMAP and Basic Needs poverty reduction efforts, $32 million (9 percent) to education, and $41 million (12 percent) to health. While SIMAP is undoubtedly the best agency to respond quickly to the immediate needs of the poor, it will have to be further strengthened to absorb more funds than currently allocated. Investments in education and health are dominated by one large IDB project each, rehabilitation of primary education ($25 million) and of the Georgetown hospital (Health Care II, $22 million). In both sectors, current funding is insufficient to address the extensive rehabilitation needs, but technical assistance for institutional strengthening should have priority. In education, a project to rehabilitate technical and vocational schools is proposed to start in 1995, for which financing of $4 million is being sought. In health, two projects to rehabilitate communal and district hospitals are proposed to start in 1995, for which financing of $10 million is being sought. In addition, there is scope for the private sector, communities, and nongovernmental organizations to offer services to complement public investments.

Summary policy agenda

The key tasks facing the Government are to (1) consolidate the macroeconomic and incentive framework in support of private sector-led growth, but also to (2) initiate a comprehensive public sector reform to reflect the changing role of the state under the ERP and (3) rehabilitate the country's basic economic and social infrastructure. Only if the Government succeeds in all of these areas will Guyana experience the economic growth necessary to raise the population's living standards and to substantially reduce poverty over the coming decade.

The Government has expressed its commitment to maintaining a sound macroeconomic framework and preserving the recent improvements in the incentive framework for private sector development. It has also initiated the public sector reform process in the context of the IDA's Public Administration Project. But this reform process must be carried further, including privatization; strengthening public sector administration; enhancing resource mobilization; and improving the efficiency of resource allocation. And the PSIP process needs to be strengthened to facilitate rehabilitation of the country's basic economic and social infrastructure. In this context, the priority items on the Government's policy agenda are as follows:

▲ A comprehensive privatization strategy needs to be developed and rapidly implemented. In addition to nonfinancial enterprises, the Government needs to divest itself from its financial sector holdings. In both instances, privatization needs to be accompanied by the establishment of an appropriate regulatory framework.

▲ Public service pay needs to be improved, accompanied by measures to reduce labor redundancies, especially at lower levels. In particular, the salary structure must be made transparent, and the salary scale decompressed to provide incentives to technical and professional personnel. The implementation of the IDA's Public Administration Project would be an important contribution to addressing this objective.

▲ Tax and customs administration needs to be strengthened, and the tax and duty structure needs to be revised as follows:

• The tax base needs to broadened through elimination of remissions under the consumption tax, reduction of remissions under import duties, and the curtailment of concessions under the income tax.

• The development levy for commercial companies should be discontinued and, subsequently, the top personal income and company tax rates unified at 33 to 35 percent.

• The revised CET should be adopted on a fast track, as agreed with CARICOM, and the revenue impact offset by the elimination of remissions as recommended above.

▲ Cost-recovery measures need to be strengthened to finance essential public services. In the medium term, enhanced user charges should yield an additional $28 million, equivalent to about 10 percent of 1992 GDP.

▲ Government transfers to the GEC need to be discontinued, based on more efficient operations, increased tariffs consistent with long-run marginal costs, and accompanied by private sector participation in the power sector.

▲ The shortfall in operations and maintenance has to be addressed urgently. A comprehensive assessment should be undertaken to establish adequate levels of operations and maintenance expenditures, and a plan developed to reach these levels within the coming years, to be financed by cost-recovery measures. In this connection, consideration should be given to contracting out operations and maintenance activities to the private sector.

▲ The budget process needs to be revised and oriented toward activities and programs. As a complementary measure, expenditure control and management also need to be improved through the implementation of adequate financial management systems and procedures.

▲ Project implementation needs to be improved. In particular:

• Project execution units should be consolidated and given more autonomy.

• A core PSIP comprising a set of selected priority projects should be identified, and a task force supported by higher-level officials should be established to ensure its speedy implementation.

• The lack of counterpart funds should be addressed through shifting resources from local projects and pooling and pari passu disbursement of local counterpart funds.

• The IDB project to develop a project cycle management system should be rapidly implemented.

▲ Drainage and irrigation systems need to be rehabilitated in a sustainable manner. Such an effort involves:

• Rehabilitation of the drainage and irrigation infrastructure with donor assistance.

• Improved drainage and irrigation operations and maintenance through radical institutional reform—for example, the establishment of water associations.

• Introduction of cost-recovery measures.

A more detailed summary of Guyana's policy agenda, describing policy issues, strategies, and recommended actions can be found in the attached policy matrix. Each of the issues addressed in this matrix is developed in more depth in the body of the report.

Notes

1. The PSIP only covers proposed investments, excluding technical assistance requirements, by the Central Government and GEC. Investments of the other public enterprises have been excluded, partly because their plans are on hold on account of the privatization program, and partly because they operate under private management contracts (sugar, bauxite) with a high degree of autonomy.

2. The PSR does not analyze the sugar sector, because GUYSUCO operates under a private sector management contract with a high degree of autonomy and is scheduled for privatization under IDA's Sugar Rehabilitation Project. This also applies for the bauxite sector.

3. The PSR does not include a chapter on the power sector, which is only discussed in the context of the PSIP. A more detailed analysis on power sector issues can be found in the World Bank's Guyana Infrastructure Sector Review, dated August 14, 1992, and in a number of IDB studies and issues papers.

Policy agenda matrix

Policy area/issue	Strategy	Main recommendations and actions
Macroeconomic policies and external debt		
Incentive policies	Maintain reform policies under the Economic Recovery Program in line with 1992-94 Policy Framework Paper.	Deepen the cambio (private foreign exchange) market, with a view to including all foreign exchange transactions.
		Continue trade liberalization policies, including rapid introduction of the revised Common External Tariff and elimination of remaining import restrictions and prohibitions.
		Reduce direct involvement of public sector in economic activity.
Financial sector policies	Improve the conduct of monetary policy.	Strengthen the role of the Central Bank and shift to more flexible monetary instruments.
	Increase the efficiency of financial intermediation through increased competition and private sector participation.	Encourage new private entrants into the financial sector, including through granting new bank licenses as soon as possible, and reduce the role of the public sector. In parallel, strengthen the regulatory framework and improve supervision.
External debt	Seek debt relief.	Approach the Paris Club for enhanced Toronto concessions and ask non-Paris Club creditors to also apply these terms.
Public finance		
Revenues	Reduce overall deficit and improve efficiency of resource mobilization and allocation.	Strengthen tax and customs administration, and broaden tax base through elimination of exemptions, remissions, and concessions under the various taxes (see resource mobilization).
		Strengthen cost recovery measures to finance essential public services, in particular in drainage and irrigation (user fees), power (tariffs), road transportation (fuel tax, vehicle licenses), water and sanitation (tariffs), sea defenses (levy), education (tuition), and health (user fees).
Expenditures		Revise and reorient budget process toward activities and programs, and implement adequate financial management systems and procedures to strengthen expenditure control (see resource allocation).
		Improve public service pay for qualified staff in a sustainable manner, accompanied by measures to reduce labor redundancies.
		Assess and address shortfall in operations and maintenance, and increase efficiency by contracting out to the private sector.

Policy area/issue	Strategy	Main recommendations and actions
Expenditures (cont.)		Discontinue transfers to the Guyana Electric Company based on more efficient operations, increase tariffs consistent with long-run marginal costs and private sector participation, and review membership to international and local organizations in light of associated costs and benefits.
Public enterprises	Reduce direct involvement of the public sector in economic activity and increase the role of the private sector.	Implement rapidly a comprehensive privatization strategy that addresses both nonfinancial and financial holdings. Follow transparent procedures. Establish appropriate regulatory framework for to-be-privatized entities.

Public Sector Investment Program (PSIP)

PSIP planning, implementation, and monitoring	Increase absorptive capacity through improving the PSIP process. Facilitate, in particular, implementation of key projects.	Improve coordination among agencies involved in PSIP process. To this end, pursue the merger of the State Planning Secretariat and the Department of International Economic Cooperation and centralize project information and effective responsibility in one subunit of the Ministry of Finance.
		Facilitate speedy implementation of the Inter-American Development Bank project to develop a project cycle management system, and request additional technical assistance for enhanced training opportunities.
		Provide, through the State Planning Secretariat, a set of updated guidelines and basic macroeconomic indicators to inform project selection by line agencies.
		Introduce a budget system that integrates capital and current budgeting and allows monitoring of recurrent cost implications of capital expenditures.
		Improve project implementation by consolidating project execution units while increasing their autonomy in addressing implementation problems, establishing mechanisms to shift counterpart funds to projects as needed, and focusing and coordinating donor conditionality.
		Formulate a core PSIP composed of a set of priority projects, and establish a task force, supported by high-level officials, to support implementation of this core PSIP.
Donor coordination	Improve donor coordination to avoid project overlap and to allow for more efficient use of donor assistance and local counterpart funds.	Facilitate a more systematic exchange of information based on a project list approach, including timetables for implementation and analysis of implementation problems.

Policy area/issue	Strategy	Main recommendations and actions
Donor coordination (cont.)		Facilitate Government planning through multiyear commitments or indications of future aid flows and assistance in estimating disbursements.
Private sector and community participation	Increase the role of the private sector and of communities in the PSIP process.	Pursue contracting-out of works. Request technical assistance to enhance legal and monitoring capabilities.
		Provide block-grants to allow nongovernmental organizations and communities to undertake rehabilitation works on their own.

Public sector administration

Public sector administration and institutional setting	Initiate a comprehensive public sector reform program to reflect the changing role of the public sector under the Economic Reform Program.	Implement IDA's Public Administration Project as a first step toward public sector reform.
	Ensure institutional correspondence in authority, responsibility, execution, and accountability.	Review the rationale of the various public sector entities with a view to streamline the organization of the public sector. In particular, reconsider the role and status of semi-autonomous agencies, privatize public enterprises and financial holdings, and transfer the functions of the Cooperative Financial Institutions Agency (COFA) to the Central Bank.
		Pursue internal reorganization within the ministries to clarify functional responsibilities. In particular, institute a modern financial management system.
Decentralization and regional administrations		Define the appropriate role of regional administrations and ensure their ability to carry out assigned functions.
		Clarify lines of authority between Regional Executive Officers and Regional Democratic Councils.
		Examine staffing levels, technical assistance and advice, and training in the regions.
		Establish the link between revenue generation and expenditure responsibilities.
Public service management		Strengthen public service management through the institution of a personnel records system and the implementation of a comprehensive personnel policy and management system.
Public service employment		Introduce a transparent salary structure to remove distortions in public service pay.
		Improve incentives for professional and higher-level technical personnel, including decompressing the wage scale.

Policy area/issue	Strategy	Main recommendations and actions
Public service employment (cont.)		Improve allocation of personnel across the public sector through reclassification, reduction of labor redundancies, and retraining.

Resource mobilization: institutional aspects

Tax structure	Improve tax structure to minimize distortions and disincentives to economic growth while ensuring adequate revenue collection.	Reduce remissions under import duties, accompanied by measures to ensure that imported inputs embodied in exports are not taxed.
		Eliminate all remissions under the consumption tax to transform the tax into a pure revenue levy free of protective effects.
		Curtail concessions under the income tax.
		Discontinue the 10 percent development levy on commercial companies and unify the top personal income and company tax rates.
		Extend the consumption tax to services other than hotel accommodations.
		Adopt the tax credit method of collection for the consumption tax.
Inland Revenue Administration	Strengthen Tax and Customs Administrations to improve revenue collection.	Computerize income taxes and vehicle licenses.
		Verify taxpayer information on a regular basis in the field, in particular in relation to companies and the self-employed.
		Introduce a bonus system for Inland Revenue staff based on the difference between the tax due on the declared income and the tax paid on the finally assessed income.
		Introduce an annual sticker to be fixed on the windscreen of each motor vehicle to strengthen administration of vehicle licenses.
Customs administration		Simplify and streamline the system for processing import and export documents, including the elimination of minor charges.
		Computerize the consumption tax to provide for the issue of returns and reminders, and the early identification of nonpayers.
		Review the arrangements for the collection and audit of consumption tax returns, to establish a proper system of records and filing for registered manufacturers.
		Introduce a simplified entry, together with an exemption limit, for the "barrel" traffic.
		Issue consumption tax assessments based on earlier returns, backed up by distraint action in the event of delayed payment.

Policy area/issue	Strategy	Main recommendations and actions
Customs administration (cont.)		Adopt a proper level of penalties for failure to furnish consumption tax returns, and the institution of interest charges based on market rates on any outstanding tax.
		Institute an enhanced training program to reinforce the control over valuation, tax liability, and smuggling, together with an accountancy and audit course.
		Provide sufficient equipment and vehicles to equip an antismuggling task force.

Resource allocation: institutional aspects

Budget process	Improve quality and effectiveness of the budget as a planning tool.	Start the planning and budget cycle early in the current year so as to issue the budget within the fiscal year.
	Short term	Forward projections of anticipated resources and major expenditure obligations, and indications of priorities to support sector ministries in the formulation of their budget submissions.
		Formulate and review budget submissions guided by Government priorities and the need to ensure resources to complete important ongoing projects and programs.
	Medium term	Introduce a budget system upon program criteria, and integrate the capital and recurrent estimates in the context of a three-year rolling budget.
		Introduce a regular midyear budget review to enable adjustments as necessary to keep essential programs and projects on track.
Expenditure control	Improve control and management over public expenditures.	Discontinue current informal procurement practices and reintroduce the system of local purchase orders.
	Short term	Strengthen the inspection wing of the Treasury through the adequate provision of staff, equipment, and vehicles.
		Implement immediately the measures proposed under the Public Administration Project, including utilizing technical assistance to aid in the timely generation of public accounts, the elimination of coverage of overdrafts to budgeted expenditures, the reduction in nonbudgeted and unaccounted-for expenditures within the ministries and Regional Administrations, and the reestablishment of an effective Public Accounts Committee.
		Review and update the Financial Administration and Audit Act of 1973 to ensure tighter control over public expenditures.

Policy area/issue	Strategy	Main recommendations and actions
Expenditure control (cont.)	Medium term	Carry out an in-depth review of the Accountant General's Department, the Office of the Budget, and the Auditor General's Department to streamline and computerize their operations.
		Contract out the auditing of all outstanding accounts and ensure that future audits are carried out within twelve months.

Agriculture

Policy area/issue	Strategy	Main recommendations and actions
Drainage and irrigation	Provide for sustainable rehabilitation of drainage and irrigation systems.	Rehabilitate physical drainage and irrigation infrastructure.
		Improve operations and maintenance of drainage and irrigation systems through the establishment of a ministerial task force to make detailed proposals on institutional reform, preparation of enabling legislation to enact reform proposals, and investment in equipment and facilities.
		Introduce cost recovery measures.
Other short-term production constraints	Support measures to enhance short-term productive capacity.	Strengthen the planning and budgeting process in the Ministry of Agriculture.
		Pursue land reform granting farmers long-term leasehold or freehold on farm land under public ownership.
		Improve institutional credit services to farmers.
		Rehabilitate the hydrometeorological service.
Production base	Enhance and diversify production base.	Strengthen the agricultural extension services.
		Support the National Agricultural Research Institute.
		Support crop diversification through research, seed sales, support for processing services, and market intelligence.
		Review the institutional arrangements for rice marketing, grading, and export.

Sea and river defenses

Policy area/issue	Strategy	Main recommendations and actions
Rehabilitation	Facilitate the early start and continuation of the donor-funded rehabilitation projects.	Establish a joint Project Execution Unit for sea and river defenses.
	Short term	Institute a transparent accounting system for the Project Execution Unit.
		Ensure competition and investments in the quarry industry to lower prices and improve quality.

Policy area/issue	Strategy	Main recommendations and actions
Rehabilitation (cont.)		Identify and announce an explicit sea defense cost recovery method and program, for example, a general sea defense levy, to be implemented in the medium term.
	Medium term	Seek further finance for sea defense works not covered under the current rehabilitation projects.
Maintenance	Improve the maintenance of the existing sea defenses.	Continue the ongoing emergency repairs to minimize and to repair breaches.
		Identify financial resources for sea defense maintenance and upgrading of the working methods for maintenance and repairs.
		Identify funds for the Project Execution Unit and the ongoing sea defenses maintenance over the coming years.
		Start a program that aims for maximum involvement of local contractors, and decide on a time schedule for phasing out the Hydraulics Division's equipment, workshops, and stores.
Policies and strategies	Design an integral and effective sea defense policy by identifying priorities, selecting appropriate design methods and encouraging the coordination between the Government of Guyana and donors.	Follow up on the coordination between the Government of Guyana and donors.
	Short term	Decide on the type of design that will be applied for repair, maintenance, and rehabilitation works.
		Identify priorities for additional studies and apply to donors for funding.
	Medium term	Develop medium- and long-term strategies, possibly in the context of a coastal zone management program designed by a to-be-established Coastal Zone Management Authority.
		Carry out an inventory and set priorities for the rehabilitation (or demolition) of the drainage structures in the sea defense.
		Carry out an inventory and set priorities for the protection of the river defenses.
	Long term	Promote self-sufficiency in rehabilitation and maintenance of the sea and river defenses.

Transport

Policy area/issue	Strategy	Main recommendations and actions
National planning	Establish national-level planning that emphasizes the intermodal nature of transportation.	Update the 1975 National Transportation Plan.
		Strengthen the Central Transport Planning Unit.

Policy area/issue	Strategy	Main recommendations and actions
Institutional reform	Pursue institutional reform to better support efficient use of resources in transportation.	Recentralize the responsibility for road operations and maintenance in the Roads Division of the Ministry of Public Works (MOPWCRD).
		Integrate the planning of sea defense and road construction.
		Create an autonomous Airport Authority to more efficiently manage the airports, and a Civil Aviation Authority to exercise regulatory functions.
		Investigate the creation of a Regional Airworthiness Authority to replace the costly UK Civil Aviation Authority.
		Expand the range of options for a Port Authority of Guyana studied under IDA's Infrastructure Rehabilitation Project to include the creation of a port company with private sector participation.
		Improve technical training for MOPWCRD staff.
Immediate interventions	Intervene immediately in selected priority areas with short-term needs.	Facilitate implementation of the main road rehabilitation projects proposed by CDB, IDA, and IDB.
		Improve aviation facilities at Timehri Airport to comply with minimum international safety standards.
		Design a short-term program to rehabilitate hinterland airstrips to ensure continued access.
		Improve port and river navigation, including reintroduction of night navigation for deep sea vessels. To this end, acquire a buoy tender, several fast patrol boats, and tamper proof replacement navigation aids, and create an independent Pilotage Authority.
		Coordinate the plans for an off-dock container freight station.
Private sector participation	Encourage private sector participation in transportation.	Encourage the creation of a Contractors' Association, promote local contractor participation in road rehabilitation, and privatize the General Construction Co., Ltd.
		Ensure competition and investments in the quarry industry to lower prices and improve quality.
		Privatize GAC and have its domestic routes served by private aviation.
		Devolve the development of Ogle Airport to the private sector.

Policy area/issue	Strategy	Main recommendations and actions
Private sector participation (cont.)		Reconsider the expansion of public ferry services in view of the evolving services by private taxi boats and pontoon barges.
		Privatize the loss-making public shipping companies.
Cost recovery	Introduce cost recovery measures that are explicitly linked to the use of transport infrastructure to increase efficiency in usage and to cover operations and maintenance expenditures.	Introduce an annual sticker to be fixed on the windscreen of each motor vehicle to strengthen administration of vehicle licenses.
		Increase the Demerara Harbor Bridge tolls and apply the resulting revenues directly to its operation and maintenance.
		Consider the introduction of a fuel surcharge or of efficiently administered road tolls to fund road operations and maintenance.
		Review airport user charges in the context of the establishment of an Airport Authority and permit revenues to be applied to services.
		Review navigation and port charges in the context of the establishment of Port and Pilotage Authorities and permit revenues to be applied to services.
		Ensure proper cost recovery for the public ferry services.
Hinterland development	Take a long-term view on hinterland development.	Improve hinterland air access and defer the completion of the Mabura-Lethem road until further study.

Water and sanitation

Rehabilitation	Pursue the following objectives in the context of the ongoing and new donor-financed water projects: (1) rehabilitation of existing facilities to bring service levels over the medium and long term to minimum internationally acceptable standards; (2) restructuring of the regulatory framework and institutional strengthening; and (3) improvement of sector finances and financial management practices to attain self-sufficiency in the long term.	Set priorities for facilities to be rehabilitated, replaced, or maintained in line with sectoral institutional and financial absorptive capacity.
Operations and maintenance		Initiate an intensive program of recruiting and training qualified personnel to operate and maintain the systems facilities.
		Improve operations and maintenance in accordance with a preventive maintenance program and linked to monitorable targets for the reduction of unaccounted-for water and for water quality.
Institutional reform		Strengthen sector planning and management, and reorganize the water sector with emphasis on legal, financial, and managerial autonomy of the water agencies.

Policy area/issue	Strategy	Main recommendations and actions
Cost recovery		Introduce more efficient cost recovery policies to reduce the level of subsidies with a view toward their eventual elimination, in conjunction with improved collection procedures and financial and budgetary practices.
Private sector participation		Introduce and foster the participation of the private sector in the operation and maintenance of water and sanitation facilities.
Donor coordination		Coordinate donor activities to minimize duplication of effort and to facilitate a common approach in the resolution of sector problems.

Poverty reduction efforts

Poverty assessment and targeting of measures	Continue efforts to alleviate poverty and assess options after completion of the Income-Expenditure and Living Standards Measurement Surveys.	Facilitate implementation of SIMAP and Basic Needs projects.
		Facilitate implementation and speedy analysis of Income-Expenditure and Living Standard Measurement Surveys.

Education

Planning	Identify priorities and develop a medium-term policy framework.	Draft and approve medium-term education sector policies, strategies and priorities under the responsibility of the Ministry of Education and with cooperation of the Regional Administrations.
Resource availability	Introduce cost recovery measures.	Prepare a strategy for introducing user fees at higher-education institutions and secondary schools, determine appropriate fee levels, and detail collection mechanisms.
		Reduce support to the University from the Ministry of Education.
		Introduce limited cost-recovery for textbooks in secondary schools.
Institutional capacity	Improve management practices in the Ministry of Education and Regional Administrations, especially planning, monitoring, and budgeting functions.	Provide training in key management areas.
		Improve programming and budgeting procedures, expenditure control and auditing, and inventory management.
		Improve data collection, analysis, and evaluation.
		Improve the flow of information between regions and the Ministry of Education.
Resource allocation	Reduce inequities inherent in public subsidies.	Examine closely the distribution of benefits under the present subsidy system.
		Reduce subsidies to higher education levels and reallocate funds to primary and nursery levels.

Policy area/issue	Strategy	Main recommendations and actions
Resource allocation (cont.)		Determine regional disparities in resource bases and establish systems for targeting additional resources from the center to regions with fewer resources.
Teacher quality	Improve training and conditions of service so as to retain qualified teachers.	Establish salary and career incentives to attract and retain qualified teachers. Eliminate supplementary emoluments funded by schools.
		Improve quality of preservice and in-service teacher training.
		Develop and enforce examinations as accreditation vehicle for teachers.
Textbooks and teaching aids	Improve production, acquisition, and distribution of textbooks.	Improve the capacity to design and produce primary texts.
		Improve the availability of secondary-level texts.
		Provide individual schools with the capacity to purchase necessary teaching aids.
		Expand cost-recovery for textbooks.

Health

Policy area/issue	Strategy	Main recommendations and actions
Planning	Identify priorities and develop a medium-term policy framework.	Draft and approve medium-term education sector policies, strategies, and priorities under the responsibility of the Ministry of Health and with cooperation of the Regional Administrations.
Resource availability	Introduce cost recovery measures, and use part of the resulting revenues to improve salaries.	Establish a system of user charges by health care level.
		Identify fee collection and auditing mechanism.
		Develop ability to charge insurers for full cost of services.
		Make salaries competitive with those offered by private facilities, and eliminate emolument system.
Institutional capacity	Improve management practices in the Ministry of Health and Regional Administrations, especially planning, monitoring, and budgeting functions.	Provide training in key management areas.
		Improve programming and budgeting procedures, expenditure control and auditing, and inventory management.
		Improve data collection, analysis, and evaluation.
		Improve the flow of information between regions and the Ministry of Health.
Resource allocation	Reallocate funds to regional (primary) health care services.	Reallocate a proportion of user fee receipts from the Georgetown area to regional hospitals and primary health care facilities.

Policy area/issue	Strategy	Main recommendations and actions
Resource allocation (cont.)		Provide incentives to attract qualified health care personnel to regional facilities.
		Support mobile services to smaller outlying communities.
Preventive health care	Strengthen the administration of preventive health care programs, and increase funding.	Invest some proportion of revenues from user fees to this function.
		Provide additional training to staff.
Pharmaceutical and medical supplies	Eliminate chronic shortages of basic pharmaceuticals and medical supplies.	Decentralize the procurement of drugs to the regional level.
		Permit regional hospitals to apply for drug import licenses or to collaborate with private facilities in drug procurement.
		Introduce cost-recovery for drugs in hospitals and clinics.
		Strengthen management and budgeting capacity at hospital level to facilitate management of the system.

PART I: MACROECONOMIC FRAMEWORK

CHAPTER II.   MACROECONOMIC POLICIES

A.   BACKGROUND

2.1   After its independence from Great Britain in 1966, Guyana followed a "corporate state" model of development. All major economic activities were state-dominated, either directly through state ownership, or indirectly through price, credit and foreign exchange controls. As a result, Guyana's macroeconomic performance following independence and prior to the shift towards market-oriented policies under the ERP was dismal. Real GDP growth averaged only 0.4% per year during 1966-89, the lowest growth rate in the Commonwealth Caribbean. At the same time, the Government became unable to meet its debt service obligations, and, by end-1988, the public sector (including the Bank of Guyana) had accumulated external arrears of US$1,031 million on its external debt of then US$1,760 million.

B.   THE ECONOMIC RECOVERY PROGRAM

2.2   In mid-1988, the Government of Guyana announced its medium-term ERP, which called for a fundamental shift in economic policies towards a market-oriented economy. The broad objectives of the ERP were to: (i) restore the basis for sustainable economic growth and a viable balance of payments position over the medium-term, (ii) reintegrate the parallel economy into the official sector, and (iii) normalize relations with external creditors. To achieve these objectives, the Government began implementing a set of far-reaching adjustment measures and structural reforms in the areas of incentive policies, fiscal and monetary policies, public sector reform, and sectoral policies:

- price controls were removed, except for domestic sugar;

- import prohibitions and restrictions were eliminated, except for some food stuff and inputs to the manufacture of carbon dioxide;

- the structure of external tariffs was simplified with the introduction of the CARICOM Common External Tariff (CET), and the Government has agreed to introduce the revised CET by mid-1993, which foresees a gradual decrease in the maximum tariff rate to 20% by January 1, 1997;

- a free *cambio* market for the sale of foreign exchange was established in 1990, and the *official* and the *cambio* rates have subsequently been unified;

- tax reform measures were put in place and a number of exemptions were eliminated to improve the efficiency of the tax system and increase revenues;

- public sector expenditures were controlled, and fiscal deficits were reduced considerably;

- a shift to market-based instruments of monetary control was initiated, including a flexible interest rate policy based on competitive treasury bill auctions;

- a process to rationalize the public administration was initiated, including a reduction in the number of ministries from 18 to 11 and of non-critical positions;

- a privatization program was initiated for a large group of public enterprises, with a number of them sold, closed or leased;

- rationalization and restructuring towards privatization of the operations in the bauxite and sugar sectors begun; and

- a social impact amelioration program was launched to mitigate the social impact of the adjustment process.

2.3   The ERP has received the support of the international community. A Support Group of donors was established to help obtain external financing. With the assistance of the Support Group, Guyana secured financing to clear its arrears to the International Monetary Fund (IMF), the World Bank, and the Caribbean Development Bank (CDB). The Government also agreed with the multilateral agencies on major programs of support and with its major bilateral donors on debt rescheduling.

C.   ECONOMIC PERFORMANCE UNDER THE ERP, 1989-92

1.   <u>Growth Performance</u>

2.4   During 1989-90, the Government implemented key measures of the ERP, in spite of disruptions which adversely affected economic growth and delayed the expected recovery. In 1989, real GDP declined by 3.3% as protracted strikes in the sugar and bauxite sectors[1], generalized power shortages, and shortfalls in the disbursement of balance of payments assistance curtailed activities in all sectors (Table 2.1). In 1990, real GDP declined further by 2.5%. Unusually heavy rains constrained output of sugar, rice and bauxite, and the economy's performance was further weakened by the sharp rise in world oil prices during the Gulf crisis. In addition, Guyana's export performance was affected by the overvalued official exchange rate applied to traditional products until the *cambio* and official exchange rates were unified in 1991.

2.5   In 1991, economic activity began to recover and real GDP increased by 6.0%, as the ERP solicited a strong supply response and weather conditions were favorable. Price and exchange rate liberalization and improved incentives for private sector development had a significant impact on increasing production in all sectors and on integrating the parallel into the official economy. Rice paddy production increased by 61%, to 251,000 metric tons, in response to availability of imported inputs, removal of price controls, shift of rice exports to the *cambio* market, and large increases in paddy prices paid to farmers by the recently-privatized rice mills. In the

---

[1]   Work-days lost in the sugar and bauxite sectors amounted to 684,340 in 1989, equivalent to about five-times the losses of 1987.

sugar sub-sector, production increased by 32%, to 174,000 metric tons, as a result of the installation of private management, subsequent wage increases which significantly improved industrial relations, replanting, and favorable weather conditions.   Production of calcined bauxite, which fetches four-times the price of chemical and metal grade bauxite, increased by 14%, to 360,000 metric tons.   Recorded gold production increased by 36%, to 58,000 oz., reflecting in large part increased returns from legal sales to the Gold Board compared to smuggling.   A similar response was evident in other export-oriented activities as well.

Table 2.1: SELECTED ECONOMIC INDICATORS
(in percent)

	1980-88	1989	1990	Est. 1991	Prel. 1992
	----------- average growth rates -----------				
Real GDP (Factor Costs)	-2.9	-3.3	-2.5	6.0	7.5
Agriculture	-1.0	-1.7	-13.5	11.5	14.0
Mining	-8.5	-11.3	19.9	17.9	-11.0
Industry	-5.1	-8.9	-12.1	11.1	5.0
Construction and Services	-2.0	-1.3	1.4	0.1	3.9
Real Gross Domestic Investment	-10.3	35.3	27.3	-4.7	-3.6
Central Government	-7.6 a/	7.4	47.5	-54.5	36.2
Public Enterprises	...	67.3	22.9	-24.1	...
Private	-10.0	39.1	-7.6	270.7	-13.8 d/
Real Consumption	-2.8	-9.0	-5.3	4.9	0.1
Central Government	-4.9	-21.0	-19.3	-2.0	1.0
Private	-2.1	-2.9	0.4	7.2	-0.2
Real Exports of GNFS	-5.7	-0.9	-8.8	17.5	28.0
Real Imports of GNFS	-8.0	-5.5	2.8	-2.5	18.4
Urban Consumer Prices (end-period)	19.7 b/	104.7	75.9	81.5	14.2
	-------------- shares in GDP ---------------				
Consumption	83.6	79.4	79.5	76.4	62.9
Central Government	25.6	23.0	19.6	17.6	20.7
Private	58.0	56.5	59.9	58.8	42.2
Gross Domestic Investment	29.5	29.5	41.6	41.6	34.5
Central Government	21.9 a/	10.9	17.7	8.5	9.9
Public Enterprises	...	14.2	19.3	15.4	...
Private	5.8	4.5	4.6	17.8	24.7 d/
Gross Domestic Savings	16.4	20.6	20.5	23.6	37.1
Resource Balance	-13.2	-9.7	-21.1	-18.0	2.6
Exports of GNFS	58.8	90.4	83.6	122.4	132.1
Imports of GNFS	72.0	100.2	104.6	140.4	129.5
External Current Account	-25.7	-43.2	-56.4	-56.1	-29.8
External Debt c/	147.9	806.2	743.9	856.9	675.5
Scheduled Debt Service	54.8	106.4	83.8	68.6	50.9

a/ Fixed capital formation, including public enterprises.
b/ Annual average.
c/ Outstanding and disbursed.
d/ Including public enterprises

Source: Statistical Appendix

2.6   In 1992, the economic recovery continued, and real GDP is estimated to have increased by 7.5%. The main contributors to GDP growth were sugar (53% increase), rice (11%), timber (22%) and gold (34%) production. Also contributing to the strong growth performance was manufacturing (5%), including non-rice and non-sugar related activities which benefited from the improved investment climate and the increased availability of foreign exchange. Among Guyana's major products, only bauxite output declined by an average of 40%, as a result of structural and financial problems in the industry.

2. Demand Management and Adjustment

2.7   The adjustment process was accompanied by a sharp increase in inflation which only subsided in the second half of 1991, to an estimated 14% in 1992. Among the principal factors contributing to the rapid rise in inflation were the continued large domestic borrowing requirements of the public sector *including* the Bank of Guyana, facilitated by accommodative monetary policies. This process also led to a decline in real money demand and propelled the depreciation of the exchange rate which further accelerated inflation.

2.8   In the public sector, control of non-interest expenditures and increases in revenues in the course of the adjustment process led to a substantial improvement in the primary current account balance during 1988-92 (Table 2.2). Nonetheless, net domestic borrowing requirements of the public sector, *including* the Bank of Guyana remained large, reaching about 26% of GDP in 1991 and 1992. These large domestic borrowing requirements mainly reflect the increase in the debt service burden in local currency units resulting from the depreciation of the Guyanese dollar.

Table 2.2: SUMMARY OF PUBLIC SECTOR OPERATIONS a/
(percent of GDP)

	1987	1988	1989	1990	Est. 1991	Prel. 1992
Primary Account Balance	27.1	15.5	18.1	16.9	27.9	32.2
Current Account Balance	-8.5	-15.7	-25.6	-28.7	-20.8	-10.9
Capital Expenditure	-28.4	-18.2	-25.6	-36.8	-23.9	-23.1
Overall Balance After Grants b/	-34.0	-32.5	-47.9	-58.2	-32.8	-28.4
Net Domestic Borrowing Requirements	-2.2	15.0	12.3	17.0	25.6	25.7

a/ Includes non-financial public sector and Bank of Guyana.
b/ Includes divestment proceeds.

Source: Statistical Appendix

2.9   Money supply in nominal terms expanded sharply during the adjustment process, by 53% per year on average during 1988-91 (Table 2.3). At the same time real money demand fell severely, and velocity increased from about 1 in 1988 to 1.6 by mid-1991. This financial disintermediation, stimulated by high rates of inflation and controlled negative rates of interest until mid-1991, in turn fed back into the inflationary process.

Table 2.3: MONEY AND CREDIT
(growth rates)

	1987	1988	1989	1990	Est. 1991	Prel. 1992
Domestic Credit (nominal)	27.7	26.4	26.5	12.5	-6.1	5.7
Public (non-financial)	25.3	20.9	19.3	-1.4	-36.5	-23.9
Private	46.5	61.2	61.3	62.1	60.4	30.9
Broad Money (nominal)	34.3	37.3	50.3	52.0	72.8	60.4
Monetary Liabilities	46.2	45.3	43.8	44.0	75.1	28.8
Time and Savings Deposits	28.2	32.4	54.7	57.1	71.4	79.0
Broad Money (real) [Index, 1987=100]	100.0	80.9	40.5	30.8	28.1	41.3
Velocity (GDP/BM) [ratio]	1.2	1.0	1.2	1.2	1.6	1.3
Memorandum Items						
Urban Consumer Prices (end-period)	34.6	51.5	104.7	75.9	81.5	14.2
Nominal Exchange Rate [G$/US$]	10	10	33	45	121	126

Source: Statistical Appendix

2.10   These trends began to be reversed beginning mid-1991, following
the unification of the exchange rate system.   In an attempt to curb excess
liquidity, the Bank of Guyana increased interest rates to reflect market
conditions, absorbed 75-80% of the excess reserves of the banking system
through the forced sale of debentures, and raised reserve requirements. At
the same time, domestic credit to the non-financial public sector was strictly
contained. As a result of these measures and the more stable macroeconomic
environment, confidence in the financial system recovered during 1992, and
real money demand began to increase and the composition of broad money began
to change in favor of time and savings deposits.

2.11   Up to June 1991, it was difficult to conduct effective monetary
policies, as the Government set its interest rates with little reference to
market conditions, resulting in highly negative rates, and was not able to use
the sale of treasury bills as an instrument of monetary control.   In June
1991, the Government shifted its policy and introduced a system for
competitive bidding of treasury bills at monthly auctions which allowed for
market-determined interest rates.   The rate prevailing in the treasury bill
auctions is currently used to adjust the bank rate for rediscounting loans and
other administered rates, such that the overall interest structure is
ultimately tied to the treasury bill rate.

2.12   Since the introduction of the auction system, treasury bill rates
have been positive in real terms (Figure 2.1). However, with the recovering
confidence in the financial system and facilitated by the relative stability
of the exchange rate over the last eighteen months, real treasury bill rates
have declined significantly during June 1991-92.

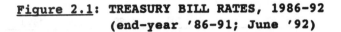

Figure 2.1: TREASURY BILL RATES, 1986-92
(end-year '86-91; June '92)

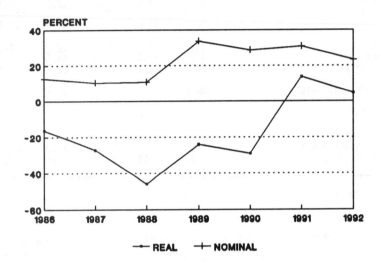

2.13   Guyana's foreign exchange system has been profoundly reformed under the ERP, and both the nominal and real rates have been subject to substantial depreciation. The parallel market for foreign exchange was legalized in March 1990 with the introduction of the *cambio* system. This allowed banks and non-bank dealers to trade foreign currency at freely determined rates. During most of 1990, a dual exchange rate system existed with an *official* rate which was substantially more appreciated than the *cambio* rate, and the *cambio* market only applied to nontraditional exports and nonessential imports and services. In June 1990, the range of application of the *cambio* rate was further extended. In February 1991, the *de facto* unification of the exchange rate occurred, when the *official* rate was adjusted to match the *cambio* rate, albeit only on a weekly basis. Since September 1991, those foreign exchange transactions which continue to be conducted by the Bank of Guyana are based on the *cambio* market rate on the day the transactions take place.

2.14   As discussed above, Guyana's nominal exchange rate depreciated considerably in the course of the exchange rate liberalization, from G$10/US$1 in 1988 to about G$120/US$1 in 1991. Since mid-1991 the nominal exchange rate has been relatively stable, and stood at G$126/US$1 by end-1992. Despite rapid domestic inflation, this process has had a positive impact on Guyana's growth prospects. The exchange rate liberalization led to a significant depreciation of the real effective exchange rate, by about 40% during 1988-92 (Figure 2.2), and strengthened Guyana's international competitiveness considerably.

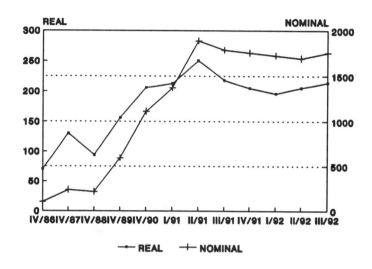

Figure 2.2: EFFECTIVE EXCHANGE RATES, 1986-92
(Indices, 1980=100)

3. External Accounts

2.15   Guyana's external financial position has improved significantly under the ERP, but remains precarious on account of the debt service implications of country's large public debt overhang of US$1793 million at end-1992.

2.16   In 1991, exports of goods and non-factor services increased by over 17% in real terms, largely based on the improved performance in the bauxite, sugar, rice and gold sectors. At the same time, imports of goods and non-factor services decreased by 2.5% in real terms, mainly on account of a 9% drop in the price of imported fuel, which accounts for about 30% of total imports. As a result, the resource balance improved from a deficit of 21% of GDP in 1990 to a deficit of 18% of GDP in 1991. In 1992, this development is projected to have continued. Exports increased by an estimated 28%, in spite of a 2% decline in average export prices and a sharp decline in bauxite exports. Import growth resumed in line with the continued expansion of economic activities, and reached 18% that year. Consequently, the resource balance recorded a surplus of 3% of GDP.

2.17   The current account of the balance of payments continued to record large deficits, estimated at US$79 million or 30% of GDP in 1992, of which 25% of GDP corresponded to interest owed on external debt. Nonetheless, the overall balance of payments recorded a surplus, estimated at about US$49 million in 1992. Accordingly, the Bank of Guyana further accumulated (gross) foreign reserves, estimated at over six months imports-equivalent by the end of 1992. This cushion of reserves will be needed to ensure repayment of Guyana's debt service obligations over the coming years.

Table 2.4: SUMMARY BALANCE OF PAYMENTS
(US$ millions)

	1987	1988	1989	1990	Est. 1991	Prel. 1992
Current Account	-119	-100	-121	-163	-127	-79
Merchandise Trade (net)	-21	-1	-8	-46	-7	26
Exports, f.o.b.	241	215	205	204	239	312
Bauxite	86	80	72	75	79	55
Sugar	90	75	83	75	82	133
Rice	16	15	12	14	17	33
Other	48	45	37	41	60	91
Imports, c.i.f.	-262	-216	-212	-250	-245	-286
Fuel	-77	-74	-70	-87	-78	-96
Other a/	-185	-142	-142	-162	-167	-190
Service (net) a/	-109	-112	-127	-130	-134	-119
o.w: Interest on Public Debt b/	-81	-85	-94	-101	-98	-66
Net Private Transfers	11	13	14	13	14	14
Capital Account	-14	-17	237	546	167	123
Non-financial Public Sector						
Capital Official Grants	10	6	7	15	8	4
Medium- and Long-term Debt	-23	-28	236	522	86	-5
Disbursements	39	29	68	225	79	55
Amortization	-134	-130	-175	-121	-43	-70
Rescheduling/Debt Relief	72	73	343	418	50	10
Short-term Debt (net)	0	0	-3	0	0	0
Sale of Assets	0	0	1	4	29	10
Official Development Banks (net)	6	1	0	0	0	0
Private Sector/Commercial Banks a/	-7	4	-5	5	44	114
Errors and Omissions	-4	11	1	1	1	5
Overall Balance	-137	-106	-117	385	41	49
Financing	137	106	117	-385	-41	-49
BoG Net Foreign Assets (incl. IMF)	77	32	29	-18	-41	-49
Non-financial Public Sector Arrears	56	70	-156	-265	0	0
Private Sector Commercial Arrears	4	4	10	-101	0	0

a/ Excludes activities related to major gold projects and petroleum exploration.
b/ On an accrual basis, including interest on principal in arrears.

Source: Statistical Appendix

2.18   Guyana received substantial debt relief under the ERP to finance its external current account deficit and reduce its external arrears during 1989-92. It benefited from two rescheduling operations from the Paris Club, the latest in September 1990 under *Toronto Terms*. Rescheduling arrangements also were concluded with various Non-Paris Club creditors. In particular, Guyana's debt to Trinidad and Tobago (currently US$413 million) was rescheduled, and negotiations on further relief have been initiated. Some bilateral lenders have canceled the debt owed to them unilaterally, including the United States (US$112 million), Canada (US$34 million), and the United Kingdom (US$9 million). In 1992, Guyana was able to buy-back its total public debt owed to commercial banks, amounting to US$93 million, with a US$11 million grant envelope provided by IDA. On the whole, debt relief amounted to US$418 million in 1990, US$51 million in 1991, and US$10 in 1992, while new loans contributed US$225 million in 1990, US$79 million in 1991 and US$55 in 1992 to support Guyana's balance of payments. In addition, the composition of Guyana's debt has changed in favor of long-term concessional loans, which currently amount to 31% of the total external debt outstanding, compared to 24% at end-1990.

2.19   The impact of past debt rescheduling and cancellations not-withstanding, Guyana's debt indicators are still alarming (Table 2.5), and point to the need for further generous debt relief. At the end of 1992, total public and publicly guaranteed external debt outstanding and disbursed is estimated to amount to US$1793 million, or 675% of GDP. Debt service payments recorded in the balance of payments as a ratio to exports of goods and non-factor services declined, but still amounted to 36% in 1992. Debt service payments as a ratio to Central Government current revenues amounted to 149% in 1991 and 105% in 1992, and remained far in excess of the Central Government endogenous capacity to serve them. As a result of these large debt service obligations and the need to address outstanding arrears, the gross foreign financial assistance listed above translated into negative net transfers of US$4 million in 1991 and US$67 million in 1992.

Table 2.5: EXTERNAL DEBT INDICATORS

	1987	1988	1989	1990	Est. 1991	Prel. 1992
	---------------- US$ million ---------------					
Total Public Debt	1722	1760	1852	1940	1853	1793
Scheduled Debt Service (Balance of Payments)	-215	-215	-269	-222	-141	-135
Change in Arrears	60	74	-147	-367	0	0
Net Transfers a/	-37	-37	-9	171	-4	-67
	---------------- in percent ---------------					
Debt/GDP	496	421	806	744	857	675
Scheduled Debt Service/GDP	62	51	117	85	65	51
Scheduled Debt Service/Exports GNFS	76	82	107	89	48	36
Scheduled Debt Service/Current Revenues	184	129	249	184	149	105

a/ Official capital inflows to the public sector after debt service and repayments of arrears.

Source: Statistical Appendix

D. THE MACROECONOMIC POLICY AGENDA

2.20   The key items of the current Government's macroeconomic policy agenda are described in the recently approved 1992-94 Policy Framework Paper. In this document, the Government expresses its strong commitment to the fundamental principles of the ERP to sustain the reform policies described above, including the pursuit of a sound macroeconomic framework and sectoral policies in line with the principles of a market-oriented economy. The main macroeconomic reforms 2/ to advance the adjustment process include the following:

- The *cambio* market needs to be deepened with a view to include all foreign exchange transactions (sugar, bauxite, and fuel).

2/   Defined broadly as covering incentive and financial sector policies; a more extensive analysis of privatization, trade and financial sector issues can be found in the report on Guyana: Private Sector Development. Fiscal and public sector reform policies are discussed in more detail in Chapter III and Part III of this report.

- Trade liberalization policies need to be continued, including adoption of the revised CET on a "fast-track" as agreed with CARICOM and elimination of the remaining import prohibitions and restrictions

- Direct involvement of the public sector in economic activity needs to be reduced further to increase efficiency and focus scarce government resources on economic and social infrastructure. To this end, the Government needs to move rapidly on a broad-based program to privatize public sector assets in the major economic sectors. Privatization needs to follow transparent procedures and be accompanied by the establishment of an appropriate regulatory framework in industries that are not sufficiently competitive or that provide significant public goods.

- Fiscal performance needs to be improved by strengthening tax administration, broadening the tax base through elimination of exemptions and improving expenditure control (see Chapter III).

- Monetary policy needs to be improved by strengthening the role of the Central Bank, shifting to more flexible monetary instruments including open market operations, and broadening the range of treasury-bill maturities.

- Financial sector efficiency needs to be increased through encouraging new entrants into the financial system and reducing the role of the public sector in this area. This process must be accompanied by efforts to strengthen the regulatory framework and improve the effectiveness of supervision.

2.21   In addition to sound economic policies, Guyana also requires further financial assistance, including enhanced concessions for debt rescheduling and debt forgiveness, to achieve external viability in the medium-term. In this connection, continued adjustment along on the lines described above will not only improve the country's economic performance and increase its population's income and consumption levels, but will also help establishing the case to the donor community to grant such assistance.

CHAPTER III. PUBLIC SECTOR FINANCES

A. OVERVIEW

3.1   Public sector finances continue to be under great stress on
account of Guyana's large debt service burden.   Control of non-interest
expenditures and increases in revenues in the course of the adjustment process
led to a substantial improvement in the primary account balance, from 16% of
GDP in 1988 to an estimated 32% of GDP in 1992.   To a large extent, this
improvement reflects improved Central Government finances and underestimates
the progress achieved in the public enterprise sector, as a number of
profitable enterprises have been divested.   The net domestic borrowing
requirements of the public sector *including* the Bank of Guyana remained large,
at about 26% of GDP each in 1991 and 1992, which can be traced back to very
high debt service obligations, amounting to about 45% of GDP during 1991-92.

Table 3.1: CONSOLIDATED PUBLIC SECTOR FINANCES a/
(in percent of GDP)

	1987	1988	1989	1990	Est. 1991	Prel. 1992
Primary Current Account Balance	27.1	15.5	18.1	16.9	27.9	32.2
Interest Obligations	-35.6	-31.2	-43.7	-45.5	-48.6	-43.1
Domestic	-12.2	-11.6	-12.2	-12.0	-9.5	-12.8
External	-23.4	-19.6	-31.5	-33.5	-39.1	-30.3
Current Account Balance	-8.5	-15.7	-25.6	-28.7	-20.8	-10.9
Capital Revenue b/	0.0	0.0	0.5	2.5	7.9	1.4
Grants	2.9	1.4	2.8	4.7	4.0	2.0
Capital Expenditure	-28.4	-18.2	-25.6	-36.8	-23.9	-23.1
Overall Balance After Grants	-34.0	-32.5	-47.9	-58.2	-32.8	-30.6
Net Domestic Borrowing Requirements	-2.2	15.0	12.3	17.0	25.6	25.7

a/ Includes non-financial public sector and Bank of Guyana.
b/ Includes divestment proceeds.

Source: Statistical Appendix

B. CENTRAL GOVERNMENT FINANCES

1. Overview

3.2   Central Government Finances showed a continued improvement under
the ERP. The primary current account balance of the Central Government
improved considerably from 4% of GDP in 1988 to over 15% in 1992.   The
current account deficit also decreased, from 27% of GDP in 1988 to 12% in
1992, in spite of continued large interest obligations, amounting to about 28%
of GDP in 1992.   These developments, together with lower-than-expected capital
expenditures on account of financing and implementation constraints, resulted
in a substantial decline in the overall deficit of the Central Government,
from 37% of GDP in 1988 to 23% in 1992.   Similarly, the Central Government's

net domestic borrowing requirements also decreased from 35% of GDP in 1988 to 7% in 1992.

Table 3.2: CENTRAL GOVERNMENT FINANCES
(in percent of GDP)

	1987	1988	1989	1990	Est. 1991	Prel. 1992
Primary Current Account Balance	-1.3	4.4	5.6	11.1	14.3	15.4
Current Revenue	32.8	39.7	38.7	40.7	40.2	48.6
Non-Interest Current Expenditure	-34.1	-35.3	-33.1	-29.6	-25.9	-33.2
Interest Obligations	-34.7	-31.4	-42.5	-45.8	-38.2	-27.7
Domestic	-27.7	-24.4	-30.0	-29.0	-13.9	-12.5
External	-7.0	-7.0	-12.5	-16.8	-24.3	-15.2
Current Account Balance	-36.1	-27.0	-36.8	-34.7	-23.9	-12.3
Capital Revenue a/	0.0	0.0	0.5	2.5	8.2	1.4
Grants	2.9	1.4	2.8	4.7	1.2	1.4
Capital Expenditure	-16.6	-11.3	-14.4	-18.6	-10.4	-13.9
Overall Balance After Grants	-49.8	-36.9	-48.0	-46.1	-24.9	-23.3
Net Domestic Borrowing Requirements	n.a.	-34.6	-34.6	-7.3	-5.8	-7.0

a/ Includes divestment proceeds.

Source: Statistical Appendix

2. Revenues[3]

3.3   Under the ERP, the Government introduced a number of reform measures to increase the efficiency of the tax system. In this endeavor, it attempted to reduce the distortionary effects of the tax system and preserve its capacity to mobilize resources. In 1988, the Government introduced a sugar levy in lieu of regular taxes to capture part of the differential between the EC preferential and the world market price. In 1989, the Government converted some specific consumption taxes to an ad valorem basis and eliminated exemptions specific to public enterprises. In 1990, it eliminated exemptions relating to fuel and imports of agricultural, forestry and mining equipment, and extended the tax coverage to previously prohibited imports. In 1991, it drastically simplified the personal income tax by replacing allowances and deductions by an income threshold and by reducing the number of tax bands from six to three, improved the company tax structure through the adoption of a single company tax rate of 35% of gross profits instead of two sets of rates of up to 45% and 55%, respectively, introduced a 15% withholding tax on interest on resident savings in lieu of taxation of personal income, charged a 15% rice export levy on exports to the EC, and reduced the consumption tax rate to 40% for most commodities previously taxed at 50%. In 1992, consumption taxes were eliminated for basic items and further reduced for a number of luxury items. In 1993, the personal income tax was further simplified, by introducing a single rate of 33 1/3 percent on all taxable income in excess of a fixed allowance of G$120,000 per year. A

3/   See also Chapter VII for a more detailed discussion of the tax system and of tax and customs administrations.

10% development levy was imposed on companies, and the consumption tax extended to cover hotel accommodations at a rate of 10%. Further, a number of consumption tax and import duty exemptions were granted.

3.4   In spite of the significant improvements in the tax system, the tax burden continues to fall on a narrow base with relatively high rates. Extensive fiscal concessions are granted in the form of tax holidays up to 10 years under the income tax, depreciation allowances, exemptions of dividends from the withholding tax during tax holidays, and remissions from consumption tax and import duties for a wide variety of purposes at the discretion of the Government. There also remains a large, untaxed parallel economy. Hence, the Government needs to further widen the tax base to improve revenue performance. In this connection, the future emphasis should be on eliminating exemptions and strengthening the tax and customs administrations to improve revenue collection. In considering other reforms, while they may be desirable *in principle*, attention needs to be given to the costs of perpetuated uncertainty by the private sector about the impact of the tax system.

3.5   The imposition of a development levy, which effectively increases company taxes from 35% to 45%, is a step back in the effort to improve the incentive framework for private sector development and has increased the distortions arising from the gap between personal income and company taxes. Hence, it is recommended that the Government remove this levy and subsequently unify the top income and company tax rates.

3.6   On average, current revenues amounted to 40% of GDP during 1988-91, with little variation over the years, before increasing to 48% of GDP in 1992. There also were some shifts in the revenue composition during this period. *Personal income tax* revenues declined from about 4% of GDP in 1988 to less than 2% of GDP in 1991. This reflected both lower tax rates and weaknesses in tax administration which resulted in a very narrow effective tax base consisting mainly of employees working for the public sector or for large companies. With the strong economic recovery, however, the personal income taxes rebounded to 4% of GDP in 1992. *Company tax* revenues remained comparatively stable, between 9-11% of GDP. They could probably be increased through covering smaller companies and sample verifications of tax assessments. Revenue losses are also incurred by overly generous fiscal concessions granted to new companies. The contribution of the *consumption tax* to revenues increased from about 10% of GDP in 1988 to 13% of GDP in 1992, reflecting the shift to an ad-valorem base and the elimination of exemptions specific to public enterprises. This contribution could be increased further if remissions were eliminated, if taxes on imports were charged at the point of entry instead of ex-factory gate, and if the tax were extended to services other than hotel accommodations. As a complementary measure, customs administrations need to be strengthened and consideration should be given to lowering rates on some items to decrease the benefit of tax evasion. Revenues from *taxes on international trade* have increased from 4% of GDP in 1988 to 6% of GDP in 1992. This trend is likely to be affected by the revision in the CET. However, a large percentage of imports enter Guyana on a duty-free basis, and elimination of remissions could compensate for ensuing potential decrease in revenues. Thus, *other things equal*, elimination of exemptions combined with a reduction in the average tariff rate to 10% would yield an increase in revenues from international taxes of about 50%. Another important source of revenue is the *sugar levy*, amounting to 1% of GDP in 1992. This revenue source needs to be preserved *in principle*, notwithstanding changes in the ownership structure of the sugar sector.

Table 3.3: CENTRAL GOVERNMENT REVENUES
(in percent of GDP)

	1987	1988	1989	1990	Est. 1991	Prel. 1992
Current Revenue	32.8	39.7	38.7	40.7	40.2	48.6
Direct Taxes	12.7	15.1	14.5	15.3	13.5	17.1
o.w. Company Tax	6.9	9.5	10.8	11.2	9.3	10.3
o.w. Personal Income Tax	4.5	4.3	2.4	2.6	1.9	3.9
Indirect Taxes	16.9	21.4	19.9	23.1	23.2	28.9
o.w. Consumption Tax	11.4	10.5	11.0	12.1	13.1	12.8
o.w. Tax on International Trade	4.3	3.8	5.3	6.2	6.0	5.9
Non-tax Revenue	3.1	3.2	4.3	2.3	3.5	2.6
Capital Revenue a/	0.0	0.0	0.5	2.5	8.2	1.4
Total Revenue	32.8	39.7	39.2	43.2	48.4	50.0

a/ Includes divestment proceeds

Source: Statistical Appendix

3.7   A further important source of revenue has been the divestment proceeds, amounting to about 8% of GDP in 1991 and an estimated 1.4% of GDP in 1992. While the argument for further privatization is mostly based on efficiency grounds, this positive revenue impact -- together with the release of scarce public funds for investments in economic and social infrastructure -- strengthens the case for privatization in a situation were the Government is forced to make difficult decisions regarding its priorities on account of stringent fiscal constraints (see Section C below).

Table 3.4: CURRENT AND TARGET REVENUE FROM COST RECOVERY a/
(US$ million)

SECTOR	MAIN SOURCE	MAIN USE	CURRENT	TARGET
Drainage and Irrigation	User Fees	O&M Expenditure	<0.5	5.0
Power	Tariff	Operating Expenses	19.0	27.0
Road Transportation	Fuel Tax/Veh.Lic.	Road O&M Expenditure	1.3b/	0.0
Water and Sanitation	Tariff	Operating Expenses	<0.1	2.0
Sea Defenses	Levy	O&M Expenditure	0.0	5.0
Education	Tuition	Recurrent Expenditure	~0.0	1.0
Health	User Fees	Recurrent Expenditure	~0.0	3.0
TOTAL			20.9	49.0
TOTAL (Share in 1992 GDP)			7.9%	18.2%

a/ Based on full recovery (100%) of targeted expenditures, except for education (15%, 40%, and 60% for primary, secondary and tertiary education, respectively) and health (30%) expenditures.
b/ Budgeted for O&M.
~   means approximately.
<   means smaller than.

Source: Mission Estimates

3.8   A hitherto neglected source of revenues, and a means to increase efficiency in the consumption of public goods and services, are user charges

and other cost recovery measures (see also Part III). Currently, the
provision of public services in almost all areas is either totally or
partially subsidized. As a result, the Government lacks the funds to maintain
the quality of these services. While in some areas services may need to be
improved prior to implementing cost recovery measures, their revenue potential
in the medium-term is large (Table 3.4). An indication of this revenue
potential is the willingness of consumers to buy services from private sources
where public delivery fails, as, for example, in health and education.
However, to avoid transferring the cost of inefficiencies in public service
delivery to consumers, private sector involvement in all areas should be
encouraged.

3. Expenditures

3.9   Central Government expenditures have been dominated by debt
service obligations stemming from Guyana's debt overhang. With interest
obligations ranging from 31% to 45% of GDP, the Government's financing
constraints have imposed drastic reductions in non-interest current
expenditures. Consequently, personal emoluments have decreased steadily from
15% of GDP in 1987 to an estimated 9% of GDP in 1992. Expenditures on other
goods and services have followed a similar path and have declined from 12% of
GDP in 1987 to an estimated 10% of GDP in 1992. At the same time, the
Government has spent increasing amounts on transfers, from 7% of GDP in 1987
to 14% of GDP in 1992, including transfers to the Guyana Electricity Company
amounting to 3% of GDP in 1991 and an estimated 4% of GDP in 1992. Capital
expenditures have been determined both by financial and institutional
constraints. As a result, they have not followed a clear path and ranged
between 10% to 19% of GDP under the ERP.

Table 3.5: CENTRAL GOVERNMENT EXPENDITURES
(in percent of GDP)

	1987	1988	1989	1990	Est. 1991	Prel. 1992
Current Expenditure	68.9	66.7	75.5	75.4	64.1	60.1
Personal Emoluments	15.4	14.4	10.0	10.2	8.3	9.4
Other Goods and Services	12.0	13.4	13.0	9.5	9.3	9.5
Interest Obligations	34.8	31.4	42.5	45.8	38.2	27.7
Transfers and Refunds	6.8	7.4	10.1	10.0	8.3	14.3
Capital Expenditure a/	16.6	11.3	14.4	18.6	10.4	13.9
o.w. Capital Formation	14.2	9.7	10.6	16.9	8.2	9.4
Total Expenditure	85.5	78.0	90.0	94.0	74.5	74.0

a/ Excludes transfers to the private sector.

Source: Statistical Appendix

3.10   While fiscal adjustment usually requires reductions in
expenditures on goods and services, in the case of Guyana they have been so
severe as to impair the efficient functioning of the Government. However,
this effect has been reinforced by a budget process which is oriented towards
line-items, as opposed to activities or programs, and which makes it difficult
to assess the impact on budget cuts on the actual operations of the government
ministries and agencies. As a complementary measure, expenditure control and

management needs to be improved through the implementation of adequate financial management systems and procedures. Also, the continuation of transfer payments to the Guyana Electricity Company (GEC) and significant expenditures on membership fees to a large number of local, regional and international organizations without assessment of their benefits indicate that the impact of the Government's limited resources could be further strengthened.

Personal Emoluments

3.11   The key constraint impeding the efficient operation of the Government is the deterioration in the quality of the public service.[4] The principal cause for this deterioration has been the sharp decrease in real emoluments, which declined by about 25% on average during 1987-92 (Table 3.6). Moreover, regular salaries have decreased even more rapidly for higher level staff, which suffered losses in real income (excluding allowances) of almost 60% during that same period. Consequently, vacancy rates are particularly high for technical positions, amounting to over 40% of budgeted positions. At the same time, over 70% of budgeted positions are for low-level positions in grades 1-5, resulting in a very bottom-heavy public service. In this setting, the Government is not able to adequately carry out such basic functions as data collection and analysis, accounting and cost control, and essential service delivery. Hence, the overriding concern for the Government with regard to public sector employment is to provide wage incentives to fill vacancies of technical positions while reducing labor redundancies, especially at lower levels. The implementation of IDA's proposed Public Administration Project (PAP), which includes upgrading of the current salary scale and measures to eliminate labor redundancies, would be an important contribution to meeting this objective.

Table 3.6: CENTRAL GOVERNMENT PERSONAL EMOLUMENTS

	1987	1988	1989	1990	Est. 1991	Prel. 1992
Number of Budgeted Positions	25384	24391	22034	18656	17821	18236
Personal Emoluments (G$ million)	535.2	602.5	754.8	1191.1	2192.3	3287.8
Wages and Salaries	422.6	439.8	511.9	696.1	1473.7	2201.8
Allowances and Contributions	112.6	162.7	242.9	495.0	718.6	1085.9
Average Nominal Emoluments (G$ per month) a/	1757	2058	2855	5320	10251	15024
Average Real Emoluments (1987-G$ per month)	1757	1359	921	975	1035	1320
Average Real Emoluments Index (1987=100)	100.0	77.3	52.4	55.5	58.9	75.1
Real Wage Index for Grade 16	100.0	n.a.	n.a.	n.a.	38.6	41.4
Real Wage Index for Grade 1	100.0	n.a.	n.a.	n.a.	58.2	62.3

a/ Based on budgeted positions disregarding vacancies (estimated at 37% in 1992).

Source: Government of Guyana and IMF

3.12   Constraining expenditures on personal emoluments has to be regarded as a necessary element of the adjustment process in view of the

---

4/   For a more detailed discussion, see Chapter VI of this report.

severe fiscal imbalances inherited from a long period of economic
mismanagement. However, the fall in real wages of the public service has been
excessive, and has led to an outflow of professionals. This has been
undermining the ability of the Government to provide adequate support for the
economic recovery process. To correct this situation, the Government has
undertaken commendable efforts in improving salaries and, since 1990, has
increased public service pay by 209% in nominal terms, and recorded some gains
in real wages. Nonetheless, current public service salaries are still low
when compared to those in the public enterprises and in the private sector,
especially for higher level positions.

3.13   The Government has employed a variety of mechanisms in an attempt
to selectively ameliorate its staffing problems. These include allowances and
other salary enhancements outside the formal grading system which, during
1987-90, have increased much more rapidly than expenditures on regular wages
and salaries, and have resulted in the payment of significantly different
salaries for similar positions across government agencies. This has fostered
resentment and low morale, decreased labor mobility between government
agencies, and has undermined accountability due to the lack of transparency of
these arrangements.

3.14   Another problem with public employment is the high number of
support and other low-level staff relative to professional and technical
staff. Over 70% of budgeted and over 75% of filled positions correspond to
grades 1-5. Often, several employees with lower skills are asked to perform
activities that should be carried out by a more qualified staff who cannot be
attracted at existing salary levels. Overall, evidence points to significant
labor redundancies, especially at lower levels and once higher level positions
will have been filled as a result of upgrading the salary scale.

3.15   In this connection, the PAP suggest decompressing and upgrading
the salary scale, so that by end-1993 real wages for low-level positions
recuperate from currently 60% to up to 76% of their 1987 level, and high-level
positions from currently 40% to up to 71% of their 1987 level. The PAP
further proposes additional measures to attract key and critical personnel
while addressing labor redundancies in non-critical positions. However, the
set of measures proposed will not suffice to address all the needs perceived
by the Government, and the public service will have to be further restructured
to focus on key tasks carried out by adequately qualified staff, while leaving
a greater range of activities to the private sector.

Operations and Maintenance

3.16   Operations and maintenance expenditures have declined sharply
during 1987-90, and have recovered only slightly during 1991-92, amounting to
less than two-thirds of their 1987 level in real terms. This decline in
allocations has prevented adequate maintenance, and has led to the
deterioration of public services and infrastructure in all sectors of the
economy. For example, the maintenance and rehabilitation backlog for sea
defenses is about 20 years-equivalent, and the life-span of drainage and
irrigation systems in Guyana is about 9-12 years, a fraction of the life-span
common in Asian countries (see also Chapters IX and X). As a result, new
investments often reflect capitalized maintenance expenditures. As it is
generally estimated that returns to maintenance compare well with those to new
investment, this reflects a rather inefficient use of scarce resources.

3.17   The shortfall in operations and maintenance has to be addressed urgently. To that end, a comprehensive assessment should be undertaken to establish the adequate level of operations and maintenance expenditures for each sub-sector of the economy, and a plan developed to reach this level within the coming years. In view of the fiscal constraints, in the short-term, funding for increased operations and maintenance will have to come mainly from reallocations within the budget, for example from savings on transfer payments or deferring locally funded capital projects. Also, donors should be encouraged to include provisions for operations and maintenance in their project financing. Over the medium-term, necessary funds should increasingly be raised through cost recovery measures. However, this will only be politically feasible after the users will have benefited from some of the improvements in the delivery of services which better maintenance should yield. At the same time, consideration needs to be given to contracting operations and maintenance activities to the private sector, especially in view of the continued shortage of properly qualified staff in the public sector.

Table 3.7: CENTRAL GOVERNMENT EXPENDITURES ON OPERATIONS AND MAINTENANCE

	1987	1988	1989	1990	Est. 1991	Prel. 1992
Operations & Maintenance (G$ million)	248.1	313.5	601.9	644.8	1516.0	1931.8
Operations	165.3	221.1	443.1	438.8	946.6	1283.8
Maintenance (including Rentals)	82.8	92.4	158.8	206.0	569.4	648.0
Real O&M (1987-G$ million)	248.1	206.9	194.1	118.2	153.1	169.7
Real O&M Index (1987=100)	100.0	83.1	78.2	47.6	61.7	68.4

Source: Government of Guyana

Functional Classification

3.18   The functional classification of expenditures underlines again the dominance of interest payments in current expenditures (Table 3.8). However, it also shows a considerable increase in the share of expenditures on transfers from 3% of current expenditures in 1987 to 14% in 1992 at the same time that the share of expenditures on economic and social services declined from 18% in 1987 to 13% in 1992. The increase in transfers mainly stems from two sources: the decision to subsidize the inefficient operations of GEC, and the increase in G$-contributions to international organizations on account of the exchange rate depreciation. The apparent trade-off between transfers and service expenditures underlines the opportunity costs of subsidizing GEC and point to the urgent need for electricity tariff increases and efficiency improvements in GEC's operations. Room for further savings could be identified through an assessment of costs and benefits of active membership in the broad range of international and local institutions to which it is currently contributing. Given the weak accounting in most sector-ministries, it is also recommended that contribution payments should be channeled through the Ministry of Finance. A reallocation from transfer to economic and social service expenditures would yield high returns in view of the underfunding of operations and maintenance activities and social sector services (see Part III).

Table 3.8: CENTRAL GOVERNMENT FUNCTIONAL EXPENDITURES a/
(in percent of total current expenditure)

	1987	1988	1989	1990	Est. 1991	Prel. 1992
Economic Services b/	4.3	5.1	5.2	2.6	2.6	3.4
Agriculture	1.2	1.3	1.3	0.7	0.4	0.6
Infrastructure Maintenance	1.9	2.2	2.4	1.2	1.4	2.0
Transport and Communications	1.2	1.6	1.5	0.7	0.8	0.8
Social Services b/	13.5	16.4	16.8	10.1	7.0	9.3
Education	6.6	8.4	8.5	5.3	3.8	5.4
Health	4.8	6.2	6.2	3.6	2.4	3.2
Social Security and Welfare	2.1	1.8	2.1	1.2	0.7	0.7
Other Services b/	26.6	21.4	25.3	16.0	18.5	18.8
General Public Services	17.8	12.0	15.7	10.7	14.5	12.9
Defence, Law and Order	8.7	9.3	9.4	5.2	3.9	5.7
Trade	0.1	0.1	0.2	0.1	0.1	0.2
Transfers	2.9	4.1	13.2	9.1	10.4	14.2
GEC	0.0	0.0	9.4	5.2	4.6	5.2
Local Organizations	2.3	3.4	3.4	2.1	2.5	4.3
International Organizations	0.6	0.7	1.4	1.8	3.3	4.7
Interest Payments	51.3	51.7	38.0	61.3	60.7	53.3
Other	1.3	1.3	1.4	0.8	0.7	0.8
Electricity	0.8	0.8	0.8	0.4	0.4	0.5
Telephone	0.5	0.5	0.6	0.4	0.3	0.3
Total Current Expenditure	100.0	100.0	100.0	100.0	100.0	100.0

a/ On a cash basis; not comparable to tables 3.2 and 3.4.
b/ Net of all expenditure sub-headings listed explicitly in this table (transfers, telephone, et.al.).

Source: Government of Guyana

C. NON-FINANCIAL PUBLIC ENTERPRISES AND PRIVATIZATION

1. Overview

3.19   Non-financial public enterprises in Guyana comprise about 20 companies supervised by the Public Corporations Secretariat (PCS), including the GEC, and a few independent companies such as the sugar company GUYSUCO, and the bauxite operations BERMINE and LINMINE, formerly GUYMINE (Box 3.1).[5] Trends in public enterprise finances are largely determined by developments in GEC, GUYSUCO, and BERMINE and LINMINE, which together account for about 60% of the total operating revenue of public enterprises. Years of state ownership and inefficient management have left these and other enterprises in extremely poor condition. To rehabilitate them will require investments of hundreds of million US dollars which are not at Government's disposal. Privatization of the public enterprises to improve efficiency, generate resources, and further enhance the role of the private sector in Guyana's economy is one of the most important tasks facing the Government.

---

[5]   In addition, the Government dominates the financial sector, where it holds over 50% of all financial assets through ownership of, or participation in seven financial institutions (see the report Guyana: Private Sector Development, op. cit.).

2. Public Enterprise Finances

3.20   Under the ERP, there has been some progress in the operations of public enterprises. Following a set-back in 1990, which was mainly owed to unusually heavy rains which caused production losses in the sugar, rice and bauxite sectors, the financial position of the public enterprises improved markedly in 1991 (Table 3.9). Increased competitiveness through the depreciation of the exchange rate, favorable weather, and continued efforts to restructure the main public enterprises all contributed to this improvement. Considerable progress has been made under the private management contract toward restructuring GUYSUCO, and the company's performance benefited from improved industrial relations and favorable weather conditions in 1991. GUYMINE's financial position strengthened somewhat on account of cost-cutting measures associated with the closing of a mine and the reduction of its labor force by about one quarter. There was also some improvement in the performance of GEC, even though its operational losses continued to be very high, on the order of 4% of GDP. Finally, the accounts underestimate the progress achieved, as some profitable enterprises have been divested, notably the telecommunications firm GTT which had contributed 3-4% of GDP to the operating cash balance of the public enterprise sector. In 1992, this trend is estimated to have continued, in spite of the decline in bauxite production (see Chapter II). Nonetheless, the prospects for sustained improvements of the public enterprises are limited as long as these entities remain under state control subject to political interference and constrained in their access to funds required to undertake urgently needed rehabilitation investments.

Table 3.9: PUBLIC ENTERPRISE FINANCES
(percent of GDP)

	1987	1988	1989	1990	Est. 1991	Prel. 1992
Operating Cash Balance	25.4	15.1	18.8	14.1	16.3	n.a.
Current Account Balance	23.1	6.2	8.9	3.9	9.9	14.6
Capital Expenditure	-13.5	-8.1	-13.5	-19.1	-14.4	-9.2
Overall Balance After Grants	9.7	-1.9	-6.3	-17.1	-1.7	3.1
Memorandum Item: Divestment Proceeds	0.0	0.0	0.5	2.5	8.2	1.4

Source: Statistical Appendix

Privatization[6]

3.21   The state continues to control a wide variety of economic activities through its about 30 non-financial public enterprises and financial holdings. Years of state ownership and inefficient management have left these entities in extremely poor condition. To rehabilitate them will require investments of hundreds of million US dollars which are not at Government's disposal. Without comprehensive privatization, these enterprises will increasingly become a burden for the successful continuation of the ERP.

---

[6]   See the report on Private Sector Development, op. cit., for a more extensive discussion on privatization.

3.22   The former Government began a process of privatization that was successful in increasing the role of the private sector in the economy. By October 1992, it had divested some 14 public enterprises and all rice mills operating at the time. Divestment proceeds amounted to about 8% of GDP in 1991, and are estimated at 1.4% of GDP in 1992. However, the divestment procedures were flawed by a lack of transparency. In the 1992-94 PFP, the current Government has committed itself to continue the process of privatization while making an effort to improve on the procedures. In this connection, the Government should issue a policy document setting out (i) its privatization strategy and (ii) a list of entities to be privatized. It is essential that this strategy be comprehensive to improve efficiency, generate savings, and further enhance the role of the private sector in the economy. It should also be rapidly implemented to avoid a deterioration in the

Box 3.1: PUBLIC ENTERPRISES
Non-financial Public Enterprises
Berbice Mining Enterprise Ltd.
Guyana Airways Co.
Guyana Electricity Co.
Guyana Fisheries Ltd.
Guyana Glassworks Ltd.
Guyana Liquor Co.
Guyana National Engineering Co.
Guyana National Printers Ltd.
Guyana National Shipping Co.
Guyana Oil Co. Ltd.
Guyana Pharmaceutical Co.
Guyana Post Office Co.
Guyana Rice Export Board
Guyana Soap & Detergent Co.
Guyana Stockfeeds Ltd. (Farm Processing Unit)
Guyana Stores Ltd.
Guyana Sugar Co. Ltd.
Hope Coconut Industries Ltd.
Linden Mining Enterprise Ltd.
Mards Workshop
National Edible Oil Co. Ltd.
National Padi & Rice Grading Center
Sanata Textiles Ltd.
Financial Institutions
Guyana Agricultural & Industrial Dev. Bank
Guyana Bank for Trade & Industry
Guyana Cooperative Insurance Society
Guyana Cooperative Mortgage Finance Bank
Guyana National Cooperative Bank
Guyana National Cooperative Bank Trust
National Bank for Industry & Commerce

performance of public enterprises due to their uncertain status and lack of capital, and to reduce uncertainty among interested private investors. At the same time, care should be taken to ensure that the procedures adopted generate confidence in the program. In addition to non-financial public enterprises, the Government also needs to divest itself from most of its financial sector holdings. In both instances, however, privatization needs to be accompanied by the establishment of an appropriate regulatory framework.

D. RECOMMENDATIONS

3.23   Further improvement of public sector finances should be pursued in the context of a comprehensive public sector reform, including (i) strengthening the public sector administration; (ii) enhancing resource mobilization; (iii) improving the efficiency of resource allocation; and (iv) pursuing privatization. The main recommendations specific to public finances and public enterprises are as follows:

- Public service pay needs to be improved, accompanied by measures to reduce labor redundancies, especially at lower levels. In particular, the salary structure must be made transparent, and the salary scale decompressed to provide incentives to technical and professional personnel. Current wages are not sufficient to attract or retain qualified higher level personnel, and the resulting low quality of the public service is a key constraint to efficient operation of the public sector. The implementation of

IDA's Public Administration Project would be an important contribution to addressing this objective.

- Tax and customs administration need to be strengthened and the tax structure needs to be revised. Lack of qualified staff, inadequate equipment and inefficient procedures hamper collection efforts in tax and customs administration and need to be addressed urgently. The tax base is too narrow and needs to broadened through elimination of remissions under the consumption tax, drastic reduction of remissions under import duties, and the curtailment of concessions under the income tax. To improve the incentive framework, the development levy on companies should be removed and the top rates for personal income and company taxes unified at 33-35%. Further, consideration should be given to extending consumption taxes to services other than hotel accommodations and charging taxes on imports at the point of entry instead of ex-factory gate.

- Cost recovery measures need to be strengthened to finance essential public services. Currently, most public services are either totally or partially subsidized. In the medium-term, enhanced user charges could yield an additional US$28 million, equivalent to about 10% of the 1992 GDP.

- The budget process needs to be revised and oriented towards activities and programs. Currently, the budget process is oriented towards line items, which makes it difficult to assess the impact on budget cuts on actual operations. As a complementary measure, expenditure control and management also needs to be improved through the implementation of adequate financial management systems and procedures.

- The shortfall in operations and maintenance has to be addressed urgently. Operations and maintenance expenditures have decreased by about 40% in real terms during 1987-92, preventing adequate maintenance to such extent that new investments often reflect capitalized maintenance expenditures. A comprehensive assessment should be undertaken to establish adequate levels of operations and maintenance expenditures, and a plan developed to reach this level within the coming years, to be financed by cost recovery measures. In this connection, consideration should be given to contracting operations and maintenance activities to the private sector.

- Government transfers to GEC need to be discontinued in line with the 1992-94 PFP, based on more efficient operations, increased tariffs consistent with long run marginal costs, and accompanied by private sector participation in the power sector. Membership in international and local organizations should be reviewed based on an assessment of associated costs and benefits and payments channeled through the Ministry of Finance. During 1987-92, there has been a considerable increase in the share of expenditures on transfers at the same time that the share of expenditures on services continued to decline. A reallocation from transfer to economic and social service expenditures would yield high returns

in view of the underfunding of operations and maintenance
activities and social sector services.

- The Government's privatization strategy should be comprehensive
  and implemented rapidly. In addition to non-financial
  enterprises, the Government also needs to divest itself from its
  financial sector holdings. In both instances, privatization needs
  to be accompanied by the establishment of an appropriate
  regulatory framework. The state continues to control a wide
  variety of economic activities through its about 30 non-financial
  public enterprises and financial holdings, which are in extremely
  poor condition and require rehabilitation investments of hundreds
  of million US dollars which are not at Government's disposal.
  Without comprehensive privatization, these enterprises will
  increasingly become a burden for the successful continuation of
  the ERP.

CHAPTER IV.   THE 1993-96 PUBLIC SECTOR INVESTMENT PROGRAM

A.   INTRODUCTION

4.1   The development strategy underlying the ERP entails that the role of the public sector is to provide the basic economic and social infrastructure to facilitate private sector growth. To support this strategy, a 1993-96 Public Sector Investment Program (PSIP) is being proposed with projected disbursements of US$343 million, or US$86 million per year on average, including transfers of US$18 million from externally financed projects to provide foreign exchange to the private sector. Provided the policies and measures suggested in this report are pursued, the size of the proposed PSIP is in line with the country's financial and institutional absorptive capacity. The PSIP emphasizes, first, the rehabilitation of the dilapidated state of the economic infrastructure, and, second, investments in social sectors. Much of the suggested investments are in fact capitalized maintenance expenditures. If implemented, this PSIP will allow the Government to provide the base for private-sector led growth of about 5% per year during the 1993-96 period.

4.2   After a long period in which the economic and social infrastructure has deteriorated, Guyana's immediate investment needs far exceed its own financing and institutional absorptive capacity. This implies that the country needs to both attract new commitments and more effectively use the limited resources available. To this end, it needs, first, to well define -- and focus on -- its investment priorities coherent with the country's development strategy. Second, it needs to strengthen the institutional framework for the implementation of the PSIP. Third, it will have to leverage its scarce resources as much as possible through international concessional assistance.

4.3   The aim of this chapter is to discuss the PSIP, analyze the its process, identify its financing requirements, and present a set of recommendations regarding its planning, implementation and monitoring.

B.   SIZE AND COMPOSITION OF THE PSIP

1.   The Proposed PSIP

4.4   The proposed public sector investment program is based on the Government's 1993 capital budget submissions of February 1993 and its rolling 1994-96 PSIP dated November 1992 with amendments as discussed below. It includes the investments undertaken by the Central Government as well as the core investments for GEC. Investment plans of the other public enterprises have been excluded, partly because their plans are on hold on account of the privatization program, and partly because they operate under private management contracts with a high degree of autonomy.

Table 4.1: PUBLIC SECTOR INVESTMENT PLAN FOR 1992 AND 1993-96
(1992 US$ million)

	Actual 1992	Budgeted 1993	1994	1995	1996	1993-96	PERCENT
Economic	10.1	12.2	11.4	10.8	9.0	43.3	12.6%
Agriculture	10.1	12.2	11.4	10.8	9.0	43.3	12.6%
Ongoing	..	11.6	10.2	7.3	3.3	32.3	9.4%
New	..	0.7	1.2	0.0	0.0	1.8	0.5%
Unidentified	..	0.0	0.0	3.5	5.6	9.1	2.7%
Infrastructure	16.1	20.3	37.4	56.9	66.6	181.2	52.8%
Power	5.3	5.3	8.8	11.0	5.5	30.6	8.9%
Ongoing	..	5.3	5.5	5.5	0.0	16.3	4.8%
New	..	0.0	3.3	5.5	5.5	14.3	4.2%
Unidentified	..	0.0	0.0	0.0	0.0	0.0	0.0%
Transportation	6.4	7.5	16.1	27.5	35.2	86.2	25.1%
Ongoing	..	4.8	6.5	7.9	7.7	26.9	7.8%
New	..	2.7	9.6	14.2	18.8	45.4	13.2%
Unidentified	..	0.0	0.0	5.3	8.6	13.9	4.1%
Water	1.3	2.9	3.8	6.5	9.1	22.3	6.5%
Ongoing	..	1.6	0.7	0.9	5.3	8.6	2.5%
New	..	1.3	3.0	5.6	3.8	13.7	4.0%
Unidentified	..	0.0	0.0	0.0	0.0	0.0	0.0%
Sea Defenses	2.9	2.9	8.1	11.3	16.1	38.4	11.2%
Ongoing	..	0.2	2.0	3.0	4.8	10.0	2.9%
New	..	2.7	6.1	8.3	11.3	28.4	8.3%
Unidentified	..	0.0	0.0	0.0	0.0	0.0	0.0%
Urban	0.2	1.8	0.6	0.6	0.7	3.7	1.1%
Ongoing	..	1.8	0.6	0.6	0.7	3.7	1.1%
New	..	0.0	0.0	0.0	0.0	0.0	0.0%
Unidentified	..	0.0	0.0	0.0	0.0	0.0	0.0%
Social	10.7	22.0	20.1	28.3	29.5	99.8	29.1%
Poverty	1.4	6.7	7.8	7.8	4.8	27.0	7.9%
Ongoing	..	3.6	2.9	2.4	1.1	10.0	2.9%
New	..	3.0	4.9	5.4	3.7	17.0	4.9%
Unidentified	..	0.0	0.0	0.0	0.0	0.0	0.0%
Education	4.1	6.0	5.6	9.1	11.5	32.2	9.4%
Ongoing	..	5.2	5.6	7.6	9.0	27.4	8.0%
New	..	0.8	0.0	0.0	0.0	0.8	0.2%
Unidentified	..	0.0	0.0	1.5	2.5	4.0	1.2%
Health	5.2	9.3	6.7	11.4	13.2	40.6	11.8%
Ongoing	..	8.5	6.7	7.0	7.7	29.9	8.7%
New	..	0.8	0.0	0.0	0.0	0.8	0.2%
Unidentified	..	0.0	0.0	4.4	5.5	9.9	2.9%
Other	7.5	6.7	4.0	3.9	4.0	18.6	5.4%
Other	..						
Ongoing	..	6.6	3.0	2.9	3.0	15.4	4.5%
New	..	0.2	1.0	1.0	1.0	3.2	0.9%
Unidentified	..	0.0	0.0	0.0	0.0	0.0	0.0%
TOTAL GROSS PSIP	44.3	61.2	72.9	99.8	109.0	342.9	100.0%
Ongoing	..	49.1	43.8	45.1	42.6	180.6	52.7%
New	..	12.1	29.1	40.0	44.1	125.4	36.6%
Unidentified	..	0.0	0.0	14.7	22.3	37.0	10.8%
o.w. Transfers	6.8	7.0	6.9	4.1	0.0	18.0	5.3%
TOTAL NET PSIP	37.5	54.2	66.0	95.7	109.0	324.9	94.7%
Memorandum Item							
Identified Net PSIP/GDP	14.2%	17.6%	19.0%	20.9%	20.2%	19.5%	
GDP Growth	7.5%	5.5%	5.0%	4.5%	4.5%	4.9%	

Source: Annex II

4.5   Of the projected total disbursements of US$343 million, US$325 million (95%) are allocated for project funding and the remaining US$18 million (5%) for on-lending to the private sector (Table 4.1). Disbursements are expected to increase over the 1993-96 period. In particular, while the budgeted expenditures of US$61 million in 1993 imply a substantial increase over the actual expenditures of US$44 million for 1992, they only amount to 18% of the total four-year PSIP. This reflects the limited present absorptive capacity, and the expectation that measures will be undertaken in the course of 1993 which will facilitate the implementation of the more ambitious program for 1994-96. However, a substantial part of the projected disbursements for 1995-96, amounting to US$37 million, or 11% of the total PSIP will have to come from not yet identified sources.

4.6   The amendments to the Government's original PSIP proposed by the mission are based on (a) updated commitments by donors (sea defenses, SIMAP), (b) changes in expected disbursement profiles (agriculture, water supply and sewerage), and (c) the inclusion of proposed new investments with unidentified financing considered important by the *Public Sector Review* mission (see below). In view of the financing constraints facing the Government, it is also proposed to defer expenditures for the Mabura-Lethem Road project, amounting to US$13 million over the period 1993-96 (see Chapter XI). Other apparent changes in sectoral allocations reflect a more detailed break-down of multi-sector projects into their components. On the whole, the proposed total PSIP expenditures exceed the disbursements projected by the Government by US$2 million.

2. Sectoral Composition of the PSIP

4.7   In general, the composition of the PSIP is consistent with the development strategy underlying the ERP. The PSIP emphasizes, first, infrastructure, which accounts for 53% of total gross expenditures *excluding* rehabilitation of Drainage and Irrigation (D&I), and, second, social sector investments, which account for 29% (Table 4.2). Investments in economic support services are limited to the agriculture sector. Its share in the PSIP (13%) includes transfers to the private sector (5%), D&I rehabilitation investments (3%) and other investments (5%). Investment in Government buildings, public safety and other expenditures account for the remaining 5% of the PSIP.

4.8   Projected disbursements in <u>agriculture</u> amount to US$43 million, or 13% of total gross investment, including transfers of US$18 million (5%). Externally funded projects cover area development (IFAD), fishery facilities (CIDA), agricultural research (UNDP) and general sector support (IDB). The priority need in agriculture pertains to D&I rehabilitation, which promises considerable returns in terms of productivity gains. This is not adequately reflected in ongoing and new externally funded investments. Therefore, this PSIP includes a proposal for additional D&I rehabilitation investments with unidentified financing of US$9 million (3%). These investments should, however, be contingent on institutional reform in the D&I sub-sector to strengthen operations and maintenance, as previous investments have not been adequately sustained on account of blurred responsibilities in this sub-sector. In particular, there should be private participation in the management of D&I systems in the form of water user associations.

Table 4.2: PUBLIC SECTOR INVESTMENT PLAN FOR 1992 AND 1993-96
(in percent)

	1992	1993	1994	1995	1996	1993-96
Economic	27.5	19.9	15.6	10.8	8.2	12.6
Agriculture	27.5	19.9	15.6	10.8	8.2	12.6
Infrastructure	39.2	33.2	51.3	57.0	61.1	52.8
Power	9.7	8.6	12.1	11.0	5.0	8.9
Transportation	19.8	12.2	22.1	27.5	32.3	25.1
Water and Sanitation	3.2	4.7	5.2	6.6	8.4	6.5
Sea Defenses	5.7	4.7	11.1	11.3	14.8	11.2
Urban	0.8	2.9	0.9	0.6	0.6	1.1
Social	19.1	35.9	27.6	28.3	27.0	29.1
Poverty	3.4	10.9	10.7	7.8	4.4	7.9
Education	10.5	9.7	7.7	9.1	10.6	9.4
Health	5.2	15.2	9.2	11.4	12.1	11.8
Other	14.2	11.0	5.5	3.9	3.6	5.4
Other	14.2	11.0	5.5	3.9	3.6	5.4
TOTAL GROSS PSIP	100.0	100.0	100.0	100.0	100.0	100.0
o.w. Transfers	16.7	11.4	9.5	4.2	0.0	5.3
TOTAL NET PSIP	83.3	88.6	90.5	95.8	100.0	94.7

Source: Annex II

4.9   In the expectation that the Government pursues private sector participation in the power sector, the PSIP only provides for the most urgent investment needs to prevent the imminent collapse of the power sector. It includes disbursements of about US$31 million (9%), allocated to the ongoing power rehabilitation project and an emergency transmission project funded by the IDB, which is well below the estimated rehabilitation and expansion needs of about US$100 million over the next four years.

4.10   The power sector in Guyana is in a severe crisis. The existing generation, transmission and distribution facilities are worn out, supply is unreliable, and capacity does not meet peak demand. While the IDB continues to finance an institutional rehabilitation program for GEC, improvements will not be sustained without a reform of the institutional set-up in Guyana's power sector. The poor performance of the public electricity company GEC suggests that this entity cannot be charged with the responsibility for the power sector. In particular, GEC suffers from weak management compounded by a fragmentation of responsibilities between Board, the General Manager and a consultants' team financed by IDB. Also, staff morale is extremely low. In the meantime, GEC is heavily dependent on Government transfers, amounting to about US$10 million, or 3.5% of GDP in 1992. This is partly a result of tariffs which are well below the estimated long run marginal costs (LRMC), and partly a reflection of the inefficient operations which result in short-term operational costs well above LRMC.

4.11   In view of this situation, the Government must seek immediate private sector participation in the power sector. As a first step, there needs to be a private management contract which allows autonomous management of GEC. At the same time, the Government should invite short-term private power generation to supplement GEC's limited capacity, e.g. under a Build, Own and Operate (BOO) scheme. To finance such purchase of energy and to cover

GEC's cost of operations also requires an increase in electricity tariffs of about 50% on average. As a second step, the Government should privatize transmission and distribution systems and allow competition in energy generation, accompanied by the formulation of an adequate regulatory framework.

4.12   Projected disbursements in <u>transportation</u> amount to US$86 million (25%) to cover the basic needs in road, air and water transport infrastructure. These investment needs reflect the severe deterioration of transportation infrastructure and services over the past decade, which is a severe impediment to private sector activities. Existing main roads have not been rehabilitated and are in need for full rehabilitation. Feeder roads have deteriorated and do not allow adequate access to and from production areas. Similarly, airport and port facilities need immediate attention in some areas and will need to be upgraded to successfully facilitate export development. Ongoing projects by the EC focus on the reconditioning of ferries and the rehabilitation of the essential Demerara harbor bridge, while new projects by IDB and IDA mainly provide for the rehabilitation of the main roads in Guyana. In addition, investments of about US$14 million with unidentified financing are proposed to cover, in particular, critical feeder roads and airport rehabilitation. However, to sustain the rehabilitated infrastructure, provisions should be made for operations and maintenance and institutional strengthening. Further, more room should be given to private provision of services to replace public investments, for example in water transport.

4.13   Projected disbursements in <u>water supply and sanitation</u> amount to US$22 million (7%), including an ongoing project to develop a Master Plan for the Georgetown water supply (IDB) and new projects for Georgetown emergency water supply, water improvement, and technical cooperation (all IDB) and rural water supply and institutional reform (IDA). While the overall rehabilitation needs in the sector are estimated at US$45-50 million, the proposed investment should cover the key needs in this sector over the 1993-96 period, and further allocations to the water sector should be contingent on improving its weak absorptive capacity. In view of the successful operation of the Eccles Plant facilities, further private sector involvement should be sought to complement or replace public investments.

4.14   Projected disbursements in <u>sea defense</u> rehabilitation amount to US$38 million (11%), financed by the EC, CDB, IDA and IDB. There are over 300km of man-made sea defenses in Guyana, many of which have served their design life time. The rehabilitation backlog is about 20 years, which makes investments in this sector an important priority. All investments included in the PSIP are funded, and the allocation for capital works is considered adequate in view of the competing investment needs in the country. However, the complete rehabilitation of the sea defenses is estimated to require some US$300 million, and the country will continue to depend on donor support in this sector for some time to come.

4.15   Projected disbursements in the <u>social sectors</u> amount to US$100 million (29%), of which US$27 million (8%) are allocated to SIMAP and Basic Needs poverty reduction efforts, US$32 million (9%) to education, and US$41 (12%) million to health. SIMAP projects (IDA, IDB) typically focus on rehabilitation of school, health and community infrastructure, vocational training and child nutrition projects. While it is undoubtedly the best agency to respond quickly to the immediate needs of the poor, it will have to

be further strengthened to absorb more funds than currently allocated. The
Basic Needs project (CDB) basically follows the SIMAP approach. Investments
in education and health are dominated by one large IDB project each,
rehabilitation of primary education (US$25 million) and of the Georgetown
hospital (Health Care II; US$22 million). In both sectors, current funding is
insufficient to address the extensive rehabilitation needs, but technical
assistance for institutional strengthening should have priority. In
education, a project to rehabilitate technical and vocational schools is
proposed to start in 1995, for which financing of US$4 million is being
sought. In health, two projects to rehabilitate communal and district
hospitals are proposed to start in 1995, for which financing of US$10 million
is being sought. In addition, there is scope for the private sector,
communities, and non-governmental organizations to offer services to
complement public investments.

C. PSIP PLANNING, IMPLEMENTATION AND MONITORING

4.16   PSIP planning, implementation and monitoring has improved over the
1990-92 period. One indicator reflecting this improvement is the increase in
the implementation ratio from 58% over 1990-91 to 88% in 1992. This has been
the result of a more realistic assessment of expected disbursements combined
with a more adequate allocation of counterpart funds, and of some improvements
in project implementation. Nonetheless, addressing Guyana's extensive
investment needs will strain the country's absorptive capacity, and will
require further improvements in the country's PSIP planning, implementation
and monitoring process, greater donor coordination, and enhanced private
sector participation.

1. The PSIP Process

4.17   What appear to be project-specific problems, often have their root
cause in more fundamental weaknesses in the PSIP process. *Until recently*,
this has been the case in Guyana. In theory, the State Planning Secretariat
(SPS) is responsible for coordinating all aspects of the investment program.
However, in practice, information and responsibilities have been fragmented
and scattered throughout the public sector. All projects are basically
identified, prepared and selected by the line agencies with little prior
feedback to SPS. Projects with external funding have been managed by two
sections of the Department of International Economic Cooperation (DIEC) under
the Ministry of Finance, with little involvement by SPS. There have been no
formal arrangements linking the current and capital budget process which would
allow to monitor recurrent expenditure implications of capital projects. As a
result, the PSIP has been only of limited use as an instrument to facilitate
planning, implementation and monitoring of projects.

4.18   While it is appropriate that the primary responsibility for
project identification rests with the more knowledgeable line agencies, it is
important that this process is guided by clear criteria and in line with the
resource availabilities. In this connection, it should be the role of SPS to
provide a set of updated guidelines and basic macroeconomic indicators which
should inform the decisions of the line agencies. At the same time, the
selection of projects should feed back to the budget and planning process in
the form of provisions for counterpart funding and future maintenance
expenditures. Without such feedback, it is extremely difficult to make
rational decisions between projects or to avoid problems in counterpart

funding as they afflicted, for example, the IDB primary education and health projects which were temporarily stalled in 1991 because of insufficient counterpart funds.

4.19   Project implementation is primarily the responsibility of the executing agency. Their execution units face a variety of problems. Often, their Government counterparts are responsible for a large number of projects, and thus do not react quickly to emerging problems pointed out to them by the execution units. In addition, execution units themselves may not be staffed adequately, as donors focus on funding of capital works. At the same time, donors often demand that each project has its own execution unit, instead of promoting joint execution units for similar projects. In this connection, consolidating execution units while giving them some more autonomy to address the problems they face would greatly facilitate implementation. This effort should be complemented by a Government task force to ensure speedy implementation of selected priority projects. Another implementation constraint arises from lack of counterpart funds for projects which advance more quickly than expected, even though there may well be funds allocated for local or non-performing externally financed projects. In this case, shifting resources from local projects and pooling and *pari passu* disbursement of local counterpart funds would improve the implementation record. Further, project implementation may be stalled on account of conditionality. While an important instrument do ensure that agreed-upon project objectives are being achieved, conditionality should be coordinated between donors to avoid duplication of efforts by the Government to satisfy marginally different conditions, or even contradictory requirements. At the same time, conditions should be focussed, and cross-conditionality should be avoided as it has proven to unjustifiably slow down project implementation.

4.20   SPS is charged with monitoring project execution. This is facilitated through submission of reports when execution agencies request monthly releases of local funds for their projects. However, SPS lacks the necessary and qualified staff to accomplish its monitoring responsibilities. This situation is aggravated by the even more severe shortage of technical personnel in the line agencies which should update SPS on cost overruns and delays in implementation schedules. In addition, SPS has no accurate records for projects where donors disburse funds directly to suppliers, contractors or consultants. This should be easily rectified, given that SPS will become an integral part of the Ministry of Finance.

4.21   A first step to reform the institutional set-up for the PSIP is currently being undertaken through the merger of the SPS and the DIEC into the Ministry of Finance. However, improvements in the information flow will depend on the specific arrangements that would centralize project information in one sub-unit of the Ministry of Finance. In this context, it should also be possible to better incorporate the recurrent cost implications of capital expenditures into the budget and planning process. For a set of selected priority projects (core PSIP), a task force recruited from this sub-unit but supported by higher-level officials should be established to ensure speedy implementation. Further, an IDB project to develop a project cycle management system is scheduled for 1993, which aims to provide computerized monthly information on all projects from pre-feasibility to post-implementation stage. Additional technical assistance is required to enhance training opportunities. Also, measures to strengthen the line agencies are needed to ensure the smooth implementation of the ambitious 1993-96 PSIP. However, as long as the salary issue is not addressed, qualified staff will continue to leave SPS or the line agencies and endanger the sustainability of these reform efforts.

2. Donor Coordination

4.22   With the implementation of Guyana's ERP and the resulting significant increase in external donor support, the need for close donor-coordination has assumed increasing importance. One important forum for this are the meetings of the Caribbean Group for Co-operation in Economic Development (CGCED). In November 1991, the World Bank, in collaboration with UNDP, also instituted a framework for closer coordination of donor-assisted programs in Guyana, which provides for periodic reviews at the technical and policy levels, on a monthly and quarterly basis, respectively.

4.23   While, in many aspects, these reviews have worked well, there is scope for improvement. In particular, there should be a more *systematic* exchange of information on programs of assistance and project implementation, both among donors and between the Government and the donor community as a whole in the context of the quarterly reviews. This could be facilitated by a *project list* approach with details of ongoing, new and future projects, including time-tables for implementation and analysis of implementation problems. Such an approach should help identify systemic problems in project implementation, and allow for a more balanced future investment program. At the same time, there is a need for mechanisms to follow up on agreements reached in donor meetings, for example in the form of progress reports.

4.24   Donors would also facilitate Government planning by (i) making their commitments on a multi-year basis, in particular for commodity assistance, or by providing, at least, qualified indications of future aid flows; and (ii) assisting the Government in making more accurate estimates of expected disbursements in the context of the Government's budget process.

4.25   As indicated above, enhanced donor coordination would also contribute significantly to a more efficient use of scarce resources on the project level. This pertains, first, to the establishment of joint project execution units; second, to pooling and *pari passu* disbursement of local counterpart funds; and, third, to consistent donor conditionality. Also, given Guyana's financial and technical skill constraints, donors should agree to assume operations and maintenance expenditures, on a declining basis over time, as an integral part of any project.

3. Private Sector and Community Participation

4.26   The private sector should not only be encouraged to substitute or complement public investments, it should also be employed to facilitate the implementation of public investments. In a number of areas, for example in sea defenses, implementation of projects by local contractors compares favorable with the performance of public sector agencies. Hence, increasing the scope of private sector participation over the project cycle would increase absorptive capacity and help ensure the realization of the ambitious PSIP. However, this would still require strong core project execution units or institutional strengthening of public sector agencies which have the legal and monitoring capabilities to conduct business with private contractors.

Box 1: COMMUNITY PARTICIPATION IN PUBLIC INVESTMENT

The components of rural development are always the same, i.e. roads, electricity, water supply, small irrigation, markets, schools, health posts and services, etc. The projects are usually small and often quite simple, and widely dispersed. But experience has shown that central planning for hundreds of differentiated localities cannot succeed because of the complexity problems arising from the location specificity of needs. Therefore, community participation in planning has been advocated and elaborate methodologies have been developed. A successful first step in a number of countries has been to establish Social Funds -- the approach followed in Guyana with the establishment of SIMAP. In the short-term, and in an environment where community participation was not encouraged and Government agencies are very weak, Social Funds can achieve impressive rates of execution and relatively successful targeting.

In the medium-term, however, a more promising approach may be to take community participation a step further and overcome the complexity problems through fiscal decentralization with community based project execution. As interventions lose their "emergency" character, Social Funds seem to be severely threatened by "improvements" of project design, selection, procurement, and disbursement rules, which are intended to reduce potential or real abuses, but in the end may well convert the management of the Funds into giant Project Execution Units, familiar from the traditional rural development experience. What is required instead, is the systematic improvement of the local decision mechanisms and rules so that they ensure real authority of the local level over the execution and the financial resources, the transparency of decisions, and include innovative mechanisms for auditing by the communities themselves.

A good example of the benefits of a truly community based approach is Mexico's Solidaridad program. Prior to the implementation of that program, rural municipalities and smaller communities had virtually no own revenue sources and received only very limited financial support from the states. Virtually all local investment was executed by state or federal line agencies on whom local groups were completely dependent for funding. Under the "fiscal systems" approach of Solidaridad, the following measures were implemented or are under implementation:

- A revision of revenue sharing formulas in favor of the poorer states and municipalities.

- Increases in own revenue generation of municipalities and states combined with greater transfer of fiscal investment resources from the federal level to states and municipalities.

- A systematic lowering of the execution and control level of investment execution and money.

- A reform of the money flows and of the systems for money release form the Central Government to states, municipalities and other executing agencies, in which each sub-project operates with a special account, and cumbersome ex-ante controls are replaced by ex-post auditing.

- Special allocation of investment resources (e.g., US$50,000) to municipalities for small projects under community control, with donated community labor and materials, and extremely simple procurement procedures,. These municipal funds operate with a special manual which ensures a transparent project selection process at the community level.

- A reform of state auditing institutions and mechanisms, with much greater involvement of private sector auditors.

- Clear rules assuring that the line agencies maintain control for approving (not designing) technical designs of all but the simplest projects, for program quality standards, and for other regulatory functions.

The program built on many institutional features, including the requirement of community contributions to costs, usually in the form of donated labor, which essentially gives the poor veto power over projects.

The impact has been tremendous, with resources for poverty-alleviating investments in rural areas and urban slums more than doubling over three years. More than 12 million people were connected to potable water and electricity, and had their school improved in a period of about three years. The most outstanding success, perhaps, were the municipal funds, which operated in 1100 municipalities, and which execute 30-40 thousand small projects annually, at very low fiscal costs. In Guatemala the earmarking of eight percent of national fiscal revenue for municipal investments (not payroll) has also had similar, but less well documented impacts. The incredible impact of the municipal funds in Mexico is clearly due to the fact that, small as they are, they removed a critical constraint to community action, i.e. their total fiscal incapacity.

Source: Hans P. Binswanger: Central Planning vs. Fiscal Systems Approaches to Rural Development, Unpublished Note, The World Bank, 1992.

4.27   SIMAP has been very successful in integrating communities and non-governmental organizations into the PSIP process for small local projects. For the time being, it continues to be the most effective means to that end. However, over the medium-term, community participation could be increased further by following the example of other countries (Mexico, El Salvador) and providing block-grants at a local level so that non-governmental organizations and communities can undertake rehabilitation works on their own (Box 4.1).

D. PSIP FINANCING REQUIREMENTS

4.28   The total PSIP financing requirements amount to US$343 million over the 1993-96 period, of which US$306 million, or 89% are identified. . External finance is projected to provide about US$227 million, or 74% of identified financing requirements. Domestic finance is projected to provide about US$79 million, or 26% of the identified financing requirements. This implies a significant increase in leverage, compared to 1990-91 and 1992, when domestic finance accounted for 31% and 45% of the financing requirements. It also is projected to be in line with the capacity to mobilize domestic resources. In particular, any unexpected shortage of counterpart funds could be addressed by reallocating funds from local projects, which account for US$41 million. A *project financing gap* of US$37 million, or 11% of total financing requirements, remains for proposed key projects in agriculture, transport, education and health for which financing has not yet been identified and towards which new project assistance should be directed on a priority basis. Assuming that Guyana aims to leverage its domestic counterpart funds for new projects at a ratio of 1:9, this would imply the need for further donor disbursements of about US$33 million over the 1993-96 period (Table 4.3).

E. RECOMMENDATIONS

4.29   In sum, the main recommendations to improve the PSIP process are as follows:

*   The PSIP process, information flows and responsibilities, needs to be better coordinated among the agencies involved. To this end, the merger of DIEC and SPS should be pursued, and project information centralized in one sub-unit in the Ministry of Finance. This unit should also be assigned effective responsibility for the PSIP process.

*   The speedy implementation of the IDB project to develop a project cycle management system should be facilitated to strengthen the institutional base for PSIP planning, implementation and monitoring. In this context, additional technical assistance should be requested to enhance training opportunities.

*   SPS should provide a set of up-dated guide lines and basic macro-economic indicators which should inform the project selection process by line agencies.

*   A budget system should be introduced which would integrate capital current budgeting and allow monitoring of the recurrent cost implications of capital expenditures.

<u>Table 4.3</u>: **PSIP FINANCING REQUIREMENTS, 1993-96**
(US$ millions)

	1993	1994	1995	1996	1993-96	PERCENT
Identified Financing:	<u>61.2</u>	<u>72.9</u>	<u>85.1</u>	<u>86.7</u>	<u>305.9</u>	<u>89.2%</u>
External:	42.1	53.7	65.6	66.0	227.4	66.3%
CDB	0.7	1.8	2.9	4.0	9.4	2.7%
EC	1.2	5.5	7.6	9.2	23.5	6.8%
IDA	6.6	10.3	12.0	9.9	38.8	11.3%
IDB	25.6	35.9	42.9	42.7	147.2	42.9%
UNDP	3.0	0.2	0.2	0.2	3.6	1.0%
Other	5.1	0.0	0.0	0.0	5.1	1.5%
Domestic:	19.1	19.2	19.6	20.7	78.5	22.9%
o.w. Counterpart	9.6	8.8	9.0	10.0	37.4	10.9%
Unidentified Financing:	<u>0.0</u>	<u>0.0</u>	<u>14.7</u>	<u>22.3</u>	<u>37.0</u>	<u>10.8%</u>
Total Gross PSIP	<u>61.2</u>	<u>72.9</u>	<u>99.8</u>	<u>109.0</u>	<u>342.9</u>	<u>100.0%</u>
o.w. Transfers	7.0	6.9	4.1	0.0	18.0	5.3%
Total Net PSIP	<u>54.2</u>	<u>66.0</u>	<u>95.7</u>	<u>109.0</u>	<u>324.9</u>	<u>94.7%</u>

<u>Source</u>: Annex II

- Project implementation needs to be improved through (i) consolidating execution units for similar projects while giving them more autonomy to address implementation problems; (ii) mechanisms to shift counterpart funds to projects as needed, including pooling and *pari passu* disbursement of local counterpart funds and using funds from locally financed projects; and (iii) focussing and coordinating donor conditionality.

- A core PSIP comprised of a set of priority projects should be formulated and a task force, supported by high level officials, be established to ensure speedy implementation of the core PSIP.

- Donor coordination needs to improved through more systematic exchange of information in the context of quarterly review meetings based on a *project list* approach, including time-tables for implementation and analysis of implementation problems. Donors should also agree to assume operations and maintenance expenditures on a declining basis over time, and design cost recovery mechanisms as an integral part of any project.

- Donors should help facilitate Government planning by (i) make (tentative) commitments on a multi-year basis or providing qualified indications of future aid flows; and (ii) assisting the Government in making more accurate estimates of expected disbursements.

- The role of the private sector in the PSIP process needs to be increased, in particular through contracting-out of works. As this requires enhanced legal and monitoring capabilities, technical assistance should be requested from donors. Also, block-grants should be made available on a local level so that non-governmental organizations and communities can undertake rehabilitation works on their own.

CHAPTER V. <u>ECONOMIC OUTLOOK, FINANCING REQUIREMENTS, AND DEBT RELIEF</u>

A. INTRODUCTION

5.1   Medium- and long-term economic prospects for Guyana are promising, provided that the Government maintains a sound macroeconomic framework, drastically reduces the size of the public sector and its command over the country's economic resources, pursues sector strategies supportive of private-led growth, and improves public sector management and administration. Projections presented in this chapter show a moderate slowing down from the high GDP growth rate of 7.5% in 1992, to 4-5% per year on average during 1993-2001. However, to finance such growth, Guyana will continue to need substantial foreign capital inflows supported by generous debt relief.

B. ECONOMIC OUTLOOK

5.2   After a decade of stagflation, Guyana is experiencing economic recovery. Real GDP growth increased from -3% per year on average during the 1980s to 7% per year on average during 1991-92, and inflation fell from 76% in 1990 to 14.2% at the end of 1992. To sustain this recovery, adjustment policies and market-oriented structural reforms need to remain on track. In particular, the Government needs to sustain fiscal and monetary discipline -- supported by cost recovery for all services, including the provision of energy -- continue to privatize the still large public enterprise sector, and focus on implementation of investments that provide the base for private-led growth. Further privatization is necessary to increase efficiency of the enterprises, to raise the capital necessary for large rehabilitation investments, and to provide finance for a well focussed public investment program in support of sustained private-led growth. In addition to sound economic policies and public sector reform, Guyana will also need further external assistance, including enhanced concessions for debt rescheduling and debt forgiveness, to achieve external viability over the medium to long term.

5.3   Guyana also needs to increase productivity in the sugar, rice and bauxite sectors, while at the same time exploiting the opportunities for diversified growth in non-traditional agriculture, forestry, gold mining, selected manufacturing (textiles) and services.

5.4   The projections presented below, in particular the good growth performance, assume that Guyana follows the economic policies recommended in this report and receives a further three-year (1993-95) rescheduling on Enhanced Toronto Terms for its Paris Club and Trinidad and Tobago debt. The projections also assume that, supported by private equity investment and management, Guyana will be able to expand its sugar and rice exports beyond its current EC and U.S. quotas, rehabilitate its bauxite sector, and at the same time develop a broader base for its economy.

5.5   The price projections are based on the World Bank's commodity projections, adjusted for the preferential agreements benefiting Guyana's sugar and rice exports to the EC and U.S. markets. The merchandise terms of trade are projected to decline by about 14% over the projection period. Inflation is projected to decrease further on account of the increasing

openness of Guyana's economy, to about 9% per year on average during 1993-
2001, slightly above the levels expected to prevail in the industrial
economies. At the same time, the real exchange rate is projected to remain
constant, implying a moderate devaluation of the nominal exchange rate over
the projection period.

Table 5.1: ACTUAL AND PROJECTED MACROECONOMIC INDICATORS

(in percent)

	Prel. 1992	Projected 1993-96	Projected 1997-2001
	--------- average growth rates ---------		
Real Gross Domestic Product (Market Prices)	7.9	4.9	4.1
Real Gross Domestic Income	12.5	2.9	2.2
Real Gross Domestic Investment	-3.6	3.8	1.4
Central Government a/	36.2	11.9	-0.4
Private	-13.8	-0.1	2.5
Real Consumption	0.1	4.3	2.0
Central Government	1.0	2.5	1.5
Private	-0.2	4.8	2.2
Real Exports of GNFS	28.0	8.0	5.6
Real Imports of GNFS	18.4	7.4	4.2
Urban Consumer Prices (end-period)	14.2	9.3	8.4
	------------ share of GDP ------------		
Consumption	62.9	70.7	69.5
Central Government	20.7	16.7	16.0
Private	42.2	54.0	53.4
Gross Domestic Investment	34.5	34.3	30.4
Central Government a/	9.9	13.3	11.2
Private	24.7	21.1	19.3
Gross Domestic Savings	37.1	29.3	30.5
Resource Balance	2.6	-5.0	0.1
Exports of GNFS	132.1	131.5	139.5
Imports of GNFS	129.5	136.5	139.4
External Current Account	-29.8	-31.4	-18.7
External Debt b/	675.5	623.7	501.0
Scheduled Debt Service	50.9	34.2	29.1

a/ Excluding PSIP social sector expenditures.
b/ Outstanding and disbursed.

Source: Mission Estimates

5.6   Under these assumptions, Guyana's real GDP is projected to grow at
5% per year on average during 1993-97, and at 4% of GDP thereafter (Table
5.1). This projected growth path is based on annual average growth rates of
about 3% in agriculture, 4% in manufacturing, 5% in mining, and 8% in
services, and is supported by the projected moderate growth in public
infrastructure and private investments of 2% per year on average.
Consequently, the share of investment in GDP falls from currently 35% in 1992
to 29% by the year 2001. This allows consumption, including Central

Government social sector expenditures, to grow at a rate of 3% per year on average.

5.7   Central Government finances are projected to improve significantly over the projection period. In particular, Government savings are projected to increase steadily from a deficit of 12% of GDP in 1992 to a surplus of 4% of GDP by the year 2001. While revenues as a share in GDP are projected to remain high, only declining to 43% in 2001, current expenditures are projected to fall more rapidly as interest payments on domestic debt are reduced and transfers to public enterprises discontinued. Similarly, the Government's overall fiscal deficit is projected to narrow, from 23% of GDP in 1992 to 11% of GDP by the year 2001. This improvement is, however, in part contingent on privatization receipts of about US$10 million per year over the projection period, mainly reflecting staggered payments for sugar and bauxite assets.

5.8   With the projected strong overall economic performance, and the ensuing increase in confidence in the economy, money demand is projected to increase and the velocity of money to decline. As a result of the projected fiscal improvement and the private sector orientation of its economic policies, the Government is expected to reduce its stock of domestic debt, and the ratio of Central Government credit to GDP is projected to decline from about 26% in 1992 to below 1% by the year 2001. In turn, this will allow credit to the private sector to increase by about 19% per year on average without generating inflationary pressures.

5.9   Real exports of goods and non-factor services are projected to grow at about 7% per year on average during the projection period. Initially, during 1993-96, export growth is projected to exceed 8% per year on average, propelled mainly by increasing rice, gold and timber exports. As discussed in Chapter IX of this report, Guyana has the potential to significantly increase rice production. There is also a potential demand for its rice, as Guyana is already exporting rice outside the EC quota to Curacao and Aruba, and should be able to recover its previously dominating position in the CARICOM market. Gold exports are projected to increase mainly on account of the OMAI gold mine, which is expected to come on stream in 1993. Finally, given Guyana's vast timber resources and the recent privatization of its timber industry, there is considerable scope for expanding timber exports over the next decade and until production will reach its long-term sustainable level.

5.10   During 1997-2001, export growth is projected to slow down to about 6% per year on average. The main exceptions to this trend are bauxite exports, which are projected to benefit from the progress in the industry's rehabilitation program, and sugar exports, which are projected to continue to grow steadily over the whole projection period as production improves on account of rehabilitation investments and as Guyana is likely to benefit from the expansion of the EC quota to cover Portugal, and may replace other Caribbean producers both in international and regional markets.

5.11   Real imports of goods and non-factor services are projected to grow faster than GDP during 1993-96, at 7% per year on average to cover increasing private consumption and investments. During 1997-2001, both imports and GDP are projected to grow at 4% per year on average. At the same time, the resource balance is projected to deteriorate slightly compared to the surplus of 3% of GDP in 1992, recording a deficit of 5% of GDP during 1993-1996 and only a small surplus of 0.1% during 1997-2001.

Table 5.2: ACTUAL AND PROJECTED SUMMARY BALANCE OF PAYMENTS
(US$ million)

	Prel. 1992	Projected 1993-96	Projected 1997-2001
Resource Balance a/	6.9	-16.4	0.6
Exports	350.6	425.4	633.6
Imports	343.7	441.8	633.0
Net Factor Payments	-99.9	-102.9	-119.5
o.w: Interest on Public Debt b/	-65.7	-70.0	-70.0
Net Private Transfers	14.0	16.7	33.7
Current Account	-79.0	-102.6	-85.2
Capital Account	122.8	124.9	116.5
Capital Official Grants	4.0	33.0	30.3
Medium and Long-Term Debt	-5.3	57.3	25.2
Disbursements	54.5	77.2	89.6
Amortization	-70.4	-40.2	-64.4
Rescheduling/Debt Relief	9.8	19.6	0.0
Sale of Assets	10.4	5.7	13.0
Foreign Direct Investment	35.0	28.9	48.0
Other	83.6	0.0	0.0
Errors and Omissions	5.0	0.0	0.0
Change in Reserves c/	-48.7	-22.3	-31.3

a/ Excludes activities related to major gold projects and petroleum exploration.
b/ On an accrual basis, including interest on principal in arrears.
c/ "-" indicates increase.

Source: Mission Estimates

C. EXTERNAL FINANCING REQUIREMENTS

5.12   Guyana will continue to require substantial foreign capital
inflows to finance its PSIP, to comply with the debt service obligations, and
to provide the foreign exchange needed to sustain import levels concomitant
with the projected economic growth. Despite the favorable projections for the
resource balance, the current account of the balance of payments will continue
to record substantial deficits, projected to average US$103 million per year
(31% of GDP) during 1993-96 and US$85 million per year (19% of GDP) during
1997-2001. To a large extent, these deficits reflect projected interest
payments *prior to debt rescheduling* averaging US$70 million per year during
1993-2001.

5.13   Capital inflows required to finance the projected current account
deficit and to cover amortization payments (excluding IMF purchases and
repurchases) average US$165 million per year during 1993-1996 and US$180
million per year during 1997-2001. The major sources of financing will need
to be private capital inflows, in large part generated from privatization;
grants and concessional loans for balance of payments support and project
assistance; and debt relief.

5.14   Foreign direct investment is projected to average about US$29
million per year during 1993-96 and US$48 million per year during 1997-2001.
These projected levels, however, are contingent on the implementation of a
comprehensive privatization program, which would be accompanied by major
rehabilitation investments in the former public enterprise sector, in
particular in sugar and bauxite during the second half of the 1990s.

Similarly, the projections also include privatization receipts of US$6 million per year on average during 1993-96 and US$13 million per year on average during 1997-2001. Without these projected inflows through privatization, Guyana would not be able to generate sufficient foreign exchange to afford the imports necessary to sustain growth and to service its external debt.

5.15   Guyana's total aid requirements *after* private capital flows during 1993-96 amount to US$446 million, or US$111.5 million per year on average. Of this amount, only US$295 million, or US$74 million per year on average have been identified in the form of loans or grants. This leaves an *external financing gap for 1993-96 of US$151 million*, of which US$33 million represents proposed projects with unidentified external financing. This financing gap increases considerably to US$92 million per year on average during 1997-2001, when the grace period granted under the previous debt rescheduling operations expires. Further balance of payments support or debt relief beyond the assumed 1993-95 rescheduling on Enhanced Toronto Terms for Paris Club and Trinidad and Tobago debt would be required to fill this gap to avoid jeopardizing Guyana's growth prospects.

Table 5.3: PROJECTED EXTERNAL FINANCING REQUIREMENTS
(US$ million)

	1993	1994	1995	1996	1997-2001
Financing Requirements	-168	-179	-162	-153	-180
Current Account	-119	-106	-97	-89	-85
Amortization	-53	-43	-32	-33	-64
Net Reserves	4	-30	-33	-31	-31
Financing Sources	168	179	162	153	180
Foreign Direct Investment	34	24	23	35	48
Sale of Assets	5	2	6	10	13
Rescheduling/Debt Relief	15	43	20	0	0
Grants	34	34	33	32	30
Identified	29	8	10	9	0
Unidentified	5	26	23	23	30
MLT Loans	79	75	81	75	90
Identified	60	58	66	51	27
Unidentified	19	16	15	24	63
Memorandum Item:					
Total Aid Requirements	112.8	108.6	112.4	112.3	119.9
o.w. PSIP (identified)	42.1	53.7	65.6	66.0	0.0
Identified	88.4	66.0	75.1	66.0	27.5
MLT Loans (identified) a/	59.7	58.4	65.6	56.6	27.2
Grants (identified)	28.7	7.6	9.5	9.4	0.3
Canada (project)	1.6	0.0	0.0	0.0	0.0
Canada (grant)	11.2	0.0	0.0	0.0	0.0
EC/EDF (projects)	1.2	5.5	7.6	9.2	0.0
EC (BoP support)	1.7	1.7	1.7	0.0	0.0
UK (BoP support)	2.9	0.0	0.0	0.0	0.0
US (BoP support)	7.5	0.0	0.0	0.0	0.0
Other (projects)	2.6	0.4	0.2	0.2	0.3
Unidentified	24.4	42.6	37.3	46.3	92.4
MLT Loans	19.1	16.2	14.8	23.7	62.4
Grants	5.3	26.4	22.5	22.6	30.0

a/ For a breakdown by sources for project finance, see Chapter IV, Table 4.3.

Source: Mission Estimates

D. DEBT RELIEF

5.16   Guyana's large external debt continues to be a burden on economic recovery. Despite previous debt relief and two Paris Club debt rescheduling operations on Toronto terms, this debt amounted to US$1793 million, or 675% of GDP at the end of 1992 (Tables 5.4. and 5.5). Of this debt, 48% is held by bilateral donors, 31% by multilateral agencies excluding the IMF, 9% by the IMF and 12% by others. The single largest creditor is Trinidad and Tobago, with US$413 million in loans outstanding, equivalent to 23% of Guyana's total external debt. By contrast, the combined Paris Club debt only amounts to US$174 million, equivalent to 10% of Guyana's total external debt. Debt service payments in 1992 amounted to US$135 million, or 51% of GDP.

Table 5.4: TOTAL EXTERNAL DEBT OUTSTANDING AND DISBURSED, END-1992

CREDITORS	US$ million	Percent
Bilateral Donors	867	48.4
Paris Club	174	9.7
Canada	6	0.3
Germany	15	0.8
Netherlands	18	1.4
United Kingdom	103	5.7
United States	21	1.2
Other	11	0.6
Non-Paris Club	693	38.7
Brazil	27	1.5
CMCF (Caribbean)	160	8.9
China	8	0.4
Trinidad and Tobago	413	23.0
Venezuela	14	0.8
Other	71	4.0
Multilateral Agencies	550	30.7
CDB	59	3.3
EC/EDF/EIB	17	0.9
IDA/IBRD	193	10.8
IDB	216	12.0
Other	65	3.6
Private	51	2.8
IMF	149	8.3
Other Short-term Debt	176	9.8
TOTAL	1793	100

Source: World Bank Debt Reporting System

5.17   Guyana's external debt is projected to grow in US$ terms over the projection period, from US$1793 million by end-1992 to US$2111 million by end-1996 and to US$2434 million by end-2001. To a significant extent, this increase in US$ debt reflects the continued need to borrow in order to cover the scheduled debt service payments, projected to average US$110 million per year (34% of GDP) during 1993-96, and US$134 million per year (29% of GDP) during 1997-2001 (Table 5.5). The projections assume a further 1993-95 rescheduling of Paris Club and Trinidad and Tobago debt on Enhanced Toronto terms, which will yield a relief of US$20 million per year on average during 1993-96.

Table 5.5: ACTUAL AND PROJECTED DEBT INDICATORS

	Prel. 1992	Projected 1993-96	Projected 1997-2001
	------------- US$ million -------------		
Total Public Debt	1792.7	2013.1	2262.0
Scheduled Debt Service	-135.2	-109.5	-134.0
Debt Relief (Paris Club)	9.8	19.6	0.0
	------------- in percent -------------		
Debt/GDP	675.5	623.7	501.0
Scheduled Debt Service/GDP	50.9	34.2	29.1
Scheduled Debt Service/Exports GNFS	36.1	24.3	19.7

Source: Mission Estimates

5.18   The recent (May 1993) 1993-95 rescheduling of Paris Club debt on Enhanced Toronto Terms is an important contribution to the alleviation of Guyana's debt burden. However, as the projections presented above imply, Guyana's tight external finances will require further debt relief in the near future. At a minimum, and consistent with the provisions under Enhanced Toronto Terms, such debt relief could take the form of 100% rescheduling of the principal by 1998. In addition, Guyana would need to apply these terms not only to its Paris Club debt but also to the debt it owes to Trinidad and Tobago. Under such a scenario, Guyana's debt service payments would be reduced by an additional US$34 million per year during 1998-2001, and would amount to 25% of GDP by the year 2001, compared to 34% in the base case scenario. Similarly, its debt at the end of the projection period would amount to US$2299 million (439% of GDP), compared to US$2434 million (465% of GDP) in the base case scenario (Table 5.6).

Table 5.6: IMPACT OF FURTHER (1998) RESCHEDULING ON DEBT AND DEBT SERVICE a/

	Base Case 1996	Base Case 2001	Second Rescheduling 1996	Second Rescheduling 2001
	-------------- US$ million --------------			
Total Public Debt	2111.2	2433.6	2111.2	2298.7
Effective Debt Service	105.4	176.9	105.4	132.7
	-------------- in percent --------------			
Debt/GDP	585.7	464.9	585.7	439.1
Effective Debt Service/GDP	29.1	33.8	29.1	25.3
Effective Debt Service/Exports GNFS	20.1	22.6	20.1	17.0

a/ Assuming 1998 rescheduling of 100% of the principal for Paris Club and Trinidad and Tobago debt consistent with the provisions under Enhanced Toronto Terms.

Source: Mission Estimates

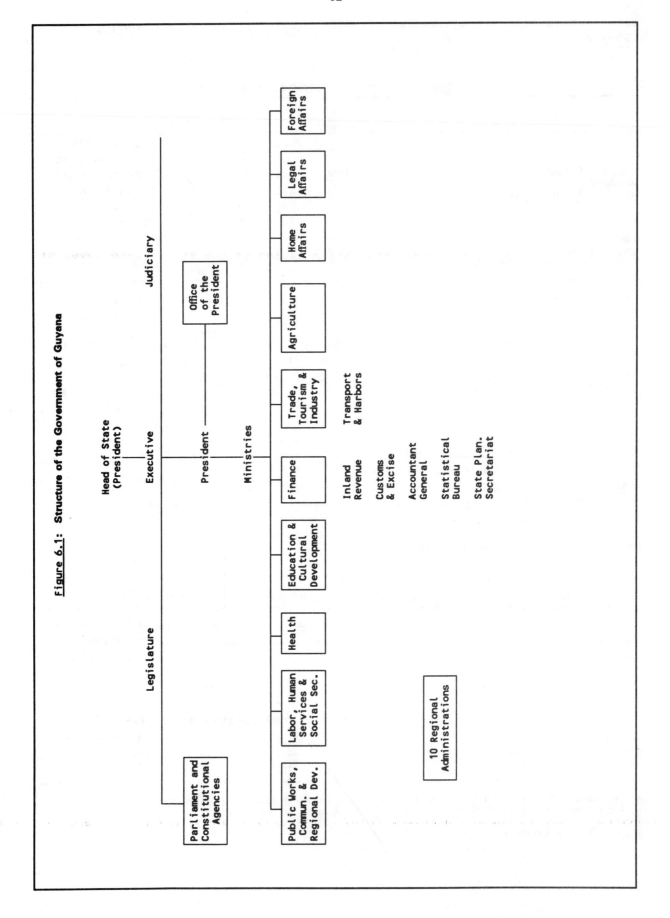

Figure 6.1: Structure of the Government of Guyana

PART II: PUBLIC SECTOR MANAGEMENT AND ADMINISTRATION

CHAPTER VI. PUBLIC SECTOR ADMINISTRATION

A. INTRODUCTION

6.1   The current effort of economic reform has profound implications for the role of the state, and requires an appropriate institutional setting to enable the public sector to deliver the services needed to sustain private sector-led economic growth and to address social concerns. It is in this context that the need for public sector administration reform arises. Administrative reform cuts across all functions and levels of the public sector and requires the prioritization of governmental functions, the reform of the organizational structure, the determination of the appropriate level of governmental action, and the rationalization of resource use.

6.2   In addition, improving the performance of the public sector requires careful attention to the quality and character of public service employment. While economic growth has resumed as a result of the ERP, the public sector remains drained of skilled managers, unable to supply basic services, and as a result, continues to constrain private sector development and economic recovery. The inability of Government to attract and retain the skilled managers and technicians necessary to ensure sound management, relegates the operation of basic services and the planning, implementation and monitoring of the PSIP to a very weakened state.

6.3   Recognition of the need for public sector reform is evident in the 1991 initiation of an ODA supported "Public Service Reform Program," focussing particular attention on the restructuring and reorganization of the Central Government ministerial structure and the strengthening of Public Service Management. The reduction of the number of ministries from 18 to 11 and the elimination of some non-critical vacancies are meaningful first steps in this process. However, the impact of these changes has been limited and much remains to be done to improve public sector performance: the size of public sector employment has not been reduced sufficiently; the quality of public servants and incentives for performance have not improved markedly; rationalization of systems and procedures has not followed from the reduction in the number of ministries; key public sector management and information systems have not been put in place; and accountability in the public sector has not been effectuated.

6.4   Guyana needs a comprehensive Public Sector Reform Program (PSRP) to deepen and broaden the reform efforts initiated in 1991 and those envisioned in IDA's Public Administration Project (PAP). Such a PSRP can be conceptualized in five interlocking elements:

- Administrative Reform
- Public Sector Management Reform
- Decentralization/centralization
- Deregulation/regulation
- Divestiture/privatization

6.5   Regarding administrative reform, a fundamental functional review
is necessary to eliminate outdated activities and permit resource utilization
to be more focused, particularly with respect to Semi-Autonomous Agencies. In
addition, the PSRP should develop explicit linkages to the ERP, ensuring that
administrative reform reflects national priorities, particularly in relation
to improvements in basic infrastructure, in health, and in education.

6.6   Public sector management reform should aim at improving decision-
making capabilities and strengthening the operational environment for the
execution of policies and programs. In this context, the PSRP can be thought
of at three levels. At the **normative** level, reform should focus on policy
making authority and the legal framework for that authority. At the
institutional level, there is a need to ensure that the institutional
framework corresponds to policy authority and the legal framework. At the
operational level, there is a need to focus on the efficient execution of
policies and programs. This suggests the need to strengthen the entire system
of financial management with initial efforts aimed at ensuring adequate
accounting systems as the basis for public accountability. A second critical
element of public sector management reform is to focus attention on the
demands of revenue collection. In this context, a revision of the tax system,
including better enforcement of existing taxes and modifications in the tax
structure to generate revenues while eliminating disparities in incentives, is
required.[7/]

6.7   Public sector reform in Guyana also depends upon the optimal
distribution of functions among the Central Government, centrally controlled
local administration, and locally elected government. It is rarely a simple
question of centralization versus decentralization. Consistency requires
central control, demands of diversity require local autonomy, and successful
institutional development depends on balance between centralization and
decentralization. If a function is decentralized without local democratic
control, then planning, resource allocation, and review mechanisms must
reflect central accountability. If a function is subject to local democratic
control, local accountability must be allowed to operate, and variations in
local standards of service delivery may well result. In Guyana, there is a
major conflict between effective local authority and the deconcentration of
service delivery subject to central authority in the Ministries. While
theoretically subject to local democratic control, the reality of
institutional arrangements and resource transfers belies the possibility of
that control. To address this issue will require decisions about the
responsibilities of the Regional Administrations and the development of
coherent operational procedures for their activities.

6.8   Further reforms include improving the incentives for, and
facilitating the effective functioning of, the private sector and reducing
state involvement in those activities that are more appropriately performed by
the private sector. This is discussed in more detail in Parts I and III of
this report. This chapter will focus on critical issues in the public sector
administration in Guyana and make recommendations for reform regarding the

---

7/   See Chapter VII of this report and the parallel report <u>Guyana: Private
Sector Development</u>, op. cit..

institutional setting, decentralization, and public service management and employment.

B. INSTITUTIONAL SETTING

6.9   Since 1970, and the creation of Guyana as a Cooperative Republic within the British Commonwealth, the public sector experienced dramatic expansion in both its functions and its size, a consequence of the interventionist and paternalistic policies that characterized its model of "cooperative socialism." As a result, the Government assumed responsibilities not only for basic infrastructure and basic social services, but also committed itself to undertake activities in the productive sectors traditionally considered the domain of the private sector. This expanded role was evident in the expansion of the Central Government and in the dramatic growth of Semi-Autonomous Agencies, Constitutional Agencies, Public Corporations, and Public Financial Entities. At the same time, the more recent creation of Regional Administrations (1980; RAs) added another layer of governmental action to the already complex fabric of the public sector without providing a clear vision of the state's appropriate roles in stimulating economic development, and assuring internal efficiency and accountability. The result has been that the institutional apparatus of the state is unmanageable, with organizational and functional responsibilities that have grown in an inchoate manner and in response to legal prescriptions that restrict its effectiveness.

6.10   This expansion of the apparatus of the public sector over the past two decades has resulted in a number of institutional problems, among them:

- the overextension of government;

- incoherent and overlapping jurisdictional and functional responsibilities within the Central Government, resulting in poor coordination among lines of authority within the Executive branch;

- weak financial management control;

- multiple and sometimes contradictory lines of authority and responsibility over the decentralized administration, particularly with regard to autonomous institutions and RAs, that result in ill-defined operational responsibilities and weakness in operational capacity;

- a weakening of the administrative capacity of the parliamentary function to make informed decisions necessary to perform its appropriate political role;

- lack of effective control over the expansion of public sector employment; and

- a dramatic deterioration in the quality and composition of public employment, particularly at management and technical levels, because of a failure to provide adequate and transparent incentives to performance.

6.11   The Constitution of 1980 provides the legal framework for the activities of Parliament, the Executive branch, and the RAs. The President has complete control over the structure of Government and its Ministries. The Local Democratic Organs Act of 1980 provides for the creation of ten regions with RAs and Regional Democratic Councils as areas of local government. The Act also gave the Minister in charge of local government authority to divide the country into sub-regional units, as well as broad authority over local democratic organs. In 1991, reorganization of the Ministry of Regional Administration as a directorate within the Ministry of Public Works, Communications, and Regional Development (MPWCRD) transferred that authority to the MPWCRD. Finally, the Constitution establishes a number of Constitutional Agencies which have specific functions to ensure probity in the conduct of public affairs, and defines the legislative and judicial systems.[8/] Other governmental entities include the Semi-Autonomous Agencies, Financial Entities, and the Public Corporations all of which were established by specific legislative acts.

6.12   Until recent reorganization efforts, the organizational structure of government was characterized by a high degree of functional overlap, a lack of coordination, great dispersion and fragmentation of responsibilities and authority that prevented effective governance. This fragmentation resulted in a number of problems, including:

- several ministries with similar responsibilities for government policy leading to a loss of coherence in policy formulation;

- duplication and overlap of tasks, particularly in central ministries;

- the need for excessive inter-ministry coordination, resulting in slow response time and decision-making;

- a lack of coordination between ministries and RAs;

- managerial, professional, and technical expertise spread too thinly;

- inflated staffing caused by the proliferation of administrative support functions; and

- inefficient use of accommodation and material resources.[9/]

6.13   With the assistance of ODA a program of reorganization was carried out and the number of ministries was reduced from 18 to 11 and appropriate

---

8/   These Constitutional Agencies include the Office of the Auditor General, the Office of the Ombudsman, the Public and Police Service Commission, the Parliament Office, the Office of Public Prosecutions, the Public Service Appellate Tribunal, the Elections Commission, the Teaching Training Service, and the Judicial Service Commission.

9/   KPMG Peat Marwick McLintock, <u>Government of Guyana Public Service Review</u>, "Report No. IV: Restructuring and Rationalisation." June, 1990, pp. 31-37.

functions were restructured and consolidated (Figure 6.1). While this reorganization has proved effective in reducing the complexity of the ministerial structure, there remains a need for internal reorganization within ministries to clarify functional responsibilities. The creation of fewer and larger ministries has allowed for a degree of consolidation of central services, but the hope that this in turn would lead to labor savings through the reduction of personnel has not been fulfilled. In large part, "reductions" have been limited to the elimination of non-critical posts that were vacant at the time. This need for further reorganization is recognized by the Government and is evident in the recent decision to reorganize the State Planning Secretariat (SPS). Formerly a Semi-Autonomous Agency, the SPS would be absorbed within the central ministerial structure to link macroeconomic investment planning and sectoral planning closer to the ministries responsible for these activities and to link current and capital budgeting responsibilities and analyses (Finance and the Sectoral Production Ministries).

6.14   In addition, the need for further restructuring and strengthening for efficiency and accountability within the ministerial structure is evident. For example, the current accounting system and the lack of an effective financial management information system throughout the line ministries result in a total absence of effective control of the financial system. The need to institute a modern financial management system with institutional correspondence in authority, responsibility, execution, and accountability requires the strengthening and restructuring of this management and accounting capacity within the ministries and at the central level (Ministry of Finance).

6.15   The goal of improved inter- and intra-ministerial coordination has begun to be evident in some ministries. Perhaps the clearest example is in the new MPWCRD through which regional works now are coordinated by a single ministry that oversees RAs and public works activities. That this reorganization has been effective is evident in the fact that it has become easier to recognize the limits of RAs in the provision of maintenance activities associated with public works, and has fueled discussion of the possibility of reorganizing the site at which this activity takes place. This will be discussed further in a later section of this chapter.

6.16   In addition to the Ministries, Departments, and RAs of the Central Government, the incremental expansion of state activity over the past two decades has resulted in the existence of a number of Semi-Autonomous Agencies, Public Corporations, and Public Financial Entities. The Semi-Autonomous Agencies (SAAs) are each created through an Act of Parliament, controlled by a supervisory board, and report directly to the subject ministry to which they are responsible. However, the SAAs have substantial operational autonomy, particularly with regard to pay and employment policies. As entities outside of the public service, SAAs determine their respective employment and wage policies subject to the constraints of resource transfers from the national budget. The rationale for the presence of a number of these SAAs as entities within the public sector needs to be reviewed. Mostly, it appears to be based on historical circumstance rather than on clear distinctions of function or economic logic. While the economic logic of their presence under the public sector can be made for some (eg., the University of Guyana), in several cases the nature of the service and the operation of SAAs would make them likely candidates for complete autonomy from the public sector altogether (eg., GUYWA and the General Construction Company).

> **Box 6.1: SEMI-AUTONOMOUS AGENCIES**
>
> Ayangana Construction Limited
> Bureau of Standards
> Central Housing and Planning Authority
> Civil Defence Commission
> Consumer Affairs
> Cooperative Finance Administration
> Economic Recovery Programme Unit
> Forestry Commission
> General Construction Company
> Guyana School of Agriculture
> Guyana Agency for Health, Education,
>   Environment & Food Policy
> Guyana Manufacturing & Industrial
>   Development Agency
> Guyana Water Authority (GUYWA)
> Mahaica Mahaicony Abary Project
> National Insurance Scheme
> National Relief Committee
> National Dairy Development Programme
> National Agricultural Research
>   Institute
> National Congress of Local Democratic
>   Organs
> National Frequency Management
> New Guyana Marketing Corporation
> Plant Maintenance and Hire Division
> Policy Complaints Authority
> Public Corporations Secretariat (PSC)
> Public Utilities Commission
> Regional Programme for Animal Health
>   Assistance
> Social Impact Amelioration Programme
>   (SIMAP)
> Statistical Bureau
> University of Guyana

6.17   One consequence of the independence in employment policies of SAAs has been the creation of numerous salary scales and allowance structures across the public service and the loss of consistent and transparent wage and employment practices with the incumbent costs associated with the exercise of multiple wage regimes. Consideration should be given to the rationalization of the salary structures of some of the SAAs, possibly in the form of stated parities with public service grades. This would preserve their autonomous nature in allowing them to determine the desired parity of their staff to public service grades, but would eliminate the need for incurring the high transaction costs of renegotiating each salary structure independently. While such a practice does imply that each salary increase announced for the public service will automatically have a wider application and greater budget cost, this process actually makes the total costs of an announced public service salary increase more transparent and calculable up front. Further, dependence on Central Government transfers has reduced institutional incentives in SAAs to pursue cost-recovery measures. As a result, most SAAs are a drain on the central budget.

6.18   There are a large number of Public Corporations (PCs), governed by the 1988 Public Corporations Act. PCs are created by the Ministry charged with responsibility and are subject to the approbation of Parliament for their existence and dissolution. At the end of the 1980s, PCs were responsible for the employment of fully two-thirds of all public employees and contributed a parallel portion of total GNP. Three PCs (GUYMINE, GUYSUCO, and GEC) alone account for some 60% of the total operating revenue of all public enterprises, and are clear candidates for inclusion in the list of enterprises to be privatized or altered in terms of the operational relationship to the public sector. The current Government has committed itself to further privatization in the context of the 1992-94 PFP. Its privatization program should be comprehensive and rapidly implemented.

6.19   Perhaps the most troublesome relationship of entities to the public sector exists in the Public Financial Entities (PFEs). All of the important non-bank financial institutions, with the exception of the New Building Society, are state-owned and are part of an umbrella organization, the Cooperative Finance Administration (COFA).[10] COFA's role is to provide support to the public sector financial institutions in mobilizing and channeling financial resources into the appropriate areas in order to foster economic growth. COFA clearly does not have the institutional capacity to perform its assigned supervisory functions, which include holding Government shares in the PFEs; providing an advisory role for the PFEs; and giving policy directions. COFA has never undertaken an examination of the institutions under its jurisdiction, and appears to have limited influence over their activities. COFA's regulatory functions should be transferred to the Central Bank and that its supervisory role in the privatization of PFEs be eliminated.

C. DECENTRALIZATION AND THE REGIONAL ADMINISTRATIONS

6.20   According to Section 3 of the 1980 Local Democratic Organs Act, the general objectives of the systems of local government were to "involve as many citizens as possible in the task of managing and developing the communities in which they live and ensure popular participation in organizing the political, economic, social, and cultural life of the communities." While six tiers of local government were contemplated, to date only Village Councils, RAs and Regional Democratic Councils have been created. Under Article 72 of the 1980 Constitution, the government was required to create ten regions in the country, each with a Regional Administration to take responsibility for the management of operational responsibility for education (nursery, primary and secondary), the day-to-day workings of the health system,[11] and the operation and maintenance of roads, river and sea defenses, irrigation and water facilities. Broad policy and planning functions, technical advice, monitoring, and construction activities remain centralized, and operate through the line ministries (health, education, agriculture, and the infrastructure sectors). To further facilitate the

---

10/   There are six institutions under COFA's jurisdiction: the development bank (Guyana Cooperative Agricultural & Industrial Development Bank-- GAIBANK), the mortgage finance institution (Guyana Cooperative Mortgage Finance Bank--GCMFB), the trust company (GNCB Trust Corporation), the commercial bank (Guyana National Cooperative Bank--GNCB), the social security organization (National Insurance Scheme--NIS) and the insurance service (Guyana Cooperative Insurance Service--GCIS).

11/   Some programs, mostly those with a high foreign aid component, like maternal and child health care and the malaria program, are administered directly by the center.

linkage between the Central Government and the regions, the RAs were to be staffed by public servants on rotation from the central offices who could implement central policies. To assure local responsiveness, each region has a elected, party-based Regional Democratic Council. In addition, each region has a Regional Executive Officer, appointed by the Minister of MPWCRD on the recommendation of the Regional Democratic Council.

Table 6.1: DISTRIBUTION OF PUBLIC SERVICE EMPLOYMENT

GRADES	1-5	6-9	10-14	15-Spec.	TOTAL
Positions Approved	13,501	3,321	1,505	281	18,608
Ministries & Departments	8,821	2,332	1,159	239	12,551
Regional Administrations	4,576	891	218	0	5,685
Constitutional Agencies	104	98	128	42	372
Positions Filled	8,782	1,905	875	198	11,760
Ministries & Departments	5,775	1,420	707	165	8,067
Regional Administrations	2,943	433	89	0	3,465
Constitutional Agencies	64	52	79	33	228
Vacancies	4,719	1,416	630	83	6,848
Ministries & Departments	3,046	912	452	74	4,484
Regional Administrations	1,633	458	129	0	2,220
Constitutional Agencies	40	46	49	9	144
Vacancies/Approved (%)	35	43	42	30	37
Ministries/Departments	35	39	39	31	36
Regional Administrations	36	51	59	0	39
Constitutional Agencies	38	47	38	21	39

Source: Government of Guyana

6.21   As the system currently operates it is unwieldy, inefficient, and suffers from poor articulation of the relationship between authority, responsibility, and effective implementation capacity. The RAs have weak capacity to carry out their operational mandate. There is wide disparity among the regions in terms of the level of staffing. For example, in regions 1, 2, 7, 8, and 9 there is approximately one approved public service post for every 32-51 persons, while in regions 3,4,5,6, and 10 there is approximately one approved post for every 84 persons. Further evidence of the weakness of the staffing for the RAs is the high level of vacancies for posts (Table 6.1). On average, 39% of the approved posts are vacant. More significant still, at the level of technical and senior technical posts, the percentage is even higher. Some 59% of posts at grades 10-14 are vacant, and 51% for grades 6-9. The problem is most acute in Regions 1, 8, and 9. To illustrate, in Region 8 in agriculture only one position, and that at grade 3, is filled! In Region 9 in education only four positions are filled, all at grade 1 (a cook, caretaker, janitor, and cleaner)! Thus, weaknesses in staffing are both a quantitative and qualitative issue. This staffing weakness is critical given that the Regional Sectoral Officers are responsible for the implementation of central programs.

6.22   The capacity issue is more than simply a question of weak staffing. Financial constraints in the regions prevent any effective compliance with their stated responsibilities. While some 30% of approved public sector positions are located at the regional level, only 5% of the total current budget is dedicated to the regions, primarily dedicated to wages and salaries.

6.23   There are no effective mechanisms to link lines of accountability or to assure consistent relationships between ministries and RAs, and the sectoral planning process suffers from weak integration. The relationship between RAs, Regional Democratic Councils, Regional Executive Officers and the Central Government is fraught with difficulty. Regional Executive Officers are appointed by the Minister of MPWCRD at the recommendation of the Regional Democratic Councils. Sectoral Personnel in the region report to the Regional Executive Officer who has financial authority for programs in the sector. Regional Executive Officers are responsible for the formulation of budget bids which are forwarded to the SPS, but not subject to clearance or approval by the sectoral ministries at the center. Further, transfers move from the Ministry of Finance, in accordance with SPS advice, to the control of the Regional Democratic Councils. Little authority for ultimate implementation rests with the Regional Democratic Councils, yet the determination of the priorities for expenditures at the regional level rests with them. The 1991 ODA study clearly shows the failure to link authority and responsibility: "...the planning process generally ceases to involve the ministry at the point at which the budget bid is decided by the regional administration and negotiations take place directly with the Ministry of Finance and the Planning Secretariat."[12] The Ministries have no downstream control of policy implementation and effectively are left in the dark as to implementation in some cases.

6.24   Further confusing these relationships is the fact that staff themselves are not clear as to lines of authority and accountability. Sectoral personnel in the region are often uncertain as to whether they are accountable to Regional Executive Officers or to the ministry. "For example, a number of Regional Health Officers considered that the Medical Director, Regional Health Services, based in the Ministry of Health was their boss, whereas the formal position is that they are accountable to the Regional Executive Officer. A few Regional Executive Officers considered that they might in some way be accountable to the Permanent Secretary, Ministry of Regional Development [now in the MPWCRD], whereas they are accountable to the Regional Democratic Council."[13]

6.25   If ineffective linkage and control of RAs is evident in the planning and budget process, it is equally evident in the Central Government's inability to assure financial accountability over resources transferred to the regions or even to monitor compliance with stated budget appropriations. The absence of any financial management system, the use of cash management rather

---

12/   KPMG, op. cit., p. 113.

13/   Ibid, p. 112.

than accounting procedures, the absence of legislative oversight of RAs, and the absence of any linkage between revenue generating capacity and expenditure responsibilities at the regional level, virtually guarantee distortions in financial practice.

6.26   Given the fundamental weaknesses and distortions described above, it is not surprising that the result is a lack of effective action at the regional level. Nowhere is this more evident than in the area of maintenance of infrastructural systems that theoretically are the responsibility of the regions. In the agriculture sector, for example, the absence of effective operation and maintenance activities in Drainage and Irrigation, either de facto in the Ministry of Agriculture or formally in the RAs, has meant output losses exceeding 25% (see Chapter IX).

6.27   Reform of the current system of Regional Administration is imperative and urgent. The system fulfills neither the promise of participation nor the necessity of effective implementation. There is a need to re-examine the relationship between activities at the regional level and the responsibilities of sectoral ministries. Further, the role that the Department of Regional Administration within MPWCRD plays in the provision of technical assistance and coordination needs to be strengthened. While the consolidation of the Regional Development and infrastructure functions in the MPWCRD are an important first conceptual step, in practice little coordination with the regions occurs yet. The relationship between Regional Executive Officers and Regional Democratic Councils needs clarification in terms of lines of authority. Appropriate qualified staffing levels, technical advising, and training in the regions needs to be examined carefully. The lack of financial accountability in the regions needs to be rectified. The link between revenue generating capabilities and expenditure responsibilities in the regions needs to be established.

6.28   All of the above suggests the urgent need to reconsider the objectives and organizational content of decentralization efforts in Guyana. In particular, it raises the questions of (a) whether to recentralize certain functions now formally resident in the regions, (b) how to redefine the political and administrative relationships at the regional level, and (c) how to integrate national and sectoral policies across levels of government. These issues should be subject to a detailed analysis in the near future.

D. MANAGEMENT OF THE PUBLIC SERVICE

6.29   One of the most critical areas for reform in Guyana is the need to improve personnel policy, particularly as it relates to providing the incentive framework for the civil service. The primary weakness of the public service system has been the sharp deterioration in public salaries. Between 1987 and 1992 real wages in the Central Government declined by about 40 percent (see Chapter III). Salaries in high level administrative and technical positions have been particularly affected by this decline, as reflected in the change of compression ratio[14] from 9:1 in 1987 to about 6:1 in 1992 (see Section E).

14/   The compression ratio is the ratio of the midpoint of the monthly salary for the highest salary grade to the midpoint for the lowest.

6.30   However, providing an equitable, consistent, and transparent salary system is but one aspect of the larger issue of appropriate personnel management for the public service. It is more appropriate to think of personnel management as the broader concern for policies, processes and procedures that address individuals in the working environment. This encompasses an entire range of activities from recruitment, performance appraisal and evaluation, training and development, remuneration, and the terms and conditions of employment.

6.31   Currently, there are two distinct entities who are charged with personnel management and exercise somewhat ambiguous authority over the personnel function. Public Service Management (PSM) is to have executive responsibility for the management and development of the personnel function -- even though authority to carry out these activities is not clearly demarcated. The Public Service Commission (PSC) is responsible for the recruitment, promotion, removal, and discipline of personnel. In addition, each ministry and region has a personnel unit, reporting to the Permanent Secretary and Regional Executive Officer, respectively, and is theoretically responsible for operational matters within guidelines set by PSM and PSC. In fact, however, the current personnel system does not serve a management function involving the formulation, implementation, and monitoring of human resource policies. Personnel "policy" has remained an unarticulated goal and is little more than the mechanical exercise of appointment and assignment.

6.32   Even as an administrative service, Public Service Management lacks a system for the maintenance of accurate and updated information on approved posts, budgeted positions, numbers of employees, and salaries. While a job evaluation exercise is currently underway, the existing evaluation scheme has been in place since independence. With each additional new requirement, job titles have simply been added. The result is a system of cumbersome and complex classifications with an extraordinary proliferation of over 1,300 job titles without comparability across entities in either pay or classification. As a result, public officers responsible for personnel management at different levels are not held accountable. Employees are often unclear as to their job responsibilities, routine procedures are in disarray, and the highly centralized personnel management system is incapable of providing effective and flexible response to personnel needs of line ministries. Even basic procedural matters are referred to the central administration. Efforts focus on compliance with procedure rather than ensuring that personnel issues are addressed. Under these constraints, the fundamental aspects of personnel policy and administration, including the design of the public service salary scale and recruitment strategy, can not be adequately managed.

6.33   One of the major tasks of the technical assistance provided through ODA was to provide recommendations and actions for the creation of the institutional and procedural infrastructure to address the issues described above. Since 1991, several steps have been taken to implement these recommendations. A Presidential Task Force was established which now directs the ongoing reform program, and has begun to strengthen the institutional capacity of Public Service Management, particularly in the areas of job evaluation and salary administration, personnel systems development and management services. This has been a positive step; the current proposed PAP is intended to build on this effort and provides significant resources for implementation of effective reform for the personnel management function.

6.34 More concerted action, however, is required to achieve transparency, equity, and consistency in recruitment, employment, and promotion. To achieve this, a number of actions are recommended:

- the establishment of clear authority to recruit below the central level;

- standardization of recruitment and evaluation procedures;

- a clear system of information regarding vacancies for competitive searches and for communicating the results of recruitment;

- procedures for monitoring recruitment and appeals processes; and

- transparent procedures for the evaluation of performance and for linking incentives to performance.

E. PUBLIC SERVICE EMPLOYMENT

6.35 There is perhaps no issue more critical for effective government action than the provision of the framework for the utilization of human resources in the public sector. The absence of such a framework, and the failure to create appropriate incentives for public sector employment in Guyana has resulted in gross distortions in employment practices and pay, and wide-spread demoralization in the work place.

6.36 The issue of equitable, meaningful, and transparent pay structures requires immediate action. The absence of such pay structures has led to inability of qualified public sector employees to earn an appropriate wage comparable to skill levels and job demands; a predominance of manual and clerical level workers over higher level officers; and high vacancy rates, especially of technical personnel, which impede effective delivery of services by the public sector. Until pay issues are resolved, there is little prospect of attracting and retaining the permanent body of qualified professionals needed to manage an efficient and effective public sector.

6.37 Real wages in the Central Government severely deteriorated in the initial phase of the adjustment, by almost 50% between 1987-89. In recent years, the Government has made commendable efforts in improving salaries. Since 1990, public service pay has been increased four times: January 1991 (50 percent over December 1990 level), July 1991 (13 percent plus G$800 per month), January 1992 (10 percent), and July 1992 (12 percent), and a further increase of 9 percent for 1993 has been envisioned in the 1992-94 PFP. Nonetheless, salaries in real terms are still well below their 1987 levels.

6.38 More importantly, real salaries of higher level management and technical personnel have declined even more rapidly than for lower level personnel. An unskilled worker at level 1 is today earning 62 percent of what his/her real earnings were in 1987, and specialists at level 12 or heads of division at level 16, are earning 44 and 41 percent of what their real earnings were in 1987, respectively. This disparity in the development of wages is also reflected in the compression ratio (of the highest and the lowest civil servant salaries): from a ratio of 9:1 in 1987, the ratio has worsened to 6:1. International comparison indicates that an efficiently functioning civil service has a compression ratio in the range of 9:1 to 12:1.[15]

6.39   Official public service salaries for high level positions are also extremely low when compared with those in the Public Corporations and in the private sector. While average salaries for support staff and low-level technical staff in the Public Corporations are 1.5-2 times their level in the public service, senior level management can earn 3-5 times more in some Public Corporations, and even more in the private sector. These comparisons illustrate the strong incentive for professionals to leave the public service, as has been the case.

6.40   As a result of the deterioration in wages, professional and technical personnel in the public sector are in short supply, and vacancy rates are extremely high. At the same time, the public service has become too bottom-heavy. Of the total of 18,608 positions approved, there are 11,760 public sector employees, or 63% of approved positions. Of the 11,760 filled positions, 68 percent are in the Ministries (including the affiliated Departments), 29 percent are in the Regional Administrations, and 2 percent are in the Constitutional Agencies. Overall, vacancies are highest in grades 6 through 9 and 10 through 14, where most technical and senior technical staff appear to be graded. The government is not able to carry out adequately such basic functions as data collection, management and analysis, accounting and cost control, sector planning and essential service delivery. High vacancy rates of technical staff are particularly prominent in the Regional Administrations where, on average, 51 percent of approved positions at grades 6 through 9 and 59 percent of approved positions at grades 10 through 14, are vacant (Table 6.1 above).

6.41   Some of these vacancies are for positions that are "key and critical" to the efficient functioning of the public sector.[16] In the Ministry of Agriculture, for example, all of the vacancies in grades 10 through Special (9 positions in all) appear to be key and critical positions. In the Ministry of Public Works, of the 12 vacancies in grades 10 through 14, five are key and critical posts (specialist engineers), and of the 6 vacancies in grades 15 through Special, one is key and critical (deputy chief road officer). In this context, the PAP is proposing several measures to secure and retain positions that are essential to the efficient functioning of the public sector, including: (i) shifting all key and critical positions to the appropriate grades to establish appropriate incentives; (ii) filling vacancies in these posts, while freezing positions in some other posts; and (iii) providing a special recruitment program targeted at professionally qualified Guyanese nationals residing in Guyana and abroad.

15/   Barbara Nunberg and John Nellis, "Civil Service Reform and the World Bank," World Bank, PPR Working Paper No. 422, May 1990.

16/   "Key positions" range from the level of Permanent Secretary to heads of divisions on which each entity depends for strong management and coordination of its activities. "Critical positions" are those posts that require scarce technical skills that cannot be attracted given the public service's existing salary structure, such as engineers, accountants, economists, and medical personnel.

6.42   In an effort to attract and retain qualified staff, the Government has introduced multiple pay systems which, because of their lack of transparency and unofficial nature, have fostered resentment and low morale, and distorted wages. These schemes include (a) shifting positions into higher salary grades, (b) establishing "special" salaries and allowances for selected higher level staff; (c) giving "market supplements" to key professional and technical posts; (d) allowing staff to "act up," that is giving staff "acting up" allowances in exchange for assuming responsibilities of a higher level position; (e) hiring personnel as "acting" staff in positions that have "not yet" been officially approved; and (f) filling posts on a temporary basis while the position remains officially vacant.

6.43   Another category of benefits that has a major impact on compensation levels is that of "benefits and allowances." This category, which includes entertainment, home, travel, telephone, and other allowances, accounted for 28 percent of total employment costs in the 1992 budget. These costs are particularly significant for the Ministry of Foreign Affairs, the Police, Guyana Defense Force, National Hospitals, Health in Region 6 and the Office of the President, which accounted for 85% of the budgeted benefits and allowances in 1992 (Table 6.2).

Table 6.2:   BENEFITS AND ALLOWANCES AS PERCENTAGE OF EMPLOYMENT COSTS
(G$1000)

	Benefits and Allowances	Employment Costs	Percent
All Entities	823,626	2,944,272	28
Ministries & Departments	696,351	1,834,468	38
RAs	62,510	750,944	8
Constitutional Agencies	2,389	31,775	8
Other a/	62,376	327,085	19
Selected Entities			
Ministry of Foreign Affairs	390,103	585,726	67
Police	172,440	406,726	42
Guyana Defence Force	51,756	263,964	20
National Hospitals	44,688	114,815	39
Region 6 – Health	22,574	82,742	27
Office of the President	21,144	83,182	25

a/   Includes the Guyana Defense Force, the Guyana National Service, and the Public Utilities Commission.

Source: Statistical Appendix

6.44   These distortions in salaries and in the relationship between jobs and positions have created a personnel records system that is neither transparent nor consistent. This lack of transparency leads to a lack of accountability and puts upward pressures on the budget. The responsible agencies in the personnel system are unable to track positions and there are few means to evaluate performance or link pay to performance. The agencies responsible for internal and external financial control, therefore, have little opportunity to exercise their function in accounting for wages and salaries accurately.

6.45   The Government, supported by the PAP, proposes to incorporate all special contracts, allowances, and other salary enhancements into the formal grading system, and to establish a new salary structure designed to link higher salaries with higher specialized skills and/or management responsibility. However, even with the proposed upgrade, which would change the compression ratio (ratio of the highest and the lowest civil servant's salaries), from 6:1 to 8.5:1, real salaries of higher level staff still will represent only about 70 percent of the 1987 salaries. Under this scenario, a number of vacant technical and managerial posts are not likely to be filled, and existing filled positions may become vacant in the future.

6.46   The overriding concern of the Government with regard to public sector employment is to fill vacancies in professional and technical posts, and to reduce labor redundancies. Stringent policies with regard to the salary structure are called for, and staffing levels need to be assessed to determine the right composition necessary to meet expanding sectoral priorities and changing needs. The salary structure of the public service will need to be decompressed even further than what is proposed, to attract and retain qualified professional and technical individuals. Adequate staff training and incentives for good performance through career development, are also important. Redundant staff will need to be either redeployed or offered incentives for voluntary departure.

6.47   In addition, given the scarcity of professional personnel, the Government may need to take extraordinary measures to attract expertise from Guyana and abroad to fill gaps, primarily in managerial skills. Several inexpensive mechanisms could be considered, such as (a) training programs through local universities, (b) international executive programs of technical assistance, (c) UN Volunteer Programs; (d) short-term assignments of professional Guyanese abroad; and (e) twinning arrangements with external training institutions.

6.48   At the other end of the employment spectrum, public sector employment is too bottom heavy. On average, about 70 percent of approved positions in the Ministries and 80 percent of approved positions in the Regional Administrations, are in grades 1-5 (typically, clerical and office support, and semi-skilled operators and unskilled workers). These positions account for 92, 77 and 73 percent of approved positions in the Ministries of Home Affairs, Public Works, and Agriculture, respectively. While some ministries, such as the Ministry of Finance, the Office of the President and the Ministry of Foreign Affairs, have much lower shares of positions in grades 1-5, this results from the practice of raising salaries by shifting positions into higher salary grades, and therefore may not reflect a lower concentration of support staff. The high concentration of low level positions in some cases results from the need to hire several individuals with lower skills to perform activities that should be carried out by a higher skilled individual who cannot be attracted at existing salary levels.

6.49   Overall, this implies that there will be increased labor
redundancy at lower levels, once higher level positions are filled as a result
of upgrading the salary scale. It is essential for the fiscal viability of
any public sector reform effort that measures should be undertaken in parallel
to upgrading the salary scale to eliminate labor redundancy, including: (i)
canceling all existing vacancies in grades 1 through 5, (ii) freezing or
canceling all new vacancies in these same grades, and (iii) redeploying and
retraining existing staff. The Government will need to systematically review
staffing patterns and identify positions that need to be either expanded or
contracted to meet changing needs. Also, it would need to consider reducing
the size of its permanent work force through incentive packages for voluntary
departure from public service, among others.

6.50   Finally, there are distortions across ministries and departments
in terms of staffing. The sectoral staffing composition may not be adequate
given the sectoral priorities. Table 6.3 shows the sectoral distribution of
staffing for the Ministries and Regional Administrations, combined. The
social sectors employ the largest number of staff (37 percent), followed by
law and order (31 percent), administration aspects of the Regional
Administrations (11 percent), and production (10 percent). This composition
may respond more to the interventionist and paternalistic policies that
characterized Guyana's model of "cooperative socialism" since 1970, than to
realistic staffing objectives in the current policy environment. There are
several entities where staffing levels appear to be exceptionally high. These
include the Ministry of Home Affairs (5,225 approved positions), and the
Ministry of Health and Regional Health combined (4,594 approved positions).
Conversely, in the ministries in the production sector, 59 percent of all
positions in grades 6 through 9 are vacant, and in the social sector, 53
percent of positions in grades 10 through 14 are vacant. To provide for
staffing increases in sectors with expanding programs, the Government will
need to review staffing levels of various programs. Redeployment of staff
across sectors may be appropriate with adequate training. The Government will
also need to review staffing in the Ministry of Home Affairs, where there
appears to be high labor redundancy (of the 5667 approved positions, 5149 are
in grades 1-5, and of these, only 3170 positions are filled).

Table 6.3: SECTORAL DISTRIBUTION OF PUBLIC SERVICE EMPLOYEES
Ministries and Regional Administrations Only

GRADES	1-5	6-9	10-14	15-Sp.	TOTAL
Positions Approved	13397	3223	1377	239	18236
Office of the President	15	233	87	23	358
Ministry of Finance	114	679	293	61	1147
Production	1537	182	119	20	1858
Social Well Being	4611	1466	708	49	6834
Law and Order	5149	356	98	64	5667
External Affairs	137	112	51	22	322
RAs (Administration)	1834	195	21	0	2050
Vacancies/Approved (%)	35	43	42	31	37
Office of the President	47	36	30	22	34
Ministry of Finance	36	38	36	36	37
Production	37	59	34	15	39
Social Well Being	33	46	53	43	38
Law and Order	34	19	11	36	33
External Affairs	77	45	18	0	51
RAs (Administration)	36	62	62	0	39

Source: Statistical Appendix

F. RECOMMENDATIONS

• The current effort of economic reform has profound implications for the role of the state, and requires an appropriate institutional setting to enable the public sector to deliver the services needed to sustain private sector-led economic growth and to address social concerns. Hence, a clear commitment by Government to a comprehensive Public Sector Reform Program (PSRP) is a sine qua non for effective economic recovery.

• Such a reform program should include careful consideration of the following interlocking elements: Administrative Reform; Public Sector Management Reform; Decentralization/centralization; Deregulation/regulation; and Divestiture/privatization.

• The past twenty years have witnessed the inchoate expansion of state activity without regard to either logical or functional integrity of the "parts." As part of the PSRP, the rationale for the various public sector entities should be carefully reviewed, and the current organization of the public sector further streamlined. In particular, the role and status of the Semi-Autonomous Agencies needs to be reconsidered, and public corporations and financial entities should be privatized, and COFA's functions should be transferred to the Central Bank.

• Administrative reform should also include internal reorganization within the ministries to clarify functional responsibilities. In particular, there is need to institute a modern financial management system with institutional correspondence in authority, responsibility, execution, and accountability. This effort requires the strengthening and restructuring of the management and accounting capacity within the sectoral ministries and at the central level (Ministry of Finance).

- Efforts at decentralization have created a system that is unwieldy, inefficient, and suffers from poor articulation of the relationship between authority, responsibility, and effective implementation capacity. In particular, there is a need to address the appropriate role of Regional Administrations and their ability to carry out assigned functions; to clarify lines of authority between Regional Executive Officers and Regional Democratic Councils; to examine staffing levels, technical advising, and training in the regions; to rectify the lack of financial accountability in the regions; and to establish the link between revenue generating capabilities and expenditure responsibilities in the regions.

- The management of the public service requires immediate attention. Public Service Management needs to be strengthened, and its role clarified. To accomplish this requires the institution of a personnel records system, and the implementation of a longer term comprehensive personnel policy and management system.

- The dramatic deterioration of wages in the public sector effectively undermines any attempt to provide a human resource dimension to the public service. Pay and employment conditions cannot continue in their current state. Recent efforts to improve wages are commendable, but only provide a stop-gap response.

- In particular, the salary structure must be made transparent, with consistency between position and pay guaranteed across the public service, and with appropriate decompression of the wage scale to provide incentives to professional and higher technical personnel.

- Parallel to this effort, there is a need to examine the allocation of personnel across the public sector. Currently, the employment structure is much too bottom heavy, with administrative and support personnel in numbers well beyond those needed for the effective management of the Government's responsibilities. Appropriate reclassification of personnel, reductions in labor redundancy, and retraining of existing personnel are in order.

CHAPTER VII.   RESOURCE MOBILIZATION: INSTITUTIONAL ASPECTS

A.   INTRODUCTION

7.1   Of Guyana's three main tax categories -- income taxes, taxes on production and consumption, and taxes on international trade -- the first two dominate the tax structure, each contributing about 35 percent to tax revenue (Table 7.1).   Export levies on sugar exports to the EC, which attract higher prices than world market prices, also make a sizable contribution to revenue.

Table 7.1: CENTRAL GOVERNMENT TAX REVENUES

	1976	1981	1986	1991
	--------------------- G$ million ------------------			
Income Tax	105.6	192.7	366.3	3453.2
o.w. Companies	67.0	130.1	238.1	2444.1
o.w. Personal Income	38.6	62.6	157.8	492.6
o.w. Withholding	--	--	13.7	457.2
Taxes on Production and Consumption	73.5	178.6	395.1	3459.5
o.w. Consumption Tax	49.9	139.3	324.8	3271.6
o.w. Excises	23.6	39.3	53.2	92.6
Taxes on International Trade	53.3	66.3	148.8	1586.3
o.w. Import Duties	52.0	46.9	81.3	1167.5
Levies	76.2	--	--	1071.7
Sugar Levy (net)	76.2	--	--	962.1
Rice Levy (net)a/	--	--	--	109.6
Other Tax Revenue	27.9	41.9	62.5	228.9
Total Tax Revenue (incl. Rice Levy)	336.5	479.5	1029.3	9788.8
Memorandum Items	-------------- percent of total tax revenue -----------			
Income Tax	31.4	40.2	41.1	35.2
Taxes on Production and Consumption	21.8	37.2	38.4	35.3
Taxes on International Trade	15.8	13.8	14.5	16.2
Levies	22.6	0.0	0.0	10.9
Other Tax Revenue	8.3	8.7	6.1	2.3
	-------------------- percent of GDP ------------------			
Income Tax	9.3	12.1	12.2	13.0
Taxes on Production and Consumption	6.5	11.2	11.4	13.1
Taxes on International Trade	4.7	4.2	4.3	6.0
Levies	6.7	0.0	0.0	4.1
Other Tax Revenue	2.5	2.6	1.7	0.9
Total Tax Revenue (incl. Rice Levy)	29.6	30.0	29.6	37.1

a/   Included under non-tax revenues in Table 3.3.

Source: Statistical Appendix

7.2   Recent years have seen major reforms of the tax system.   These have included considerable simplification of income taxes, the 1991 reduction in CARICOM's Common External Tariff (CET), the restoration of proper exchange rates for the valuation of imports for duty purposes, widespread reduction in the rates of consumption tax, and the replacement of specific by ad valorem tax rates for the excises.   The tax structure that has resulted is broadly satisfactory.   The main priority should now be on broadening the coverage and on improving the administration of different taxes.   Aside from economic growth, it is the progress made in these areas that will largely determine the prospects for revenue growth over the next few years.

B. TAX STRUCTURE

1. Income Taxes

7.3   Income taxes are narrowly-based: only about 2,000 companies, 18,000 self-employed and 30,000 employees are assessed. Companies account for 80 percent of total revenue from income taxes.

Personal Income Tax

7.4   In a drastic simplification of the personal income tax in 1991, a single basic allowance that varies with income replaced all other allowances (which ranged from child allowances to deductions for savings). The basic exemption was G$72,000 (US$571) or one-third of income, whichever was higher. The first G$50,000 (US$397) of taxable income was taxed at the rate of 20 percent, the next G$50,000 at 30 percent, and the remaining income at 40 percent. In 1993, the personal income tax was further simplified, by introducing a single rate of 33 1/3 percent on all taxable income in excess of a fixed allowance of G$120,000 per year. This reform has raised the maximum effective rate from 27 to 33 1/3 percent. Taxable income from employer-provided housing is estimated at standardized rates; for example, income from unfurnished accommodation of up to 1,000 sq. ft. is estimated at G$0.84 (US cents 0.7) per square foot, while that for accommodation of over 3,000 square feet is taken as G$1.28 (US cents 1.0) per square foot. Bank interest received by both individuals and companies is not subject to further taxation once it has borne a withholding tax of 15 percent. There is a separate assessment of married couples.

Withholding Tax on Interest

7.5   The introduction of a withholding tax on interest was a significant measure, since deduction of tax at source tends to improve the enforcement of taxes. On the other hand, the appropriateness of the overall tax treatment of interest is difficult to evaluate. Ideally, interest income should be aggregated with other income and taxed in the same manner as other income (with credit given for any withholding taxes). Consequently, the current approach can only be justified if it is believed that the proper taxation of interest would result in a substantial outflow of capital.

Company Taxes

7.6   The simplification of income tax extended to corporate taxation: the taxation of companies through a combination of corporate and income taxes was discontinued, the distinction between industrial and other companies was abolished, and depreciation allowances were raised to more realistic levels. However, in 1993, the Government proposed a 10% development levy on "commercial" companies, which effectively increases their company taxes from 35% to 45%, as a short-term expedient to raise additional revenue. This measure has only a limited revenue potential, and should not replace the efforts to broaden the tax base. In addition, it has increased the distortions arising from the gap between personal income and company taxes.

Hence, it is recommended that the Government discontinue this levy and subsequently unify the top income and company tax rates.

7.7   The country's previous company taxes, though much higher and complex, were integrated with the personal income tax to some extent. The present system of corporate taxation, by contrast, is completely separate from the personal income tax. A major result is that corporate-source income bears higher taxation than other incomes, and the extent of overtaxation is higher the lower the income (mainly because all distributed profits are taxed at a uniform rate of 15%). The objective of reform should be to achieve complete integration of corporate and personal income taxes in the taxation of distributed profits. This can be achieved by requiring the aggregation of (gross-of-tax) dividends with other income and permitting shareholders to claim credit for corporation tax deducted from distributed profits against their income tax liability. The suggested approach is likely to result in a loss of revenues and may need to be introduced in a phased manner and only after the Government's fiscal position is sufficiently strengthened.

Concessions

7.8   Fiscal concessions in Guyana take the form of tax relief from one or more taxes. Under income tax, the tax concessions take the form of: a tax holiday of up to five years, with a possible extension by a further five years; accelerated depreciation allowances; exemption of dividends from the withholding tax during the tax holiday period and the subsequent two years; and the carryover and set-off of losses suffered during the tax holiday period against profits following the tax holiday period without limitation. These are supplemented by an export allowance, which reduces the tax payable by the same proportion as the fraction of total profits from non-traditional exports to non-CARICOM countries; the reduction is restricted to one-half of the tax payable.

7.9   Tax concessions need to be curtailed, taking account of the arrangements elsewhere in the region. The concessions are bound to be costly in terms of the revenue foregone. For example, since depreciation allowances start after the end of a tax holiday period, the concessions may exempt a firm from taxation for a considerable period of time. Now that the corporate tax rate is much lower than in the past, the need for generous concessions would seem to be less.

2.   The Consumption Tax

7.10   Consumption duties were introduced in 1969 to counteract the revenue loss resulting from the removal of import duties on goods originating from the other members of CARIFTA. Their scope as well as the range of tax rates was widened substantially in August 1973, when CET, which was much lower than Guyana's then prevailing tariff, was originally adopted. Subsequent tariff reforms also prompted modifications of CET. The consumption tax will have to continue to help cushion the revenue impact of the trend toward lower tariffs in the CARICOM.

7.11   The consumption tax applies equally to local and imported goods. Section 18 of the Consumption Tax Act confers powers to remit the tax. Goods utilized as materials by registered manufacturers are exempt from tax. This is ensured by exempting *all* registered manufacturers from consumption tax on *all* directly imported inputs, and on *all* domestically produced inputs purchased from other registered manufacturers. Exports are exempt from the tax. Imports account for seventy-five percent of the revenue; fifty percent of the revenue from domestic goods comes from alcoholic beverages and tobacco (Table 7.2).

Table 7.2: **REVENUE FROM THE CONSUMPTION TAX, 1991**

Category	G$ Million	Percent of GDP
Imports	2,501.4	9.5
Oil	1,346.1	5.1
Other	1,155.3	4.4
Domestic Goods	811.6	3.1
Alcoholic beverages	174.4	0.7
Tobacco	239.5	0.9
Other	397.7	1.5
TOTAL	3,313.0	12.6

Note: Raw data, differ slightly from Table 7.1.

Source: Customs and Excise Department

7.12   For imports, the consumption tax is levied on the c.i.f. import value plus the import duty payable, whereas the price realized by the manufacturer in the "open market" constitutes the base for domestically produced goods. The tax rates, which are now all ad valorem, range from zero to 100 percent, but most goods are taxed at the rates of 10 percent and 30 percent. Recent reforms have lowered some tax rates and exempted a number of necessities.

7.13   The consumption tax, by its exemption from tax of materials used in production, embodies the essential characteristic of value added taxes. Where it differs from most value added taxes is in its method of tax collection. This *exemption* method is not widely used these days because of the possibility that a proportion of tax-free inputs may be sold for profit rather than used in production. Most countries use the *tax credit* method, under which taxes paid on inputs can be set off against the tax due on output. A major implication in the Guyana context would be that the consumption tax would be payable on imported inputs at the time of importation, but registered manufacturers would be able to deduct the tax paid from the tax payable on their sales. Apart from advancing some tax payments, the credit method makes **tax avoidance more difficult** and is, therefore, worth considering.

7.14   The credit method also permits a more satisfactory treatment of machinery and exports. Value added taxes normally exempt from taxes all purchases by firms, including machinery. In Guyana, while duty *remissions* (full or partial exemptions from prescribed rates) have been widely used for machinery, not all machinery utilized in the production of goods subject to consumption taxes has been exempt from (consumption) taxes. The credit method can deal with machinery quite satisfactorily, since credits in excess of gross tax liabilities can be carried forward.[17] Machinery should be exempted from the consumption tax (that is, it should be treated in the same manner as intermediate goods) when the revenue situation permits.

7.15   Several reviewers of Guyana's tax system have suggested the extension of the consumption tax to services. The kind of services that are frequently taxed are hotel rooms and meals, telephones, air transport, water and electricity. A first step in this direction has been the introduction of a 10% tax on hotel accommodations.

7.16   The range and number of consumption tax rates need to be limited. The best indirect tax from the viewpoint of economic efficiency will be the tax that leaves the allocation of resources undisturbed. Too wide a range of highly divergent tax rates tend to induce distortions by taxing close substitutes differently and tax avoidance by creating the temptation to misclassify goods. Hence, it is advisable to set only three to four rates that are not widely dispersed.

Table 7.3:   **REMISSIONS OF IMPORT DUTY AND CONSUMPTION TAX MARCH-NOVEMBER, 1992**
(G$ thousands)

	Import Duty	Consumption Tax	Total
Fishing	2,164	2,641	4,805
Mining	216,021	312,725	528,746
Agriculture	2,733	4,678	7,411
Forestry	24,807	37,000	61,807
Migrants and Emigrants	73,038	178,440	251,478
Private Companies	512,711	441,892	954,603
Public Sector	99,724	94,220	193,944
Consultants, Specialists, etc.	411	483	894
Charitable Organizations	4,185	1,888	6,073
Mini-buses	10,805	76,541	87,346
Petroleum Products	378,635	161,085	539,720
Other	173,095	102,332	275,427
TOTAL	1,498,329	1,413,925	2,912,254
Remissions/Revenue Collected	133%	42%	65%

Source: Customs and Excise Department

17/   For exports, the normal practice is to make cash refunds when credit exceeds gross tax liability.

7.17   In the interests of a flexible tax policy, it is desirable that there should be one tax solely for revenue purposes. Pursuit of several objectives through each tax tends to complicate revenue mobilization. The most suitable tax for revenue purposes is the consumption tax, given that it has a much wider base than any other tax and can be made neutral in production. It is important, therefore, that all remissions under the consumption tax are eliminated, so that the tax is converted into a pure revenue levy with no protective effects. Remissions are also pervasive under the import duty. Given that remissions are equivalent to about 65% of consumption tax revenue and import duty collected (Table 7.3), elimination of remissions under the consumption tax and drastic reduction of remissions under the import duty would be the most significant measures that could be taken to improve the efficiency and revenue of the tax system.

7.18   Broadening of the base of consumption tax acquires added significance in the context of the proposed reductions in CET. Loss of revenue from the phased reductions in CET would have to be partly made up through higher taxes on domestic incomes and production. Since the personal income tax plays a limited role, it follows that the revenue loss would have to be offset primarily through the consumption tax. This, in turn, must mean a shift in taxation from inputs to final outputs, since the consumption tax does not tax inputs, and from imports to domestic production. Given that inputs are significant in the import structure, and local goods contribute a modest proportion of revenues from the consumption tax, the task of recouping the revenue loss would be eased if the coverage of the consumption tax is broadened to the maximum extent possible. This strengthens the case for confining exemptions under the consumption tax to the basic necessities, and for eliminating all remissions.

3. Excises

7.19   Excises are imposed on domestic production and imports of alcoholic beverages and matches. The tax rates range from 5 percent on "sweets" (local wine made from fruit) to 30 percent on some liqueurs. Most revenue comes from beer and rum, which are taxed at 20 percent. Excise revenue has stagnated -- its share in total tax revenue fell from 8 percent in 1981 to 0.8 percent in 1991 -- because the duties have been specific in nature. With the adoption of ad valorem rates in 1992, the contribution of excises to tax revenue should grow.

7.20   Current excises do not have protective effects because they apply to only final goods and cover both local production and imports of those goods. It does not matter much, therefore, whether excises remain a separate tax or are merged with the consumption tax. However, some time in the future, it may be useful to utilize excises on domestic production to reduce protection. In the context of CET, a Member State that wishes to provide greater protection than available under CET can do so by exempting machinery and materials used in production. No similar mechanism exists to lower protection. An excise confined to domestic production would enable a Member State to reduce protection below that provided by CET if it is so desired.

4. Import Duties

7.21   The rates of CET adopted by Guyana in early 1991, vary from zero to 45 percent. These rates are generally lower than those they replaced, but not markedly so. Except for a few goods (some alcoholic beverages, spices, perfumery and matches), to which community rates of import duty apply, goods originating from other members of CARICOM are not subject to tariffs. Import duties in Guyana contribute much less to the revenue (about 10 percent) than in other countries at a similar stage of development, primarily because of a widespread use of remissions as part of fiscal incentives.

7.22   Both CET and national legislation provide for remissions. The list of conditional duty exemptions in CET permits Member States to provide exemptions from duty for a wide variety of purposes. In the case of new investment or substantial expansion of an enterprise, machinery, equipment and materials for use in approved industry, agriculture and mining may be exempted. Furthermore, Guyana's Customs Act, under Section 12, permits the Government to make partial or full refunds of duties if it is "just and equitable" to do so.

7.23   As is the case for the consumption tax, the estimated cost of import duty remissions is considerable. According to the import duty data for 1990, the latest year for which detailed data are available, out of the import duty collectible of G$1 billion, only G$510 million was collected, suggesting that remissions were as great as the collections. In addition, the use of special exchange rates for valuation purposes during most of the year held down remissions as well as collections.[18] More recent data, albeit less complete, confirm the high cost of remissions. For the period March-November 1992, remissions under import and consumption duties amounted to G$2.9 billion, accounting for 65 percent of the total revenue collected (Table 7.3). Hence, as stated before, the most significant measure that can be taken to improve the efficiency and revenue of the tax system is a drastic reduction in remissions.

7.24   The reduction in remissions under import duties would need to be accompanied by measures to ensure that imported inputs embodied in exports are not taxed. The rationale for this is that any system of protective tariffs would be biased against exports unless export production can, at the very least, rely on tax-free inputs. If exports were not relieved from indirect taxes, then this would mean that while import-substitution industries were being protected, exports were being taxed. Manufacturers can be refunded import duties paid on inputs utilized in export production through rebates based on actual rates (that is, actual taxes paid) or at standardized rates (frequently derived from surveys). The latter method is preferable because it tends to be administratively simpler, and does not discourage the substitution of domestic for imported inputs.

7.25   In October 1992, the CARICOM Member States decided to lower CET in stages to the 0-20 percent range between July 1, 1993 and July 1, 1997. In the first stage, the "More Developed Countries" in the region, including Guyana are expected to reduce the tariff range to 0-30 percent. It is envisaged that at the end of the five-year process, there would be only four main tax rates in the More Developed Countries: 5 percent (non-competing primary, intermediate and capital inputs); 10 percent (competing primary and

---

18/   For a more detailed discussion of remissions, see F.J. Crittle, "A Review of the Application and Administration of Consumption Taxes in Guyana" (mimeo), Georgetown, Guyana, 1991.

capital inputs); 15 percent (competing intermediate inputs and non-competing final goods); and 20 percent (general manufactures, garments and agro-industry). With lower duties, the need for remissions will be less. In this connection, it is recommended that Guyana adopt the revised CET on a fast-track and tackle the adverse revenue implications of tariff reform through elimination of remissions under import duties and consumption tax.

5. Levies

7.26   Export levies on sugar and rice are meant to capture part of the gains arising from the preferential access to EC markets that Guyana enjoys as a signatory to the Lomé Convention. The sugar levy makes a substantially higher budgetary contribution. The sugar levy formula siphons off part of the difference between the EC price and the world price. Rice exports are subject to a tax, in conformity with the EC requirement, equal to 50 percent of the difference between the EC and world prices. Proceeds from this tax are returned to the millers. However, receipts from a supplementary tax of 15 percent of one-half of the difference between the EC and world prices flow to the budget. While export levies cannot be relied upon as a growing source of revenue, they should be retained for the time being as they provide welcome budgetary support.

C.   INLAND REVENUE ADMINISTRATION

1.   Departmental Background

Organization

7.27   The Inland Revenue, which is part of the Ministry of Finance, is not only responsible for the income and company taxes but also for vehicle licenses and the purchase tax on vehicles. The Department is headed by a Commissioner, assisted by a Senior Deputy Commissioner and a Deputy Commissioner. The main office in Georgetown is responsible for the administration of company tax and vehicle licenses throughout the country as well as the assessment of individuals residing in Georgetown. The branch offices in Linden, Amsterdam and Corriverton, which are responsible to the deputy commissioners, undertake the assessment of individuals in their areas.

Staffing and Remuneration

7.28   In 1991, the Inland Revenue had 453 staff positions, of which 367, or about 80 percent, were filled. Staff turnover was about 20 percent. During the year, 71 positions were filled, while 68 staff left through resignations or dismissals. Many staff leave after receiving training, with the result that most staff are young (under 25 years) and inexperienced. Of the 88 vacancies, 16 were for senior technical personnel.

7.29   Better salaries will be needed to reduce staff turnover and to induce skilled staff to stay on longer. Annual salaries range from G$1.1 million (US$8,730) for the Commissioner to G$72,000 (US$571) for a clerk. Salaries in the private sector are estimated to be twice as high as these for jobs requiring similar skills.

7.30   One way of increasing salaries without increasing jealousy among other civil servants and without affecting the budget is to introduce a bonus system for the staff of the Inland Revenue. The bonus could take the form of a percentage of the difference between the tax payable on declared income and the tax collected on assessed income. To safeguard against possible abuses of this system, assessments under dispute or appeal should not be taken into account. Initially, the appropriate percentage could be arrived at by forming a judgment on the possibilities of raising additional tax revenues through greater vigilance and initiative. Subsequently, the actual results could provide guidance. The total amount of the bonus could then be distributed free of tax among all staff members of the Inland Revenue Department each year in addition to regular salary. To ensure regular payments, the amount available to be paid as a bonus must be retained by the Inland Revenue and not remitted to the Treasury.

Office Accommodation

7.31   Office accommodation at all locations is inadequate. Assessments take place in long rooms with a large number of staff in each room (in Georgetown, 25 persons in one room and 15 in another; in New Amsterdam, 25-30 persons; and in Corriverton and Linden, about 10 each), with the result that interviews with taxpayers can be overheard. There are no proper filing facilities; the tightly stacked files in wooden buildings create a high fire risk. This issue needs to be addressed, as even a minor fire would necessitate a general tax amnesty (see below).

7.32   Office accommodation in Georgetown, Linden and New Amsterdam should be improved; at the very least, it should be possible to interrogate taxpayers in the absence of witnesses. More space should also be provided for the storage of files. When circumstances permit, in the interest of the flow of information, sections dealing with individual and company taxation should be located in the same buildings.

7.33   The Inland Revenue's new office building in Corriverton, expected to be completed in August 1993, will be too large for its present needs. Consideration should, therefore, be given to transferring the assessment of companies in New Amsterdam and Corriverton from Georgetown to Corriverton. This should help improve the assessment of companies by facilitating verification of information in the field.

Equipment

7.34   Most of the equipment at the disposal of the Inland Revenue is below the levels needed for a satisfactory performance of its duties. The computer facilities need to be strengthened, and more office equipment and motor vehicles need to be acquired. These investments in equipment can be expected to have a high payoff.

7.35   Computer facilities were installed in 1987. The facilities comprise a mainframe IBM 36, type 5360, with 16 terminals, of which only a few are connected. Besides these facilities, the Inland Revenue possesses four personal computers with an internal memory of 384 KB. It was only in 1991 that a generator, obtained through the UNDP Emergency Funding Program, was installed. The only use that has been made of the computing facilities so far has been to print notices of assessment and assessment lists, based on the recording of manually calculated assessments. In addition, one personal computer serves to print the checks for refunds.

7.36   IDA's PAP and IDB's tax administration project, expected to be implemented in 1993, will help with the computerization of company taxation and vehicle licenses. Under these projects, the suitability of the existing mainframe computer and software are also to be investigated. Availability of personal computers at the Linden, New Amsterdam and Corriverton branches, by permitting exchange of information on floppies, would increase the effectiveness of the computer facilities. To ensure the success of the projects, a electronic data processing specialist should be immediately recruited to participate in the implementation of the project and to subsequently assume the responsibility for the needed modifications and updating of software.

7.37   Only a few calculators are provided at the offices, though some staff utilize their own battery-operated calculators. Most of the calculations relating to tax returns and assessments are done manually. There is no copy machine available even at the main office in Georgetown, which has to rely on the Post Office copy machine in the case of emergency. Only a few typewriters are available; despite this, not even personal computers are used as word processors for lack of software. Calculating machines should be made more widely available, and there should be at least one copy machine in every building. All personal computers should be provided with a word processing program.

7.38   The Inland Revenue has only three cars, two in Georgetown and one in New Amsterdam. In the absence of better transport resources, verification of taxpayer information, particularly outside Georgetown, will continue to be hampered.

2. Revenue Functions

Income Taxes

7.39   _Assessments_. The income tax system emphasizes the deduction of tax at source and the payment of tax in advance. Employees are subject to "pay-as-you-earn" (PAYE), under which the employer deducts the tax from salary. The self-employed must pay the tax in advance, based on the previous year's earnings, by quarterly installments on April 1, July 1, October 1 and December 31. Companies are required to pay the corporation tax by quarterly installments on March 15, June 15, September 15 and December 15, based on the taxable profits of the previous year, though the Commissioner has the powers to require payments based on the actual income. The present system of assessment could be strengthened through computerization of taxpayer data and periodic verification of such data at locations where taxpayers reside or work.

7.40   _Card Index (File) of Taxpayers_. There are large gaps in the current information concerning potential taxpayers, particularly where the self-employed are concerned. There is collaboration between the Inland Revenue and the Registrar of Companies, so that basic information about all registered companies can be taken to be available. Most employees can be expected to come under the PAYE system. The only means of gathering information about the self-employed are sample surveys and population censuses. In this context, the forthcoming population census would provide a valuable opportunity to update the existing data. Computerization of income tax, which will ease the task of compiling, updating and exchanging information, is strongly recommended.

7.41   Verification in the Field. The absence of verification of taxpayer data in the field, particularly for companies and the self-employed, is a serious shortcoming of tax administration. It is only through periodic visits to the taxpayer's place of business that it is possible to make a judgment on the plausibility of the details supplied. At present, since all companies are assessed in Georgetown, the assessments depend solely on the documents submitted. Although the self-employed are assessed at branch offices as well as in Georgetown, the opportunity to verify data in the field is not utilized. Verification of data in the field should be undertaken for each taxpayer every three to four years. The department's transport facilities should be improved to implement this policy.

7.42   Objections and Appeals Against Assessments. The arrangements regarding appeals against assessments seem to be working satisfactorily. A taxpayer wishing to dispute an assessment must object, stating the grounds of objection, to the Commissioner within 15 days from the date of service of the notice of assessment. The Commissioner may revise or confirm the assessment. If the taxpayer is still not in agreement with the assessment, he may appeal to the Board of Review or to the Judge in Chambers.

7.43   Within 15 days from the date of the refusal of the Commissioner to amend the assessment, the taxpayer who remains aggrieved may file a notice of appeal to the Board of Review. The taxpayer must pay two-thirds of the tax in dispute before the appeal can be heard. The Board may confirm, reduce, increase or annul the assessment. If the taxpayer is still dissatisfied, he may appeal to a Judge in Chambers.

7.44   An appeal may be lodged with a Judge in Chambers within 30 days of the decision of the Board of Review or of the decision of the Commissioner of Inland Revenue. No appeal can be made to a Judge in Chambers unless the taxpayer has paid the whole amount of the tax which is in dispute. The decision of the Judge is final, except on questions of law. Appeals on questions of law lie to the Court of Appeals.

7.45   These arrangements seem to be working satisfactorily. In 1991, there were only 840 objections against the assessments and 23 appeals to the Board of Review; there were no appeals to the Judge in Chambers. All appeals were either withdrawn or settled in favor of the Internal Revenue.

7.46   Arrears. Arrears of tax are considered to be a serious problem but, in the absence of the computerization of tax data, their magnitude is not known. Computerization of the card index of arrears is urgently needed. Systematic prosecutions, which can bring about considerable improvement in the recovery of arrears, presuppose the existence of up-to-date data. Computerization is also necessary for security reasons; at present, there are no duplicate data, so that even a minor fire can necessitate a general tax amnesty.

7.47   Delinquent Accounts. The recovery of unpaid taxes may require a court judgment. A simple procedure has been adopted in this connection. A certificate of the amount due is sent to the taxpayer, together with a statement of the intention to obtain a judgment for the sum due after the expiration of ten days. The certificate can be registered in the High Court. When so registered, the certificate is treated as a judgment in favor of the Government for the tax due, together with appropriate interest.

7.48   Conclusion. All in all, there can be little doubt that the collections of personal and company taxes fall far short of their potential. A fuller realization of their revenue potential will require greater attention to the recruitment and retention of skilled staff, compilation and collation of information, and to the improvement in the physical facilities. The recent simplification of the tax structure places Inland Revenue in a good position from which to combat tax evasion and avoidance.

Motor Vehicle Licenses

7.49   The License Revenue Division administers the collection of motor vehicle and other licenses, and the purchase tax on cars. The road toll fees, for which it also used to be responsible, were a minor source of revenue and were abolished in 1992. In 1991, the purchase tax (a once-for-all tax on the acquisition of a car) yielded G$95.7 million and motor vehicle licenses (payable annually) G$29 million.

7.50   The buyer of a vehicle must report the purchase of the car to the License Revenue Division. The buyer is assigned the number of a number plate, but he must himself procure the number plate. The evidence of payment of the annual license fee must be kept in the vehicle, but no sticker is attached to the windscreen. Certain changes relating to the vehicle must be reported to the licensing authority by the owner.

7.51   The card index of the License Revenue Division should be computerized without delay, with a backup copy kept at another location. At present, all information is kept in a card index without a duplicate copy. Further, these is no regular thinning of cards, so that the number of vehicles in the country cannot be estimated with certainty. Such problems can be tackled through computerization. The entire file of taxpayers can be stored on a personal computer with a hard disk capacity of 100 MB. The programs should facilitate the recording and updating of basic data, the annual follow-up of unpaid licenses, compilation of statistics, etc.

7.52   The receipts from vehicle licenses could most likely be doubled by introducing an annual sticker to be attached to the windscreen of each vehicle. There are probably 50,000–60,000 vehicles in Guyana, of which only about 32,700 (1991) are licensed. To reduce possibilities of fraud, the owner's name and the characteristics of the vehicle (make of the vehicle, chassis number, and engine size) should be indicated on the sticker, and a sticker of different color should be issued each year. The purchase tax can also be verified and collected at the time of the issue of the first sticker. To ensure proper enforcement of the licensing requirements, the police could be provided an incentive to check the vehicles (e.g., a bonus amounting to a proportion of the tax for the detection of each vehicle without a valid sticker). In addition, the Government should announce a terminal date for voluntary licensing after which vehicles are subject to an additional fine.

D. CUSTOMS ADMINISTRATION

1. Departmental Background

Organization

7.53   Customs and Excise in Guyana are responsible for the collection of consumption tax, import duties, export duties, excise duties and a range of liquor license duties. The Department, headed by a Comptroller, is responsible to the Minister of Finance. The Comptroller is assisted by two Deputy Comptrollers, one of whom is responsible for Operations and the other for Administration, Enforcement and the Excise. An Assistant Comptroller, responsible for Inspection and Audit, reports directly to the Comptroller, as does a Legal Counsel.

Staffing

7.54   The approved complement for the Department is for 384 staff. Currently the staff of the Department is some 20 below this figure, but the shortfall has been as high as 80 in past years. The shortfall is spread evenly over the staffing structure.

7.55   The bulk of the staff is split in two streams: Customs and Excise Officers Grades I to III (some 140 staff); and Patrol Officers Grades I to III (some 120 staff). Basically the more technical work of assessing and collecting duty is undertaken by the Customs and Excise Officer grades, while the Patrol Officers perform search, patrol and safeguarding duties, often assisting the technical grades in their work.

7.56   Most of the staff are allocated to the collection of duties on imports and exports, and to the safeguarding of the revenue and the prevention of smuggling. Only some 24 staff are allocated to the collection and assessment of the excise duties and the domestic consumption tax. This position is exacerbated at times of staff shortages when the staffing required to process import and export documentation has to take priority over other commitments. But taken overall, the approved complement should provide sufficient resources to match the main departmental requirements and responsibilities.

Remuneration

7.57   The average monthly wage of a Customs Officer is between G$5,000 (US$40) and G$6,000 (US$48) but, in addition, some 100 staff have the opportunity to earn overtime varying between G$5,000 (US$40) and G$10,000 (US$80) per month. Staff working on enforcement, who have a commitment to a possible 24-hour working day, are not paid overtime, but can be paid a 10 percent Revenue Protection based on the amount of fines collected for revenue offenses, etc.

7.58   However, the comparative cost of living in Guyana is high (e.g., a one-bedroom flat can cost G$4,000 (US$32) per month, and the cost of transport and utilities are also high), making it extremely difficult for staff to manage on their monthly wages. This may well be a major factor behind the widely publicized allegations of bribery and corruption within the Customs and Excise Department.

Training

7.59   The Department has a Training Academy and an annual training program which is intended to provide comprehensive and systematic training arrangements for the various grades. However, over the past two years, training has been constrained by financial limitations and, in 1992, only three courses were run.

7.60   The Academy also lacks such basic equipment as an overhead projector as well as its own duplicating and photocopying facilities. It has a VCR but has none of the latest videos on such aspects as car and container search currently available elsewhere.

7.61   Currently some 80 percent of the staff have less than eight years of service; this represents a considerable training effort in the future and will inevitably require additional financial and staff support. Staff working on consumption tax audit would also benefit from a basic accountancy and audit course which is not catered for under the present training program.

7.62   All the main training courses have an examination at their conclusion, the results of which are a major factor in determining candidates for promotion. Senior staff are also required to attend the university to obtain a Diploma in Management Studies.

Equipment

7.63   The Department currently faces significant shortages in a wide range of the necessary equipment to enable it to perform its duties effectively. There are at present seven vehicles in service but, of these, two are in need of urgent replacement. A minimum of four extra vehicles and two replacement vehicles are essential to ensure effective use of resources, and particularly to combat the threat of smuggling.

7.64   The Department has a motor launch based at Georgetown, but it has been out of commission since August 1992. It is capable of carrying at least 10 persons but, with a top speed of 10 knots, it is no match for the average smuggler's boat, which can achieve at least 20 knots. There are also two smaller boats which can be equipped from a supply of outboard motors seized in previous anti-smuggling operations.

7.65   There is no radio communication equipment to permit surveillance and effective anti-smuggling operations. Staff also lack such basic items as binoculars and other basic search equipment.

7.66   The Department lacks an adequate supply of calculating, photocopying and duplicating machines. The cashier only has a single machine for the essential recording of payments and the numbering of import and export entries and shipping bills. This machine is now obsolete and needs to be replaced urgently, preferably by two machines to spread the workload at peak periods. Ideally there should also be a third backup machine. There are frequent failures in the supply of electricity and a generator should also be available to allow the essential cashier function to be maintained without recourse to the much slower manual fallback system.

7.67   Some of these deficiencies would be remedied by the IDB tax administration project, which proposes not only additions to equipment (e.g., vehicles and a launch) but also the computerization of the consumption tax and the entry processing system. IDA's PAP also has proposed the introduction of a module to assist with the administration of the consumption tax. To derive maximum benefits from such initiatives, it is essential that the various systems currently in operation are simplified before they are computerized, and that both projects are properly coordinated to prevent any confusion or overlap. It is of utmost importance that the Department is left with the appropriate expertise for the continued operation of the systems, which must also be capable of simple modification to meet possible tax changes in the future.

Laws and Instructions

7.68   The law relating to the Department is in need of revision and many of the staff do not have copies to refer to in the course of their duties. There is also a lack of formal departmental instructions setting out how the staff should perform their work. The revision of the present laws, coupled with the preparation of departmental instructions, needs early attention.

Management

7.69   Senior staff are often heavily involved in the day-to-day work of the Department, and this often precludes them from exerting an effective management over their staff. There is a section responsible for inspection but lack of resources and transport has limited this activity. It is an essential prerequisite in a revenue department that the staff are closely supervised and are subject to surprise checks as well as to regular inspection.

7.70   There is also a section to investigate complaints against the staff, including offenses of bribery and corruption. Over the past years, a number of staff have been obliged to resign, but it appears that it is difficult in cases of inefficiency or dilatoriness to obtain the dismissal of staff who have successfully completed their period of probation.

2. Revenue Functions

The Administration of Consumption Tax

7.71   The tax is charged on goods at importation and on sales made by domestic producers of taxable goods. All eligible manufacturers can be registered and are permitted to import materials free of consumption tax by quoting their registration number on the import documentation. Registered manufacturers are also permitted to buy goods tax-free from other registered manufacturers. This, in effect, provides a tax-free ring with the consumption tax being raised when the goods are sold to an unregistered person. There is also no consumption tax charged on goods that are exported from Guyana.

7.72   Presently all manufacturers of chargeable goods are obliged to apply for registration irrespective of their size -- the earlier minimum registration limit of G$10,000 (US$79) per annum (G$50,000 (US$397) for manufacturers of furniture) no longer applies. Registered manufacturers are obliged to submit monthly returns but only 130 of the 430 registered manufacturers regularly submit returns. While this figure is likely to include the bigger taxpayers, there does not seem to be any formal system of issuing reminders or effective follow-up action over failures to render returns or to pay the full amount of tax due. In one recent case, a reconciliation of returns and payments revealed an underpayment of G$6.3 million. Reintroduction of a minimum registration limit (say, G$100,000 (US$794)) should facilitate the strengthening of administration.

7.73   Registered manufacturers are also obliged to give a bond for the security of the likely tax but, with rapid inflation, this safeguard can quickly lose its effectiveness. It is also a heavy burden on smaller manufacturers who are often obliged by the bank to deposit the equivalent in cash before they can be given the requisite bond.

7.74   The monthly Consumption Tax Return Form 3 requires details of quantity and value of opening stock, and of goods manufactured, exported and sold locally, together with the closing stock of finished products. A similar return is required for manufactures of goods free of consumption tax. The completion of these returns places a heavy burden on the manufacturers; at the same time, the complexity of the returns does not allow for easy verification or cross-checking by Customs staff.

7.75   There also seems to be no formal central record of the registered manufacturers' activities, accounting system or of audit visits and checks, and the results obtained (e.g., underpayments). The Department's Annual Report shows that only 25 percent of the target for audit visits was achieved over recent years. Effective control over the larger taxpayers would require at least an annual audit and, preferably, further check visits during the year. Audit checks are also often carried out in the Customs House, and this prevents an effective correlation between the manufacturers' premises and activities with the books presented. Lack of staff and transport is the main reason given for this practice and also for the shortfall in visits.

7.76   Enquiries are in hand with a number of unregistered manufacturers, but lack of resources and transport has limited this activity; this could lead to further losses in revenue. Regular audit activity and visits to unregistered shops are also a means of providing evidence of unregistered manufacturers, but these are not a regular part of the present system of control.

7.77   Physical checks are also made on importations of textiles by registered manufacturers and samples are taken of the imported cloth. However, the results of these checks are not filed in a readily accessible fashion and, in any case, are probably of limited value for control purposes. A record is also kept for all registered manufacturers of the goods they have imported as materials free of consumption tax. The record is cross-referenced to the actual documentation, but retrieving it for audit purposes can be time-consuming and could easily be overlooked.

7.78   Each registered manufacturer has a file for returns and one for correspondence. This documentation is filed in cabinets in the office but the files are often full and need to be weeded periodically to avoid congestion and to allow lost documents to be more easily retrieved.

7.79   The consumption tax does not seem to be managed and controlled as well as it could be. An immediate review of the arrangements for the collection and audit of consumption tax returns and payments is needed. The object should be, _inter alia_, to establish a proper system of records and filing for registered manufacturers. Imputed (estimated) assessments in the absence of returns, and adequate penalties and charges for tardy returns and tax payments also need to be provided for. Computerization can assist in the performance of these tasks.

The Administration of Excise Duties

7.80   Excise duties are now levied on an ad valorem basis, but the present system of control is based on that required for specific duties. It should be possible to introduce relaxations in control and, if this can be coupled with laying of the responsibility for the security of warehoused goods on the distiller, it should be possible to reduce the present staff commitment.

Import Entry Procedures

7.81   Both import duties and consumption taxes on imported goods are collected through the same documentation. All goods imported into Guyana are reported on arrival. This is normally done by attaching a copy of the manifest for the ship or aircraft to the official report which has to be lodged with Customs on arrival.

7.82   Each importation is then declared to Customs on the appropriate entry form, which has to rendered in quadruplicate. Details are given of the goods, their value and quantity, together with the appropriate tariff classification and duty rate (where applicable), and the amount of duty and consumption tax where this is payable. Each entry has to be accompanied by the appropriate documentation (e.g., commercial invoice, bill of landing, etc.). Entries must be prepared by licensed brokers, who are approved by Customs and required to give security.

7.83   The documentation is examined and dated on receipt and then checked in detail by the passing officer. His work is, in turn, examined by the assessing officer before the entry is returned to the broker either for correction or for payment of the duty and tax to the cashier. The cashier records the duty and tax paid and the entry is formally numbered and dated by machine.

7.84   The duty-paid entry is then taken to the manifest section, which compares it with the manifest and records it. The entry is returned to the broker who then takes it to the examining officer to have the goods examined. If the examining officer is satisfied, an out of charge note authorizing the delivery of the goods from the transit shed is issued. The original entry, together with a receipt for the goods, is then returned for filing in the manifest section.

7.85   A copy of the import entry is sent to the Statistical Office, which is responsible for preparing details of importations. Entries are also subject to a 100 percent check by an internal audit section and by the State Auditor. Errors discovered by the internal audit section amount to an average of some G$550,000 (US$4,356) per month.

7.86   There are a variety of entry forms to cope with different kinds of traffic (e.g., goods for warehousing or transhipment). Where the importer declares that he does not have an invoice, the goods are entered on a provisional entry and the customs officer examining the goods has to determine an appropriate value. Under the present system, two officers are required to examine such importations; smaller importers seem to prefer this system to the normal entry system, which requires the production of the actual invoice.

7.87   The "barrel" traffic, normally private importations of used clothing, foodstuffs and gifts sent by relatives abroad, is entered on appraisement entries as the exact contents are generally unknown to the recipient. Each consignment has to be examined internally by a customs officer to assess both the tax liability and value. In general, officers apply a rather arbitrary value of say G$2,000 or G$3,000 (US$16-24), which attracts a charge for import duty and consumption tax of G$1,770 or G$2,655 (US$14-21), respectively. Such traffic tends to peak at the Christmas season but, taken overall, it represents something like one-half of the import entries. The resources involved in handling this traffic are, therefore, not inconsiderable. Simplified assessment, combined with an exemption limit of, say G$5,000 (US$40), could save sizable staff resources.

7.88   Goods may also be entered under a permit for immediate delivery, a system originally introduced for perishables (e.g., hatching eggs), where the time for normal clearance could lead to the deterioration of the goods. This system, which allows for delivery against a bond, had in the past been extended to a wide range of goods and there was evidence of a failure by importers to finalize their entry documentation properly and pay the duty due. The system is, once again, limited to perishables only.

7.89   The Department faces difficulty in checking the valuation of imported goods. Currently suspect values are examined by a committee of two experienced officers who are able to access information from previous importations and trade publications. However, this does not provide an adequate data base, and neither does it meet the problem of determining the correct value when there is an association between the importer and his supplier. Neither is the verification of value at the importer's premises part of the normal system of control.

7.90   There are, in addition to import duty and consumption tax, a number of smaller charges. Where an import license is required, there is a charge of G$1 per G$1,000 of the import value. This raises something like G$1.7 million (US$13,492). In addition, where goods are not entered within 30 days of arrival, Want of Entry charges are raised, which are based on the cubic capacity of the goods and on the assumption that the goods will be removed and stored in the State Warehouse. However, at the present time, the goods are stored in transit sheds as the State warehouse can neither offer secure storage nor protection from the elements. But, in any case, the threat of seizure of unentered goods is probably as effective as any system of charging. The amount raised annually from Want of Entry charges is about G$3 million (US$23,810).

7.91   The average daily throughput of import entries is about 250 per day, but the figure can rise to almost 1,000 in peak periods. The Department aims to clear import documentation through the Customs House in 24 hours for private importations, and in 72 hours for commercial importations. Obviously, the other aspects, including examination, will extend this period and this must result in constant pressure on the Department from importers anxious to obtain clearance of their goods. This is evidenced by the number of visitors present in the Long Room at any one time.

7.92   Tight control is also exerted over goods exported from Guyana, with all exports being declared and often examined. All imports by post are examined and duty is raised where appropriate; all packages for export are also examined internally.

7.93   In conclusion, the import entry system provides a secure method of ensuring that the duty and tax are raised on all goods imported into Guyana. However, it is expensive in terms of the resources deployed, and there is little sign of any selectivity in checking and examination. For instance, an entry can be checked as many as six times; moreover, every importation is examined, on occasion by two officers. The delays and costs imposed on industry by the operation of the system must also be significant. Simplification of the present system would release resources which could be redeployed more effectively in anti-smuggling activities. Selective checking and examination should be the cardinal features of the modified system.

Control and Smuggling

7.94   Control Over Arriving Ships and Aircraft. Currently all ships and aircraft are boarded on arrival in Guyana to secure the bonded stores and to obtain declarations from the crew. Modern practice is for a selective approach, leaving the onus on the master of the ship to secure his stores and to ensure that any crew member liable to pay duty does so. As many vessels and aircraft visit regularly, control can be concentrated on non-regular traffic or suspect vessels.

7.95   Airport Traffic. All passengers arriving from abroad by air at Timehri Airport are obliged to complete a written customs declaration. Customs practice a system of "confrontation," which means that each arrival can be questioned and, where necessary, be subject to examination of the baggage. Where duty and tax are assessed, the appropriate amount must be paid to the cashier before the person can leave the airport with the baggage.

7.96   Modern practice is to institute a red/green system whereby passengers make their declaration by selecting the appropriate channel. However, to be successful, the physical layout of the airport must be such as to preclude the possibility of arrivals seeing into the green channel before they make their choice.

7.97   The pattern of arrivals at the airport requires staff early in the morning and in the evening. To meet this commitment, staffing has to be on a 24-hour basis, and staff are paid four hours' overtime on each 12-hour shift. Inevitably, there are long periods when there is no productive work possible and the introduction of a red/green system would allow for a reduction in the overall level of staff employed (presently some 26 staff are required to cover the 24-hour period). It would be more economical if a mobile force could be deployed on occasion from Georgetown on a random basis to reinforce the level of control that would normally be exercised by the reduced staff necessary for a red/green system.

7.98   State Warehouse. The warehouse is intended for the storage of seized goods and of unentered goods. The warehouse is presently in a dangerous condition, containing hazardous chemicals and with a leaking roof allowing the floor timbers to rot. The warehouse lacks overall security and the general level of activity hardly justifies the full-time employment of the five staff based there.

7.99   Smuggling. Given the extensive land boundaries with Venezuela, Brazil and Surinam, smuggling into Guyana is always likely, and particularly when there is little or no cooperation with the neighboring customs services. The border with Surinam, based as it is on the high water mark on the Guyana side of the Corentyne river, presents special difficulties, and there is strong evidence here of commercial smuggling activity. However, recent seizures at the New Amsterdam ferry and at the border demonstrate what can be achieved by determined customs action.

7.100   Staff are being discouraged from challenging goods on retail sale for evidence of duty payment. While entering busy street markets to make challenges could produce a strong public reaction, there is no reason why such checks should not be made at established retail premises or at the homes of known market traders. Such checks would also provide evidence to verify the correct payment of consumption tax on home produced goods. It should also be possible to institute random checks on road traffic using the main access roads from the borders.

E. RECOMMENDATIONS

7.101   The following measures are recommended:

Tax Structure

- Drastic reduction of remissions under import duties, accompanied by measures to ensure that imported inputs embodied in exports are not taxed.

- The abolition of all remissions under the consumption tax to transform the tax into a pure revenue levy free of protective effects.

- The curtailment of tax concessions under the income tax.

- The discontinuation of the 10% development levy on commercial companies and, subsequently, the unification of the top personal income and company tax rates at 33-35%.

- The extension of the consumption tax to services other than hotel accommodations.

- The adoption of the tax credit method of collection for the consumption tax.

Administration of Income and Motor Vehicle Taxes

- The computerization of personal and company income taxes and vehicle licenses.

- Regular verification of taxpayer information in the field, particularly in relation to companies and the self-employed.

- The introduction of a bonus system for the staff of the Inland Revenue Department based on the difference between the tax due on the declared income and the tax paid on the finally assessed income.

- The introduction of an annual sticker to be fixed on the windscreen of each motor vehicle as a means of strengthening the administration of vehicle licenses.

Customs Administration

- The introduction of a more simplified and streamlined system for the processing of import and export documents, including the elimination of minor charges.

- Early computerization of the consumption tax system to provide for the issue of returns and reminders, and the early identification of non-payers.

- An immediate review of the arrangements for the collection and audit of consumption tax returns and payments, with a view to establishing, inter alia, a proper system of records and filing for registered manufacturers.

- The introduction of a simplified entry, together with an exemption limit (say, G$5,000), for the "barrel" traffic.

- The issue of a consumption tax assessment based on earlier returns, backed up by distraint action in the event of non-payment, where returns are not furnished by the due date.

- The adoption of a proper level of penalties for failure to furnish consumption tax returns, and the institution of interest charges based on market rates on any outstanding tax.

- The institution of an enhanced training program, incorporating the latest techniques, to reinforce the control over valuation, tax liability and smuggling, together with an accountancy and audit course to improve the control over the consumption tax.

- The provision of sufficient equipment and vehicles to equip an anti-smuggling task force, possibly using resources freed from rationalization of the assessment of import, excise and export duties.

CHAPTER VIII.   RESOURCE ALLOCATION: INSTITUTIONAL ASPECTS

A.   INTRODUCTION

8.1   Guyana has an extensive legal framework for its budget and expenditure control processes, to allow for rational resource allocation by Government and guarantee accountability to the public.   In practice, however, these processes suffer from a number of deficiencies which undermine their objectives and urgently need to be addressed.   This chapter describes the procedures underlying budget and expenditure control and contrasts them with the existing practice to make recommendations for improvement.

B.   THE BUDGET PROCESS

8.2   Budgeting in Guyana is done on an annual basis and covers the period January 1 to December 31 of each financial year.   The Financial Administration and Audit Act of 1973, as amended, outlines the procedures for the receipt, control, and disbursement of public monies and related matters. It requires, _inter alia_, the keeping of two separate accounts in relation to the Consolidated Fund, namely, a Consolidated Fund Current Account and a Consolidated Fund Capital Account.   Consistent with this requirement, the budget consists of two parts – a recurrent budget and a capital budget which are currently prepared by the Ministry of Finance and the State Planning Secretariat, respectively.   In the Ministry of Finance, responsibility for the preparation, execution and management of the budget is vested in the Office of the Budget, headed by a Director.

8.3   Budget preparation usually commences in September with the issuance of a series of circulares addressed to _all_ Ministries, Departments and Regions that incur capital and recurrent expenditures; the Inland Revenue and Customs and Excise Departments as well as other public agencies responsible for the collection of current and capital revenues, all public corporations and the public financial entities.   In some cases, though not routinely, the circulares may include general information on macroeconomic projections, for example, exchange rate, interest rate, inflation rate and wage increases (where these have already been negotiated in advance.)   While, in general, responsibility for budget preparation rests with the Office of the Budget the latter may delegate a number of its functions to other agencies. This has frequently been done in the past since the Office lacks adequate manpower and resources.   Thus, _capital expenditure_ is undertaken by the SPS; _financial operations of the public sector corporations_ by the Public Corporations Secretariat (PCS); _financial operations of the public banking and non-banking sector_ by COFA.

8.4   The Ministries/Departments/Regions are given about six weeks to submit their estimates of current and capital revenues and expenditures.[1] Submitted estimates are checked for conformity with the approved guidelines,

---

[1]   The public corporations and financial institutions work within a timetable set by their respective umbrella organizations.

consistency and accuracy. Rejected estimates are returned with a list of the defects identified for correction and re-submission. This exercise lasts between two to three weeks on average, but has taken much longer at times. Upon completion, the various agencies are invited to meet with the ad hoc Budget Committee in order to: (i) review the activities and programs of the spending agencies for the current year; (ii) discuss the agency's plans and programs for the next financial year; and (iii) present to the agencies a preliminary picture of the economic outlook for the next year and how that may influence their final budgets. However, budget formulation and submission at the Agency level does not allow for effective correlation between programs and activities and the budget. Line-item submissions are not presented in relation to priorities and programs, and the process of effective "program management" and evaluation through the use of the budget is non-existent. Agencies are encouraged to prioritize their proposals in order for rational decisions to be made. Internally this may occur, but often this advice is ignored by spending agencies in the hope that all their line items will eventually be funded. This often results in the Budget Office making across-the-board cuts without reference to program priorities. Thus, budget determination in relation to program activities is based more on intuition and experience with the process rather than the application of known techniques such as cost-benefit analysis and cost effectiveness.

8.5   During the Minister of Finance's review a series of meetings are usually held with a wide range of interest groups, including business organizations, the trade union congress, and the consumers' association. The meetings are intended to inform the Minister about issues affecting the groups and to elicit their suggestions and recommendations. They also provide a forum for the Minister to: (i) interface with the wider society and achieve a better understanding and appreciation of the problems that require the Government's attention; and (ii) involve the groups and consequently, the people they represent, in the fashioning of policies and measures and the future direction of the economy.

8.6   The meetings with interest groups are followed by a meeting of the ad hoc Wider Budget Committee. At this meeting, the Minister of Finance presents the: (i) consolidated financial operations of the central government; (ii) consolidated financial operations of the public corporations; (iii) consolidated financial operations of the public sector; (iv) gross domestic product at factor cost and current prices; (v) balance of payments; (vi) monetary survey; and (vii) a summary of the issues and recommendations arising from his meetings with various interest groups. Following the Wider Budget Committee meeting, the Minister of Finance then presents his proposals and recommendations to the Cabinet for consideration. The Cabinet's deliberations are often elaborate and lengthy and it is rare for a Cabinet decision to be made after one meeting.

8.7   Once the final decisions are made by the Cabinet and the policies and measures are agreed, the Minister of Finance begins the drafting of his speech, while the technical staff of the Ministry prepare the **Estimates of Revenues and Expenditures, as Presented to the National Assembly.** On Budget day, the Estimates are "laid" before Parliament, the speech is read, and business is suspended for five days during which parliamentarians review the Estimates and prepare their interventions for the debate. While the debates may result in minor changes, Parliament does not, however, have the power to alter the Estimates, as presented. If changes are agreed, they will eventually be incorporated in the final document: **Estimates of Revenues and Expenditure, as Passed, by the National Assembly.** Parliament will also pass a Bill that authorizes spending up to the limits approved by the National Assembly. Statutory payments (debt service, some types of emoluments and pensions) do not require such actions, since they have automatic claims on the Consolidated Fund.

8.8   Upon approval of the Estimates of Revenue and Expenditure by the National Assembly, the various concerned agencies are informed of the outcome together with a request to each spending agency to submit to the Office of the Budget, a detailed monthly breakdown of expenditure as a basis for monthly allocations to be made by the Current Releases Committee and the Capital Releases Committee.

8.9   This budget process is complex, and would seem to suggest a great deal of formal intricacy in detail. However, given the absence of technical capacity, the use of the line item budget, and the diffusion of responsibilities, the process is neither timely nor transparent. Currently, responsibility for the preparation of the budget is diffused among a number of agencies (the Office of the Budget, SPS, PCS, etc.). There are also a number of ad hoc arrangements involved in the budget review process (e.g., the Budget Committee) where membership, procedures and guidelines have either not been properly defined or lack transparency. In order to streamline the budget process and improve the overall efficiency of the system, both the Office of the Budget and the budget functions in line agencies need to be significantly strengthened both in terms of staffing and equipment to enable them to cope with the additional workload entailed. This can be addressed through the proposed redeployment of staff from SPS (which is slated to be abolished) and the provision of technical assistance and additional equipment under the PAP. The credibility and effectiveness of the budget process should also be considerably enhanced if steps were taken to institutionalize the various arrangements associated with the budget review process and more importantly, if a set of transparent and properly defined guidelines were developed to ensure that the review process is carried out on a systematic basis, consistent with the Government's stated priorities.

C.   EXPENDITURE MANAGEMENT AND CONTROL: THE REGULATORY FRAMEWORK

1.   The Regulatory Framework

8.10   Formally, the management and control of public expenditures are regulated by various constitutional provisions, standing orders and specific acts approved by the National Assembly. In fact, however, the amalgam of formal rules governing expenditure management are inadequate for a modern financial management system, and are often honored more in the breach.

8.11   For example, Articles 221 and 222 of the Constitution requires the public debt and the salaries and allowances of certain office holders such as the President, the Speaker of the National Assembly and the Auditor General to be charged to the Consolidated Fund as "statutory expenditures", not subject to parliamentary approval, while Article 223 provides for the appointment of an Auditor General, accountable to the National Assembly, to be responsible for auditing and reporting on the public accounts. Of significance also is

Standing Order No. 70(2) which establishes a Public Accounts Committee to consider the appropriation accounts and other matters referred to it by the National Assembly; however, this Committee is incapable of performing its assigned function given its extant technical weaknesses. Further weakening legislative input into the process of expenditure control is the power of the Executive to withdraw funds from the Consolidate Fund in the absence of legislative appropriations. The Act authorizes the Minister to withdraw monies from the Consolidated Fund for up to three months from the beginning of the fiscal year or the coming into operation of the Appropriation Act, whichever is earlier. Furthermore, and to meet urgent and unforeseen contingencies for which no other provision exists, the National Assembly established by resolution in 1974 a ceiling on the Contingencies Fund, equivalent to 2 percent of estimated expenditure in the preceding financial year. In the absence of timely passage of appropriations, the determination of the use of funds occurs without appropriate legislative oversight. In addition, reports of the Auditor General are constitutionally required and The Financial Administration and Audit Act of 1973, which outlines procedures for the receipt, control, and disbursement of public monies and related matters, provides responsibilities for the Auditor General, the Ministry of Finance, and the Secretary of the Treasury, some of which are inadequate or inappropriate, and others which are not fulfilled.

8.12   The Act gives comprehensive powers, including powers of inspection, to the Minister of Finance over such matters as authorizing expenditure, collecting revenues, investing public monies, and borrowing by means of advances from banks and through the issue of Treasury bills. In addition, the Act authorizes the Minister to issue instructions and to make regulations regarding such matters as the preparation of the Estimates, the opening of bank accounts for public monies and requires the Minister to submit annual statements to Parliament on revenues and deposits, expenditures and loans, public debt and government guaranteed loans as regulated under the Guarantee of Loans (Public Corporations and Companies) Act, 1971.

8.13   The Financial Administration and Audit Act also requires the Secretary to the Treasury to designate accounting officers to be responsible for accounting of public expenditure and revenue and empowers the Secretary to the Treasury to levy a surcharge against any public officer who fails to perform such duties efficiently. In fact, however, no such disincentive has been utilized in any systematic way, and the control is not credible. Similarly, the treasury function at the level of line ministries (accounting officers) is technically weak as well.

8.14   While Article 223 of the Constitution establishes the Office of Auditor General, Sections 26 to 35 of the Financial Administration and Audit Act set out the functions, powers, and responsibilities of this office. The Act gives comprehensive powers to the Auditor General to inspect, at any time, all records on financial matters and to summon persons, whether public officers or not, to give information regarding receipt or expenditure of public monies. Section 7(2) of the Act requires the Accountant General, accounting officers, and principal receivers of revenue to submit the various statements and accounts to the Auditor General, within a period of four months, after the close of each financial year. In practice, however, there have been substantial delays in finalizing these accounts and statements. Special reports of the Auditor General to Parliament for the years 1982/85 show that large portions of expenditure by Ministries and Regional

Administrations could not be accounted for by supporting documents. In October 1991, a Special report of the Auditor General noted that he was not in a position to issue the required official Annual Report for 1985! In general the quality and reliability of expenditure management and control is poor and needs to be overhauled. In formulating measures to modernize the existing system, consideration should also be given to computerize those aspects that are currently handled on a manual basis.

2. Organizational Arrangements, Supervision and Monitoring

8.15 In addition to weaknesses in the legal framework guiding the budget and expenditure control process, there are organizational inadequacies in the financial management system. Of the four existing divisions of the Office of the Budget, two -- the multilateral financial institutions division and the budget division -- are directly involved in the budget process. The multilateral institutions division essentially is responsible for keeping track of relations and assistance from the multilateral institutions to Guyana while the budget division is charged with controlling the disbursement of funds. The latter division examines ministries' requests for funds in relation to the recurrent budget on a month-by-month basis and authorizes disbursements. The division is responsible for checking that actual disbursements are in accordance with authorizations. For this purpose, each accounting officer is required to certify by the seventh day of each month that expenditures during the month under review have not exceeded those authorized. The division also prepares quarterly reviews on the progress of the recurrent budget. The division considers requests for "virement" in relation to recurrent expenditure, that is, requests for authority to meet an overrun on one subhead by transferring savings from another subhead under the same head.[2] The responsibility for capital expenditures lies with the Capital Releases Committee, which includes representatives from SPS and authorizes disbursements and monitors progress of capital projects.

8.16 The Accountant General's Department is organizationally separate from the Ministry and it is included under a separate head in the Estimates. The Accountant General's statutory functions are not set out in a single consolidated piece of legislation, but references to his responsibilities are made in a number of acts, the most important of which is the Financial Administration and Audit Act, 1973. The Act requires the Accountant General to operate the detailed accounting arrangements in relation to the consolidated funds and to furnish statements on them to the Auditor General. Accounting is mainly on a cash basis. In spite of the broad scope and complexities of the statutory responsibilities as well as heavy workload, the entire functions of the Accountant General's are carried out on a manual basis, the Department is seriously understaffed and the prevailing levels of remuneration contribute little towards needed improvements in staff morale. Moreover, most of the Departments enabling legislation, regulations, procedures and guidelines are obsolete and in urgent need of revision. The existing accounting requirements and reporting format could also benefit from some improvement.

---

[2] Transfers between heads require parliamentary approval and virement is not permitted between recurrent and capital items.

8.17   Public Service Management and the State Planning Commission and its Secretariat have powers and responsibilities relevant to the budgetary process. Public Service Management (PSM) forms part of the President's portfolio and is responsible for personnel matters such as numbers, grades, and general pay issues in the public service. PSM is responsible for reviewing, inter alia, the organization and staffing of ministries and departments in order to ensure that existing staff resources are being used efficiently and to verify the justification for any additional staff. However, decisions on staff increases and other matters likely to have a significant budgetary impact are normally considered in the wider budgetary context. The State Planning Commission was established by legislation in 1977 and has wide-ranging powers and responsibilities in relation to the preparation, implementation, and review of development plans. The Commission is served by a full-time Secretariat which is not included within the public service proper. The Secretariat is divided into four divisions, with functions ranging from planning at the macroeconomic level to planning of specific productive and infrastructure projects. In recent years, attention has focused more on short-term planning through, for example, the annual capital budget rather than on medium-term development planning for the economy as a whole.

8.18   Under sections 46–51 of the Bank of Guyana Act of 1985, the Bank of Guyana is required to act as banker to the Government and is also, empowered to lend to the Government, subject to the conditions and limits specified in the Act. The legislation provides that the amount of advances outstanding cannot exceed 15 percent of the average annual revenue for the preceding three years. Advances cannot be outstanding for a total of more than 350 days in a year. The amount of securities held by the Bank cannot exceed 30 percent of average annual revenues during the preceding three years. The rates of interest are settled by negotiation between the Bank and the Ministry of Finance subject to a minimum specified in the Act. The Bank provides regular reports to the Ministry of Finance, on financial matters.

8.19   The existing public corporations are also integrated into the budgetary process. A special subcommittee of the Budget Committee examines their operations and proposals in the context of the annual budget. The public financial institutions report to the Minister of Finance; the other corporations report to individual ministers and, in addition, are coordinated by PCS, which reports to the President. A number of public corporations also operate under the control of supervisory councils established under the 1985 Budget Speech.

8.20   The Budget Committee and a subcommittee coordinate the inputs of the various ministries and agencies. The Budget Committee is chaired by the Minister of Finance and is made up of representatives from each of the ministries and agencies involved with major inputs or with responsibility for major policy areas in the budget, including PSM, SPS, and PCS. The Committee may alter its structure and procedure, as warranted. The subcommittee of the Budget Committee examines the proposals and performance of the public corporations in the context of the preparation of the budget and reports to the Budget Committee. It is chaired by the Governor of the Bank of Guyana and includes representatives from the Ministry of Finance, SPS, and PCS.

8.21   While the Estimates are being considered in the National Assembly, the Ministry of Finance usually requests each accounting officer to submit a return showing a phased monthly breakdown of the allocation in the estimates for each recurrent and capital subhead. This information provides the basis for the release of funds for each subhead and capital project throughout the year. For a broad subhead that covers a range of expenditures, the Ministry would normally require an itemized breakdown.

8.22   Each month the budget division of the Ministry of Finance obtains a return from each ministry, showing actual monthly expenditures against the phased breakdown submitted earlier and the ministry's requirement for the current month. The ministries provide the actual expenditure data for these returns mainly from their manually operated records, usually the vote account book. Because the data are obtained from manual records, aggregate amounts rather than itemized statement are all that can be submitted within the time period available for preparing returns. In addition to the manual statements a computerized system is in operation to facilitate the preparation of central government accounts in fuller detail from payments and receipts vouchers for each individual transaction. This system is operated in the Ministry of Finance for the use, initially, of the Accountant General. Detailed accounting records could potentially be obtained from this system, but inaccurate coding and classification of data by the accounting units outside the Ministry of Finance have caused serious delays.

8.23   The manually prepared monthly returns, however, serve as important controls on the disbursement of funds. As mentioned earlier, each accounting officer is required to certify by the seventh day of each month that the funds provided for the previous month had been disbursed in accordance with authorizations. In addition to the current month requirement, the returns project expenditure for the rest of the year to facilitate the identification of areas where supplementary estimates or virement may be required. Capital expenditure is administered by the Capital Releases Committee which monitors expenditures and inflows of project funds and authorizes the release of funds for the individual projects as the year progresses. The object of these tasks is to avoid situations in which over-optimistic assumptions about project aid inflows give rise to excessive demands on domestic sources of funds.

8.24   At quarterly intervals, the budget division prepares a report on the progress of the recurrent budget which is submitted to the higher levels in the Ministry. Similar information about the capital budget is also made available. These submissions include brief explanations of major deviations from the planned path, but they are not comprehensive and do not take account of the impact of changes in the overall macro-economic environment.

D. DEFICIENCIES OF THE EXISTING BUDGET AND EXPENDITURE CONTROL PROCESS

8.25   A major deficiency of the existing budget process is the lack of any systematic attempt to develop the budget within a well-defined annual or medium-term economic framework. As currently conceived, the budget process reflects the outcome of a series of negotiations rather than the product of properly costed programs within an overall macroeconomic framework, including an assured financing plan. The process seems to place greater emphasis on compliance with formalities rather than on efficiency in the use of scarce resources. Most of the draft estimates by line ministries or agencies are prepared by poorly qualified and inexperienced staff. There is very little attempt, if any, to base the proposed expenditures in the draft estimates on any clearly defined objective or set of priorities of the respective ministries/agencies. Moreover, each line ministry or agency seems to approach the budget exercise on the assumption that the process is meaningless rather than as a serious exercise aimed at properly defining and tailoring their plans to what is realistically required and achievable within the budget period. Officials of line ministries and agencies tend to rely on past budget allocations with little regard for the prevailing macroeconomic environment. In general, budget proposals from the ministries and agencies tend to be inflated in the expectation of across-the-board cuts. In reviewing the various sectoral estimates, the Ministry of Finance, on the other hand, uses an incremental approach, that is, adjusting the various proposals to the previous year's levels, with appropriate increases for inflation. The practice whereby SPS had to rely on input from the Ministry of Finance for an assessment of multilateral capital inflows and from the Department of International Economic Co-operation for bilateral inflows in the formulation of the capital budget also reflects the absence of a systematic approach. This is, however, expected to be rectified with the merger of SPS and Department of International Economic Cooperation staff with the Ministry of Finance.

8.26   Equally important, current practice undermines the democratic process by effectively constraining legislative functions in the budget process. Articles 216 and 217 of the Constitution of the Cooperative Republic of Guyana provide for the creation of a Consolidated Fund for the receipt of all monies and for parliamentary control over disbursements. Article 218 requires the Prime Minister or other Minister designated by the President to place revenue and expenditure estimates before the National Assembly no later than 90 days after the commencement of the financial year in question. Upon approval by the National Assembly, the authorized expenditures are set out under an Appropriation Act. Similarly, approved expenditures under a supplementary estimate are also contained in a supplementary Appropriation Act. However, under Article 219, the Minister responsible for finance could withdraw funds from the Consolidated Funds for up to four months until the Appropriation Act, is passed while Article 220 enables the National Assembly to establish a Contingencies Fund from which funds may be withdrawn to meet urgent and unforeseen expenditures for which no other provision exists and which cannot be postponed "without prejudice to the public interest", until adequate provision is made by the National Assembly.

8.27   Recent experience suggest that the 90-day deadline is the exception rather than the norm. The routine delay in submitting each year's budget to the National Assembly for approval well after the commencement of the financial year undermines its effectiveness both as a planning tool and as a medium for ensuring Parliamentary control of taxation and public expenditures.

8.28   There appears to be broad consensus among most key Government officials regarding the need for timely steps to be taken in order to ensure greater order over public expenditure and more importantly, to improve the system of monitoring so as to verify that the goods, services and works for which expenditures were incurred had, in fact, been procured and utilized for the purposes for which the expenditure were authorized.

   •   Procedural consistency is lacking. There is a need to undertake
        an early review and updating of the existing legislation relating
        to budgeting, accounting and auditing, and to integrate these

procedures in a readily accessible Manual for the guidance of those charged with responsibility for administering the process.

- Operations are impeded by the lack of computerization. The efficiency in the performance of the key functions described above for each of the named agencies could be considerably enhanced with computerization. This is particularly urgent in the case of the Accountant-General's Department where most of the existing accounting forms and filing system are poorly designed, obsolete, and in need of modernization.

- Expenditure management is open to abuse. Two areas that lend themselves to potential abuse are expenditure made under Category 3 or 1 "Other Charges" of the Approved Estimates, specifically those under Sub-Heads 309 and 314. The current widespread practice whereby advance purchases of goods and services are made on the basis of mutual trust in the hope that payment would be made, at a later stage, is unsatisfactory and should be discontinued.

8.29   These deficiencies in the budget process and in the control of **running expenditures** are complemented by serious shortcomings in public **sector accounting** and auditing practices which even prevent an ex-post control over **expenditures** and are in stark contrast to the official procedures described **above.**

- The accounting system broke down in 1981 and since then no official financial statements for the public sector have been produced. In fact, actual recording of accounts is not currently taking place; and accounting practice has been largely in the form of cash management. There are plans to re-establish the accounting system, but in an overly centralized form, implying that all bookkeeping will be done by the Accountant General Department of the Ministry of Finance.

- The audit of accounts has been severely hampered and inordinately delayed, and control is therefore ineffective. Special reports of the Auditor General to Parliament for the years 1982/85 show that large portions of expenditures of Ministries and Regional Administrations could not be accounted for by the presentation of supporting documentation. In October 1991, a Special Report of the Auditor General noted that he was unable still to issue the required official Annual Report <u>for 1985</u>!

- While the authorization of disbursements occurs through the Executive function of the Releases Committees, in the absence of financial statements for audit examination, the public and Parliament have had no means to monitor appropriated funds. Overdrafts exist in bank accounts of Ministries, Departments, and Regional Administrators, suggesting weak Treasury response as well. The legislative function, through the Public Accounts Committee, has not functioned in years, and there has been no external audit function as a result.

E. RECOMMENDATIONS

1. A Modified Approach to the Budget Process

8.30   Since the budget affects and is affected by the overall state of the economy, there is a need to carry out a proper evaluation of the prevailing economic environment before budgetary commitments are made. **At present, there is no regular forum for staff of the various ministries and agencies to exchange information on critical economic indicators such as current and projected revenues, expenditures, and aid inflows.** Greater dissemination of such information would sensitize staff about the constraints imposed by the overall macro-economic environment and, in turn, elicit a more professional and realistic approach on their part in the formulation of their budget proposals.   Donors could facilitate this process by (i) making their commitments, particularly of commodity aid on a multi-year, rather than on an annual basis or, at least, by providing qualified indications of future aid flows; and by (ii) assisting the Government in making more accurate estimates of disbursements, prior to the finalization of the budget preparation process.

8.31   Another difficulty in the budget process is the lack of timely and adequate local funding of approved projects under the PSIP. This results in slow project aid disbursements, particularly in cases where external financing does not cover total project cost, and in the suspension of some projects for which adequate financing could not be provided under the budget. Some donors have resorted to various measures in order to "insulate" their projects from the adverse consequences of the shortage of local counterpart funding. In the typical case, donors have insisted on earmarking all or part of the local currency proceeds generated under their financial assistance programs for the financing of the local costs of projects supported under their respective project assistance programs. Other donors have resorted to the creation of revolving funds, with provision for their automatic replenishment in order to protect their programs. While these devises can be useful in protecting individual projects, they place a major constraint on the Government's ability to allocate local resources within the budget and ultimately could make it more difficult for the Government to achieve its overall development objectives.

8.32   The availability of realistic and regularly updated estimates of available resources should also support the formulation of a <u>core investment program</u> comprised of a set of priority projects that are of critical importance to achieve the Government's development objectives.

8.33   Recurrent expenditures and capital expenditures are integrally linked. In particular, the capital budget has major repercussions on the current budget in future years when maintenance and servicing costs will be incurred. To accomplish the integration of the two sets of expenditures in the budget requires thinking of the budget as a process and planning tool with changing exigencies over time. The effectiveness of the budget as a planning tool can be enhanced if efforts were made to develop each year's budget as an integral part of a <u>multi-year rolling program</u> within a properly defined macroeconomic framework. The assessments would roll forward each year as a new fiscal year commences, and adjustments could be made in order to accommodate changes occurring in each current year.

8.34   All of this is to suggest the need to think of the budget process as more than simply a mechanism for control. It is the ultimate expression of political intent, decision and consensus on the content of government strategy and should reflect programmatic content, targets, and the required flexibility to respond to changing macroeconomic conditions.

2.   Overall Recommendations for Resource Allocations

8.35   In order to improve the quality and effectiveness of the budget as a planning tool and also the management and control over public expenditures, it is recommended that the authorities consider the introduction of a number of reforms.   These proposed reforms are discussed under two categories, namely: (a) those that can be implemented in the short term; and (b) those that may require further study and could therefore only be implemented over the medium term.

Short-term Measures

- Start the planning and budget cycle early in the current year so as to allow enough lead time for the budget process to be completed for submission to the National Assembly by the beginning of the new financial year.

- As part of the planning process and prior to the start of the budget cycle, the Ministry of Finance should prepare and forward to the various sectoral ministries and agencies, etc. projections of anticipated resources and major expenditure obligations for the next two to three years and also, preliminary indications of plans for the allocation of available resources, based on the Government's stated priorities, among the various sectors.

- The review and any resulting reductions in the various sectoral ministries' and agencies' proposed estimates should similarly be guided by the Government's stated priorities as well as by the need to protect additional resources that are required to complete on-going programs/projects that are critical to the Government's overall development objectives.

- Develop within the PSIP a core program, based on the Government's development objectives on the clear understanding that its funding will be accorded priority consideration in the event of any shortfall in the availability of resources.

- Discontinue the current informal domestic procurement practice whereby local suppliers provide goods and services to ministries and agencies against verbal assurances that they will receive payment at a later stage and reintroduce the system "Local Purchase Orders" with adequate built-in safeguards to ensure greater expenditure management and control.

- Strengthen the inspection wing of the Treasury through the provision of additional staff, equipment and vehicles to facilitate closer and more effective monitoring of public expenditures.

- Under the proposed Public Administration Project, several short-term goals are intended, including technical assistance to aid in the actual generation of public accounts and the timely provision of accurate accounting information to assure compliance with the preparation of official annual accounts; the elimination of current practice of coverage of overdrafts to budgeted expenditures (monitored semi-annually); the reduction in non-budgeted and unaccounted-for expenditures within the ministries and Regional Administrations (monitored semi-annually); and the reestablishment of an effective Public Accounts Committee within one year of loan effectiveness. These measures should be done immediately.

Medium-Term Measures

- Review and update the Financial Administration and Audit Act of 1973 with a view to ensuring tighter control over public expenditures.

- Carry out an in-depth review of the Accountant General's Department, the Office of the Budget and the Auditor-General's Department with a view to recommending measures for streamlining and computerizing their operations.

- Introduce a budget system upon program criteria, and integrate the capital and recurrent estimates and develop budget in the context of a three-year rolling program.

- Introduce mid-term review of budget on a regular basis to enable adjustments to be made as necessary, to keep essential programs/projects on track.

- Contract-out the auditing of all outstanding accounts so as to clear back-log, and introduce measures to ensure that future audits are carried out no later than twelve calendar months _after_ the completion of each financial year.

PART III: SECTOR STRATEGIES AND EXPENDITURES

CHAPTER IX. AGRICULTURE

A. INTRODUCTION

9.1   Agriculture is the single most important sector in the economy and the main source of employment. Production is concentrated in the coastal strip with most of the cultivated area serviced by a series of irrigation and drainage canals and protected from saline water intrusion by sea defenses. Sugar and rice are the most important crops cultivated in terms of area, value of production and contribution to export earnings. Most sugar production is currently under the parastatal GUYSUCO, which, since 1991, has been run under a private sector management contract with Booker Tate. Rice production is held wholly in the private sector where the majority of farms are small, below 25 acres, with a few large farms of over, sometimes well over, a thousand cultivated acres.[3/] Production of both crops declined dramatically during the 1980s due to poor economic policies.

9.2   Since the liberalization of the economy under the ERP initiated in 1988, there has been a rapid turnaround both in the performance of the sector and in the prospects for continued growth. Helped by good weather, sugar output increased by over eighty percent during 1992, and, at about 250,000 tons, reached a level which allows Guyana to supply more than its domestic and external preferential markets. Rice production has responded quickly to the removal of price controls in 1991 and the improved profitability of exports consequent to the devaluation following the removal of exchange rate controls. Preliminary, perhaps optimistic, estimates indicate a sown area approaching 160,000 acres for the first crop of 1993 compared to a harvested acreage of 127,000 for the first and second crop in 1990. Such growth will provide much-needed foreign exchange through rice sales to the protected markets in the Caribbean and Europe as well as a basis for growth in other crops, services and manufacturing through domestic expenditure linkages. The new Government elected in October 1992 has a clear commitment to development of the agriculture sector and this convergence of political and economic interest provides a real opportunity for growth.

9.3   As in other sectors, the neglect of the productive infrastructure during the 1980s has created the need for substantial rehabilitation investment for which, however, resources are very limited; it is this combination of extreme scarcity of investment resources and massive rehabilitation needs which dictates the need for the most careful prioritization of public expenditure. At present, the fragmented and ad hoc approach to planning is a considerable barrier to sectoral prioritization. It constrains the efficient allocation of public investment and the equally vital issue of institutional reforms necessary to promote cost recovery and complementary private investment.

3/   The last sample census of agriculture was for 1978 when nearly 90% of the 24,635 farm households cultivated below 25 acres.

9.4   In reviewing these public expenditure issues, this chapter takes careful account of other recent studies, issues dealt with elsewhere in this report and the need to focus on the Ministry itself as a revenue generating and expenditure unit. This has four implications. First, since the agriculture sector has recently[4] been reviewed by the World Bank no attempt is made to provide a comprehensive sector review. Chapter I of that review discussed the performance of the agricultural sector during the 1980s and the reforms undertaken. In summarizing sectoral issues, this chapter draws heavily on the earlier study taking account of developments in the 13 months between the field missions. Secondly, sea defenses, although the responsibility of the Hydraulics Department and therefore of the Ministry of Agriculture, are such a critical issue for the overall economy and involve such substantial investment sums that they are treated separately in the following chapter. Thirdly, and for similar reasons, investment on rural roads, which is crucial for agricultural growth prospects, is reviewed in Chapter XII, Transportation. Fourthly, the sugar industry and the forestry sub-sector are not reviewed; public investment in both is outside the remit of the Agriculture Ministry and, in both cases, there are other studies and private sector investment proposals which are currently being reviewed. The focus of this chapter is on rice production but it also covers, fisheries, milk production and other crops which are the productive sub-sectors directly under the Ministry.

9.5   Figure 9.1 is an organizational chart of the Ministry and, with the exception of sea defenses, shows the main sub-sectors covered here. In support of this analysis there is also discussion of other institutions involved in: regulation and support of crop production and export; agricultural credit; and, operations and maintenance of irrigation and drainage systems.

B. SECTOR OVERVIEW[5]

1. Rice

9.6   With the adoption of the ERP in 1988 the Government of Guyana began to implement the measures needed to reverse the stagnation and decline that characterized the agriculture sector during the preceding decade. Rice prices were raised substantially in 1989 and all price controls were removed in 1991 triggering a rapid response in planted area. Area harvested increased by forty six percent from 1990 to 1991 and rice output increased by over sixty percent to 151 thousand metric tons. In addition to price liberalization several other measures have contributed to a mood of great optimism concerning growth potential in rice. The freeing of the exchange rate was fundamental to the re-installation of price incentives. IDB and World Bank estimates suggest that the combined implicit taxation of rice production through price and exchange rate control had been between 60 and 100 percent throughout the

---

4/   World Bank, Guyana Agricultural Sector Review, June 1, 1992.

5/   As described above, Sea Defenses, technically within the Ministry of Agriculture, are dealt with in Chapter X. Sugar and Forestry are not the direct responsibility of the Ministry of Agriculture and are not included in this report.

1980s. Accompanying these measures were the sale of much of the Rice Milling and Marketing Authority's (GRMMA) milling capacity and a major reduction in their direct intervention in paddy and rice marketing. Both the domestic and export markets are now principally served by the private sector at all points in the marketing chain. Agricultural inputs are also completely privatized and the availability of farm machinery was greatly aided by an IDB Agricultural Rehabilitation loan which made over US$14 million available for private sector purchases related to rice production, the balance of which is scheduled to be used in 1993 and 1994.

Figure 9.1: MINISTRY OF AGRICULTURE ORGANIZATION

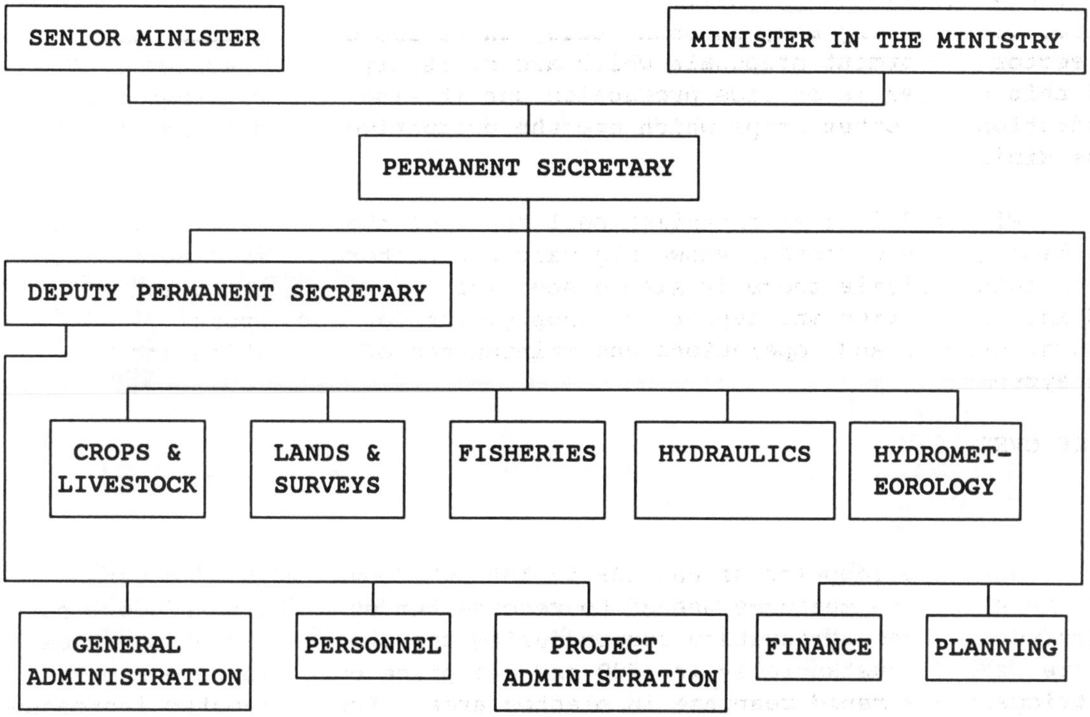

Source: Government of Guyana and KPMG Management Consulting

Table 9.1: ESTIMATED MARKETABLE SURPLUS OF PADDY

Year	Paddy Production (MT)	Seed, feed and wastage	Domestic Consumption a/	Marketable Surplus
1984	301 833	37 729	84 000	179 804
1985	256 167	32 021	84 150	139 996
1986	275 500	34 438	84 000	157 062
1987	243 399	30 425	83 990	128 984
1988	226 761	28 345	83 900	114 516
1989	237 183	29 648	83 700	123 835
1990	155 740	19 468	83 650	52 622
1991	251 322	31 415	83 600	136 307
1992a/	260 000	32 500	83 500	144 000

a/   Estimated.

Source: Rice Sector Review, (Draft) December 1992, Planning Division
         Ministry of Agriculture

9.7   As Table 9.1 indicates, although there has been an impressive
turnaround in rice production and marketable surplus over the last two years,
output is still well below the 1984 level which, in turn, is much below the
potential. A number of important constraints within the sector inhibit
farmers from realizing this potential. These are listed here and discussed
more fully in Section E.[6]

- The drainage and irrigation infrastructure is in need of extensive
  rehabilitation.

- The institutional basis for operations and maintenance of drainage
  and irrigation systems is wholly inadequate. There is a very poor
  collection rate on the existing very low water charges because
  service provision is so poor.

- Yield and quality losses in rice production are likely to be
  greater than 25 percent because of these drainage and irrigation
  constraints which also effect the ability of farmers to make
  efficient use of farm machinery and agro-chemical inputs.
  Furthermore, there is a reduction in planted area directly
  resulting from inadequate drainage and irrigation.

- Many farmers lease their land from the State on very short leases
  which inhibits land development and restricts access to credit.

---

[6]   The World Bank Agriculture Sector Review (Report no.10410), dated June
      1992, provides a fuller discussion of these constraints.

- Credit availability is limited and many farmers are dependent on informal credit, often from rice mill owners.

- Research and extension services are both severely under-financed and are failing to provide an adequate service to farmers. There is no prospect of cost-recovery mechanisms being introduced until performance to farmers improves considerably.

- In certain regions, it appears that there is a danger of virtual monopsony control of paddy purchases by large rice mills. Combined with millers' roles in credit provision and, with the inadequacy of control over grading standards, there is a danger that price incentives to farmers will be watered down by the rent-seeking behavior of large millers.

2. Fishing, Milk Production and Other Crops

9.8   Despite the severe resource constraints faced by the Fisheries Department and the disincentives to exports as a consequence of the overvalued exchange rate the fisheries sub-sector has continued to develop during the 1980s with substantial assistance from CIDA through the fisheries equipment facility project and the artisanal fisheries development project providing on-shore facilities for fishermen's cooperatives. Since liberalization the growth rate in this sector has improved and continuing support from CIDA both directly through the fisheries technical assistance project and through a regional project (CARICOM Fisheries Research and Management Project) is expected to further promote growth. There was an increase in artisanal fish landings from 27,685 tons in 1981 to 32,538 tons in 1991. This constituted nearly 80 percent of total fish and shrimp production in 1991; industrial (large scale) capture of fin fish contributed 5.9% and the remaining 13 percent, by weight, was from shrimp capture. The Fisheries Department estimates that the total value of fish and shrimp exports in 1991 was over US$22 million.[1] The major contribution to these export earnings comes from shrimp exports which totalled nearly US$17 million in 1991. Costs of production have been adversely effected by increases in the consumption tax on fuel but have benefited from reductions in the export levy and in license fees. However, more detailed information is required on costs of production in order to make a reasonable assessment of the possible contribution of enhanced public revenues from the fisheries sector.

9.9   In the livestock sector the principle area of growth has been in milk production through the National Dairy Development Program. The program has focused on the development of improved pastures and the provision of artificial insemination services to smallholders. The program has been successful with an increase in milk production from less than 13 million liters in 1983 to over 36 million liters in 1991. This program has resulted in substantial foreign exchange savings and considerable improvement in the availability of milk and milk products to Guyanese consumers who were adversely effected by import restrictions during part of the 1980s. This program has also indirectly helped beef production, and both milk and beef

---

[1]   Other estimates of fisheries contribution to GDP suggest that export earnings may have been lower but there is considerable uncertainty about the basis for such estimates.

production have benefited from the increase in prices following the freeing of exchange rates. The pork and poultry product sectors do not appear to have benefited however, since they are hardly developed and have not demonstrated a capacity to compete with imports. The NDDP is currently evaluating alternative models of dairy development and seeking funding for expansion of its improved pasture and artificial insemination programs. It seems probable that continued growth will be recorded in the production of milk and milk products. And, since these products typically have reasonably high income elasticities of demand, it is likely that price incentives will remain strong. The future development of the rest of the livestock sector is much less clear; although beef exports remain a promising opportunity there are serious restrictions with regard to facilities for slaughter, marketing, transport and quality control.

9.10   In Guyana, the "other crops" sector refers to all crops other than sugar or rice. These crops have been relatively insignificant in relation to rice and sugar and this continues to be the case though some efforts are now being made to develop both domestic and export markets. In 1991, exports of other crops were valued at US$1 million and figures for the first three quarters of 1992 indicate that a similar performance is likely. The principle export has been pineapples although in 1992 heart of palm has grown to be a significant contributor to export earnings. More than 2 dozen other products are also exported but only in small quantities. There are serious constraints on shipment facilities which lead to major quality control problems. The regional (Caribbean) markets also have trade restrictions which adversely effect export opportunities. In the domestic market, growth of other crops, particularly vegetables and fruits, has been reasonable and is expected to improve further in response to the expenditure linkages generated through growth in other sectors including rice and sugar production. Production of other crops is severely constrained by the limited availability of publicly provided crop production services including research, seed production, extension and support for private sector development of marketing, processing and packaging facilities. The new Guyana Marketing Corporation serves as an export promotion agency but itself faces severe resource constraints.

9.11   In addition to the specific constraints identified above the Ministry itself also faces three key limitations as a service organization promoting private sector agricultural growth.

- Planning activities within the sector are undertaken by a range of actors and this fragmentation causes inconsistencies and tensions which are often exacerbated by poor information flows. Moreover, the data base for proper planning is absent.

- Low salaries and inadequate facilities have resulted in the Ministry operating well below establishment levels and with very limited resources to design policies or to implement them. Some departments are barely functioning. Inadequate accounting practices and weak planning have led to limited benefits from those financial resources that are available.

- The budget process of agreeing current and capital financial estimates for the following year with the Ministry of Finance is not related to sectoral priorities which are anyway poorly defined.

These limitations all serve to reduce the absorptive capacity of the Ministry of Agriculture which is a major factor determining the appropriate size and composition of the public investment plan. In particular, the limited absorptive capacity requires a focus on a relatively small number of core constraints on growth. Success on these will help strengthen commitment and morale. Whilst the core problem on morale is that salaries and facilities are insufficient to attract or retain adequate levels or quality of staff in almost all grades these changes will help boost morale within the Ministry by energizing the planning process.[8/] More widespread strengthening of Ministry of Agriculture service provision depends on the availability of sufficient trained personnel with adequate facilities to plan and to budget for effective allocation of public sector resources between the main sub-sectors.

C. INSTITUTIONAL AND REGULATORY FRAMEWORK

9.12   There are a large number of institutions with regulatory and other responsibilities within the agricultural sector not all of which come directly under the Ministry of Agriculture. The largest corporation in Guyana, GUYSUCO, responsible for the sugar industry operates independently of the Ministry of Agriculture. Similarly, in the forestry sub-sector, development and regulation is the responsibility largely of the Guyana Forestry Commission and the Guyana Natural Resources Agency. In the rice sector there are three semi-autonomous public agencies involved in marketing, export regulation and quality control which, for budgetary purposes, come under the Ministry of Finance. The Guyana Rice Milling and Marketing Authority (GRMMA) had a substantial role to play prior to liberalization but now its role is severely restricted; there are only two rice mills left under its authority and there are proposals for divestiture or leasing of these. In future GRMMAs main role, if any, will be the provision of market information and data on the sector relating to production, costs, etc. Control and promotion of exports and certification for export purposes is undertaken by the Guyana Rice Export Board (GREB). For this service they receive a three percent export levy for which there is apparently little accountability and which is the subject of criticism from rice millers and producers. The National Paddy and Rice Grading Center (NPRGC) is responsible for setting grading standards and for assisting in their implementation. It is under-resourced, under-staffed and under-equipped and much grading is in fact done on an ad hoc basis at mill level. Nevertheless, NPRGC has responsibility for an important function in terms of fair pricing and improvement of quality. The future development of the sector will require strengthened capability to perform this function.

9.13   For rice production, and for many other crops, the most important regulatory agencies outside of the Ministry of Agriculture are those responsible for irrigation and drainage. The first group of these are the Water Conservancy Boards which are responsible for maintenance of the conservancies and the release of water from the conservancies. The second group are the Regional Democratic Councils which have taken over the functions of the Drainage and Irrigation Boards. They are responsible for maintenance

---

8/   There are government-wide plans being implemented to gradually try and remedy this situation. They involve rationalization of the salary structure, of the establishment level and of the salary levels. Inevitably, because of the overall financial resource constraint it will not be possible to move as far or as fast on this as might be desirable.

and operation of the drainage and irrigation systems on which most of Guyanese agriculture depends. In the Mahaica-Mahaicony-Abary land development scheme the drainage and irrigation responsibilities are held by the MMA authority which has a separate board with all the relevant agencies represented on it. The regions and the MMA-ADA are responsible for determining each year what major maintenance work needs to be undertaken and preparing budgetary estimates for the costs involved. The Ministry of Agriculture has to approve these estimates and provide a 10 percent subsidy towards these works; the rest of the costs are supposed to be met through charges to water users on a per acre basis. Various statutory provisions effect the calculation of cost shares and, with tight financial constraints, the amounts of money actually available from the Ministry are much less than the estimates submitted. Indeed, most maintenance work has been provided through PL480 counterpart funds in recent years. The Regional Democratic Councils do not themselves collect the water users' share of costs, this is the responsibility of the local authorities. Collection rates have been extremely low, sinking to below 6 percent in 1990. Since the initial amounts authorized for collection have been very much lower than the actual costs of works, the amount of money available for undertaking maintenance has been very much less than required. As a consequence service delivery has deteriorated, to the point of non-existence on some irrigation and drainage systems with the inevitable consequence that farmers have been reluctant or completely unwilling to pay charges. The problem is compounded by the fact that the areas vested under the old Drainage and Irrigation Boards, and now the responsibility of the Regional Democratic Councils, are not necessarily self-contained drainage and irrigation systems but what has been handed over from land development schemes. Very often, parts of such schemes are in fact the responsibility of district councils, the local authority themselves or private individuals. This makes coordinated management of the operational and maintenance functions impossible.

9.14   A high priority for the Government is institutional reform of operations and maintenance systems for drainage and irrigation without which the prospects for sustained agricultural growth are very gloomy. Evidence from the D&I systems which are managed privately indicate that farmers are able and willing to pay for a service which is properly provided. Evidence from other countries shows that, properly managed, operations and maintenance functions can be paid for through user fees but this depends on having an appropriate institutional framework which makes service providers accountable to water users.

9.15   The final group of agencies involved in rice and other crop production which are not under the purview of the Ministry of Agriculture are the banks responsible for agricultural credit. Some large individual farmers and corporate farms obtain credit from commercial bank sources. However, the main sources of institutional credit to the farm sector are Gaibank, the Guyana Agricultural and Industrial Development Bank and the Institute of Private Enterprise Development. These two agencies only manage to meet the credit needs of a relatively small number of farmers and an even lower share of the agricultural production costs. As of 20 November 1992, Gaibank only had 913 agricultural loans to small borrowers and at the end of 1991 IPED only had 172 loans for rice cultivation; IPED also had a number of loans for dairy farming, pig and poultry rearing and artisanal fishing. The major problem in credit provision is absence of adequate collateral which inhibits lending to small borrowers. Moreover, the absolute volume of funds available through these institutions is itself insufficient; there are proposals being considered to utilize IDB counterpart funds in addition to those already available, for example through PL 480, which would help relax the institutional credit bottle-neck.

9.16   Within the Ministry of Agriculture itself activities are divided between 5 departments; three providing indirect support services and two providing direct production support. The Hydraulics Department is responsible for drainage and irrigation system rehabilitation and sea defenses (see Chapter X). The Hydrometeorology Department is responsible for monitoring the atmospheric and water resources of Guyana in order to provide information to aeronautical, water, agricultural, mining, fishing, maritime and other agencies. This Department has been part of the Ministry of Agriculture for less than 2 years. It is scarcely able to provide any service presently because it is starved of resources. There are proposals prepared by the Department for user fees, but these have not been acted upon. The problem here, as with the user fees for D&I operations and maintenance, is the need to invest in service rehabilitation in order to provide a level of service of sufficient quality for user fees to be justified; in other words initial investments will be necessary before proposals for user fees could be negotiated successfully with user agencies.

9.17   The third department not directly responsible for production activities is the Lands and Surveys Department. The Department is responsible for mapping of land and water resources; issuing title deeds for farming and other land uses; collecting rent for leases on state and government land; and, information provision in relation to mapping etc. Though the Department has a rent collection accounting responsibility it is not directly involved in the major rent collection activities; these are undertaken by the regional administrations. In fact, rents are set at such low levels that the costs of collection frequently exceed the value of the rents and collection success rate is extremely low. Although there has been some improvement the total collected in 1991 was only G$7.4 million. A major regulatory function of the Lands and Surveys Department is the issue of leaseholds to farmers. Much of this work is actually organized through the Regional Democratic Councils who have taken responsibility for the regionally-based Lands and Surveys staff although final authority is still vested in the Commissioner of Lands and Surveys. This function is crucial with respect to the development of the agriculture sector, since, historically, many farmers have been issued with very short-term leases. Promotion of land development, and improved access to institutional credit, is very much dependent on farmers securing long-term leasehold or freehold title to their lands. This has been identified as a priority area although the funding for accelerated implementation of registration has not yet been provided.

9.18   The Fisheries Department is responsible for the management regulation and promotion of sustainable exploitation and development of the fishery resources. It has three units: The Legal Inspectorate Unit; The Research and Development Unit; and the Extension Unit. The Legal Inspectorate Unit has a key revenue generation function since it is responsible for the issue of licenses to fishermen and the collection of rent from the processing units management by fishermens' cooperatives.

9.19   The Crops and Livestock Department has a wide ranging set of responsibilities with a number of institutions operating under it. It consists of 4 divisions: The Plant and Animal Health Services Division; The Extension and Education Services Division; The Crops Services Division and the Wildlife Division. It is involved in all aspects of the development of Guyanese agriculture through service provision. From 1993, the extension services have been transferred back from the regional administrations and now operate under the direct control of the Department. Under its auspices a number of agencies operate including the National Agricultural Research Institute, The Guyana School of Agriculture, The National Dairy Development Program and The New Guyana Marketing Corporation. Its main revenue collection function is through the issuing of export permits by the Wildlife Division.

9.20   In addition to these five functional departments the Ministry at central level has Finance, Personnel, Administrative and Planning Divisions. The Planning Division should have a crucial role to play since liberalization in the provision of information and preparation of plans for the development of the productive sectors. It is not able to fulfil this role because of the gross inadequacy of resource provision. The data base for planning in agriculture is extremely limited and there are almost no regularly collected sources of reliable data.

9.21   The Ministry is responsible for a variety of revenue functions the most important of which relate to fishing licenses and land rents. In 1991 it collected nearly G$22 million. Funds from the Wildlife Division are deposited in a special fund one use of which should be for investments in wildlife conservation; in practice the fund has been used for a variety of purposes. The other revenues are transferred to the consolidated fund under the Ministry of Finance. The organization of revenue collection has recently been reviewed by the Planning Division which has made a number of recommendations to improve the efficiency and accountability of revenue collection. At present, revenue collection is often very inadequate. Certainly, any proposals for revenue generation through collection of user fees for services provided will not succeed until improved methods of revenue collection have been implemented. Critically, such improvements must include strengthened accountability of those responsible for revenue collection and transmittance.

D. SECTOR FINANCES

1. Current Expenditure

9.22   As in other Ministries, current expenditure estimates are prepared by the Ministry of Agriculture during the last quarter of each calendar (financial) year. Each department prepares its own estimate and these are consolidated by the Assistant Principal Secretary Finance. Decisions on allocations (i.e., the budget) are not usually finalized by the Ministry of Finance until February; in other words the expenditure year is already well started before departments know how much money they will have. Whilst there are standard arrangements for advances on a monthly basis until the budget is agreed, the procedure is very problematic because actual expenditure plans often depend crucially on knowledge of budgetary allocations. For example, the National Agricultural Research Institute has to plan its seasonal crop research activities for the first crop of the year in the preceding November; where there are significant differences between budgets submitted and budgets agreed, as is often the case, the delay in budget finalization can lead to serious sub-optimality in the utilization of budgetary provisions.

<u>Table 9.2</u>: MINISTRY OF AGRICULTURE CURRENT EXPENDITURE
(G$ million)

Head		Actual 1990	Actual 1991	Revised Estimates 1992	Budget Submissions 1993
Administration <u>a</u>/	Total	4.1	9.0	20.3	26.3
	Employment Related	2.5	3.1	6.1	9.7
	Other Charges	1.6	5.9	14.2	16.7
Crops and Livestock	Total	39.8	140.6	355.8	334.0
	Employment related	7.3	6.0	14.4	14.6
	Other Charges	32.6	134.6	341.4	319.4
	o.w. to intl. org.	6.9	87.9	242.1	151.1
Lands and Surveys	Total	5.4	8.1	12.5	17.6
	Employment Related	3.7	4.6	8.5	12.4
	Other Charges	1.7	3.5	4.0	5.3
Fisheries	Total	1.1	1.3	2.3	5.8
	Employment Related	0.8	0.8	1.7	3.0
	Other Charges	0.3	0.5	0.5	2.7
Hydrometeorology <u>b</u>/	Total	NA	NA	48.5	78.3
	Employment Related	NA	NA	3.5	7.9
	Other Charges	NA	NA	45.1	70.4
Total Current Expenditure		50.5	159.1	439.4	462.0

<u>a</u>/ Includes Finance, Personnel and Planning.
<u>b</u>/ Hydrometeorology became part of the Ministry of Agriculture in July 1991.

<u>Source</u>: Ministry of Finance and Ministry of Agriculture

9.23   The budget submissions prepared by the departments in the Ministry of Agriculture for 1993 are detailed in Table 9.2 together with the revised estimates for 1992 and the actual expenditures in 1990 and 1991. The very substantial increases over the period to 1992 of course reflect the high level of inflation in Guyana. The revised estimates for 1992 are in fact submissions made during the third quarter of the year; they reflect actual expenditures in the first three quarters and projections for the last quarter. To the extent that they reflect employment-related expenditures they are likely to be realistic, but, on other charges, they may overstate the final allocation agreed by the Ministry of Finance.

9.24   The "other charges" element covers all non-employment related expenditure; the ability of the departments to do anything productive with their staff obviously depends crucially on adequate provision here. In all departments, as in other ministries, there was considerable dissatisfaction with the level of provision for other charges in the recent past. It was commonly reported that allowances for services such as telephones and electricity and provision for fuel expenditure were used up within the first 5-8 months of the year.[9/] The submissions for 1993 are well in excess - with the exception of Crops and Livestock - of the 1993 target figure of 1992 plus 5 percent indicated by the Ministry of Finance. Clearly, there will have to

[9/]   Even though the budget is released on a monthly basis it is possible, through credit arrangements and virement, to spend ahead of actual cash provision.

be substantial reduction but the figures are useful in indicating - in comparison with the likely actual provision of 1992 plus 5 percent - the degree of shortfall in relation to current expenditure requirements. The departments, as a matter of course, "pad" their budget in anticipation of cuts which only undermines the ability of either the Ministry of Agriculture or the Ministry of Finance to take rational decisions with respect to prioritization of expenditure.

Table 9.3: MINISTRY OF AGRICULTURE: CROPS AND LIVESTOCK DIVISION,
LOCAL INSTITUTIONS
Current Budget Estimates (G$1000)

Institution	Budget Submissions 1993	Revised Estimates 1992	Actual Expenditure 1991
National Agricultural Research Institute	101,269	54,278	23,908
Guyana School of Agriculture	20,000	13,025	11,286
Guyana Marketing Corporation	10,325	8,433	6,853
National Dairy Development Program	11,231	7,489	5,258
Regional Educational Program for Animal Health Assistants	4,652	2,705	1,576
Total	147,477	85,930	48,881

Note: These estimates are as prepared by the Institutions themselves. They correspond approximately to the consolidated submission of the Crops and Livestock Division for 1993 though the consolidated figures for 1991 and 1992 are lower than these estimates - probably due to differences on coverage. The National Cane Farming Committee and the Guyana Society for Protection Against Cruelty to Animals have very small budgets and are not included.

Source: Ministry of Agriculture

9.25   Contributions paid to international organizations presently appear in the relevant departments current expenditure estimates under the heading "other charges". These are often very substantial and distort the picture of the actual availability of funds to the department, as in the case of the Crop and Livestock Department (Table 9.2). How misleading the inclusion of these contributions can be is well illustrated through these figures; for the 1993 budget submission there is an overall reduction in the size of the "other charges" budget but because the very substantial share of that budget going to international contributions in 1992 has been sharply reduced in 1993, the department has been able to substantially increase its allocations to other heads covered under the "other charges" budget. In particular this has allowed large increases in the budget submission for local organizations as detailed in Table 9.3 above. A similar type of situation also exists with the Hydrometeorology Department. Whilst it is clearly the Ministry of Agriculture which should determine, beyond statutory requirements, which international organizations they wish to associate with, it is misleading to have contributions to such organizations incorporated in the budget of the Ministry itself. For this and other reasons, as discussed in Section G below, reform of the budgetary process is a priority requirement for improved planning within the Ministry.

2. Capital Expenditure

9.26   The capital budget, presenting the investment program of the Ministry, should reflect the planned pipeline of investment funds for priority activities of the Ministry.   In practice of course, given the very severe financial constraints at a macroeconomic level, the investment program is largely dependent upon the availability of external finance.   Provision of local funds is usually linked to external projects and commonly dependent upon counterpart funds generated through balance of payments support activities in the past.   The investment pipeline that has been proposed for the Ministry of Agriculture[10] is outlined in Table 9.4.   It involves a total expenditure a little over G$4 billion over the 4 years 1993-1996.

Table 9.4:   SUMMARY OF IDENTIFIED AGRICULTURAL INVESTMENT PROGRAM
(in G$ million)

Source of Funding	Budgeted 1993	1994	1995	1996	Total
Local	300.6	480.4	433.9	418.5	1633.4
External	1230.8	944.2	479.0	0.0	2654.0
Total	1531.4	1424.6	912.9	418.5	4287.4

Notes: Excludes Sugar and Sea Defenses.

Source: Statistical Appendix

9.27   A detailed breakdown of capital expenditures is given in Tables 9.5 and 9.6 which separate those projects which have current external finance and those which are dependent on local finance only.   In fact the numbers in Table 9.5 give a much exaggerated impression of the actual commitment of public investment funds.   This is because the single largest item accounting for 42 percent of the external investment provision in 1993 is a private sector transfer.   On the whole, private sector transfers come to 57 percent of the 1993 external provision and 68 percent of the total external investment provision in the pipeline for the Ministry of Agriculture.   These private sector transfers will generate counterpart funds but there is no guarantee on what those counterpart funds will be used for so it is not really appropriate to incorporate them in current public investment provision.   As Table 9.4 indicates there is no external finance in the pipeline for the Ministry of Agriculture beyond 1995.   Given the crucial importance of the agricultural

---

10/   Based on the Guyana Public Sector Investment Review by the State Planning Secretariat.

sector in the economic recovery program and the substantial rehabilitation and investment needs this is of major significance.

Table 9.5: MINISTRY OF AGRICULTURE: CAPITAL INVESTMENT PROGRAMS WITH EXTERNAL FUNDING a/
1993-94
(G$ million)

		Budgeted 1993			1994			Notes
		Total	External	Local	Total	External	Local	
1.	National Agricultural b/ Research Institute - capability strengthening	130.4	100.4	30.0	115.0	0.0	115.0	Grant UNDP. FAO executed.
2.	Agricultural Rehabilit- ation - Rice and Sugar Farm Machinery	645.5	627.5	18.0	833.3	810.5	22.8	Loan IDB. PEU latest estimate. Private sector transfer.
3.	Agriculture Sector Hybrid - Technical Cooperation Component	81.8	62.8	19.0	147.0	133.7	13.3	Loan IDB.
4.	Fisheries Equipment Facilityb/	211.6	205.3	6.3	0.0	0.0	0.0	Grant CIDA. Delayed. Private sectortransfer.
5.	East Bank Essequibo Dev. Project	1521.9	1155.4	366.5	0.0	0.0	0.0	Grant IFAD.
6.	East Bank Berbice Irrigation Works	494.0	462.2	31.9	0.0	0.0	0.0	Loan
Total		3085.2	2613.6	471.7	1095.3	944.2	151.1	

a/ Hydraulics Division (Sea Defenses) is excluded (see Chapter X). No externally-funded investment in Drainage and Irrigation Rehabilitation is currently agreed.
b/ CARICOM Regional Projects excluded.

Source: Mission Estimates

9.28   Table 9.6 gives the projections of agricultural sector investment from local funding the period 1993-96. Even these rather modest amounts are by no means guaranteed since in some cases, for example the National Agricultural Research Institute, they involve substantial increases on current local funding; the presumption has been made that external funding will become available. All of the investment funds in part A of the Table relate to area development and drainage and irrigation investment and are largely linked to externally funded investment which has been completed; these expenditures represent completion of commitments. The exception to this is the first project on rehabilitation of drainage and irrigation in the regions. Whilst there has been some provision for maintenance, largely through PL 480 funds, there was no funding in 1992 for drainage and irrigation rehabilitation in the local capital budget. The projections here for 1993 through 1996 were expected to be linked to reallocation of IDB funds already committed; however, it appears likely that this commitment will now be cancelled so the future for this investment is very unclear. Leaving aside the expenditures in Part A of the Table and taking out the first item in Part B for the National Agricultural Research Institute, the remaining funds are very limited indeed. The only item greater than G$10 million is for the agricultural extension services. These have suffered substantially because of systematic neglect over the last decade. Until this year, they have been incorporated in the regional budgets and this led to their virtual immobilization. Expenditures projected here are an initial attempt to rehabilitate the service through provision of transportation and other facilities. At least some of the proposed expenditure on extension will be generated as a consequence of the World Bank support provided through the public sector reform program.

Table 9.6: AGRICULTURE SECTOR INVESTMENT PROGRAM: LOCAL FUNDING PLANNED a/
(in G$ million)

		Budgeted 1993	1994	1995	1996
A.	**Area Development, D & I Investment**				
1.	Drainage and Irrigation (Regions)	24.5	70.0	80.0	90.0
2.	Mahaica-Mahaicony-Abary Project	39.0	55.0	65.0	70.0
3.	Black Bush Poulder Rehabilitation	40.0	80.0	30.0	35.0
4.	Rehabilitation of Drainage and Irrigation Areas	36.0	20.0	0.0	0.0
Total: Area Development, D & I Rehabilitation		**139.5**	**225.0**	**175.0**	**195.0**
B.	**Agriculture - Other**				
5.	National Agriculture Research Institute	..b/	115.0	125.0	125.0
6.	Agricultural Extension Services	0.0	45.0	65.0	70.0
7.	Artificial Insemination Program	3.0	4.0	4.2	4.4
8.	Geodetic Surveys	0.5	1.8	1.9	2.1
9.	Hydrometeorological Services	5.0	15.0	15.0	15.0
10.	Land Registration	1.0	5.0	5.0	5.0
11.	Plant and Animal Quarantine	2.0	1.5	1.0	1.5
12.	Forestry Studies	20.0	32.0	30.0	0.0
Total: Agriculture - Other		**31.5**	**219.3**	**247.4**	**223.5**
GRAND TOTAL		**171.0**	**444.3**	**422.4**	**418.5**

Notes: a/ Capital expenditure estimates from Ministry of Agriculture divisions deviate both above and below these figures.
b/ 1993 is externally financed; local contributions to this and the other externally funded projects are specified in Table 9.5.

Source: Mission Estimates

9.29   The actual allocations in Table 9.6 can be compared with those in Table 9.7 listing the investment proposals emanating from the Ministry and from other planning initiatives. The total of Table 9.7 is over G$750 million compared to the actual allocation of local funding in 1993 of G$171 million. Excluding the area development and D&I investment in Table 9.6 provides a better comparison with Table 9.7 estimates since D&I investments have not been included there; on this basis, the proposals from the Ministry are twenty times greater than the actual allocation in 1993. It is evident that a great number of potential investments have been suggested - even if in a rather uncoordinated manner - which on present availability of funds have little or no prospect of leading to funded investment activity.

Table 9.7: INVESTMENT PROPOSED BY THE MINISTRY OF AGRICULTURE - CURRENTLY UNFUNDED
FOR 1993 ONWARDS
(in G$ million)

	AMOUNT	NOTES
A. Ministry Proposals		
Hydrometeorological Service Strengthening	54.8	Scaled down version of part of WMO recommendations. Full version budgeted at G$176.9 million.
National Dairy Development Program	6.0	Equipment support to Forage Improvement Program.
Geodetic Surveys	5.9	International boundaries verification, feasibility studies and rehabilitation in Lands and Surveys Department
Ministry of Agriculture, Central Office	3.0	Equipment
B. Other Proposals		
[Prepared for the Atlanta Conference on International Development (Dec. '92)]	87.5	Agro-Industry for Women
	19.0	Dairy Technology Transfer
	12.5	Forage Plot Establishment
	250.0	Support to the Agricultural Census
	39.1	Extension Service Rehabilitation
	38.2	Expansion of National Dairy Development Program
	186.9	Seed Production Support
	48.4	Land Registration Cadaster
TOTAL (A + B)	**751.3**	

Note: All proposals in Part A have been included in the Ministry of Agriculture's 1993 original capital estimates but do not appear in the PSIP at all or only in a marginal way; those in Part B are not in the PSIP.

Source: Ministry of Agriculture and State Planning Secretariat

3.   Revenue Generation

9.30   Table 9.8 describes the collection of revenue showing a total of just under G$22 M for 1991. The major contributions to this revenue are fishing licenses and rent from agricultural lands. The Fisheries Department reports reasonable satisfaction (90 percent plus collection rates) for licensing of industrial trawlers and fish processing plants. The Department reports an almost 100 percent record on export licensing but a collection rate of below 50 percent for the artisanal and fishermen's licensing. There is a felt need for a review of licensing and a belief that there is opportunity to increase revenue. This should also be accompanied by improvements in the accounting system. Revenue collection from lease of state and government lands is in a very much poorer condition. Lease rates are extremely low – with rates for land development schemes, for example, ranging from G$2 to G$15 per acre. The costs of collection often easily exceed the value of rentals and, with little risk of attempted payment enforcement, leaseholders are not inclined to pay. Most land revenues are not collected directly by the Lands and Surveys Department but through the regions which makes it extremely difficult to promote better collection procedures. Accounting is symbolic or non-existent and there is considerable scope for improvement in almost all aspects of land revenue collection, beginning with adjustments of rates to reflect inflation.

Table 9.8: MINISTRY OF AGRICULTURE CURRENT REVENUE FOR THE YEAR 1991
(Cash basis; G$)

Duty on Transportation and Mortgages	29,567
Fees and Fines etc.	1,313,236
Licenses	14,738,968
Other Loan Fees	4,799
Land Fees	7,250
Permission	25,099
Miscellaneous	726,463
Rent State Land	3,099,729
Rent Government Land	662,649
Others	36
Black Bush Polder	145,598
Garden of Eden	9,325
Soesdyke Linden Highway	80,198
Sundries	1,156,164
Sale of Empty Drums	495
Total	**21,999,576**

Source: Ministry of Agriculture

9.31   The main opportunity for generation of revenue in addition to the two sources identified above is through user fees for drainage and irrigation operations and maintenance services. As detailed in the 1992 agriculture sector review, current collection rates are extremely low. Because drainage and irrigation services are themselves extremely poor, due to lack of investment maintenance, many farmers are unwilling to pay the very low rates which are currently charged. Here also the collection is largely indirect with local authorities collecting sums due on behalf of the regional accountant. The prospects for improvement depend critically upon improvements in service delivery requiring changes in the institutional framework for operations and maintenance provision for accountable responsibility and responsibility for collection of user fees. This is the most critical area to be addressed in the whole of the agriculture sector (see next section) as it represents both an opportunity to make a substantial contribution to agriculture production as well as to meet the costs of a significant budgetary expenditure.

9.32   Several other opportunities are often mentioned as possibilities for cost recovery. The hydrometeorological service has developed such a proposal involving three sets of charges: one percent of the cost of water-related development projects reflecting the Department's role in providing data on water quantity and quality; twenty five percent of the landing charges at Timehri Airport reflecting charges for supply of meteorological information; and user charges for other provision of hydrological and meteorological information per "data piece" at a published rate. But, as discussed above, this is unlikely to succeed until rehabilitation investment is provided to ensure a more adequate level of service delivery. Similarly, the National Agricultural Research Institute and the agricultural extension services are considered to be producer related services for which user fees could be obtained. In practice, for the medium term at least, it is extremely unlikely that this would be the case. For the research service, much of their output is in the nature of a public good for which it would be difficult to collect rent. For example, seed once released can be produced and sold by private growers and farmers can re-use seed; this is certainly the case for rice and likely to be the case as well for much of the output from the tissue culture program. Eventually, when modern genetic engineering techniques are applied in agricultural research this situation could change through the development of varieties with non-heritable characteristics; this is a long way off in Guyana. In the case of the extension services the problem is more fundamentally one of the quality and relevance of the service provision. It is only in the most well developed agricultural systems that extension services are able to command satisfactory user fees and this is because they can achieve a level of professional competence that makes utilization of their services a satisfactory investment for farmers.

9.33   Instead of directly paying user fees, the contribution by farmers so far has been in the form of an export levy, which more or less exclusively benefits the Guyana Rice Export Board. However, an export levy is a very questionable device for cost recovery, as it gives rise to distortions and bears little relation to actual services delivered. In fact, the export levy is already considered by many to be excessive for the level of service provision. The Government also operates a graduated claw-back of the private sector rents obtained through the differential between the EC price for rice and the world market price. The National Agriculture Research Institute rightly argues that they have a strong claim to a share in such revenue and that given such a share they would be able to make a much more substantial contribution to the development of the rice sector than is currently possible with the limited resources that budgetary constraints currently allow them. In this case, and in the case of the proposals from the Hydrometeorological Department whose service users are largely in the public sector at present, implementation of the proposals would amount to a transfer of revenue within the public sector. Moreover, schemes such as supporting NARI from export taxes would not easily allow the accountability to users of services provided. Thus, whilst such proposals may represent a "fairer" distribution of revenues in some senses they would not in themselves provide a mechanism that promoted efficiency of revenue utilization.

9.34   The main conclusions from this review of sector finances are as follows:

*   Current expenditure budgets are wholly inadequate even for the day to day functioning of the departments.

*   Delay and uncertainty in approving estimates results in inefficiency.

*   The pipeline for external funding of capital investment is short and narrow.

113

- Most existing proposals for external finance are in fact private sector transfers not public sector investment.

- Provision for local funding of capital investment is very small and offers little to most departments.

- Where local funding provisions are more than minimal in the estimates there is considerable doubt as to whether funding will ultimately be available.

- There are many existing proposals for capital investment emerging from the departments and elsewhere which have little prospect of funding without further external support. There is inadequate prioritization of investment proposals.

- The revenue generation function of the Ministry of Agriculture is extremely limited and, with a couple of exceptions, falls far short of potential.

- Opportunities for cost recovery through user fees are likely to remain limited for both research and extension in the medium term. For water users, better collection depends on better service and an improved institutional framework.

- The separation of collection responsibility from accounting responsibility leads to poor performance on revenue generation.

E. MAIN SECTORAL ISSUES

9.35   The Agricultural Sector Review undertaken by the World Bank in 1992 identified a number of priority issues for the agricultural sector including needs for action in relation to water resources, land tenure, rice production promotion and research and extension.[11] The prioritization in the Agricultural Sector Review, clearly, and correctly, places major emphasis on the development of rice production. The continuing responsiveness of farmers to the price incentives since liberalization during the 13 months between that review mission and the current mission provide further evidence of the growth potential in rice production. There is no data, at least for the last decade and a half, on the number of rice farmers or of their average holding sizes or cultivated areas, but, as the Rice Sector Review from the Ministry of Agriculture Planning Division states, there is much anecdotal evidence of farmers returning to once abandoned rice land and of strong producer response from both small and large farmers. The priorities identified seek to strengthen that response by providing a rice production environment conducive to continuing growth in output. The core constraint on continued growth is the poor condition of the drainage and irrigation infrastructure and the poor procedures in its operations and maintenance. Many of the irrigation and drainage canals have deteriorated to the extent that routine maintenance and activities will be insufficient to restore them to proper operating conditions. Farmers report yield reductions of 25% as being not uncommon on areas planted because of yield and quality losses. In

---

11/   The review also identified priority needs in relation to the sugar and forestry sub-sectors which are not covered in this chapter.

addition there are the losses due to areas not planted and the higher production costs associated with inability to use farm machinery and agro-chemical inputs to proper efficiency. Substantial investment in machinery and in engineering design to plan rehabilitation will be necessary. At present the very limited investments identified in Table 9.6A are all that is available for such work, and, as discussed, it is not clear that even these funds will in fact actually materialize. In many areas, completion of such rehabilitation work will be necessary before any system of user fees can be effectively implemented since reliable operation will not be possible.

9.36   The identification of rehabilitation of D&I systems as a first priority has more or less universal agreement. However, rehabilitation will not produce sustainable benefits without a solution to the two fundamental and inter-dependent problems with respect to drainage and irrigation systems operations and maintenance. First, is the difficulty in getting farmers to pay water user fees when the quality of service provision is poor - as measured by the adequacy of D&I operations and maintenance arrangements; The second problem is the difficulty of improving service without increased resource provision, e.g., from user fees. There is no doubt that a major strategy for the Government of Guyana must be to develop an improved system of cost recovery for D&I operations and maintenance; both from a revenue generation perspective and a resource use efficiency perspective such cost recovery is vital. This issue has been discussed at some length in the recent Agricultural Sector Review and elsewhere; without repeating that discussion, it is worth summarizing the main priorities for improved system performance.

- A fundamental problem is the under-resourcing of the authorities responsible for D&I operations and maintenance.

- Even though detailed proposals on necessary (rehabilitation and) maintenance work are submitted from the regions the responsible authority, the Minister of Agriculture, is not able - because of financial constraints - to approve the required works. The problem is that the Ministry has to bear a share of the costs for these works. Moreover, the areas which need the most work are the areas which provide the poorest service which further inhibits fee collection, hence, execution of work. Whilst the initial system in the Drainage and Irrigation Act for levying costs was a simple per acre basis, various ad hoc amendments have produced a rather complex system of determining user share in costs.

- The effect is that the charges levied are wholly inadequate for the costs of adequate operations and maintenance services. The degree of undercharging varies considerably.

- As a consequence of these conditions the actual collection of user fees is extremely poor. In most cases, outside of the MMA, it is local authorities who actually collect dues and turn them over to the Regional Democratic Councils. This inhibits both efficiency of collection and accountability for use of funds.

- Outside of the MMA Agricultural Development Authority it is the Regional Democratic Councils who are responsible for drainage and irrigation systems. They have inherited the powers vested in the Drainage and Irrigation Boards under the Drainage and Irrigation

Act. There are approximately 39 such boards. The RDCs have proven incapable of effectively managing the D&I systems under their jurisdiction. Each regional engineering officer has a wide range of responsibilities encompassing all civil works within the region and his office and workshop are under-resourced and over-extended.

- Not all D&I systems are "vested", that is under the jurisdiction of Drainage and Irrigation Boards. There remain district drainage canals, local authority canals and irrigation and drainage provided by private interests or controlled by GUYSUCO. Sometimes, these exist within inter-connected D&I systems which frustrates attempts at efficient overall management. It also effects investment plans, through donor supported projects for example, which can result in highly inefficient investment decisions when the proper operation of the whole inter-connecting system is assessed.

- There are five water conservancies in three geographical areas all covered by different legislation dating back as far as 1886. Two conservancies are almost entirely operated by GUYSUCO. Conservancy management has to be implemented with a view to the efficient operation of the relevant agrarian system served by it as well as by other demands on water use (drinking water and transport), and with regard for environmental considerations; resources to allow such management are not being provided.

9.37   Underlying all of these problems is the inadequate institutional framework for D&I operations and maintenance. The transfer of the Drainage and Irrigation Boards to the Regional Democratic Councils was a disaster and even the most basic records on system design have been lost in the process. There is an urgent need for an alternative authority for D&I water management. Inevitably, this must be linked to a broader strategy on national water use planning in Guyana. Box 9.1 concerns lessons on water management from Taiwan; it suggests that the methods by which efficient water delivery and collection of user fees is achieved may not depend solely on the hierarchical imposition of an authoritarian management regime. It is evident from this example that a very pragmatic approach has to be used in practice in order to achieve the objectives of efficient water use and cost recovery. Also, whilst it is clear, eg from the IFAD-supported East Bank Essequibo project and from the conditions on the IDB hybrid loan, that donors have recognized the crucial importance of radical reform of the D&I system, it is necessary for the Government to embrace this concern with more urgency and more resources. With appropriate political support it should nevertheless be possible to move fairly rapidly to rectify this situation because:

- Detailed review of proposals for the amendment of water resources legislation has been undertaken.[12]

12/   An FAO report provides a detailed discussion of such legislation and suggested alternatives; in Report No. TGP/GUY/4401(A) 1985, "Water Resources Legislation for Guyana".

- Detailed proposals have been made on institutional strengthening and operating procedures for most of the D&I System.[13]

9.38   A priority for the Government must be a review of these and other studies already prepared. Based on this, legislation should be drawn up to respond to the identified needs for an alternative institutional framework for the exercise of water management authority. Financing will then be required for equipment and facilities for the new institutional framework.

9.39   Improving credit provision and elimination of short-term leaseholds are crucial complementary activities in support of D&I rehabilitation and institutional reform to improve D&I operations and maintenance. On farm credit, at present there is very limited access to institutional borrowing. Gaibank is a development bank supported both by donors and the Government which is charged with responsibility for agricultural lending. However, in 1991, the total lending to the farm sector was estimated to be less than 5% of the total production costs for rice.[14] The commercial banks provide very limited support for rice cultivators and the only other source of institutional credit available is the Institute for Private Enterprise Development (IPED). IPED has had support from the donors, notably through PL480 funds. They have a wide ranging loan portfolio but according to their Annual Report they have only provided 261 loans for rice cultivation in the first 6 years of their activities up to 1991. A part of the explanation for low institutional borrowing by farmers lies in the production risk associated with the poor condition of the infrastructure.[15] However, poor performance of financial institutions is the underlying problem.

9.40   Neither the commercial banks nor IPED have the institutional infrastructure to be substantial farm lenders and Gaibank is the only institution likely to be able to provide substantial institutional credit for the rice production sector. Plans for the reinvigoration of Gaibank are being developed but for it to achieve a markedly improved level of service provision to farmers two issues must be addressed. First, it is technically bankrupt at the moment since it has carried the foreign exchange risk associated with donor support and, because of devaluation, has suffered foreign exchange losses of over G$800 million. Losses also occurred because the initial Gaibank policy was to charge below the market rate of interest; it now charges more or less at the prime rate for borrowing but still slightly below the commercial rate. A sound recapitalization plan and a commercial structure for interest rates is fundamental to any future role of Gaibank in farm credit provision. Secondly, Gaibank faced relatively few problems of loan delinquency (below 5 percent) with respect to their rice production loans but

---

13/   For example, see report, "Institutional Strengthening of Blackbush, Amendment 3, D&I Systems in Regions 3, 4 and 6, Manual for Operation, Maintenance and Supervision of Drainage and Irrigation Systems" March 1989. Prepared by NEDCO for the Hydraulics Department, Ministry of Agriculture.

14/   Planning Department Rice Sector Review (Draft), Section 6, 1992.

15/   For example where the infrastructure is better such as in region 2 demand is higher than in other regions (such as region 5) where the infrastructure is poor.

Box 9.1: WATER MANAGEMENT PRACTICES IN TAIWAN

Taiwanese irrigation management is often cited as a good example of efficiency in service delivery paid for through satisfied water users - largely small rice farmers. There is an elaborate organizational structure and a very detailed system of planning for the timing, volume, distribution and use of irrigation water which are often thought to explain this good performance. This note, by a social scientist with extensive experience in irrigation management, offers an alternative set of reasons for the relative efficiency of irrigation management in Taiwan. An important factor identified is the existence of a well-accounted and timely collection of fees which allows user non-payment to act as a viable indicator of localized poor service delivery.

- The localism of staff recruitment practices, which makes staff very familiar, especially after long periods of service, with the physical and human environment in which they work.

- The de facto devolution of very considerable authority to the lower levels of the official system - to Irrigation Laborers, Irrigation Supervisors, Working Station Chiefs - permitting them to make on a day-to-day basis the kinds of compromises with local physical and social factors which are essential if the system is to work at all smoothly.

- The smallness, at least at the Working Station level, of the boundaries between different job categories, permitting considerable flexibility in use of staff.

- The existence of a relatively elaborate set of working procedures and an elaborate water distribution plan which can if necessary be used as tools to check on and discipline errant field level staff, and which can provide a framework for a general tightening up of discipline, work performance and water distribution practices on those occasions when water is scarce.

- The existence of multiple channels - none perhaps individually very impressive or effective - through which farmer demands and dissatisfaction can be voiced: elected irrigation Group Chiefs with formal roles in the management system; delays in the payment of irrigation fees when rapid timely collection is an important indicator of Working Station efficiency; the elected Representative Assembly of each Irrigation Association; and the close political and social involvements of IA staff at all levels with the population they serve.

One would not want to be too eulogistic about the excellence of all Taiwanese practices. In particular, the involvement of IAs in local politics has undesirable as well as desirable effects. The broader point however is that the fact that the elaborate formalized procedures established for irrigation management - the water delivery plans, water measurement schedules, crop and water flow records, allocation of responsibility to high levels in the authority structure, democratic institutions - are widely ignored, by-passed or short-cut under normal circumstances does not mean that they are not useful or necessary. They probably play a very important role in establishing performance goals which can be arrived at if not met, in 'educating' staff and farmers into their responsibilities, and in providing a framework of procedures and practices which can be brought into play when water does become very scarce.

Source: Dr. Michael Moore, Unpublished Note, August 1983

this was achieved through insistence on adequate collateral provision which in turn meant farmers with leaseholdings were ineligible.[16] An important step is to change lease arrangements (see next paragraph) but, even with improvements on collateral arrangements, Gaibank will continue to face problems of high transaction costs in lending to large numbers of small

---

16/   In some cases homestead lands and other assets were accepted as collateral.

farmers. The underlying issue is access to information that allows loan officers to adequately evaluate risks which have co-variance and avoid problems of adverse selection and moral hazard. One strategy to help address this issue that may prove attractive is for them to develop as a second tier institution providing funds to intermediary organizations that deal directly with farmers. This is a model that has worked elsewhere and, by reducing transactions costs, increasing loan size and improving repayment rates, would help secure their commercial viability.

9.41   The absence of freehold or secure long lease title to land has received considerable attention as a constraint on farm investment and access to farm credit. Many of the front lands (generally those lands in the first 2 miles from the sea coast) are held privately but lands developed through the land development schemes are commonly held as leasehold.[17]   The Lands and Surveys Department estimate that, on all publicly owned land, 30,000 farm households will benefit from land reform. In moving to freehold or long leasehold the valuation of land will be determined according to criteria of location, land capability and services provided, i.e., the quality of D&I and infrastructure. This valuation will then provide the basis for determining an appropriate value for market sale of the land to current operators or to grant them a long term lease which will allow them to use their land as collateral for credit. A critical and sensitive issue in this process is an adjustment to the market value of the land to reflect the land development efforts undertaken by the leaseholder. A further complication is that present leasing arrangements are sometimes complex with many cases of sub-leasing or second leases granted where land has been abandoned. This also raises the question of what constitutes an economic size of holding, particularly given the high dependence on bulky farm machinery which is often too large for smallholders to operate cost-effectively except through leasing of pooling arrangements. Despite these problems the previous government developed a tentative program for the transfer of leasehold land into freehold starting with the smallholders. The implementation of this has not occurred and it is not clear yet what steps are to be taken with respect to granting improved tenurial status. Plans are being drawn up currently but the Lands and Surveys Department does not have the resources to rapidly implement any scheme at present. Experience from other countries demonstrates that land reforms, such as are being proposed in Guyana, are politically and administratively very difficult. In particular, valuation, deed registration and compensation arrangements are susceptible to widespread abuse. If Guyana is to avoid such pitfalls it will need strong and clear political commitment, a transparent publicly accountable set of procedures and a high level of integrity from the public servants responsible for implementation. A priority need is to make available the financial resources necessary for the Lands and Surveys Department to act upon plans when they are finalized.

9.42   Support for a number of other activities has already been identified as a pre-requisite for sustained growth of rice production in Guyana. Most important of these are the strengthening of rice research, (including seed production), and agricultural extension services. Although farmers do not face an absolute shortage of seed since they self provision, it

---

17/   The MMA is an important example where there are some 8-9,000 farmers. Initially, they were only granted annual leases and now there is a move to increase these leases to 25 years.

is clear that access to the most recent improved seed (Guyana 91) is at present still limited. This is a blast resistant variety developed by NARI from international germ plasm and, though not without problems particularly relating to fertilizer dosage, promises to make an important contribution to yield enhancement in Guyana. With FAO support, seed production is currently being enhanced but more resources are needed to continue this program after 1993 and to further expand it. Also, beyond the regional programs (CARICOM) which relate to non-rice activities, there is no external funding in the pipeline for NARI beyond 1993. As discussed above, there seems to be a legitimate case for support for NARI; particularly if Guyana 91 is adopted widely, it will have made an important contribution to growth in production and export earnings. Moreover, continuing variety improvement and maintenance research will be necessary to sustain improved levels of rice production.

9.43   Extension services are receiving limited support through local funding in the capital investment program. Further strengthening of extension services is a necessary corollary of support for NARI. With the return of the extension services to the Crops and Livestock Department the links between research and extension will become better, and, as NARI provides relevant output, the need for strong extension service will become greater. This is particularly true as the new varieties, illustrated by the case of Guyana 91, are usually more sensitive to exact agronomic practice and there is need for farmer education in husbandry techniques.

9.44   Fisheries, livestock and other crops will have an increasingly important contribution to make to the development of Guyanese agriculture. With support from CIDA the fisheries sub-sector made considerable progress during the 1980s and growth prospects have been improved through the liberalization program. CIDA are developing an assistance strategy for strategic sectoral support focusing on local institutional strengthening and manpower development; this is likely to enhance the ability of the Fisheries Department to address their priority needs of strengthening policy formulation and management capability for the Guyanese fisheries. However, there are conflicting views on the size of the fisheries resource and further growth in this sector will very much depend on establishing the real potential for increases in the sustainable catch. On shrimp production, there is also a question mark concerning export potential as international competition and domestic pond aquaculture restrict the opportunities for Guyanese shrimp exports. In the livestock sector the principal success to date has been the National Dairy Development Program and modest capital investments are included in the financing plan for the agriculture sector to further capitalise on this success. The priority is to achieve self-sufficiency in milk and milk products through improved breeds, improved forage and gradual adoption of improved systems of stock management. The focus is on smallholders rather than on large enterprise development as this strategy complements rice farmers' and part-time farmers' livelihoods strategies. Other developments within the livestock sector, particularly growth in beef, pork and poultry products, are likely to take longer in the face of foreign competition for both domestic and regional markets and the difficulties being faced in promotion of regional exports of beef. Nevertheless, private sector initiatives are being encouraged with the long-term goal of developing the cattle ranching potential of the Savannahs.

9.45   Relative to the fisheries and milk production sub-sectors which make substantial contributions to foreign exchange earnings (or savings) the other crops sub-sector currently makes a modest contribution of just over US$1 million. However, it is vital to recognize that the medium and long term development of Guyanese agriculture is crucially dependent upon diversification of the export base and the other crops subsector is fundamental to this. So far, only pineapple exports have provided significant export earnings and demonstrated growth potential.[18/] Much depends on the tissue culture program at NARI being able to produce agronomically suitable varieties that are available in sufficient quantities for widescale commercial adoption. The new Guyana Marketing Corporation, although severely under-resourced, is identifying the key constraints to sector development and prioritizing investment to release these constraints. Crucial amongst these are the transport limitations facing exporters who wish to supply the lucrative North American and European markets. As these are released through investment in the transport infrastructure and through development at the airport, allowing adequate storage provision and trans-shipment by large planes, the potential growth rate is high. Ultimately this may prove to be an important hedge against the uncertainties associated with the long-term availability of large rice and sugar export markets which currently enjoy protected status.

F. PROPOSED STRATEGY

9.46   In developing an expenditure strategy, the Ministry of Agriculture, like other line ministries, must acknowledge its dependence on external sources of funding. Whilst there is a clear commitment from the Government for the prioritization of agriculture it is very difficult to translate such a commitment into substantial incremental funding because of the overall financial constraints. There are very limited opportunities for further divestiture in the agriculture sector, and, as discussed above, whilst there are opportunities for cost recovery these are unlikely to be significant in the short term. Nonetheless, cost recovery for delivery of irrigation and drainage services remains an important intermediate objective for the sustainable development of the agriculture sector. In the short term, recognizing the dependence on external funding, there are three important considerations that must inform development of an expenditure strategy.

9.47   First, it is important to recognize that donor confidence is very heavily influenced by overall macroeconomic performance; specifically, if donors are persuaded that there is a disciplined commitment to meeting balance of payments objectives and overall public sector borrowing objectives they are more likely to be convinced that investments in the real economy will achieve a reasonable rate of return. The commitment of the Government of Guyana to observing targets with respect to these two key indicators, and with respect to monetary discipline and the promotion of private sector initiative, are crucial to the maintenance of confidence in any specific sectoral public investment strategy.

9.48   Second, the agriculture sector historically has received very substantial sums from donors, particularly through land development schemes. These investments have been extremely poorly managed and there is a great deal of donor fatigue with large investment programs for agricultural development.

18/   Though heart of palm exports during the last 2 years have suggested the ability of new crops to be added to this list.

Central to the problems has been the poor management of the D&I systems. Prospects for substantial donor support depend very much on conviction that the Government will implement the radical institutional reforms necessary to make sustainable and efficient use of D&I resources and promote cost recovery mechanisms.

9.49   Third, the Ministry of Agriculture must recognize as well that donors have specific preferences. These emerge either as a consequence of their history of involvement in the agricultural development of Guyana or through their assessment of what they have done best elsewhere or because of specific domestic industrial or human resource endowments they wish to capitalise on. Canadian support for the fisheries sector in Guyana is a case in point. For this reason, it would be necessary to accommodate some degree of mis-match between aggregate sectoral priorities and the specific set of activities that gets supported through external funding. This is not likely to be a seriously contentious issue but points to the need for sensitivity in negotiating external support.

9.50   Credibility with the donors also depends crucially on having a strategic approach to sector development with clearly identified roles for the public and private sectors, strategies for dealing with problems of absorptive capacity and commitment to cost recovery where feasible. There must be a clearly identified set of priorities and a vision of where the sector is going. Within the agricultural sector, the overwhelming importance of relaxing current production constraints to sectoral growth dictates a hierarchy of priorities as follows:

> **Priority 1:   Sustainable Rehabilitation of D&I Systems**
>
> **Priority 2:   Support for short-term productive capacity;**
>
> **Priority 3:   Enhancement and diversification of the production base.**

9.51   Sustainable rehabilitation of the D&I systems must have precedence over everything else. Such an effort involves principally, **rehabilitation of the D&I infrastructure.** However, currently, no donor support exists for such rehabilitation[19] and it is unlikely that donor support will be forthcoming in the absence of **improved operations and maintenance of the D&I systems.** Crucially, this requires radical institutional reform to improve the complex and muddled system of joint responsibilities within single systems that now prevails. Rehabilitation of the physical infrastructure and improvement of operations and maintenance of the D&I systems must be considered as complementary efforts. There is little prospect of the favorable growth performance of the last couple of years being maintained for very much longer unless both investment resources for rehabilitation are forthcoming and institutional reform of operations and maintenance is realized. However, once D&I systems are rehabilitated, **cost recovery** is imperative to ensure their sustainability.

---

[19]/   A number of externally-supported D&I rehabilitation investment projects have recently finished, or because of delayed disbursement, are about to finish so far as donor funding is concerned, including IFAD and IDB projects in East Essequibo and Black Bush.

9.52   A crucial element in supporting the <u>second priority</u>, strengthening short term productive capacity, is the strengthening of planning capabilities within the Ministry of Agriculture. At present, departments draw up their own plans with their own view of priorities and there is little opportunity for central coordination according to strategic goals. The Planning Department itself is often not involved in these activities; also, ad hoc planning activities occur through donor activity and through advisers to the Minister. Enhancement of resources for the Planning Division and a stronger role for the Division in drawing up current and capital expenditure plans is a necessary element in the coherent development of the sector. A complementary need is the reform of the budget process to allow Ministry of Agriculture priorities to be properly reflected in budgetary allocations. At present this does not happen; and the action proposed (see below) involves three specific changes in the budget and finance arrangement of the Ministry of Agriculture which will facilitate a more coherent planning process.

9.53   Considerable resources are needed as well to strengthen the data base on which such planning can take place. At present, there is little information available concerning important dimensions of the agriculture sector, such as the number of rice farmers, average farm sizes, costs of production and rates of return on different types of farm investment. Substantial survey work needs to be undertaken urgently. Such studies should be prioritized in relation to the hierarchy of priorities described above. Therefore, a first concern would be an inventory of rehabilitation investment needs for the drainage and irrigation infrastructure. The second priority would be a series of rice production studies. These would seek to identify the costs and returns for different socio-economic groups of farmers and different agro-ecological production conditions taking account of the different technologies employed by farmers in rice production. This is not as onerous as that description may sound since there is a relatively high degree of homogeneity in rice production conditions in Guyana. In support of this latter study and in order to interpret the results it is crucial that support be found also for the conduct of an agricultural census even if only on a sample census basis in the first instance. The last sample census was 1978 and there have been significant changes in the agricultural sector since then.

9.54   Closely related to these planning considerations is the need to rehabilitate the Hydrometeorological Department; data collection needs for agricultural planning and investment are easily ignored when expenditure constraints are tight. This has happened in Guyana and the Hydrometeorology Department is virtually incapacitated at present. In addition to agricultural benefits, air and sea transport services would be major beneficiaries from strengthening of the Department. Whilst there are rehabilitation requirements in all departments it is clear that Hydrometeorology has suffered worse than most. Very substantial investment requirements were identified during the recent WMO mission; the proposed expenditure here is a modest first step in addressing the prioritization of constraints identified in that mission.

9.55   Finally, strengthening short-term capacity also includes reforms related to the rice sector, in particular:

•   **land reform** - addressing the need for either freehold or long term leasehold of rice lands.

- **improving credit services** - to rice farmers especially small farmers.

9.56   The third priority, enhancement and diversification of the production base, has several elements which can contribute to considerably improved productivity in agriculture once the first two priorities have been adequately addressed. On **enhancement**, research and extension are obviously important components. These two activities depend very much on progress with the first two priorities in order for them to realize producer benefits and, ultimately, to allow at lest some element of cost recovery. Also important is the need to review the current institutional arrangements (GREB, GRMMA and NPRGC) for rice marketing, grading and export. It is likely that, with the revitalization of the Rice Producers Association (RPA) a realignment of responsibilities is appropriate and this should be studied. Looking to the medium term, another element in the strategy must be to address the eventual need for **diversification** of the production base. Both rice and sugar production depend on protective markets which may not always be there; also, as domestic incomes grow and as the transport infrastructure improves allowing easier access to export markets, there will be enhanced demand for other crops and for non-crop agricultural output. Although this element is a lower priority than the needs identified for enhanced rice production it is an area of great potential for private sector development; it can be promoted by relatively modest public investment in research, seed sales and support for processing services and market intelligence.

G. ACTION PLAN

9.57   To implement the strategy outlined above, and to improve opportunities for cost recovery, the following action plan is proposed (Box 9.2). The first type of action involves active pursuit of funding for investments. These funds should first be directed towards rehabilitation of D&I infrastructure. However, for this to result in sustainable improvement in crop output or better cost recovery it must be accompanied by improved service delivery.

9.58   The proposed investment plan also involves additional resources for (i) credit, (ii) land reform, (iii) agricultural planning, and (iv) hydrometeorology. These are critical complementary investments addressing the second priority, support for short-term productive capacity. Within the limitations of absorptive capacity and financing constraints, investment in these areas represents the major opportunity to strengthen growth prospects and facilitate cost recovery. Investment relating to the third priority, enhancement and diversification of the production base, should be focused on agricultural research and extension. However, their contribution is largely contingent upon progress in the rehabilitation of D&I systems. For this reason, no further support on extension and on research has been specified in this plan beyond the resources already proposed to be made available by Government. The other major item addressed in the third tier of priorities is crop diversification. This is a medium-term goal which both extension and research will eventually need to focus on; however, no investment is being proposed in this area as it will be aided by support on export promotion from the new Guyana Marketing Corporation.

9.59   The <u>second type of actions</u> pertains to institutional reforms, in particular:

- Establishment of a ministerial task force to make specific and detailed proposals on institutional reforms of D&I operations and maintenance.

- Strengthening the Agricultural Planning and Budget Process.

9.60   <u>D&I Operations and Maintenance Task Force</u>. Enabling legislation will be necessary in order to implement the radical institutional reforms likely to be needed; this could easily become a slow process. The ministerial Task Force will provide the authority necessary in order to expedite the collection of information and views necessary for development of acceptable and workable institutional reforms. The Task Force drawing upon the successful experience of other countries, could also be instrumental to donors confidence that D&I rehabilitation investments would lead to sustainable improvements in rice production and that user fees would pay for D&I operations and maintenance service delivery.

9.61   <u>Strengthening Planning and Budget Process</u>. Whilst priority areas other than rehabilitation and efficient operations and maintenance of the D&I system have been identified above, the specific actions to be taken in pursuit of these priorities depends upon development of adequate plans. Strengthening of the Planning Division, as discussed above, is a core element in development of such plans and this need is reflected in the new expenditure priorities listed in the next section. However, the planning process will also be greatly enhanced by changes in the way in which the budget is prepared.[20] More specifically, the recommendation is to:

- revise the budget presentation forms so that the Ministry of Agriculture shows a functional prioritized budget. Very often the relevant departments do have priorities but these are not clearly reflected in the forms employed nor in the processes by which adjustments to financial constraints are made. By so doing it will be possible for the Ministry of Agriculture to make transparent what they can achieve with any specified level of funding.

- strengthen the internal accounting system within the Ministry. Currently, revenue and project funds are frequently used for current expenditure needs. The formal presentation of current budget estimates bears only a distant relationship to the actual expenditures undertaken. The Auditor General is already investigating ways of strengthening accounting within the Ministry with the support of the Finance Division and it is vital for effective budgeting that reforms recommended by this review are acted upon.

---

[20]   This is true for other line ministries also. Of course, the changes discussed also require action on the part of the Ministry of Finance, responsible for issuing the forms currently being used in the budget planning exercise.

Box 9.2: **ACTION PLAN:** **AGRICULTURE SECTOR PUBLIC INVESTMENT PRIORITIES**

1. **Sustainable Rehabilitation of D&I Systems**

   - Drainage and Irrigation Rehabilitation
   - Institutional Reform to improve Operation and Maintenance of Drainage and Irrigation Systems
     - ••Ministerial Task Force
     - ••Enabling Legislation
     - ••Equipment and Facilities Investment
   - Cost Recovery for Sustainability

2. **Support for Short-term Productive Capacity**

   - Strengthen Agricultural Planning

   - Land Reform granting long Leasehold or Freehold on farm land under public ownership

   - Improving institutional credit services to farmers through recapitalization and reform of Gaibank

   - Rehabilitation of the Hydrometeorological Service

3. **Enhancement and Diversification of the Production Base**

   - Strengthening Agricultural Extension Services

   - Support for the National Agricultural Research Institute

   - Crop Diversification: Research, Seed Sales and Support for processing services and market intelligence

   - Review Institutional arrangements for Rice Marketing, Grading and Export

---

- handle contributions to international organizations through a separate budgetary heading under the auspices of the Ministry of Finance (see paragraph 9.24).

9.62   Adopting these changes will provide some salience to the budgetary process which is often now regarded as a futile planning exercise. Whilst the changes cannot of themselves help to address the resource constraints they can certainly demonstrate the impact of specific budgetary cuts and help the Ministry to specify what the priorities are using those limited resources that are available.

9.63   A _third type of actions_ relates to the implementation of studies. The Government has already drawn-up terms of reference for three studies in response to loan conditionality associated with the IDB Agriculture Sector Hybrid Loan relating to:

- improvement of water control management;
- the restructuring of Gaibank; and
- rice price policy, sector performance and competitiveness.

9.64   These are important initiatives which can lay the foundations for an effective response to some of the priorities identified. However, the study on water management does not adequately reflect the urgency of the need for improvement in water management and the complexity of achieving this objective.[21/] Hence, the terms of reference should be redesigned and the study should be used to facilitate the work of the Task Force proposal above. The other two studies are adequate. Farm credit investment, involving recapitalization of Gaibank and reform of its operating procedures, will be facilitated by the Restructuring study. The rice study will provide evidence on the distribution of benefits from price and exchange rate liberalization. It will allow informed assessment of what anti-monopoly actions, if any, are required in rice processing and marketing. It should mean that desired changes in institutional arrangements can be identified; since such changes will be low cost they may be implemented relatively quickly if firm evidence of desirable changes is produced. Nonetheless, this need has been deliberately placed third. There is good reason to believe that competitive private sector investment may obviate any need for specific anti-monopoly action, particularly if GRMMA, and now also the RPA, continue to monitor and report rice price movements.

H.   PROPOSED INVESTMENT PROGRAM

9.65   Based on the existing investment planned and the priority needs identified in this chapter the proposed expenditure plan is outlined in Table 9.9. The funded investment program for agriculture has very limited expenditures proposed for the first priority, D&I rehabilitation. Realistically, given the dependence on external support and the need to develop a specific program approach to addressing this priority, substantial investment cannot be anticipated before 1995. The program therefore involves modest funding for technical assistance for constitutional strengthening in 1994 leading to investment in physical works over the following years. The technical assistance should support the activities of the ministerial Task Force proposed above for determining appropriate institutional reform of the D&I operations and maintenance.

9.66   There are three other new expenditures indicated. Financing needs identified on planning and hydrometeorology reflect the requirements for studies, for establishment of a broader, more reliable long-term data base relating to agriculture and for an overall strengthening of planning capacity within the Ministry of Agriculture. The investments proposed specifically accommodate estimates of rehabilitation needs for the Planning and Hydrometeorology Departments. The other new investment proposed is for land reform. Land reform cannot be successfully pursued without substantial strengthening of the Lands and Surveys Department. This involves rehabilitation of their office infrastructure and funds for contracting

---

21/   As presently designed, the study is to be conducted by engineers whereas there is a crucial need for institutional development specialists, including people with extensive experience of cost recovery in other countries, to be centrally involved in all the regional studies.

private sector survey and valuation work as well as the substantial costs directly associated with the complex task of awarding freehold or long leasehold title to farmers currently operating on short leases. Finally, credit investments are left undetermined in view of the questionable performance of Gaibank whilst forming part of the proposed sector strategy.

9.67   The investment plan addresses the all the types of action specified in the Action Plan as necessary to implement the first and second priorities. Initial investments are very modest in financial terms but lay the foundations for larger investments to follow. Actions falling under the third priority, enhancement and diversification of the production base, are already addressed to some extent through current commitments. No further investment on these needs is warranted until the financing needs of the Ministry of Agriculture priorities have been met.

Table 9.9: PROPOSED AGRICULTURAL PUBLIC INVESTMENT PROGRAM
(US$ 1000)

Project	Budgeted 1993	1994	1995	1996	Agency
Ongoing Projects	11550.5	10180.1	7274.0	3334.7	
Agricultural Rehabilitation	5143.4	6639.8	3908.4	0.0	IDB
Fishery Equipment Facility	1686.1	0.0	0.0	0.0	CIDA
Natl. Agri. Res. Inst. (NARI)	1039.0	916.3	996.0	996.0	UNDP
East Bank Essequibo Dev. Prj.	1521.9	0.0	0.0	0.0	IFAD
East Bank Berbice Irr. Works	494.0	0.0	0.0	0.0	Other
Artificial Insem. Prog.	39.8	31.9	33.5	35.1	Local/PAP
Extension Svcs., Agri.	159.4	358.6	517.9	557.8	Local/PAP
Agriculture Equipment	14.3	0.0	0.0	0.0	Local/PAP
Land Registration	49.4	39.8	42.2	43.8	Local/PAP
Geodetic Survey	26.3	14.3	15.1	16.7	Local/PAP
Drainage and Irrig. (Regions)	195.2	557.8	637.5	717.1	Local
Black Bush Polder Rehab.	318.7	637.5	239.0	278.9	Local
Mahaica-Mahalcony-Abary Proj.	310.8	438.2	517.9	557.8	Local
Forestry Studies	159.4	255.0	239.0	0.0	Local
Rehab. of Drain. & Irr. Areas	286.9	159.4	0.0	0.0	Local
Hydrometeorological Svcs.	39.8	119.5	119.5	119.5	Local
Plant & Animal Quarantine	15.9	12.0	8.0	12.0	Local
Agriculture Development (Regions)	19.1	0.0	0.0	0.0	Local
Land & Agriculture Development	31.1	0.0	0.0	0.0	Local
New Projects (Identified)	651.8	1171.3	0.0	0.0	
Agri. Hybrid Loan (TCC 877)	651.8	1171.3	0.0	0.0	IDB
Total (Identified)	12202.3	11351.4	7274.0	3334.7	
New Projects (Unidentified)	0.0	0.0	3513.9	5625.5	
Hydromet. Services	0.0	0.0	215.1	111.6	
Drainage and Irrigation	0.0	0.0	2199.2	4414.3	
Land Reform - Long Lease/Freehold	0.0	0.0	1099.6	1099.6	
TOTAL	12202.3	11351.4	10787.9	8960.2	
Memorandum Item:a/	0.0	500.0	500.0	500.0	
D&I Inst. Stren. (T.A.)	0.0	300.0	300.0	300.0	
Stren. Agr. Plan. (T.A.)	0.0	200.0	200.0	200.0	
GRAND TOTAL	12202.3	11851.4	11287.9	9460.2	

a/ PSIP does not include Technical Assistance.

Source: Mission Estimates

CHAPTER X. SEA AND RIVER DEFENSES

A. INTRODUCTION

10.1   The vast majority of Guyana's economic activities (except mining and forestry) take place in a narrow coastal strip where over 90% of the population lives. Since most of this land lies between the high and low tidal levels, it is subject to flooding. Therefore the residential and cultivated areas are protected by a sea wall, which dates back to the eighteenth century. Sea defense is necessarily given a high priority by both the Government of Guyana and its donor agencies. For the next 3 to 5 years, some US$50 million has been allocated to the rehabilitation of the most critical sections in the old sea walls.

B. SECTOR OVERVIEW

1. The Coastline

10.2   The total length of the coast line is about 530 km. In the western region Barima-Waini (Region 1), there is a natural transition between land and sea via mangrove beaches. In the other, more densely populated coastal regions (2 to 6), a sea defense was built because the natural protection did not suffice to prevent flooding. For over 200 km earth dams have been constructed. At the other sections (in total about 100 km), the beach is eroded to levels below low water tide and the mangrove have disappeared. Prior to this time, the earthen dikes in these sections had been protected against erosion from wave attack but are now open to such deterioration. Table 10.1 shows the preliminary results from an inventory of the sea defenses, carried out in 1992 with EDF funding.

10.3   Although the hydraulic and geotechnical conditions are similar along the entire coast of Guyana, the sea defenses vary considerably in design character (type of protection, copings, toe construction) and dimensions (crest width, levels, slope inclinations). Most striking is the fluctuation of the dike crest elevations within short distances. The variety of sea walls dates back to the early days of land reclamation, when each landowner was responsible for their own sea defense. Two decades of low-budget maintenance and patchwork amid ongoing foreshore erosion, have added sheet-piles, boulders, sand-cement bags, gabions and mass concrete fill to the diversity of protection works.

2. Breaches and Overtopping

10.4   Breaches in the sea defenses usually occur during high spring tide, in particular when high tide coincides with wind-set-up, long waves (swell), and the strong inland winds, i.e., mainly in the period from October to March. When weak spots in the defense fail, an area is flooded and salt water enters the drainage canals. In many areas the coastal road limits the area that is flooded, and the flood water can be drained off during low tide because the land lies above the low water level.

10.5   Overtopping is the spill of waves over the crest of the sea walls.
It occurs both in gushes and spray.   In the past, overtopping has been a
normal phenomena along the sea defenses in Guyana.   For example, the
Hydraulics Division reports regular overtopping in Region 2, of 11 of the 45
km (25%) of the sea wall.

Table 10.1:   SEA DEFENSES INVENTORY

	Natural km	Earth dam km	Concrete km	Boulders km	Other km	Total km
Region 1	183.4	–	–	–	–	183.4
Region 2	9.4	17.6	15.7	4.8	6.6	54.1
Region 3	–	10.8	18.7	–	0.1	29.6
Region 4	–	29.9	31.2	–	–	61.0
Region 5	–	37.7	–	–	0.7	38.4
Region 6	24.5	56.0	1.1	–	1.7	83.3
Leguan	–	31.5	4.9	–	–	36.4
Wakenaam	–	41.2	3.2	–	–	44.4
Total	217.3	224.7	74.8	4.8	9.1	530.5
Excluding R1	33.9	224.7	74.8	4.8	9.1	347.2

Legend:
Natural   The natural sea defense consists of mangrove beach
Earth dam   Earth fill dikes, usually with a grass and clay cover
Concrete   Dikes with a protection of reinforced, not reinforced, or grouted
               boulders
Boulders   Boulder slopes include only engineered (designed) sea walls
               Emergency works are listed under "Other"
Other   Temporary works like emergency rock fill (without filter cloth),
               gabions, mass concrete fill and sheet piles

Note: Lengths are measured along a baseline. Lengths over the sea defense
        center lines will in general be slightly more.

Source: Hydraulics Division

10.6   Breaches as well as overtopping of the sea defenses cause
substantial damage to the coastal areas.   The immediate consequences of
breaches are:

- the loss of incidental field crops due to saline incursion;
- the loss of subsequent crop yields due to infertile (saline) soil
  (usually for about one year);
- damage to the infrastructure and houses;
- the loss of livestock and kitchen-garden crops;
- damage to pit-latrines; and
- damage to the sea wall itself.

Loss of life due to breaches in the sea defense is rare in Guyana. Consequences of overtopping of the sea defenses are:

- extended loss of fertility of the areas immediately behind the sea walls; and
- ongoing erosion of the crest and land side slopes of the sea wall.

An indirect effect of flooding and overtopping is a lack of interest from farmers and industry in investment in the affected areas which they consider to be unsafe.

3. Rehabilitation and Maintenance Works

10.7 Budgetary constraints and the lack of qualified staff resulted in a rising number of sea breaches until 1990 when 49 occurred. Since that time, the Hydraulics Division (HD) has received more aid from donor agencies (EDF and USAID). This increased support to Guyana's Infrastructure Rehabilitation Program (IRP) enabled the Hydraulics Division to reduce the number of breaches to about 4 per year during 1991-92. However, under the IRP only patchwork repair has been carried out and the overall condition of the sea wall is still deteriorating. A more sustainable approach would require a major rehabilitation program. This fact has been recognized by a number of donors who have committed themselves to substantial funding in this sector.

10.8 *Capital works* on the sea defenses are necessary for the following reasons:

- Many of the sea walls have served more than their design lifetime. Some structures are on the verge of collapse because the materials have degraded and erosion has undermined concrete slabs and copings (parapets). The backlog in rehabilitation works is about 20 years.

- Ongoing foreshore erosion continues to extend the length of the coastline that requires protection against flooding.

10.9 The backlog in rehabilitation works will require a few decades to be recouped. In the meantime, the more recently constructed sea walls will continue to age and wear. For medium term planning, the rehabilitation of the sea defenses will therefore have to be considered a continuous activity. At the same time, the *maintenance requirements* will remain high for the coming decades, because there is a severe backlog in the maintenance of all the sea defenses and deteriorated (not yet rehabilitated) sea defenses require more intensive maintenance. The rise of the sea level causes a number of additional problems namely:

- the increase in tidal levels necessitates the raising of dike crests;
- higher waves reach the dikes, demanding a further increase in dike crest elevations as well as a strengthening of the dike protection; and
- the likely change in coastal morphology will result in more foreshore erosion with the effects noted above.

4. River Defenses

10.10   In addition to sea defenses, there are over 400 km of river defenses. Although a systematic record does not exist, it is believed that breaches of protected banks are rare and that any damage is usually limited. Therefore the strengthening of river defenses is considered of secondary importance for short term planning. In the long-term, some river banks will probably require more permanent protection at outer bends. For planning purposes an inventory of the river defenses will be required.

5. Sluices

10.11   The land behind the sea defenses is drained via drainage structures or sluices in the sea wall. Over 300 such sluices exist, most of which are very old and are constructed of concrete and/or wood which has degraded. Only about half of the sluices are still operational and some of these leak, allowing salt water to enter the drainage channels.

10.12   Although the purpose of the sluices relates to drainage, their function as water retaining structures cannot be disregarded. Up to the present, only a few breaches in the sea defense have been caused by failure of a sluice, but the old structures represent weak spots in the sea defense. Rehabilitation and sealing of many of the structures will have to be considered in medium and long-term planning. Obviously such a program requires coordination with the drainage requirements of the hinterland.

C. INSTITUTIONAL AND REGULATORY FRAMEWORK

1. Current Responsibilities of the Hydraulics Division

10.13   After independence, the maintenance of the sea defenses was the responsibility of regional authorities, while capital works resided under the Hydraulics Division. With the revision of the Sea Defense Act in 1988, the maintenance of the sea defenses is again centralized in the Hydraulics Division of the Ministry of Agriculture. The Hydraulics Division has its main office in Georgetown and a number of regional offices with work shops and stores. The division is headed by the Chief Hydraulics Officer (CHO). Apart from sea defense, the Hydraulics Division is also responsible for capital works for drainage and irrigation (D&I) and sluices.

10.14   The sea defense tasks of the Hydraulics Division consist of:

- Maintenance, including monitoring, design, emergency response, contracting to local contractors and supervision.

- Fulfilling the role of Contracting Authority (CA) for the contractors that will be attracted through International Contract Bidding (ICB), including:
  - selection and supervision of consultants in all stages of the project;
  - review and approval of contract documents presented by consultants;
  - award of tenders, approval of payments, variation orders etc;
  - participation in site meetings;

- - liaison in relation to responsibilities on the side of the Government of Guyana related to custom arrangements, borrow areas, quarries, administration, etc.
- - protection of the interests of the Government of Guyana and liaison with donor agencies in contractual disputes and financial claims.

- Management and administration, including:
  - - identification of priorities and strategies in the sea defense areas;
  - - accounting;
  - - coordination between donor agencies;
  - - development and conservation of expertise and information related to the sea defenses; and
  - - logistical, financial and administrative functions.

10.15   The tasks identified above require engineering, legal and management expertise. However, like other public institutions, the Hydraulics Division organization has suffered severely from the departure of capable engineers, administrators and managers. In light of the donor funded rehabilitation programs that are about to start, it must be concluded that the Hydraulics Division is not equipped to meet its tasks.

10.16   One of the immediate negative effects of the lack of qualified staff within the Hydraulics Division has been the growing delay in donor funded rehabilitation projects. It is not expected that these projects will show much visible impact in 1993, and unless the institutional framework in the sector is strengthened the delays in project implementation may stretch well into 1994. This need has been recognized by the donors who have made institutional strengthening a pre-condition for the rehabilitation programs. The recommended approach for this strengthening is the establishment of a Project Execution Unit (PEU), which will become responsible for the maintenance as well as the rehabilitation of the sea and river defenses.

2.   Suggested Responsibilities of the PEU

10.17   In response to the critical situation in the sea defense sector, the ministries involved (Finance, Agriculture) decided to prepare a proposal for cabinet approval to establish a PEU with considerable autonomy. At the same time, donors tentatively agreed on the institution of only one such unit to suit the requirements (conditions) of all donors.[22/] The Government of Guyana will still have to reach an agreement with the donors on the exact design of the PEU and the role it will play for the donor funded rehabilitation projects. A tentative proposal for the establishment of the PEU and the related legal and organizational reforms has already been drafted (Technical Note No.2). Its main features are:

- The PEU will have three sections: (i) sea defense maintenance; (ii) contracting of (donor funded) rehabilitation works and special projects; and (iii) accounting.

22/   Based on a meeting in Guyana on December 17, 1992; a further meeting is scheduled for March, 1993.

- The PEU employees will be recruited at market rates for capable staff. Compensations will include good salaries (higher than the current public service salaries), mobilization fees (if recruited from abroad), and career plans (based on a human resources development plans).

- The number of employees will be kept small, to minimize the salary cost of the PEU

- The staff will be recruited as much as possible on a long term or permanent basis and the following preference ranking is adopted for the origin of qualified staff:

    (1)   Guyana;
    (2)   CARICOM countries; and
    (3)   Other.

- The establishment of the PEU will be contracted to a consultant to give it the required impetus.

- The Hydraulics Division's role in carrying out sea defense repair and maintenance works will be taken over gradually by the private construction sector in Guyana.

- The PEU will have considerable autonomy in the allocation of budget, in contracting of works to the private sector, and in developing staff policies.

- There will be a phased transition from the current to the new organization.

10.18   The EC has shown a willingness to contribute to the financing of such a PEU. In order to ensure the commitment of other donors it is recommended that at least one of the other donors involved in the sector (IDB, IDA and CDB) co-finance or co-staff the PEU. Also, the donors that will not contribute directly to the PEU, would have to confirm that:

- They will concentrate their expert and administrative services in this PEU.

- This PEU is accepted as a sufficient institution in accordance with their loan conditions, and that it can act as the Contracting Authority for their rehabilitation program.

10.19   The institution of such a PEU will require the Government to initiate a number of legal reforms, to legalize its authority in sea defense policies, staffing and budgeting.

3.   Suggested Responsibilities of the Hydraulics Division

10.20   The establishment of a PEU for river and sea defenses implies that the responsibilities of the Hydraulics Division will be considerably reduced. Existing functions of the Hydraulics Division that will continue for some time are:

- management of the Hydraulics Division's equipment, workshops and stores until these have been phased out as part of a privatization program; and
- drainage, irrigation and sluices.[23]

10.21   The responsibilities of the Hydraulics Division, the Ministry of Agriculture and other governmental organizations with respect to the operation and maintenance of drainage works, irrigation works and sluices will be reviewed in line with recommendations in Chapter IX (Agriculture). Substantial reorganizations are foreseen, and therefore it is expected that the Hydraulics Division in its current form, will be either replaced, or fully restructured within the coming 5 years. The function of the CHO as a coordinator, policy maker and advisor to the ministries would be maintained until the new authorities (for sea defense, drainage, irrigation and sluices) have proven themselves. The CHO will also be in charge of designing a national sea defense policy.

4. Accountability, Authority and Autonomy

10.22   The Hydraulics Division's accounts have a reputation for lack of transparency. Although theoretical budgets exist, the distribution of costs over projects, staff, materials or regions is not at all clear. Furthermore, there is no systematic record of the results of various activities. Hence, donor agencies, unable to identify the outcome of their inputs, discontinue funding. Therefore, the establishment of a transparent and rational accounting system will be a high priority for the new PEU.

D. SECTOR FINANCES

1. General Considerations

10.23   Guyana's budgetary constraints dominate the decision making for the sea defense rehabilitation and maintenance. An economic feasibility study executed under EDF funding by DHV from the Netherlands[24], concluded that the full rehabilitation of the sea defenses and the implementation of adequate maintenance systems is economically justified. However, the shortage of funds will not allow this to be accomplished in the near future.

10.24   Presently a substantial part of donor funds is already allocated to sea defense rehabilitation. Nevertheless, with given allocations, the rehabilitation of all existing sea defenses will take a few decades to complete. At the same time, drainage and irrigation and other sectors also require substantial funding. Although there is no comprehensive general policy addressing priorities, it is safe to assume that a substantial increase in expenditures for sea defenses is not viable.

23/   Rehabilitation schemes for sluices should be coordinated with the PEU, to ensure their function as part of the sea defense.

24/   DHV Environment and Infrastructure, funded by EC/EDF under Lomé III/IV Convention.

2. Maintenance

10.25   A study by DHV has identified minimum maintenance requirements for the sea defenses. The associated costs are on the order of G$600 million per annum. Again these requirements exceed the available budget and it must be expected that the necessary maintenance will not be carried out in the coming 2 to 5 years. As a consequence of the financial situation and the backlog in rehabilitation works, overtopping and breaches will continue to occur, and further deterioration of the sea defenses will not be prevented.

3. Recent Donor Funding

10.26   Since 1988 donors have funded a number of projects related to the sea defense (Table 10.2). Without this funding, the Hydraulics Division would not have been operational.

Table 10.2: SUMMARY OF DONOR PROGRAMS UNTIL 1992

Funding	Identifi-cation	Allocated Funds US$ million	Remarks
EDF	Lomé III (IRP)	5.0	Provision of Materials, Equipment and Technical Assistance
USAID	Title 3	5.0	1991 and 1992 budgets
IDB	Hybrid	0.1	Preparation of Design Tender Documents
IDA		0.1	Technical Assistance
UNDP	Volunteers	0.1	3 Engineers
VSO	Volunteers	0.1	1 Engineer

Source: Donors and Hydraulics Division

- EDF has supported the IRP with three main activities related to the sea defense sector: provision of materials to the Hydraulics Division, provision of materials to the quarry sector and technical assistance to the Hydraulics Division. Furthermore, the EC has contracted with a consultancy company for the preparation of tender documents for the rehabilitation of 11 km of sea defense (see Section 4).

- IDB has completed the tender documents for the rehabilitation of 6 km of sea defense. It is expected that soon a consultant will be selected for the preparation of tender procedures (see Section 4).

- USAID has supported the sea defense sector since 1989. Disbursements have been on the order of: US$ 0.7, 0.75, 2.5 and 2.5 million in 1989, 1990, 1991 and 1992 respectively. Actually a substantial part of the running budget of the Hydraulics Division has been carried by these funds. The results of these inputs have not been monitored. Nevertheless, it is safe to conclude that the outcome was disappointing in terms of rehabilitated sea defense.

- **UNV** (United Nations Volunteers of UNDP) has assigned three engineers to the Hydraulics Division. These engineers work within the structure of the division and are involved in the sea defense maintenance, planning and administrative works.

- **VSO** (Voluntary Service Oversees of ODA/UK) has assigned one engineer to the Hydraulics Division until January 1993. This engineer has coordinated the design works within the Hydraulics Division and advised the CHO on technical matters.

- **IDA** has recently assigned a technical advisor to the CHO, to help get the rehabilitation programs started.

4. Future Donor Programs

10.27   Donors have committed themselves to substantial funding of this sector for the coming years. Table 10.3 provides a list of the identified financing arrangements. More details follow in the text.

Table 10.3: SUMMARY OF IDENTIFIED DONOR PROGRAMS

Funding	Identification	Allocated Funds US$ million	Remarks
Capital Works			
EDF	Lomé IV	17.0	11 km in Regions 2, 3
IDB	Hybrid	14.5	16 km in Regions 2, 6 and islands
CDB	8SFR-GU	4.7	5 km in Region 5
IDA	IRP	4.0	7 km in Region 3 or 4
Sub-total		40.2	39 km in Regions 2 to 6
Institutional Strengthening			
EDF	Lomé III	0.9	Counterpart Funds
EDF	Lomé III	0.6	Technical Assistance (extension)
EDF	Lomé IV	1.2	PEU
IDB	Hybrid	9.0	PEU, Studies and Supervision
USAID	Title 3	n.a.	BoP support (under review)
IDA	IRP	0.1	Technical Assistance (extension)
Sub-total		11.8	
Technical Assistance			
UNDP	Volunteers	0.1	3 Engineers (estimate)
VSO	Volunteers	0.0	1 Engineer (estimate)
Sub-total		0.1	
Special Studies			
IDA	IRP	1.8	Study (under review)
Sub-total		1.8	
Total Sector Support		53.9	

Note: The donors listed have indicated their commitment, but the amounts and/or the exact inputs (or length of the sea defense that will be rehabilitated) may be revised when final project designs and cost estimates have been prepared.
Source: Donor Agencies and Hydraulics Division

10.28   **EDF** is committed to the rehabilitation of 7 km of sea defense between La Resource and Golden Fleece in West Coast Essequibo (Region 2) and 5 km of sea defense between Le Destin and Windsor Forest in West Demarara

(Region 3). The project also includes support to the strengthening of the Hydraulics Division, i.e., the establishment of a PEU. EDF envisages that the rehabilitation of sea defenses in the first approach will cost between ECU10-12 million (US$13-16 million). An appraisal study has been requested for that rehabilitation program which covers not only the technical aspects (design, cost estimates and tender documents) but also the related institutional and organizational requirements (PEU organization, set-up and costs estimates). Draft reports from the study have been presented. The length of sea defense that can be rehabilitated within the available budget, also allowing for support to the PEU, is under review by the EC and the Government of Guyana.

10.29   The project funds have been allocated under Lomé IV convention. Presently consultants have been requested to adjust the proposed design to comply with the requirements of the Hydraulics Division. Tender Documents for International Contract Bidding (ICB) are expected mid 1993. The physical works are expected to start early 1994.

10.30   The most important conditions associated with the grant agreement are:

- institutional strengthening of the Hydraulics Division, i.e. the institution of a Project Execution Unit (PEU) for the maintenance of the sea defenses and as a Contracting Authority (CA) for all donor programs (see also Technical Note No.2);

- establishment of a committee for the coordination of all activities related to the rehabilitation and maintenance of the sea defenses in Guyana;

- commencement of maintenance of the sea defenses; and

- action by the Government of Guyana to achieve genuine prices for quarry products.

10.31   IDB is committed to the rehabilitation of some 3.2 km of sea defense between Bounty Hall and Reliance in West Demarara (Region 3) and some 2.8 km of sea defense between Harriet and New Calcutta in East Coast Essequibo (Region 6). The first tranche of the project funds (US$10 million) has been allocated under the Hybrid loan. The rehabilitation of another 10 km of sea defense is planned for a second stage. Presently the designs and Tender Documents for International Contract Bidding (ICB) are with the Hydraulics Division, who are reviewing the design. The capital works are expected to start in late 1993 or early 1994.

10.32   The most important conditions associated with the loan agreement that pertain to sea defenses are[25]:

- institutional strengthening of the Hydraulics Division, i.e. the institution of a PEU; and
- maintenance works to be carried out after completion

---

[25]/   There are a large number of other conditions which are not addressed here as they are mainly related to other sectors.

10.33 IDA is committed to the rehabilitation of some 7 km of sea defense between Turkeyn and Greenfield in Region 4, and Nismes to La Retraite at the west bank of the Demarara River. Presently the World Bank has assigned one Assistant to the CHO. The amount allocated to sea defense rehabilitation (US$ 5 million) is too little for the scheduled rehabilitation of 7 km of sea defense. Depending on the design works and the preparation of tender documents for ICB, the capital works may be expected to start mid-1994.

10.34 The most important conditions associated with the loan agreement are:

- institutional strengthening of the Hydraulics Division, i.e., the institution of a PEU; and
- maintenance works shall be carried out after completion.

10.35 CDB is committed to the rehabilitation of some 4.6 km of sea defense between Abary and Berbice rivers in West Coast Berbice (Region 5). The project also addresses deficiencies in the rice industry. The project funds have been allocated. Consultants have been short-listed for the preparation of designs and Tender Documents for ICB. The capital works are expected to start in early 1994.

10.36 The most important conditions associated with the loan agreement are:

- institutional strengthening of the Hydraulics Division, i.e., appointment of a Project Manager/Coordinator; and
- maintenance works shall be carried out after completion.

10.37 USAID has not yet decided on committing itself to further support to the Hydraulics Division for the repair and maintenance of the sea defense, even though allocations of up to US$2 million are possible. UNV continuation of this Technical Assistance component has been confirmed. VSO follow-up of this Technical Assistance component is expected.

E. MAIN SECTORAL ISSUES

1. Quarry Sector

10.38 The Hydraulics Division's new standard design for rehabilitation of the sea defenses involves a protective layer of boulders (rip-rap). The costs of this construction are therefore very sensitive to the cost of quarry products. In Guyana there is a huge reserve of good quality rock. The main problems in mining the rock are production capacity and transport to the coastal zone. The most strategic volumes (over 10 million tons) are located in the Bartica area upstream of the Essequibo river. This reserve is sufficient for the undertaking of the road and sea defense rehabilitation works that are envisaged for the near future, as well as for export to the Caribbean region. At the moment the market of quarry products in Guyana is dominated by a monopoly. At the same time no significant investments are made to increase the production capacity and quality.

10.39 The Government of Guyana will have to take action to get the quarry sector ready for the upcoming (donor funded) sea defense and road

projects. Production capacity must be increased and the price of rock has to
come down at the same time. Some options are:

- Allow other companies than the established Toolsie-Persaud and
  Baracara to produce rock in Guyana. One possibility would be to
  divest the existing Tepura (GNS) quarry, which has sufficient
  potential to provide the local market and allow for export as
  well.

- Give tenderers for the new projects free access to the smaller
  quarries in the Essequibo river area.

- Make the Tepura quarry an open access quarry for future tenderers.

- Support the use of rock from inland gold mines (a by-product of
  gold mining) for sea defense works.

The cost of the residual rock from gold-mines is probably more than from the
Tepura quarry, because of the substantial transport costs involved in the use
of such rock for the coastal zone. A benefit of this material is that it has
a rather high density which allows for saving on the volumes required for sea
defenses.

2. Cost Recovery

10.40   The Government of Guyana needs to introduce a cost recovery
program to help maintain sea defenses. The cost of maintaining the sea
defenses is estimated at about US$5.0 million in 1993, gradually decreasing to
US$2.5 million per annum after two decades. However, for this year, the
Government of Guyana has allocated the equivalent of about US$2 million for
the Hydraulics Division for 1993, far less than the requirements. This
situation cannot be allowed to continue for long, which makes cost recovery an
urgent matter. One option is the introduction of a general sea defense tax.
Since over 90% of the population benefits from the sea defenses, a general tax
is essentially equivalent to a user tax. Moreover, a long term neglect of the
sea defenses would necessitate an ongoing retreat to the hinterlands and would
soon create substantial problems in all sectors. The sea defense may
therefore be considered a national/state responsibility more than a sector
issue.

10.41   An increase of the land-levies may provide for a complementary
portion of the sea defense costs. This option is hardly viable on the short-
term as current incomes in the agricultural sector will not allow for
substantial duties. On the medium to long term the application of limited sea
defense levies to be incorporated with Drainage and Irrigation (D&I) charges
can be reconsidered. It is expected that the implementation of sea defense
levies will require a considerable transition period, and moreover, would be
more easily accepted by users, when the rehabilitation projects have shown
some appreciable results. In light of this, the Government of Guyana is
advised to prepare a realistic cost recovery program for sea defense
maintenance as soon as possible. Such program should identify the method, the
time of announcement and the time of implementation. This program should also
be presented to their donor agencies in view of the loan conditionalities. In
addition, the cost recovery mechanisms also need to be decided in a timely

fashion to allow for the development of adequate policies for future short-lease, long-lease or freehold titles on land.

3. Private Sector

10.42   Implementation of sea defense maintenance and small scale repair works by local contractors has been tried in Regions 3, 4, 5 and 6. In general the results are satisfactory. A gradual transition to full privatization of responsibilities for the maintenance and rehabilitation of the sea defense seems feasible. However, strong contractual and accounting skills within the PEU will be essential to the success of the privatization scheme because the local contracting industry has a great deal of expertise in these matters.

4. Policy, Coordination and Donor Conditions

10.43   At present, the Government of Guyana has no coherent strategy for the sea defense sector. Policy decisions are dominated by the conditions that are negotiated with donors. In general, these conditions reflect the priorities for the sector very well and the thrust of the conditions is very similar.

10.44   Nonetheless, the identification of a central policy for the sector would benefit clarity and consistency. It would also help the Government in future negotiations. This policy should address both implementation methods, planning, organization and financing. Donor support could then be designed to meet this central policy, providing an integral effort and preventing duplication. In this respect, the contacts and coordination between the donors has to be improved and the organization of a quarterly sea defense meeting has been recommended by the World Bank.[26]

F. PROPOSED STRATEGY

10.45   The proposed strategy for the sea defense sector has three foci:

(1)   Facilitating the early start of the donor funded rehabilitation projects. This includes meeting the donor conditions regarding PEU, quarry products, decision on design, cost-recovery etc.

(2)   Improving the maintenance performance of the Hydraulics Division (or future PEU), by ensuring not only sufficient staff, but also sufficient budgets.

(3)   Designing an integral and effective sea defense policy by identifying priorities, selecting appropriate design methods and encouraging the coordination between the Government of Guyana and donors.

The main steps necessary to implement this strategy are described in the action plan below.

---

[26]   As mentioned earlier, a first meeting will be held in March 1993.

G. ACTION PLAN

1. Short Term

10.46   The short-term action plan for the sea defense sector should be as follows.

To start the donor funded projects as soon as possible, the following actions shall be taken:

- Establish a PEU. This requires:

  - agreement between the donors on the establishment of a PEU, its form and the central role it will play in the various donor projects;
  - legal reforms to establish it and provide it with the necessary authority;
  - a time schedule for the change over of responsibilities from the Hydraulics Division to the PEU;
  - an organizational plan (covering career plans and the involvement of foreign experts); and
  - a realistic budget plan for the first 3 to 4 years, covering also donor involvement.

- Ensure competition and investments in the quarry industry to get both lower prices and better quality.

- Identify and announce an explicit sea defense cost recovery method and program.

- Institute a transparent accounting system for the PEU.

To improve the maintenance of the existing sea defenses:

- Continue the ongoing emergency repairs to minimize and to repair breaches.

- Identify financial resources for sea defense maintenance and upgrading of the working methods for maintenance and repairs.

- Identify funds for the PEU and the ongoing sea defenses maintenance over the coming years.

- Start a program which aims at a maximum involvement of local contractors in sea defense works and decide on a time schedule for phasing out the Hydraulics Divisions' equipment, workshops and stores.

To design an integral sea defense policy:

- Follow up on the coordination between the Government of Guyana and donors, as was started with the meeting of 17 December 1992, to get all donors agree with the main items of this strategy.

- Decide on the type of design that will be applied for repair, maintenance and rehabilitation works.

- Identify priorities for sea defense repairs, maintenance and rehabilitation.

- Identify priorities for additional studies and apply to donors for funding.

2. Medium Term

10.47   For the medium term, the plan of action should focus on continuation of the maintenance and rehabilitation works. The necessary actions are to:

- Institute a Coastal Zone Management Authority (CZM) to develop long term strategies for coastal defense and ensure optimum coordination between the Government of Guyana and the donors.

- Develop medium and long term strategies for sea defense rehabilitation and sustainable maintenance, i.e., CZM.

- Implement cost recovery mechanisms for sea defense.

- Finance the rehabilitation of the sea defense works that are no yet covered by the current donor programs.

- Carry out an inventory of and prioritize the rehabilitation (or demolition) of the drainage structures in the sea defense.

- Carry out an inventory of, and prioritize the protection of the river defenses.

- Develop a coastal zone management program.

- Prepare a study of the (current and potential) economic value of various agricultural, residential and industrial areas, to allow for a more accurate assessment of the priority areas for an integral sea and river defense policy.

3. Long Term

10.48   Long-term planning shall mainly focus on self sufficiency of Guyana in protecting the land and the population against attacks from the sea. The main foci are to:

- Implement maintenance and rehabilitation programs, aiming at long term safety.

- Make Guyana independent of foreign expertise with regard to sea defense management, engineering and implementation.

- Make Guyana self-sufficient in the financing of sea defense maintenance and rehabilitation works.

H. PROPOSED INVESTMENT PROGRAM

10.49   Table 10.4 shows the tentative disbursement schedule for both donor funded and locally funded undertakings. It should be noted that there is a large increase in capital expenditures from US$3.0 million in 1993 to US$22.3 million in 1994. While donors are committed to this increase, it must be recognized that it represents a very ambitious proposal heavily dependent on the implementation of the action plan outlined above.

10.50   In particular, delays in disbursement may originate from:

- delays with the Government on Guyana or the donors, in approval and tendering procedures during various stages of the different projects;
- difficulties for the Government of Guyana in meeting donor conditions; and
- delays in the establishment of the PEU, or it having insufficient capable staff, legalized authority or budget.

Experience has shown that delays can be long (years) and involve large amounts (millions of dollars). Hence, if the Government wants to realize the suggested disbursement schedule, it should move forcefully on the actions proposed.

Table 10.4:   TENTATIVE DISBURSEMENT SCHEDULE DONOR AGENCIES
(US$ 1000)

Project	1993	1994	1995	1996	Agency
<u>Ongoing Projects</u>	<u>200.0</u>	<u>2000.0</u>	<u>3000.0</u>	<u>4800.0</u>	
Sea Defenses - IRP	200.0	2000.0	3000.0	4800.0	EEC/EDF
<u>New Projects (Identified)</u>	<u>2687.7</u>	<u>6074.9</u>	<u>8310.4</u>	<u>11340.2</u>	
IRP-Sea Defenses (cap. works)	422.3	2000.0	4000.0	7000.0	IDB
IRP-Sea Defenses (cap. works)	0.0	1000.0	1700.0	2000.0	CDB
IRP-Sea Defenses (cap. works)	285.3	1140.2	1710.0	1425.5	IDA
IRP-Sea Defenses					
(counterpart funds)	1980.1	1934.7	900.4	914.7	Local
TOTAL (Identified)	<u>2887.7</u>	<u>8074.9</u>	<u>11310.4</u>	<u>16140.2</u>	
<u>Memorandum Item:a/</u>					
<u>T.A., Studies and Volunteers</u>	<u>3100.0</u>	<u>3600.0</u>	<u>3700.0</u>	<u>900.0</u>	
IDB	1700.0	2700.0	2700.0	700.0	
EDF	700.0	200.0	0.0	0.0	
IDA	500.0	500.0	800.0	0.0	
USAID (under review)	0.0	0.0	0.0	0.0	
VSO	100.0	100.0	100.0	100.0	
UNV	100.0	100.0	100.0	100.0	
<u>Maintenance Works (incl. PEU)</u>	<u>3700.0</u>	<u>4700.0</u>	<u>4800.0</u>	<u>5100.0</u>	
PEU (donor funding)	1600.0	1900.0	1300.0	900.0	
PEU (local funding)	100.0	300.0	500.0	700.0	
Maintenance of Sea					
Defenses (local funding)	2000.0	2500.0	3000.0	3500.0	
GRAND TOTAL	**<u>9687.7</u>**	**<u>16374.9</u>**	**<u>19810.4</u>**	**<u>22140.2</u>**	

a/ PSIP does not include Technical Assistance or Maintenance Works.

<u>Source</u>: Mission Estimates

10.51   Should budgetary constraints be alleviated, a challenging maintenance program that would minimize future damage to agricultural lands and more specifically, prevent further deterioration of sea defenses, is shown in Table 10.4a below.   This is based on assessments by DHV (September 1992). Even with the action plans in place, budget constraints are likely to force the Government of Guyana to spend less on maintenance and risk more damage to the agricultural sector than desirable.

<u>Table 10.4a</u>:   EXPANDED MAINTENANCE BUDGET
(US$ 1000)

Project	1993	1994	1995	1996
<u>Maintenance Works (incl. PEU)</u>	<u>6700.0</u>	<u>7100.0</u>	<u>6500.0</u>	<u>6100.0</u>
PEU (donor funding)	1600.0	1900.0	1300.0	900.0
PEU (local funding)	100.0	300.0	500.0	700.0
Maintenance of Sea Defenses (local funding)	5000.0	4900.0	4700.0	4500.0

<u>Source</u>:   Mission Estimates

CHAPTER XI. TRANSPORTATION

A. INTRODUCTION

11.1   The severe deterioration of transportation infrastructure and services over the past decade is a major constraint to economic recovery and sustainable development of Guyana's rich natural resources and agricultural base. By improving transport, costs can be lowered, new markets developed and exports increased. Therefore, the Public Sector Investment Plan emphasizes the rehabilitation of roads, river transportation and other infrastructure. However, given Guyana's limited absorptive capacity and the systemic deterioration in the country, the limited resources available for transportation must be rationally allocated to optimize the economic impact of selective improvements in the system.

11.2   The transport system of Guyana is concentrated in and along the sugar and rice growing areas of the coastal plain, with very little traffic to the interior. The main Highway system follows the coast line from the Corentyne River on the Surinam border as far west as the Pomoroon River (Charity) with a major spur south at Georgetown into Timehri International Airport and beyond to the bauxite area at Linden. Ferry services and private boat fleets provide transport across the Berbice, Demerara and Essequibo rivers, connecting the highway system. There is an important retractable (for vessel thoroughfare) pontoon bridge also crossing the Demerara near Georgetown. In addition to Timehri International Airport, there is a small general aviation airport at Ogle near Georgetown and a network of over one hundred small, many private, interior airstrips, although air access to the interior is limited. Secondary and farm access roads on the coastal plain allow transport of products along the main highway system and by river barges and coastal ships to the Georgetown area where limited port facilities are located. Most of the ton-kilometers for the internal transport of bulk materials (sugar, rice, timber, bauxite, and aggregates) are handled by the marine sector.

11.3   The interior savannas and rain forest are largely inaccessible except for a few logging roads, the aforementioned airstrips and river access to about 200 km upstream. A 345 km road from Lethem, at the Brazil border, to Georgetown is incomplete but currently passable in good weather by trucks.

11.4   In all cases, transportation infrastructure has deteriorated due to poor management and lack of maintenance. Management of transport facilities has been adversely affected by misguided policies and lack of resources. Existing main roads have not been maintained since they were constructed to their current design specification in the seventies, and are in need of full rehabilitation. Similarly airport and port facilities need immediate attention in some areas and will need to be upgraded before a serious effort at export development, particularly of non-traditional commodities, can be successful. No new facilities are warranted in the near future.

B. SECTOR OVERVIEW

1. Road Transportation

11.5   The main road network of Guyana, approximately 2576 km (1610
miles) long (excluding urban streets and minor trails), is divided
functionally into: (i) a primary network of 493 kms (19%) comprised mostly of
paved roads along the coastal area and river banks serving primarily the
agricultural sector, and the road to Linden which serves the mining and
forestry sectors; (ii) a coastal area minor road system (feeder roads) of
nearly 514 km (20%) which connects the agricultural areas along the coast to
the primary road network; and (iii) a system of interior roads and trails 1570
km (61%) serving the interior of Guyana. Approximately 88% of the primary
roads and 13% of the coastal area roads are paved. Of the total network, only
434 km (17%) is estimated to be in good condition. Table 11.1 presents a
summary of the road network statistics.

Table 11.1: GUYANA'S ROAD NETWORK (kms)
(By road classification, surface type and condition)

	PAVED				UNPAVED				TOTAL	
	good	fair	poor	sum	good	fair	poor	sum	km	%
Primary Network	152	185	98	435	–	–	58	58	493	19
Coastal Area Minor Roads	–	42	24	66	–	24	424	448	514	20
Interior Roads/Trails	–	21	–	21	282	438	829	1549	1570	61
TOTAL	152	248	122	522	282	462	1310	2054	2576	100
%	6	9	5	20	11	18	51	80	100	

Source: World Bank IRP Staff Appraisal Report and Mission Estimates

11.6   The road infrastructure is in a deteriorated state. Little or no
maintenance has been done on the primary road network for nearly 15 years
leading to its rapid deterioration particularly of those links carrying high
traffic volumes: the road between Georgetown and Timehri International
Airport (38 km, with about 13,000 vehicles per day (vpd) near Georgetown),
the Georgetown to Mahaica road (29 kms, about 5,000 to 8,000 vpd) and the
Essequibo Coast Road (3861 km, about 1,200 vpd with significant pent up demand
withheld due to the very bad condition of that road). The other paved roads,
which carry relatively low traffic volumes and are much more recently built,
are still in reasonably good condition but will need resealing, resurfacing or
overlaying soon. Rehabilitation of the above mentioned roads, as well as the

replacement of the bridges on the Linden highway will be done under IDA and IDB loans.

11.7   Most feeder roads leading to the farming areas off the primary roads and the interior roads and trails are poorly constructed, poorly maintained and nearly impassable during the rainy season. The poor condition of these roads has become a real bottleneck to the transportation of agricultural products. An example is the Black Bush Polder Road, which was never designed for truck traffic and which has now collapsed in several areas due to foundation failure. A feeder roads and trails rehabilitation and maintenance program is urgently needed. The IDB, as parts of its Agricultural Sector Loan, is rehabilitating about 1000 kms of interior farm access trails. However, no funding is currently secured for upgrading feeder roads.

11.8   In 1989 a bilateral agreement was signed between Guyana and Brazil for the construction of a road from the Guyana coast to Brazil. The purpose of the road is to facilitate the traffic of goods and people from the state of Roraima, in Brazil, to Georgetown. The road would also enable farmers in the savannas of the Rupununi district of Guyana to take their cattle and other produce directly to market in Georgetown. Paranapanema (a Brazilian construction firm) signed a contract with the Ministry of Communications and Works for the design and construction of approximately 346 kms of new road and road structures between Lethem (on the Guyana-Brazil border) and Mabura Hill. This road would then link up with the existing roads through Linden to Georgetown. As of December 1992, Phase I of the construction from Lethem to the Essequibo River is complete, 210 km (US$16 million) and Phase II (US$14 million) to Linden, is a priority for the Government of Guyana, although terms of the loan are presently being renegotiated. This road (total construction cost US$30 million) is controversial in that it is not economically justifiable at this time, or in the near future, in terms of costs and benefits to road users. In addition, the potential harmful impacts of the road on the environment and indigenous population have not been adequately studied. The IDA IRP will conduct an environmental study of this project.

11.9   The Demerara River Floating Bridge provides an extremely important river crossing connecting Georgetown and the half of the country west of the Demerara River. The 1.9 km steel pontoon bridge with an Accrow Panel deck was constructed as a temporary structure some seventeen years ago. The bridge includes a retractable portion to allow river vessels to pass. This crossing is the most efficient crossing of the Demerara, although a ferry service and private speed boats also provide access. Due to lack of sufficient maintenance, inadequate design of the anchoring system and old age, sections of the bridge have been collapsing or sinking, more frequently recently. The steel pontoons are subject to rusting in the salt water and there are inadequate maintenance funds to apply marine paint regularly. Pumping the water out of the leaking pontoons is a continuous procedure. Although the bridge is operated as a toll facility, the tolls charged do not cover the cost of administering the tolls and the receipts are not earmarked for operation and maintenance. When the bridge is out of service, or when the retracting portion is inoperable, the economic costs to the country in terms of river navigation and road access to the capital are crippling. The EC is planning a major overhaul of the bridge, but the country will need a longer term solution in the future.

11.10   The streets of Georgetown are in generally poor condition. Most of the town is flooded after heavy rains. There is evidence that some work has been done on the arterial roads. However, the local streets serving residential areas have been left unattended over the last several years. A program for city streets improvement should be considered as part of an urban project for Georgetown.

11.11   The road transport industry in Guyana is quite efficient. Public passenger transport is provided mostly by a reasonably new stock of privately owned vehicles made up of about 2400 minibuses and 7000 hire cars with enough capacity to satisfy current demand. (Figures are for 1989 and were provided by Central Transport Planning Unit of the Ministry of Public Works, Communications and Regional Development (MOPWCRD)). These vehicles came into service to replace the now-defunct, government-run Guyana Transport Services Limited. Beginning in 1985, individuals were permitted to import minibuses and in 1986 the import policy was expanded to give duty free concessions for their importation.[27] Minibus and hire car operations are licensed by the MOPWCRD to operate on specified routes. Fares are regulated; but this is not uncommon for public passenger transport and does not appear to be hurting the efficiency of the industry. In addition, there are approximately 20,500 private vehicles licensed by MOPWCRD.

11.12   Roads carry about one third of freight tonnage within the country. Road freight traffic is carried by an aging fleet of about 1,800 single unit trucks and some 140 tractor-trailers. About 6,000 tractors also yield various types of transport services on dry-weather rural roads which are generally in poor condition. Import restrictions had previously hindered the acquisition of new trucks. Spare parts are readily available but at a high price. The recent liberalization of foreign exchange is already helping to improve truck and spare parts imports. Freight transport rates are not regulated with customers and truckers negotiating prior to the provision of the service. Existing regulations govern only axle loads, vehicle dimensions and vehicle safety inspection, but these are unfortunately not strictly enforced resulting in high accident rates and excessive road wear due to overloading.

2. Air Transportation

11.13   Air transport plays an important role in Guyana due to the country's location, topography and physical layout, and the dispersed population of the interior.

Timehri International Airport

11.14   Timehri is the only international airport serving the country and is by far the main port of entry for all international passenger arrivals and departures. Very few international passengers arrive by boat or overland. Business people, international representatives, CARICOM officials, as well as the large number of expatriate Guyanese living in North America and their

---

27/   Only new vehicles were originally permitted for import, although recently this was extended to vehicles up to five years old. This policy suppresses demand to some extent because of the higher cost of new vehicles, but has environmental benefits because newer vehicles are designed for lower vehicle emissions.

families rely on Timehri International Airport for access to the capital. This airport is a critical asset in economy of Guyana as well as its link to the rest of the world. It must be considered a priority in the PSIP.

11.15   Timehri is located 38 km (approximately 50 minutes by road) from Georgetown. It has two runways; one 2,290 m long and 45 m wide with an asphalt surface, and the other 1,525 m long and 45 m wide with a concrete surface. The pavements are in good condition. This runway configuration is capable of handling a Boeing 702 size or smaller aircraft and with some restrictions, up to the Boeing 707 size aircraft. Timehri's other services include refuelling and cargo handling. There has been some discussion about extending the runway to 3,050 m to accommodate the Boeing 747 size aircraft, but traffic projections do not justify expansion at this time. The passenger terminal building requires expansion and renovation and the Government of Guyana is currently undertaking this work. However, operational and safety deficiencies at the airport are much more critical and must be addressed immediately; not only to avoid a possible incident, but to optimize the efficiency and utility of existing facilities.

11.16   A stark example of the result of inferior services at Timehri is the fact the US Federal Aviation Administration (FAA) has consistently denied US airline applications to serve Georgetown due to unsafe conditions. Another way to look at it is, if US operations were already at Timehri, conditions are such that the FAA would shut it down. (The FAA only has jurisdiction at airports serving US air carriers.)

11.17   The most critical deficiencies follow:

- Crash Fire Rescue Services. The Government has recently completed the construction of a firehall at the airport, and a previous donor project provided communication radios and basic training of fire officers. With Guyana Airways flying 707's into Timehri, the CFR Category requirement established by the International Civil Aviation Organization (ICAO) is Category 7. With the previously provided firetruck out of service (due to a roll-over), the airport is now only a Category 4 (Dash 8 size or smaller). This means that if there were an on-airport fire on a 707, even if it landed right in front of the firehall, the fire service would not be able to rescue the passengers. The airport is therefore currently operating below minimum acceptable international standards in CFR. The IDA IRP program proposes to provide a new firetruck, which should be a first-year priority in the project.

- Security. Airport security fencing is needed as facilities are often vandalized affecting aircraft operation. This is a priority of the CAD and should be funded as a priority.

- Telecommunications and Navigational Aids Maintenance. Navigational aids, communication equipment, safety aids, security equipment and other equipment have not been properly maintained. A Maintenance Management System and a Planned Maintenance System are critically needed in addition to long term technical assistance. The T&N workshop is completely inadequate and ill-equipped to maintain the complex equipment at the airport.

Transport vehicles are also needed to enable technicians to visit critical sites on a timely basis for maintenance.

- The Air Traffic Control Tower. The ATC communication console is on the verge of collapse; it is over 25 years old and is obsolete. It should be replaced immediately. A new air/ground antenna system is required for the ATC radios. Air Traffic Controllers need refresher training.

- Instrument Landing System (ILS/DME). The ILS Glide Slope and Localizer are old (20 years) but are still operating satisfactorily. Some repairs are needed. Both will have to be replaced within five years. The DME is in good condition but needs specialized repairs of the Power Amplifier. The main problem is the ILS antenna support structure, which is likely to collapse at any moment. This structure must be replaced immediately.

11.18   Other serious deficiencies include:

- Airport Management. The overall management of airport operations and facilities (buildings, airfields, ground services) must be systematized. Institutional strengthening of airport general management, financial management, revenue generation and forecasting, planned maintenance systems, procurement of equipment and spares, and training is needed.

- High Frequency (HF) Communications. The facility was hit by lightening recently and only part of the equipment is functioning. The console needs extensive repairs. The overhead control cable was damaged and part of it was also later vandalized. A new location is needed for the remote site, including a new building, fencing and standby generator.

- Navigation Beacon (VOR/DME). The VOR is in good condition but the building has been vandalized on several occasions shutting down the system. Electronic security monitoring and fencing should be installed. A new Test Unit for the DME is required.

- ILS Outer Locator. This equipment is old (over 25 years) and obsolete and needs to be replaced. A solar array should be used to supply power as the site is over water and cannot be supplied by main power lines and it is difficult to ship fuel to the diesels by boat. The site buildings need extensive refurbishing and the site needs fencing.

- Non-Directional Beacon (NDB). This equipment is also over 25 years old and should be replaced. If possible, the site should be moved because it is in an isolated area and has been vandalized several times. A new building, secure fencing and a standby generator are required.

- Meteorological Services (MET). MET services are virtually non-existent. Pilots must take unreasonable risks in estimating weather conditions, especially in the interior.

- **T&N Power System.** The power cable servicing the T&N systems runs under the runway and is 40 years old or older. It has recently failed, requiring the use of the backup generator 24 hours per day. The generator now fails several times a day. A temporary cable has been run above ground, but power in Guyana in general is most unreliable; the power has been out about 25 times in a period of only several weeks. Each time the power is out and the generator fails, the VOR, DME and ILS are off the air posing a very serious threat to air safety.

- **Cargo facilities.** Cargo facilities are practically non-existent. The present covered storage space at the airport is insufficient and results in cargo having to remain in the open, exposed to the elements until it is put on an aircraft. There are also no refrigeration facilities at the airport, and thus no incentive for air export of produce or tropical flowers.

11.19   The Government has been seeking foreign joint-venture operators to run the international airport but negotiations have failed to date. This is partly due to the poor condition of airport infrastructure and partly due to unrealistic expectations of profit potential by the foreign operators. The airport has commercial viability in terms of maximizing revenues to cover operational costs. However, base costs for minimum airport services are fixed; revenue potential increases with the volumes of traffic, but with only 250,000 passengers per year being served at Timehri, there is not the scope required for profit generation.

Ogle Airport

11.20   Ogle Airfield is located close to the coast about 8 km east of Georgetown, about 15 minutes by car. It's runway is approximately 600 m (425 m paved, 580 m usable, and 760 m cleared) by 10 m wide and has a concrete surface. It can accommodate aircraft of up to 12,500 pounds and is designed for short take off and landing (STOL) aircraft such as the Twin Otter. It is used primarily for domestic passenger service, although international flights are accommodated on a pre-arranged ad-hoc basis. There is a small terminal building, and several privately owned hangars. Traffic at Ogle now exceeds that at Timehri in terms of aircraft movements.

11.21   The airfield is owned by GUYSUCO, the national sugar company. Management is contracted out to Booker Tate of the UK. The airport land is therefore not vested to the Civil Aviation Directorate and there is no effective aviation development management. No zoning regulation have been applied, as is evident by the fact that most of the small hangars are located too close to the runway.

11.22   The ATC facilities at Ogle are primitive. The tower structure is inadequate as are the communications and navigational aids facilities. There has been one serious incident of a 707 mistaking Ogle for Timehri when the Timehri aids were out because of a power failure, and the 707 attempted to land at Ogle.

11.23   Very little credit is given to the role of Private Sector Commercial Aviation in Guyana. At Ogle, there is an active community of about 40 aircraft, a flying school, a flying club and a Private Aircraft Owners

Association. The Aircraft Owners Association is eager to develop Ogle for business, but have been blocked by government inaction.

Interior Airstrips

11.24   There are some 80 government owned and 60 private aerodromes serving the interior. Most are very simple, comprised of grass or gravel strips with few additional facilities. The most important one is Lethem airstrip with a 2,000 m, 22 m wide bitumen runway. Most airstrips are in poor condition. The Government is currently surveying the major strips at Baramita, Bemechi, Matthews Ridge, Port Kaituma, Maburuma, Kaikan, Paruima, Kamarang, Phillipai, Kurupung, Kopinang, Mahdia, Kurukubaru, Kato, Paramakatoi, Monkey Mountain, Lumid Pau, Aishalton, Wichabai, Annai Yopukari, Apoteri, Karasabai and Kaieteur for possible future upgrading.

11.25   There is only one NDB operating in the interior and that is at Kamarang. All other beacons are out of service and have been for some time. These beacons are all 25 years old or older and cannot be repaired. The VOR at Timehri can be used out to about 100 nautical miles. The Timehri NDB should work out to at least 100 miles, but the range in only about 50 miles. New equipment is needed to improve the range. Communications, except HF radio, are nonexistent.

11.26   Additional communications and navigational aids should be installed in the interior to improve flight safety and to facilitate search and rescue. Pending any dramatic traffic increases, this should concentrate on at least providing full NDB coverage. This can probably be accomplished by replacing the Kamarang NDB with a new NDB and installing two or three others. A locator should be installed at Kaieteur Falls, where tourist traffic is growing dramatically. All NDB's should be solar powered as it is very difficult and expensive to fly fuel in to the interior.

Air Services

11.27   Timehri International Airport is served by a number of airlines including Guyana Airways Corporation GAC (once a week from Miami, 3 times a week from NY), BWIA (16 flights a week from Trinidad), LIAT (10 times a week), ALM (once a week from Trinidad), SLM (3 times a week from Surinam), Cruseiro Dosul (from Brazil), and Aeropostal (twice a week from Venezuela), as presented in Table 11.2. United Airlines has applied to begin service in June of 1993, but recent discussions with CAD indicate that the FAA has denied its application (due to safety deficiencies at the airport). Timehri handles approximately 250,000 passengers per year, which is a low level of activity compared to other regional airports (i.e., Piarco International in Trinidad handles over 1.4 million passengers per year), but is significant in terms of population served.

11.28   Nearly 60% of passengers to the interior areas are transported by air. Guyana Airways Corporation has only one scheduled route and one Twin Otter aircraft. Other air services are provided on a charter basis by private operators such as Air Services Ltd., Trans-Guyana, and Kayman Sankar. All private operators have mainline businesses (mining, sugar, timber) to which air service is a sideline and thus subsidized by the main business activities.

11.29   In addition, the Civil Aviation Directorate (CAD) has been operating a Skyvan aircraft. This aircraft is intended for civil aviation duties and defence, however, it has also been operated on a commercial basis; in direct competition with private operators. This has caused some distrust of the CAD, in that the Directorate was in effect, regulating itself regarding these commercial flights. The Government is now considering moving the commercial operation of these aircraft to the Defence Department.

Table 11.2: SCHEDULED AIR SERVICE AT TIMEHRI

Airline	From	Equipment	Frequency (trips per week)
Guyana Airways	Miami	707 (135 seats)	1
	NY	707	3
BWIA	Trinidad	MD80 (150 seats)	16
LIAT	Caribbean	Avro 748 (50 seats)	10
ALM	Curacao	MD80 (150 seats)	2
SLM	Surinam	DC8 (180 seats)	2
		Twin Otter (20 seats)	1
Cruseiro	Brazil	n.a.	n.a.
Aeropostal	Venezuela	MD80 (150 seats)	2
TOTAL			36

Source: Official Airline Guide 1992

11.30   Guyana Airways Corporation is currently operating at a small profit on its international routes, but this is unlikely to be sustainable for several reasons: the 707 aircraft it operates is old and very noisy; new noise laws in North America are likely to restrict this type of aircraft from operating at North American airports in the near future. Also, the increasingly competitive nature of the international airline industry requires strong management direction, and GAC is poorly managed. Finally, the introduction of NY service by United Airways will cut into GAC's NY market share.

11.31   GAC's domestic service is seriously inadequate; only one of previously 12 scheduled route service is being maintained with only one Twin Otter aircraft.

11.32   The Government is considering the divestment of GAC. The Ogle Aircraft Owners' Association has made a proposal to government to take over domestic air services, including medical, education and mail services to the interior, as well as expanded services in aerial seeding, eco-tourism and commuter service to mining, timber and agricultural sites. This proposal should be seriously considered by the Government. International operations should be divested to private interests (most likely foreign) but still under government regulation. Another option to be considered is the elimination of GAC entirely, opening Guyana to unregulated "open skies".

3. Coastal and River Transportation

Deep Sea Activity

11.33   Ports in Guyana handling deep sea vessels in order of importance
are: Georgetown, Linden and New Amsterdam. Bulk commodity handling for
exported bauxite and sugar and imported petroleum products and flour account
for the largest volumes of cargo and totals one to two million tons per year.
Bulk exports of bauxite (about 1.1 million tons in 1992) and sugar (about
230,000 tons in 1992) represent about two thirds of the total value of
exports. Breakbulk handling of exported timber and rice (about 77,000 tons in
1992) and imported fertilizer also takes place in small quantities. While
general cargo handling is mostly containerized, containerization is not part
of Guyana's internal transport system. All containers are stuffed and
destuffed adjacent at the berth face. Principal general cargo imports are:
cars, frozen chicken, consumer goods while principal general cargo exports are
frozen fish, rum, and frozen shrimp. Volumes data are not available because
national marine activity statistics are not collected.

11.34   Draught constraints and, for some commodities, shipment size
limitations have encouraged the use of very small vessels; the largest vessels
are approximately 25,000 deadweight tons (dwt) capacity. There are no
Guyanese registry vessels significantly involved in overseas trade. A few
small coasting general cargo vessels of Guyanese registry trade regionally to
the Caribbean and neighboring countries. There are five vessels ranging from
522 dwt to 1350 dwt; two are owned by John Fernandes & Sons Ltd. and three are
owned by Sherman Stoll.

11.35   Most of Guyana's exports and imports are handled by foreign
shipping companies. Because bulk exports are carried by competitive charters
and imports are carried by liners, Guyana's capture of ship cost savings
through improved port facilities is likely to be highest for facilities
investments directed to Guyana's bulk exports.

11.36   Shipping lines calling at Georgetown include: TechMarine (the
most active in Guyana), Mitsui, Harrison, Seafreight, and Bernuth. Nedlloyd
has suspended service to Guyana and Blue Carib Line has recently ceased
calling. Although Guyana has some direct container service to Europe and the
Western Pacific, most containers are handled by way of intermediate container
ports at Port of Spain, Kingston and Miami. Trade with North America appears
to showing the greatest growth. Expatriate populations in Canada and the U.S.
have recently become a noticeable presence in the logistics of liner trade
between Miami and Georgetown. General cargo trade to and from Guyana is
characterized by numerous small scale private commercial importers and
exporters. Guyana trades in a region that has had moderate growth in
container activity. The Caribbean and Central/South America region's
container fleet grew by 10.4% in the period from 1990 to mid-1992 compared
with world wide growth of 24.8% in the same period.

Table 11.3: GUYANA'S MAIN TRADING PARTNERS
(% of total by value)

Exports to:	1986	1991	Imports from:	1986	1991
UK	24.2	26.9	USA	16.4	31.3
USA	22.6	36.0	Trinidad and Tobago	32.1	12.8
Germany (West)	9.1	3.0	UK	9.7	15.8
Japan	8.7	6.2	Germany	4.2	2.2
Canada	5.6	9.3	Japan	3.7	6.7
Trinidad and Tobago	6.8	2.0	Canada	1.6	4.8

Source: IMF, Directory of Trade Statistics

Internal Maritime Transport

11.37   Coastal general cargo vessels operating between Georgetown and the regions and ferries for river crossings carry people, consumer goods and, bagged rice and bulk sugar for export. Because of intersecting rivers and the lack of roads, most agricultural inputs (eg. fertilizers), people, vehicles and consumer goods travelling within Guyana must use marine transport for part of the journey. Government owned ferries and one government owned coastal cargo vessel operate and compete with private water taxis and coastal cargo vessels. However, only publicly owned ferries are capable of carrying vehicles. The Government's aged, slow and unreliable ferries and coastal vessels are being rehabilitated through an EC funded program. Because an aids tender is no longer available, the government's vessels are diverted to aids maintenance from time to time. An aid tender is a vessel specialized to the purpose of lifting heavy buoys (eg. 5 tons) out of the water for re-furbishing. For reasons of safety and of cost recovery of government services, private operations require more regulation. Water taxis have no safety equipment and appear to often overload their vessels.

11.38   Significant quantities of bulk commodities travel by water within Guyana. On the Berbice River, bauxite bulk barges link loading facilities for ocean-going vessels at the river mouth terminal to mining operations 195 km upstream. 98% of the 230,000 tons per year of sugar are delivered by barge from the various production areas for export from Georgetown. Sugar barges are in three size classes depending on delivery route; 180 to 190 tons, 68 to 70 tons and 27 to 30 tons. Similarly, most of the internal transport of rice is by water. Aggregates are delivered to Georgetown by barge.

11.39   Pontoon barges and riverine small craft use the Demerara, Berbice, Corentyne, and Waini Rivers. Rivers are the primary means for timber to be brought to sawmills in the Georgetown area and are important for the re-supply of interior communities. Several sawmills are located on the Demerara and Essequibo Rivers to receive raw logs for processing. Some 1,000 km of river waterways are reported to be commercially significant for navigation. Drainage canals are also used for the collection of sugar cane by barge on plantations and for personal travel in small craft.

11.40   Internationally registered Guyanese vessels include: 10 general cargo coasting vessels; 5 ferries ranging from 160 to 612 gross registered tons (grt); 2 tugs of 100 grt each; 1 tanker of 125 grt; 1 roll-on roll-off (RORO) vessel of 848 grt; 1 hopper dredge of 1500 grt; 35 deep water fishing vessels in the 101 to 108 grt size range.

Georgetown Harbor

11.41   Approach. Entry of all vessels to the port of Georgetown on the Demerara River is governed by the depth of water on the bar; once past the bar there is ample depth in the 70 m wide main channel into the main port area for any vessel which can cross the bar itself. Depth on the bar at high water varies from 4.91 m to 6.23 m on spring tides. On the tide, ships with draughts up to 6.7 m can cross. The River is navigable as far as Linden, 96 km from the entrance. Pilotage by Transport and Harbors Department pilots is compulsory and all ships regardless of their destination in Guyana must come to the pilot station off Georgetown's harbor entrance to pick up their pilot before proceeding to their destinations. No tug assistance is available. The main part of the harbor was last surveyed by the Canadian Hydrographic Service in 1974. Anchorage locations are available in the harbor but the lack of mooring buoys forces risky reliance on the soft mud bottom against the strong tide assisted currents.

11.42   Vessel Accommodation. There are six principal wharves ranging from 59 m to 228 m in length with depths of 4.88 m to 6.10 m at low water. There are also sawmills with loading facilities and shrimp freezing depots. Vessels discharge with their own gear because the narrow timber wharves with their low bearing capacities are not suitable for heavy equipment. The La Penitence improvement project has been completed for the Guyana National Shipping Corporation. The wharf is 231 m long providing accommodation for two vessels of limited lengths. Bauxite vessels use Georgetown as a topping up port having first loaded a part cargo upstream at Linden. Bauxite bulk carriers moor in 6.9 m depths against a permanently vessel that acts as a transhipment station to receive their final cargo allotments. Barges are also used to bring bauxite against anchored vessels awaiting topping up. Lloyds' vessel database reports that in 1990, 689 international vessels of 4,873,252 dwt visited the port. (The average dwt for these vessels was 7,072.) The Transport and Harbors Department reports that in 1991, 1545 vessels (both Guyanese and international) subject to harbor dues entered Georgetown. Exempt from paying harbor dues are tugs, barges, fishing trawlers and small craft.

11.43   Cargo Handling. General cargo handling is slow and constrained at an estimated handling rate of about 80 tons per shift. There are six cranes of 2 t to 30 t and two 20 ft container movers. Containers are not normally moved away from the berth face because city roadways are inadequate. John Fernandes & Sons Ltd. handles about 3,600 Twenty-foot Equivalent Units (teu's) per year and GNSC handles about 2,400 teu's annually (the teu is the standard measuring unit for container traffic). Smaller but unknown amounts are handled at other terminals. Cargo storage space is limited; only 9858 m^2 of covered storage and 8,370 m^2 of open storage space is available. Oil storage terminals owned by Shell, Texaco, Esso and Guyana Oil Co. Ltd. are situated on the east bank of the Demerara River.

11.44   Reported bulk handling rates are: bauxite 500 tons per hour at topping up stations; flour 60 tons per hour (each of two vacuum discharge hoses); sugar 500 tons per hour; bagged fertilizer 65 tons per hour; bulk fertilizer 30 tons per hour; bulk alcohol 100,000 liters per hour

Linden Harbor

11.45   Approach. All vessels must enter by travelling 96 km up the Demerara River after passing Georgetown. The main navigational limitations are Georgetown's entrance bar, the unreliable opening of the Demerara River floating bridge, and depth limitations at various locations of the river. Notable shallow spots include the area near the floating bridge and several locations on the journey to Linden. The controlling depth is at the bridge while the rest of the river offers deeper water at 5.2 m to 6.4 m in most of the channel. Generally two tides are required to make the passage. While waiting for tides, designated anchorages are available in the River. Pilotage from the upstream harbor limit at Georgetown to Linden is handled by a separate group of river pilots employed by the Guyana National Engineering Corporation.

11.46   Vessel Accommodation. The berth face at Linden is 274.3 m long and will accommodate two ships of 152.3 m alongside. Vessels use the 175 m diameter turning basin but siltation has reduced the basin's effective size. While the principal commodity handled is bauxite in deep sea bulk carriers, there is also a container service by TechMarine Lines and visitations by a small oil/bulk vessel. The oil/bulk vessel delivers oil to Linden and backhauls bauxite on its outward journey.

11.47   Cargo Handling. The bauxite shiploader at Linden and the materials handling system supporting it can deliver at a peak rate of 500 tons per hour, compared to 900 tons per hour in Suriname or 1,400 tons per hour in Trinidad.

New Amsterdam Harbor

11.48   Approach. Vessels cross the New Amsterdam Bar drawing 0.38 m more than the predicted tide for the Georgetown Bar and can proceed 192 km up the Berbice River depending on size and tonnage. New Amsterdam itself is located 8 km upstream on the Berbice River. Compulsory pilotage requires vessels to divert to Georgetown to pick up a pilot before approaching at New Amsterdam. (In many countries the pilot moves to meet the ship rather than moving the ship to meet the pilot. Pilot time charges are usually much less than vessel time charges.)

11.49   Vessel Accommodation. For New Amsterdam, vessels discharge to lighters at anchorage in the river in 3 m to 5.8 m of water. At Everton, situated further upstream ocean-going vessels are handled at bauxite loading facilities of Guyana Mining Enterprises Ltd. Their wharf is 98.4 m long with a minimum depth alongside of 5.8 m. Small oil tankers are handled at Heatherton for the Guyana Oil Co. and at Providence for Shell Oil Co. Both facilities have depths of 4.88 m to 5.49 m. Lloyds' vessel database reports that in 1990, 20 international vessels of 157,537 dwt entered the harbor. (The average dwt for these vessels was 7,877.)

Dry Docks and Ship Repairs

11.50   Three companies (all fully or partly government owned) provide dry docking and ship repair facilities for smaller local commercial vessels at Georgetown, the Marzaruni River and New Amsterdam (at Everton). Larger international trade vessels at Georgetown can have hull and engine repairs carried out while at anchor.

Table 11.4: DRY DOCK AND VESSEL REPAIR FACILITIES

Location	Type of Facility	Length (m)	Breadth (m)	Capacity (tons)	Cranage	Owner
Georgetown	dry dock	62.55	14.00	–	1 @ 10t	GNEC a/
Georgetown	dry dock	79.60	11.50	900	–	GNEC
Georgetown	slipway	45.00	–	700	–	GNEC
Georgetown	slipway	26.00	–	500	–	GNEC
Mararuni River	dry dock	48.76	10.67	–	–	Government
New Amsterdam	floating dock	42.67	15.24	600	–	GMEL b/

a/ Guyana National Engineering Corporation.
b/ Guyana Mining Enterprise Ltd.

Source: Lloyds Dry Docks

4. Rail Transportation

11.51   There is no national rail system in Guyana. A government owned standard gauge railway 133 km long operates to serve bauxite mining operations between Linden and Ituni and Coomacka. Local business interests are promoting the reestablishment of rail service along the abandoned right-of-way along the coast, but all such attempts should be discouraged. It is not economically feasible to reestablish rail service which would, in effect duplicate road and coastal boat services, and double maintenance requirements.

C. INSTITUTIONAL AND REGULATORY FRAMEWORK

11.52   The Ministry of Public Works, Communications and Regional Development has overall responsibility for the planning, construction, improvement, operation and regulation of the transport sector. The Ministry of Agriculture participates in the development of the farm and feeder road system. The Ministry of Finance is responsible for reviewing and allocating budgetary funds for the sector's agencies while the State Planning Secretariat (SPS), soon to be subsumed by the Ministry of Finance, has been responsible for putting together the public sector investment program. Urban roads are technically the responsibility of the Municipality.

11.53   The purpose of the Central Transport Planning Unit (CTPU) of the MOPWCRD is to control the development of the transport sector by integrating the investment proposals of the modal agencies. CTPU is also mandated to establish priorities among projects, propose transport policy changes, and review tariffs and charges. However because the CTPU is seriously understaffed, it does not have full control of its transport coordination function. Only one of six approved positions are currently staffed. The modal agencies tend to submit budget requests directly to the Ministry of Finance completely bypassing CTPU. Tariffs and charges are set and collected by the Ministry of Finance, often without the benefit of technical analysis. Development of the CTPU will be essential in the effective implementation of needed transport policy changes and institutional reform.

11.54   MOPWCRD Roads Division (RD) falls under the Public Works Branch and is responsible for the planning, construction and operation of pubic roads, as well as vehicle licensing. Currently responsibility for road maintenance is decentralized to the regions. This has been less than successful in the past due to lack of resources, equipment and technical capability in the regions. It is proposed that legislation be passed to recentralize responsibility for maintenance of the main roads system to RD. Roads Division currently has four professional staff, but there has been virtually no road development over the past decade.

11.55   The Demerara Harbor Bridge Project also falls under the Communications Branch and is responsible for the repair and maintenance of the bridge. The project structure works well given the on-going rehabilitation projects funded by the EC.

11.56   The Civil Aviation Department (CAD) of MOPWCRD, Communications Branch, has responsibility for development, maintenance and operation of all airports and airstrips, for the regulation of air transport, for the licensing of aircraft and pilots and for setting rates and tariffs. It is proposed that the operation and regulatory functions of CAD be separated by preparing and passing legislation creating an Airports Authority and a Civil Aviation Authority. In addition, the CAD currently contracts the UK Civil Aviation Authority (CAA) for airworthiness inspection and pilot testing, but CAA has recently ceased service due to non-payment. This regulatory function may best be undertaken at the regional level, and it is proposed that CARICOM investigate the feasibility of a Regional Airworthiness Authority. Policy development, regulatory compliance and airport licensing should remain the responsibility of CAD, but it is understaffed for complete coverage.

11.57   Guyana is a member of the International Civil Aviation Organization (ICAO), which establishes minimum standards for airport operations, airspace management and aviation related facilities and is bound by ICAO agreement to these international standards.

11.58   The Guyana Airways Corporation is administered under the Ministry of Trade and Tourism, but is regulated by CAD. If GAC is divested, air transportation regulation would remain with CAD. Negotiation of bilateral route rights is the responsibility the Transport Advisory Board of CAD. Guyana Airways Corporation is a participant in a multilateral interline agreement with the International Air Transport Association (IATA) which establishes agreements among international air carriers to carry passengers and cargo between sovereign states.

11.59   The Transport and Harbors Department (THD) of MOPWCRD under the Communications Branch, is responsible for ports, shipping and river transport. Its mandate includes provision of marine navigation services (pilots, marine navigation aids and dredging) and operation of ferries and coastal passenger/cargo services. THD is also the primary regulator in the marine sector encompassing: ship safety, vessel surveys, navigation services, channel maintenance, and policy. There is no port authority to coordinate and control port activities however, the Department has all the general powers and duties of a port and harbor authority, such as port land use and development, but it does not appear to be actively exercising this mandate. The Harbor Master's office and the Chief Pilot report to the Department General Manager. There are four main terminals at the port, two government owned and two privately owned.

11.60   As an institution, MOPWCRD suffers from the same problems systemic in the public service: low government salaries, resultant deficit in qualified personnel, lack of system information, and inappropriate accounting practices.

D. SECTOR FINANCES

1. Overview

11.61   Table 11.5 presents Guyana's transport sector expenditures from 1985 to 1992. Current expenditures have decreased in recent years, reflecting the lack of funds for maintenance. Maintenance expenditures are not recorded separately from MOPWCRD's other recurrent expenditures. Increases in the capital expenditures in 1991 and 1992 largely reflect investment in the Guyana/Brazil road and repairs to the Demerara Harbor Bridge. The percentage of total Government expenditures on transportation has steadily increased since 1986 indicating the Government's relative priority on transportation, but the current percentage of 6.2% is still low, and is distorted by the relatively large investment in the Guyana/Brazil road. A spending level of about 10-15% would be more realistic for Guyana.

Table 11.5: GUYANA'S TRANSPORT SECTOR EXPENDITURES 1985-92
(Current US$ millions)

	1985	1986	1987	1988	1989	1990	Est. 1991	Budget 1992
Current Expenditures	3.95	5.67	3.39	4.68	2.21	N/A	N/A	1.34
Capital Expenditures	3.98	3.40	2.25	4.61	6.93	N/A	11.06a/	10.26b/
Total	7.93	9.07	5.64	9.29	9.14	N/A	N/A	11.60
Share in Budget	2.16%	1.52%	1.85%	2.54%	4.30%	N/A	N/A	6.24%
Memorandum Item:								
User Charges				5.0	3.5	5.9	N/A	8.0c/

a/ Increase due to expenditure on Guyana/Brazil Road.
b/ Includes all transport related line items.
c/ Conservative estimate of vehicle registration, licenses, tolls and fuel tax (Table 11.7).

Source: Central Transport Planning Unit of MOPWCRD and 1992 Budget

2. Current Expenditures

11.62   Current account expenditures fall far short of required levels and have been decreasing since 1988 (Table 11.5). This trend reflects the crisis in transportation infrastructure maintenance. Table 11.6 present a breakdown of budgeted current account expenditures for 1992.

Table 11.6: BUDGETED OPERATIONS AND MAINTENANCE, 1992a/
(Current US$ millions)

	Road	Bridges	Other	Total
MOPWCRD RD	0.10	0.20	0.00	0.30
MOPWCRD CAD	0.01	0.00	0.10	0.11
Regions	0.67	0.18	0.08	0.93
TOTAL	0.78	0.38	0.18	1.34

a/ Excludes category "Other Maintenance" and Transport and Harbors Department which is nominally self financing.

Source: Guyana Public Accounts 1992

11.63   It is expected that less than 50% of allocations to the regions are actually spent on road maintenance, the rest being diverted to other sectors.

11.64   It is evident is there are inadequate funds in the current account for routine maintenance for roads. On average, for the 2500 km road network, the Roads Department spends less than US$120 per km on road maintenance. Even assuming funds are only spend on the main road network of 500 km, average expenditure is only US$600 per km. An average of US$2,500 per km for maintenance of paved roads is considered a minimum for South American and Caribbean standards (US$1,800 for other roads).

11.65   In aggregate, a recent World Bank Staff Appraisal Report estimates a need for US$5.77 million per year for maintenance of the road system (including the Demerara Harbor Bridge). Maintenance of a completed Guyana/ Brazil road would add another US$1 million per year. It is unlikely that the Government will be able to exceed the current US$0.3 million presently allocated (Table 11.6) in the near future.

11.66   However, most roads are so deteriorated now that full rehabilitation is needed, and funding is secured through IDB and IDA for rehabilitation of the most of the main road network. IDA, through the Agricultural Hybrid Loan, has also provided funding for the rehabilitation of 1000 miles of farm access roads. These projects include provisions for maintenance for non-project roads for the next four to five years, giving the Government a breathing period after which it is expected that the Government will be better able to commit to ongoing maintenance requirements.

11.67   Rehabilitation of feeder roads however, is not covered in either IDA or IDB's funding program (although both originally were planned to cover some sections) nor are maintenance funds available. This is a serious funding gap that the Government of Guyana will have to assume, unless other donors can be identified.

11.68   The current account expenditures also reflect the crisis in public sector salaries (which are one third that of private sector) and the difficulty in recruiting and retaining qualified technical staff. Average salaries are US$4,800 per year, or about US$80 per month. Due credit should be given to the many remaining staff who are professional and competent and who have made a commitment to assisting in Guyana's economic recovery. Most have other sources of income which enables them to remain in the Ministry. The issue of salaries and recruitment in the public sector is a systemic problem which must be addressed at the macro level.

11.69   Current expenditures by the Transport and Harbors Department and by marine related government enterprises such as the GNSC do not appear in the public accounts because of the self-financing nature of these entities. For THD total current expenditures in 1991 were US$2 million, but because Department revenues exceeded these expenditures, this amount was not represented in government accounts. The composition of the Department's current expenditures for its commercial services was: salaries and wages 16%; vessel maintenance 45%; building maintenance 7%; fuel and lubrication oil 22%; other expenses 9%.

3. User Charges

11.70   Highways expenditures in Guyana are recovered through road-user charges in the form of taxes and duties on motor fuels, lubricating oil, spare parts and tires, and imported vehicles, tolls and vehicle registration and licensing fees. Information is incomplete, but average total annual receipts estimates range from US$6 million to US$16.9 million for recent years. Table 12.7 presents a conservative estimate of road user charges. It is clear that user charges far exceed present maintenance levels, and indeed exceed even levels required for proper operation and maintenance (approximately US$5.7 million). However, these revenues contribute to general revenues for the Government, and it is unlikely the Government will be able to divert them entirely to road operation and maintenance. Nevertheless, better accounting, budgeting and stronger representation by CTPU should improve the allocations by emphasizing the magnitude of user charges, as well as the potential societal benefits of road maintenance (i.e., lower fuel consumption and vehicle wear).

11.71   Recently the tolls on all roads, except the Demerara River bridge, have been abolished by the Government, but the impact of that decision will be insignificant on receipts and in the long run beneficial to the country since the receipt did not cover the administration and accounting costs for the stations.

11.72   The current fuel consumption tax is 50% CIF (cost/insurance/ freight) for mogas, diesel and avfuel. The avfuel tax has been reduced from 140% pre 1991 to 75% in 1991 to 50% in 1992, but is still considered crippling by local operators. Oil company markups are typically 38% which some consider excessive.

11.73   Air transport user charges are collected through aviation fuel
taxes and surcharges, ticket taxes, a recently introduced US$8 departure tax,
as well as aircraft landing and parking fees and air navigation charges.
These fees are currently paid into general revenues and are not available for
aviation operation and maintenance. The CAD has for years been promoting the
establishment of a financially autonomous Airport Authority responsible for
self-financing operation and maintenance costs through user fees. The
Government has recently approved the preliminary planning for such an
Authority. The Authority could be self financing for operation and
maintenance, but not for capital expansion, which would still be the
responsibility of MOPWCRD. Self financing differs from commercially viable,
in that there are no profits made.

Table 11.7:   ROAD USER CHARGES
(In US$ millions)

	1988	1989	1990	1991	1992
Vehicle registration licenses and taxes	2.9	2.2	1.5	1.2	1.5
Tolls	0.2	0.1	0.1	0.0	0.0
Fuel Taxes	1.9	1.2	4.3	N/A	6.5 a/
TOTAL	5.0	3.5	5.9	N/A	8.0

a/ Assuming half of all gasoline and diesel fuel consumption tax collected
applies to road vehicles.

Source: IDB GY-0005, and Ministry of Finance

11.74   In 1991 revenues of the Transport and Harbors Department (US$2.10
million comprised of passenger fares 16%; cargo freight charges 15%; vehicle
and other fares 18%; barge revenues 5%; harbor dues: Pilotage 14%, light dues
10%, tonnage dues 22%) exceeded expenses to achieve a positive gross margin of
about 2%. The Department's operations combine money-losing ferry and steamer
operations with highly profitable harbor operations. Although surpluses are
being reported, it appears that the Department's accounting does not take in
account the cost of administrative overhead, dredging, vessel refits and the
backlog of maintenance needed for marine navigation systems. Accounted
expenses appear to include only wages, fuel, regular maintenance and supplies;
depreciation is not recognized.

11.75   When considered as a separate entity, the Department's ferries and
coastal vessels have a gross margin of negative 40%. All but one of the seven
major routes lost money; only the Berbice River ferry crossing generated a
surplus (US$0.22 million in 1991). The worst financial performance was for
the Berbice River service where revenues were only 24% of the US$ 117,000 in
expenses. Higher priced but faster private services (taxi boats) have
succeeded in capturing 25% to 50% of the passenger market from government
ferries and are accelerating the Department's ferry operations losses. The

taxi boat fare is more than double that of the ferry, indicating a willingness of users to pay for better service.

11.76   Harbor operations revenues are composed of Pilotage (30%), Light Dues (21%) and Tonnage Dues (48%) and amounted to US$0.95 million in 1991. From harbor operations, surpluses of US$0.58 million were generated in 1991. Harbor dues revenues exceeded the costs of pilotage and aids maintenance by a factor of about 2.5 to 1. The THD does not collect significant revenues or harbor dues from the use of wharves and terminals because they are owned and operated by other private and government enterprises.

4. Capital Expenditures

11.77   Capital expenditures have shown a significant increase in 1988/89 due to expenditures on the Black Bush Polder Road and on the Demerara Harbor Bridge, and in 1991/92 because of expenditures on the Demerara Harbor Bridge and the Guyana/Brazil Road.

11.78   The aviation sub-sector is seriously underfunded for capital upgrading. For example the CAD requested US$2.5 million for 1993 and were approved only for US$0.8 million. No plan for replacement of obsolete telecommunication and navigational equipment is even contemplated. Most equipment in the interior is already out of service, and equipment at Timehri is over 25 years old and must be replaced within three years.

Table 11.8: GUYANA'S PSIP TRANSPORT SECTOR EXPENDITURES 1992 a/
(Current US$ millions)

Timehri Airport	0.49
Stellings & Wharves	0.04
Demerara Harbor Bridge	1.31
Equipment Civil Aviation	0.09
Guyana/Surinam Ferry	0.00
Hinterland Airstrips	0.04
Land & Water Transport	0.25
Reconditioning of Ships	0.10
Roads (Regions)	0.25
Navigational Aids	0.02
Ferry Services	0.00
Reconditioning of Ferries	0.20
Bridges	0.19
Guyana/Brazil Road	5.27
Cargo Vessels - Spares	0.06
Land & Water (Regions)	0.11
Misc Roads	0.45
Bartica/Issano/Mahdia Rd	0.11
Timehri Fire Hall	0.13
Land Transp (Min of Labor)	0.01
Urban Roads & Drainage	0.32
Land/Water (Regions)	0.10
Guyana Airways Corp	0.20
Guyana National Shipping Corp	0.10
Guyana National Engineering Corp (shipping)	0.42
TOTAL	10.26
Roads	8.14
Air	0.95
Marine	1.17

a/ Several transportation items are not listed under "Transportation and Communications" category.

Source: Guyana Public Sector Investment Review, 1992

11.79   Capital expenditures by Government in the marine sector have included monies for reconditioning ferries and ships, providing vessel spares and for replacing navigation aids. Identified capital expenditures of this kind as listed in the Guyana Public Accounts were US$0.32 million in 1991 and US$0.97 million in 1992. Although nominally self-financing entities, both the Transport and Harbors Department and Guyana National Shipping Corporation (GNSC) have received such funds in 1991 and 1992.

11.80   It is interesting to compare the 1992 capital expenditures (Table 11.8) with the priorities of the new Government as presented in the document for the Meeting on Global Development Cooperation at the Carter Center in Atlanta on December 4-5, 1992 (Table 11.9). Such a comparison reveals that 1992 expenditures did not cover many of the new Government's priorities. A recommended future PSIP for transport is presented in Section H of this chapter.

Table 11.9: GOVERNMENT PRIORITIES IN THE TRANSPORT SECTOR

	Project	Gov Est (US$M)	Comment on Funding
1.	Emergency Maintenance Assistance Updating the Guyana Transport Plan Preparation on Investment Projects	3.094	IDA 1.5 roadmaintenance IDB 1.0 road maintenance Gap: Transport Plan
2.	Reorganization of Transport Functions	0.397	IDB 0.52 institutional strengthening
3.	Urban Transport master Plan Georgetown	0.554	No financing
4.	Demerara Floating Bridge Rehab	9.000	EC 9.0
5.	Rehab G/T-Soesdyke Road	10.700	IDB 5.2
6.	Rehab Timehri Airport	9.000	IDA 2.0 firetruck Financing Gap
7.	Demerara River Navigation	3.000	No financing
8.	Soesdyke-Linden Road resealing and bridges	5.500	IDA 5.0
9.	Rehab Essequibo Road	21.500	IDA 10.5 (lower design standard)
10.	Container Freight Station and Inner Port Area	6.000	IDA 0.2 study only Financing Gap
11.	Renovation of Hinterland Airports	10.000	No financing
12.	Ferries Action Plan	0.600	EC 0.27
13.	Tech Assistance for Shipyard Rehab and Concession	0.100	No financing
14.	Tech Assistance for Central Planning Unit	1.100	IDA 0.3 technical assistance
15.	Development of Inland Waterways (Feasibility)	1.500	No financing

Source: Based on "From Crisis to Sustainable Development and Democracy in Guyana".

E.   MAIN SECTORAL ISSUES

1.   General

11.81   Problems in MOPWCRD mirror those of the entire public sector: low salaries, lack of qualified staff, insufficient recruitment, a need for training, lack of a budgeting process, lack of system information, lack of clear lines of responsibility and accountability, no national-level planning, and poor donor coordination. Many of these systemic problems must be addressed at the macro level. The proposed IDA Public Administration Project is expected to target salaries and training, and the IDA and IDB sectoral projects are designed to address specific institutional and technical issues.

11.82   The lack of national planning in transport is a critical bottleneck to the efficient allocation of resources. Total transport solutions are needed which optimize modal roles and provide strategic policy and tariff bases. In all modal sub-sectors managers point out the need for training and the reestablishment of a technical training institute for mechanics, supervisors, pilots, marketing, distribution training, as well as management training.

2.   Road Transportation

11.83   The planned rehabilitation of the main road sections by IDB, IDA, and CDB over the next five years will effectively return Guyana's main road network system to acceptable standards. The issues during reconstruction are absorptive capacity of MOPWCRD and local contractors, and coordination and optimization of human and material resources. The issues after reconstruction are traffic management and, of course, provision for ongoing maintenance to prevent a return to current conditions.

Rehabilitation

11.84   Five large international contracts will be tendered within the next year for road rehabilitation; in addition, at least three contracts for sea wall reconstruction will also be tendered. The Government will want to coordinate this sizeable civil works program. For example, on the West Essequibo Coast, the road should not be rehabilitated until the sea wall is reconstructed, or the new road would be in danger of being washed out in the next breach of the sea wall. Similarly, there may be economies of scale with respect to purchase and shipping of materials needed for both sea wall and road construction, eg. stone aggregate, heavy equipment etc.

11.85   Prices for both road and sea wall reconstruction are affected by cost of quarried stone aggregate. This is an issue in Guyana because of the current monopoly status of the one operating quarry resulting in prices of about US$25 per ton; equal to the cost of imported aggregate. Aggregate is relatively so expensive, that the IDA road project on the Essequibo Coast involves a modified pavement design minimizing the use of aggregate and increasing the use of sand (which is more readily available). Production capacity must be increased and the price of rock has to come down at the same time. Some options are:

- Allow other companies than the established Toolsie-Persaud and Baracara to produce rock in Guyana. One possibility would be to divest the existing Tepura (GNS) quarry, which has sufficient potential to provide the local market and allow for export as well.

- Give tenderers for the new projects free access to the smaller quarries in the Essequibo river area.

- Make the Tepura quarry an open access quarry for future tenderers.

- Support the use of rock from inland gold mines.

11.86   The local contractor industry in Guyana is effectively dormant presently because of the paucity of work in the past decade. There are interested business people willing to rebuild their assets, or get into the industry if some minimum level of activity were assured for the future. Guyana will be highly dependent on private sector contractors in the future for maintenance, as MOPWCRD has neither staff or equipment to take on this function. Every effort should be made during the rehabilitation phase to involve local contractors.

Maintenance

11.87   Responsibility for highway administration has since 1985 been divided between the Roads Division (RD) of the MOPWCRD and the regional authorities. RD's role was restricted to the overall development of the main network and to advisory and technical support to the regions, while the regions were made responsible for the improvement, rehabilitation and maintenance of the roads in their region. The regional authorities have neither the technical capacity nor resources to perform their functions. On the other hand, RD which still has some capacity (4 professional-level staff) has practically nothing to do since there has been virtually no road development over the past decade. The maintenance funds allocated to the regional authorities are not only insufficient, but are also not necessarily spent on maintenance. Moreover those regions which try to execute maintenance are hampered by lack of technical capacity and equipment. In order to achieve any degree of successful maintenance of the soon to be rehabilitated main road system, the Government needs to recentralize the development, administration and maintenance of the main roads under the Roads Division, and allocate sufficient funds for operation and maintenance in the annual current account. Maintenance of feeder roads and trails should remain under regional responsibility, and again sufficient funds must be allocated for maintenance, and accountability for that maintenance should be monitored by RD.

Traffic Management

11.88   Improvement of the travelling surface of the main road network will significantly reduce vehicle user costs; however, it will also encourage higher travel speeds. This is an issue in Guyana because of the multi-purpose nature of roads. The coastal roads are in effect "main street Guyana" and are used as footpaths, for water hauling (on low wheeled platforms pulled by very young children), for animals, and at times the surface is completely covered by sun-drying rice paddy (hiding any potholes). The road runs through built up residential and market areas its entire length. The accident rate is currently unacceptable, and the livestock loss through accidents is significant.

11.89   IDB Report GY-0005 (Guyana Main Road Rehabilitation Project) reports that in recent years, the average number of fatalities was 191 per year. An extremely high proportion of these fatalities, over two-thirds, were accounted for by pedestrians, bicyclists and users of other non-standard transport (i.e. push carts). Over 20% of all fatalities were children. This translates into approximately 25 times the average fatality rate per 1,000 motor vehicles per year in a developed country.

11.90   The pattern of deaths and injuries on roads in Guyana is explained in part by the lack of shoulders on the trunk roads. This problem will be largely addressed in the design of the IDB and IDA road rehabilitation projects, However, some form of public education and traffic management program is needed. In addition, compliance of vehicle safety and axle loading regulations must be improved to prevent premature destruction of road surfaces and to increase safety.

Feeder Roads

11.91   Unless a donor is found for rehabilitation of feeder roads, the Government will have to budget for feeder road maintenance. The Black Bush Polder Road is a priority feeder road in need of repairs or reconstruction. The use of local traditional technologies should be examined for possible cost economies, for example, the use of "burnt earth" aggregates.[28]

Urban Roads

11.92   Urban roads are presently serviced in an ad-hoc, patch up process. Rehabilitation should be part of an overall urban development master plan. The proposed IDB Urban Rehabilitation Program is investigating the best approach.

Guyana/Brazil Road

11.93   The most significant issue with respect to financing is the proposed Government expenditure to complete the Guyana/Brazil Road (also referred to as the Mabura-Lethem Road). The cost of this road is US$30 million, financed through loans with the Government of Brazil, plus ongoing maintenance costs estimated at over US$1.0 million per year. A total of US$16 million has already been spent in Phase I (210 km). Loan terms are being negotiated now for Phase II US$14 million for 136 km).

11.94   The Government's objective in building this road is to open up the vast resources of the hinterland to development, increase trade with Brazil, enable farmers in the savannas of the Rupununi district to market their cattle and other produce in Georgetown, and to provide better medical and educational services to the Amerindians and other residents of the interior.

28/   Burnt earth is created by laying wood in an earth pit, adding a layer of local clay, then another layer of wood and setting the entire pit on fire for about three days until the clay is dried and clumped. This technology requires considerable skill and is practiced only by a few older road workers.

11.95   However, the high the cost of the road, both in capital and recurring maintenance costs, requires rigorous examination of the investment to date and the proposed benefits of completion.

11.96   The loan agreement will require a significant portion of Guyana's available external financing and will indebt the country into the 21st century. Also of concern is the likelihood that the Government will not be able to afford to properly maintain the completed road, which would result in its rapid deterioration and ultimately a decay of the investment.

11.97   The road design is already of questionable standard. The existing portion is not built for heavy loading and the quality of construction has been challenged. The Phase II section alignment has also been questioned in that it does not take advantage of a natural ridge line and sand base.

11.98   The premise of the road investment is that the cost of transport to the interior, currently only possible by air, will be greatly reduced by land transport, thus stimulating greatly increased traffic demand. Also to be considered, however, is that air service (and the associated infrastructure costs) will still be required for air access to areas not along the road, and for time dependent transport. The per trip cost from the Rupinuni to Georgetown will be greatly reduced by the availability of a road compared to current air service. However, the full economic cost of facility, including the capital cost, must be included in an analysis. It is likely that a detailed analysis will show that improved air service, through greater frequency of service and a decrease the present unit cost per passenger or ton of cargo (through economies of scale or subsidies) would also achieve an induced demand, and at lesser total economic cost. The population to be served by this road is presently less than 50,000 people; thus the effective cost of the road is over US$1000 per person.

11.99   There is no evidence of a recent economic feasibility study done for this road. However a general analysis for the 1975 Guyana National Transport Plan, was conducted using a range of forecasted traffic demands. It reports:

> "A general conclusion of the preliminary economic analysis is that for the existing and forecasted low traffic of the hinterland roads, it is not economically justified to build roads, even for the lowest standards, in order to transfer traffic from other modes of transport. On the other hand, the investment needed to improve the road leads to even greater loses. A road must therefore be justified by special development projects (eg. the Kamarang Hydropower Station). Otherwise, the construction of a road in the hinterland can be justified only by non-economic objectives, e.g., national, political, defense."

11.100   The Government is not prepared for the impact of a completed road with respect to regulation of natural resource development (mining and timber), or impact on Georgetown's urban road and port facilities. Other concerns include the possible damage to the rainforest, increased theft of livestock, smuggling, exploitation of "open-door" Amerindian communities, and transmission of disease for both humans and livestock.

11.101   The creation of a spine road may well be justified for political, unity and national defence objectives if resources were available. However, for a country with the severe financial situation of Guyana, where every dollar spent has a huge opportunity cost for competing urgent requirements, this investment cannot be justified at this time or in the near future. Hence, this investment should be deferred until a study of options for hinterland development can be quantitatively studied. Strengthening of the interior aviation system will meet the transportation requirements of the country at a lower cost, with greater flexibility and greater area covered.

3. Air Transportation

Airport Development

11.102   The role of aviation in the economic well being of the country should not be underestimated. Aviation plays a critical modal role in two areas: international passenger transport, and access to the interior.

11.103   Immediate intervention is required to improve airport safety and security; specifically in Crash Fire Rescue services, and emergency Telecommunication and Navigation repairs.

11.104   Rational, well managed airport development is constrained by the current institutional and budgeting arrangement in MOPWCRD. Airport lands are not vested with the Civil Aviation Directorate, and thus cannot be protected for appropriate zoning and future development. Ogle Airport is owned by GUYSUCO and is managed as part of the sugar industry. Revenues from aviation activities currently go directly to central government accounts and are not available for maintenance or improvement of services. Current airport management is largely oriented to caretaking and crisis control. Very little initiative is shown due to lack of training, lack of motivation, lack of funds, and lack of authority.

11.105   Because of the distance of Timehri International Airport from Georgetown, Ogle Airport has taken on increasing importance for domestic service and is best positioned for future regional service eg. to the Caribbean. Ogle, however does not have the space for eventual expansion to receive larger long range aircraft. For these reasons both airports will have to be retained for the foreseeable future.

11.106   The Government has taken an important positive step in approving study into the establishment of an Airport Authority. An Authority, to be responsible for both airports each with separate management, would be directed by a Board of Directors independent from CAD but responsible to MOPWCRD. The Authority would be self financing for operation and maintenance. CAD would remain responsible for operational safety regulation and aircraft airworthiness. This strategy should be pursued vigilantly and could be achieved within six months with some outside technical assistance in the arrangement of required legislation and the establishment of the Authority mandate. The Governments of Jamaica and Barbados have implemented the Airport Authority model, and should be consulted for assistance and valuable Caribbean related experience in this matter.

11.107   The preparation of a Master Plan for Timehri should be the first priority of the Airport Authority. Review of user fees and development possible commercial sources of revenue (eg. duty free sales, restaurants, lease of unused airport lands etc.) should be investigated. Provision of cargo sheds, refrigerated facilities and improved customs handling will also improve service and promote export opportunities.

11.108   Development of Ogle airport should be left to the private sector. Development to date has been constrained by government blockage. Ownership of airport lands should be transferred from GUYSUCO to CAD and leased liberally to private operators. The Government must create a transparent and supportive environment to encourage private sector investment in the airport.

11.109   The CAD now uses the United Kingdom's Civil Aviation Authority (CAA) for airworthiness inspections, a practice becoming increasingly expensive throughout the Caribbean. Current arrears have led the CAA to threaten discontinuation of service, as is has done throughout the Caribbean. These critical issues of safety and security in the aviation sub-sector must be addressed. Funds must be made available for these services, or alternatively, CARICOM must be encouraged to investigate the feasibility of the creation of a Regional Airworthiness Authority to replace the need for the CAA.

Air Telecommunication and Navigational Aids

11.110   Navigational aids in the country are largely non-existent or near expected service life. A replacement program must be planned and financed. Urgent requirements should be integrated into existing infrastructure rehabilitation programs.

Guyana Airways Corporation

11.111   The profitability of GAC's international operations is most uncertain given the aging aircraft and competing international service. If the Government does not want to continue subsidizing GAC (through protectionist policies and discriminatory practices) it should move quickly to divest GAC or bring in foreign joint owners in order to benefit from current negotiations among the other regional airlines LIAT and BWIA regarding privatization or creation of joint ventures with foreign operators. If GAC negotiates independently of LIAT and BWIA, it may also have an advantage because of its single entity owner; whereas LIAT and BWIA are owned jointly by many states with competing objectives. Guyana can not afford to subsidize an inefficient operation that can and should be run on a commercial basis. As a private operator, CAD would still regulate safety and service of the airline and would still represent the airline in route right negotiations.

11.112   The removal of the protectionist policy toward GAC will result in benefits and consequences that typically follow direct exposure to international competition. The Government would indeed save money, and air service frequency and choices will improve. If the airport is upgraded, US air carriers have shown interest in providing service in addition to the regional carriers. The Government, however, will have less control over service and prices.

11.113   In addition to divesting GAC, the Government is considering an "open skies" policy, whereby Guyana would open rights to operate out of Timehri to any qualified carrier that applies. Again, this would improve frequency of service, but may affect the viability of GAC. GAC's viability, however, is dependent on Government, or its private owners, making significant investment in aircraft and personnel in the next several years, which may be unrealistic in any event.

11.114   Domestic services of GAC are also of concern. It is generally agreed that the one scheduled flight offered per week is inadequate. Other users must charter aircraft at much higher cost. The Government could support GAC domestic service through the purchase of an additional aircraft and creation of additional scheduled flights, or it could turn over domestic operations to private operators. This is a case where the private sector, which already has adequate aircraft, could provide the service more efficiently and at lower overall economic cost. The improvement of hinterland airstrips, navigation and communication is also essential for improved access to the interior. The delay of the construction of the Guyana/Brazil road would free up funds for hinterland airports.

4.   Coastal and River Transportation

Navigation Aids

11.115   Guyana's marine navigation services are inadequate and unsafe by international standards. A high proportion of navigation aids and radio beacons are out of service due to lack of maintenance and vandalism. Improved navigational aids would save money for the industry in two ways: first by reducing demurrage charges, and second by doubling the effective use of Guyana's harbors and waterways by permitting nighttime operations.

11.116   Because harbor dues generate surpluses (US$0.58 million in 1991) above the costs of pilotage and other navigation services, substantial funds for sustained maintenance of navigation services are potentially available. However, these surplus harbor dues funds are now used to pay the operating losses of ferries and coastal cargo ships of the THD. Privatization or re-organization for self-financing operations of ferries and coastal cargo ships would reduce losses to the Government and funds would become available for improved navigation services. Improved navigation services, in turn, would reduce demurrage penalties and reduce freight rates thereby increasing the net price that Guyana can get for its exports.

11.117   For the size of vessels now being used in Guyana, each day of ship's time saved has a value of about US$0.40 for every ton handled. For example, the publicly owned bauxite marketing and shipping company, BIDCO, paid an annual demurrage penalty of about US$0.5 million this year to foreign ship owners for delays attributable to navigational delays. These delays occur when pilots are not available, when ships must wait for daylight because navigation lights are out, and when ships can't pass the Demerara Bridge because it won't open. In addition to demurrage, there are hidden freight rate surcharges reflecting the relative inefficiency of marine operations. Metallurgical grade bauxite, Guyana's largest volume export, currently nets about US$23 per ton to Guyana after shipping charges (ranging from US$12 to US$35 per ton) are paid. Because deep-sea shipping is highly competitive, improvements to navigation that reduce ship delays would translate to an increase in the net price that Guyana can get for its metallurgical grade bauxite. Consequently, it is recommended that navigation services be improved with the expectation of immediate returns to Guyana for its exports of bauxite and other bulk products such as sugar and rice.

11.118   Guyana's two deep sea harbors at Georgetown and New Amsterdam are shallow and loaded vessels depend on tidal assistance for entry and departure. Because Guyana's tides are semidiurnal, there is usually at least one high tide in daylight hours available for entry or exit. Providing night navigation would reduce the interval between useful high tides from 24 hours to 12 hours. Since the 96 km river journey to Linden's bauxite terminal requires two high tides in each direction, the capacity for night navigation would significantly reduce vessel cycle time and would cause a reduction in freight charges. Furthermore, shipping charges for Guyana

Waterways Development

11.119   Lack of water depth in Guyana's harbors results in the use of smaller high cost ships, which may reduce earnings potentials from the sale of bauxite, sugar and other exports and may increase the cost of imports.

11.120   Although the mandate to carry out dredging is assigned to THD, BIDCO is currently bearing the burden of paying nearly US$2 million per year to maintain existing water depths at Georgetown's harbor entrance through dredging. Dredging must be repeated at seven month intervals to maintain depths against sedimentation from silt transported by northerly currents along Guyana's shallow coast. The THD dredge does not have the capacity for the required work and consequently a Dutch dredging company has been retained. Each dredging program costs about US$1 million. In the period from May 1992 to December 1992, sedimentation at Georgetown's harbor entrance caused the limiting depth to go from 6.9 m to 6.25 m below datum. On a 12,000 tons deadweight capacity vessel, the 0.65 m change amounts to a significant loss of about 1,400 tons of carrying capacity. Indicative of the savings that could be achieved if dredging were to allow the use of larger ships is the difference in freight rates charged for Trinidad and Tobago and Guyana for sugar: for otherwise comparable sugar shipments, but with smaller vessels being used for Guyanese shipments, Trinidad and Tobago is charged US$15 per ton, while Guyana is charged US$23 per ton for transport to the UK.

11.121   Although the main entrance channel has been deepened, water depths at wharves and in the Demerara River have decreased and are restrictive. Reported depths at Georgetown wharves range from 4.9 to 6.1 m. Shallow water forces the use of smaller higher cost vessels to carry exported products with the result that net returns to Guyana are reduced. Small increases in water of depth at some terminals would significantly reduce marine freight rates. However, because of the risk of undermining their shallow timber pile wharves, the four main general cargo/container terminals have only a limited potential for deepening. Significant deepening awaits the development of a new common user general cargo/container terminal.

11.122   The net benefit of deepening the main entrance channel beyond the existing design depth of 6.9 m requires study to determine whether increasing the already high cost of maintenance dredging is justified. For example, some of Guyana's bauxite buyers require smaller parcel sizes where the capacity for larger shipments may not translate into higher revenues for Guyana. With production increases, the benefits of navigational improvements and dredging will be much greater. Investigation and economic analysis is required to determine if Guyana could attain possible shipping advantage through increased dredging.

Port/Industrial Planning

11.123   This function appears to be completely absent. For example, private and public sector terminal operators are all under severe space constraints at Georgetown's river front and are beginning the process of acquiring additional cargo storage areas. Nevertheless, no suitable expansion areas have been designated. For off-port container and general cargo facilities to work effectively, there is a need for: the provision of site services, customs services and in the integration of road access and coastal vessel access. Roadways linking wharves to off-port storage areas need to be widened and strengthened to allow containers to move in and out. These services should be provided for the common good of port users, rather that each terminal developing its own facilities at much higher cost, and possible detrimental impact to other users.

11.124   Another example of the effect of poor planning is that wharves and other structures appear to have been constructed on the Demerara River without regard to detrimental hydraulic effects causing sedimentation in front of wharves. For example, the construction of the floating bridge and a fishing wharf appear to have caused such downstream sedimentation. Dredge spoils have been deposited in areas upstream of marine facilities and have caused reductions in water depths. There is no authority for the systematic development of marine resources. This is a result of inadequate capacity by THD to manage port facilities and points to the need for some form of Harbor Authority.

Port and Harbor Management

11.125   The 1975 National Transportation Plan recommended the establishment of a National Ports and River Authority for the long term planning of port development and regulation of river transport including ferry services. This concept is still valid. An IDA study, under the IRP, will look into the feasibility of creating a "Guyana Port Authority" (GPA) having an autonomous Board of Directors, which would make all essential operating and business decisions, and retain all revenues generated by the GPA for the operation and further development of its ports and other facilities. The study will determine whether pilotage services, hydrographic surveying, dredging of ports and waterways, supply and maintenance of navigation aids, and operation of an off-dock container storage facility should fall within the proposed GPA, or be operated as separate entities. It would also be determined whether the GPA should continue to operate government owned cargo terminals, and whether GPA should be responsible for the allocation of berths, including the allocation of berths from and to privately operated terminals.

11.126   Another option in the range of possible configurations of a port authority would involve the creation of port company to own and operate its commercial port facilities. While the shareholdings of these companies are primarily owned by local authorities, the liberalization of company shareholdings creates the opportunity for wider port ownership, in particular by industry interests. Negotiations for initial setup of the port company could include assignment of shares in return for transfer of currently privately-owned facilities. The port company would be required to operate commercially, and focus on business performance and efficiency, rather than the mix of commercial and social objectives that are the norm under an elected harbor board system. Port companies do not have regulatory powers, but are able to respond to market demands and expectations.

11.127   The "private" sector (including publicly owned BIDCO and GUYSUCO) have already taken on the responsibility and the costs of dredging, provision of some navigation aids, repairs to the Demerara Bridge opening mechanism, the development of terminals, and the acquisition and development of off-port storage areas. Because the private sector has shown the willingness and capability to act, there are encouraging indications for the success of private sector participation in a port company.

11.128   Under this option, the independent port company would: own buildings, lands, wharves, warehouses and handling equipment; undertake its own port planning; maintain navigation aids and vessel traffic systems within harbor limits; conduct its own dredging within harbor limits; collect tonnage dues, light dues, wharfage and handling fees; and finance itself independently. Government would: set up an independent pilotage authority; establish the necessary legislation and regulatory framework; regulate on the basis of ship safety; and facilitate customs and bonded areas to support new development. Whatever the specific arrangement, an independent authority is needed to improve port operations and ensure optimal development in the future.

Privatization of Government Marine Enterprises

11.129   The government owned Guyana National Shipping Corporation (GNSC) operates a small coastal cargo vessel, vessel repair services, operate a shipping agency, a trailer transport service and a general cargo/container terminal.   In addition, the Guyana National Engineering Corporation (GNEC) operates dry docks, ship building yards and runs a river pilotage service. Both enterprises rely on requests for capital funds from the Government to fund equipment purchases. However, at the same time, private terminals and privately operated coastal cargo vessels profitably compete and perform the same services as the Government's commercial marine sector operations without government subsidy. It is therefore recommended that GNSC and GNEC should be privatized, thereby forcing the enterprises to operate competitively, and relieving the Government of subsidy payments. Because of the competitive nature of the marine sector it is unlikely that the cost, or level of service will be affected.

F. PROPOSED STRATEGY

11.130   The following strategy is comprised of seven elements: it suggests that the Government should focus on the establishment of national level planning, institutional reform, making some immediate interventions, establishing a role for the private sector, increasing transportation user charges, hinterland development, and longer term initiatives. The important aspect about the proposed strategy, is that it is not delineated strictly by mode; it emphasizes the inter-modal nature of transportation, the interdependencies and complementarities required for an efficient use of resources.

1. National Planning

11.131   Need for a National Transportation Plan. In an economy of extreme financial constraint, resource management is critical to optimize the impact of each investment. Investments should be complementary and synergetic. Improvements to the transportation system in Guyana must be strategically designed to contribute to the collective national recovery. The Transport Plan for Guyana 1975, prepared with the assistance of the Israel Institute of Transportation, was a comprehensive and useful plan for the time. Unfortunately, little of the plan was implemented and many of the issues and priorities still apply. This document should be updated for the 1990's and for the new Administration's vision for Guyana. A National Transport Plan will ensure that the increasing investments in transport (22 % of PSIP) are optimally allocated from a inter-modal perspective. The Plan will also provide an effective means of determining the relative priority of projects for investment. Finally a plan will encourage international and foreign investment and will be useful for the coordination of international and foreign funding agency projects. This should be the first task on the strengthened Central Transport Planning Unit and foreign technical assistance should be solicited.

11.132   Need to Strengthen the Central Transport Planning Unit. The CTPU currently has only one professional staff member. MOPWCRD needs to hire at least two more over the next year if the Unit is to have any impact on the sector's functioning. Moreover, several key issues coming up over the next two or three years will require strong contribution from the CTPU. Among these are: preparation of the National Transportation Plan, highway financing and the issue of increasing user charges, the separation of MOPWCRD's regulatory and operator's roles in river transport, the establishment of an Airport Authority and Civil Aviation Authority, the need and feasibility of establishing a national ports authority, the creation of a commercial-based off-port container terminal, and the next phase of the development of the main road arteries. In addition, the CTPU should be coordinating the budget process for all transport departments and agencies. The IDA road project proposes a component for the strengthening of the CTPU through the provision of technical assistance. The Government should hire the required staff and participate fully in the rebuilding of the CTPU.

2. Institutional Reform

11.133   Roads Division - Recentralization of Operation and Maintenance. The existing decentralized responsibility for roads to the regions is ineffective since the regions have neither the resources, staff nor technical capacity to carry out their responsibility. The recentralization of responsibilities, at least for the main road network should be undertaken immediately. The proposed IDA and IDB road projects include technical assistance for this transition, but the Government must prepare and pass enabling legislation. The Roads Division should also take over responsibility for vehicle safety, traffic management and axle loading regulations and enforcement, as well as public education regarding safety and overloading.

11.134   Integration of Sea Wall and Road Construction. There may be merit to the possibility of moving the division of the Hydraulics Division responsible for sea wall reconstruction, currently in the Ministry of Agriculture, to MOPWCRD in order to optimize overlapping skills and duties required in both road and sea wall construction and maintenance. Such functions would include design, contractor registration, contract preparation and administration, technical services, and construction supervision.

11.135   Creation of an Airport Authority and Civil Aviation Authority. The new Government has recently indicated interest in moving towards the establishment of an autonomous Airport Authority (for overall management of Timehri and Ogle airports) and a Civil Aviation Authority (which will retain regulatory functions). This initiative should proceed immediately. As autonomous authorities, the agencies will become self financing for operation and maintenance expenses, although capital improvements will remain the responsibility of central government. The Airport Authority would be run by a Board of Directors comprised of government and stakeholder members (airlines, concession owners, consumers etc.). This will promote more efficient management, increased revenues, improved services (including cargo facilities) and longer term planning due to more control over budgeting. A self-financed Authority will also require improved budget accountability.

11.136   In addition, Cabinet approval should be obtained to vest airport lands, both at Timehri and Ogle, in the CAD, in order to enforce airport zoning and to protect future land requirements. A Master Plan for both airports should also be prepared.

11.137   Investigation of Creation of a Regional Airworthiness Authority. CARICOM should be encouraged to investigate the feasibility of establishing a Regional Airworthiness Authority to replace the costly UK Civil Aviation Authority contract for inspection of aircraft in the Caribbean.

11.138   Expansion of Options for Harbor Authority. An autonomous and self-financing body that has the responsibility, will, technical and financial capability to maintain port waterways and to plan and create future facilities at the Port of Georgetown is required. The range of options for a "Port Authority of Guyana" to be studied under the IDA IRP program should be expanded to include the possible creation of a port company with shareholdings available to the private sector. The Government should participate actively in this study and support the concept of user driven port expansion.

11.139   A comprehensive port development plan for Georgetown and the Demerara River estuary needs to be developed and adopted. Based on a plan having the support of the major stakeholders, development guidelines concerning dredging, placement of dredge spoils, new bridge or wharf construction, anchorages, traffic management, need to be developed and enforced through the Harbor Master's office. Concurrent with port development plan, a marine sector information center and library should be established with the aim of facilitating technological transfer.

11.140   Improve Technical Training. In all modes, transport operators agree that there is a need to improve technical training in Guyana with respect to mechanical maintenance, management, operation, marketing and distribution skills. A Government Technical Institute has been proposed as one option. A more encompassing option is the establishment of a CARICOM Regional Aviation and Maritime Training Institute. Scope for services expands when regional.

3. Immediate Interventions

11.141   Main Road Rehabilitation. The main road rehabilitation projects proposed by the IDA, IDB and CDB will restore Guyana's main road network to economic standards while assisting in the reorganization of Roads Department. This initiative is adequately financed in the PSIP.

11.142   Improve Aviation Facilities. Civil aviation facilities cannot be allowed to deteriorate beyond minimum international standards. Because of the nature of international aviation, tolerances are not permitted for developing countries beyond minimum requirements. Crash Fire Rescue services should be improved immediately. Emergency repairs to aviation telecommunication and navigation systems should be undertaken by the Government in 1993. Funding should be sought for a longer-term T&N replacement and expansion program. An Airport Maintenance and Management System must be developed and adopted to ensure the sustainability of Timehri International Airport.

11.143   Improve Hinterland Airstrips. An immediate program to rehabilitate selected hinterland airstrips is needed. No funding is currently secured in the PSIP for this initiative.

11.144   Improve Port and River Navigation. A buoy tender, several fast patrol boats, and tamper proof replacement navigation aids should be acquired to restore night navigation for deep sea vessels. With the re-introduction of night navigation, some form of low level vessel traffic management system and the publication of a Sailing Directions document may justified. An independent self-financing pilotage authority should be created and supplied with refurbished or new pilot launches. The feasibility of introducing electronic navigation systems should be investigated.

11.145   Off-Dock Container Freight Station. There a current need for a new consolidated container/general cargo handling area away from the Georgetown's crowded river front. The IDA IRP project will study this proposal, but terminal operators are currently making their own plans; an immediate plan for coordination is needed.

4. Role of Private Sector

11.146   If the Government presents a stable and supportive environment for public sector enterprise, many of the gaps in transportation services will be filled by the private sector.

11.147   Creation of a Contractors' Association. The future PSIP civil works activities give the Government an ideal opportunity to promote the re-establishment of the contractors industry. Classification of contractors and tenders should be carried out in order to create equal competition and to avoid contract failures. The establishment of an Association of Contractors is urgently required. The Government should promote local contractor participation in the upcoming work in road and sea wall rehabilitation, such that the industry will be ready to assume maintenance contracts subsequent to the rehabilitation. Finally, the Government should consider the divestment of the government owned General Construction Company Ltd. in order to promote competition in the industry.

11.148   <u>Private Sector in Quarrying</u>. The increase in civil works proposed in the PSIP highlights the need to open the market for quarried stone required for both road and sea wall rehabilitation. There now exists a monopoly on quarry stone which results in prices that are near that of international imports. The Government should consider the privatization of Guyana National Services, but with corresponding regulation which will not permit a new cartel on prices. Also to be considered is the opening on new, smaller quarries, or free access to government owned deposits for government contracts. (See also Chapter IX on Sea Defenses.)

11.149   <u>Private Sector in Aviation</u>. Domestic air service provided by GAC is inadequate and unlikely to improve without the acquisition of additional aircraft (one twin otter) and reinstatement of several scheduled routes to the interior. However, the current fleet of general aviation aircraft more than meets expected domestic demand. Arrangements could be established with the Aircraft Owners Association to provide scheduled service in addition to essential health, mail and exploration services to the interior if Ogle Airport is developed as Municipal Airport under the aforementioned Airports Authority. The private aviation sector has shown interest and capability to do so. Rates would be monitored through competition with the existing GAC service, or through regulation by the new Civil Aviation Authority.

11.150   GAC's international operation should be divested. The Government cannot afford to continue subsidizing GAC (through protectionist policies and discriminatory practices). It should move quickly to divest GAC or bring in foreign joint owners in order to benefit from current negotiations among the other regional airlines LIAT and BWIA regarding privatization or creation of joint ventures with foreign operators. If GAC negotiates independently of LIAT and BWIA, it may also have an advantage because of its single entity owner; whereas LIAT and BWIA are owned jointly by many states with competing objectives. Guyana can not afford to subsidize an inefficient operation that can and should be run on a commercial basis. As a private operator, regulation of safety and service of the airline would still be the responsibility of CAD, and CAD would still represent the airline in route right negotiations. Ultimately, the Government should move to an "open skies" policy, opening up Guyana to service from outside airlines.

11.151   <u>Private Sector in the Development of Ogle as a Community Aerodrome</u>. The development of Ogle can be entirely devolved to the private sector. The Aircraft Owners Association of Guyana have the capacity, capability and resources to do so. Commercial arrangements will have to negotiated by the Government to fully facilitate private development while maintaining regulatory and safety control. The establishment of an Airport Authority will greatly facilitate this process.

11.152   <u>Private Sector in River Transport</u>. The ferry service need not be expanded if private taxi boats and pontoon barges can be encouraged. The proposed purchase of two new ferries by EC should be revisited by the Government as funding may be better allocated to the strengthening of the regulatory function of THD.

11.153   <u>Private Sector in Shipping</u>. The Government is maintaining a loss on two shipping companies which should be entirely divested.

5. Increase Transportation User Charges

11.154   Infrastructure improvements needed will have to be supported by increased user charges. How to implement them without adversely penalizing the people and industries the system is meant to serve is an important undertaking.

11.155   Road User Costs. The total road-user charge receipt per year fully recovers the cost not only currently spent on roads but would also cover adequately the requirements needed annually for the next five years to restore the network and prevent its further deterioration. The problem is one of allocating a sufficient portion of the user-charge receipts for operation and maintenance. This is unlikely to happen soon with existing revenues, since the Ministry of Finance relies on these charges for general revenue. The highway authorities must compete for scarce general revenue funds with other sectors of the economy. This means that they must be able to present a convincing case for their budget request and its timely release. They must also be able to show what has been done with former budget allocations.

11.156   In addition to allocation from Ministry of Finance, a surcharge on fuel has been proposed, which would be earmarked for operation and maintenance. This could take the form of an increase in consumption tax on fuels, the elimination of exemptions currently allowed to selected businesses on the consumption tax for fuels, or the introduction of a pump tax.

11.157   Other areas for possible increases in revenues are improved compliance in payment of vehicle licensing dues, or the introduction of more efficiently administered road tolls. The Demerara Harbor Bridge tolls should definitely be increased, and applied directly to operation and maintenance. Private sector involvement in the maintenance of roads directly serving mining, timber or agricultural sites might also be explored. The Government must prepare a strategy for funding operation and maintenance of the road network or deterioration will continue.

11.158   In the air sub-sector, the establishment of an Airport Authority will permit user charges (landing fees, passenger taxes, concession rents, fuel throughput charges etc.) to be directly applied to services. Charges can be reviewed and increased as appropriate. This is an less an issue of increasing charges, as it is to applying them directly to airport operations.

11.159   Similarly, in the marine sub-sector, a national port authority would be self financing; fees could be adjusted to cover the cost of services provided. If the Government privatizes the two shipping companies losses will be eliminated thus eliminating the need subsidies. For the THD ferry services, the EC is studying THD's finances, as part of its ferry rehabilitation assistance and with the Government will insist on proper cost recovery as a condition for further assistance.

6. Hinterland Development

11.160   Perhaps the most difficult tradeoff in transportation master planning is determining modal access to underdeveloped regions. The Government has promoted the construction of a main road from Georgetown to the Brazil border at Lethem which is intended to increase exports from the Rupinuni, promote trade with Brazil, increase health and education services in the hinterland, and improve national defence. The road has become a symbol of the development of Guyana.

11.161   In addition to the total US$30 million construction cost (US$16 m spent, US$14 estimated for Phase II), maintenance of the road would burden the Government with an additional US$1.0 million per year. The design standards adopted for the road appear inadequate for the type of heavy truck traffic that would use the road. All economic analysis to date show that the road is not justified economically at this time or in the near future, for the traffic projected. The Government would have to issue a port transit tax and/or toll taxes to cover the loan payment and maintenance of the road. Nor is the Government prepared for the impact of a completed road with respect to regulation of resource development, or impact on urban road and port facilities. In addition, the road may pose serious environmental hazard, will serve only the areas adjacent to the road, may be a conduit for disease and smuggling.

Box 11.1:   ALASKA HIGHWAY

The main road to the Canadian North is the famous Alaska Highway, built by the Americans in response to the Japanese bombing of Pearl Harbor and the perceived threat of an attack on Alaska during the Second World War. This road was never used for defence but served a useful public relations role in presenting an apparent defence against a desperate enemy. Fifty years later, the Alaska highway has certainly made a difficult life easier for those living along it, but it has also introduced many diseases to indigenous peoples and disrupted a valued way of life. The Alaska Highway now costs the Government of Canada over US$20 million per year to maintain and is only marginally cost effective, partially due to tourism related to the history of the road.

11.162   The alternative to a road is improved hinterland air access, in terms of improved air service and airstrips. For example, the Government of Canada has chosen air access to service much of its vast Canadian northlands as the most cost effective solution to hinterland development (Box 11.1).

11.163   Phase II of the construction of the Guyana/Brazil road should be deferred until further study. Because of the strong national appeal for the road, a detailed economic and socio-environmental study must be prepared to enable the Government to make a defensible decision. Equally important is the need to be able to explain and quantify the costs and benefits of various options to the populace.

7. Long Term Outlook

11.164   The long term strategy for the transport sector in Guyana includes the completion of the Guyana/Brazil road. In addition, new port facilities should be developed with road access bypassing the city of Georgetown. As traffic increases, Timehri International Airport should be expanded and the runway lengthened to handle wide-body aircraft. Ogle Airport should eventually be developed as a full regional airport (short range) for business, tourism and commuter services.

BOX 11.2:   SUMMARY OF PROPOSED STRATEGY FOR TRANSPORTATION SECTOR

1.   National Planning:
     Prepare a National Transportation Plan
     Strengthen the Central Transport Planning Unit of MOPWCRD

2.   Institutional Reform:
     Recentralize Responsibility for Maintenance of Main Roads
     Investigate Integration of Sea Wall and Road Construction
     Create an Airport Authority
     Investigate Feasibility of CARICOM Airworthiness Authority
     Study Feasibility of Establishing a Port Authority
     Improve Technical Training

3.   Immediate Interventions:
     Rehabilitate Main Roads
     Improve Aviation Facilities
     Improve Hinterland Airstrips
     Improve Port and River Navigation

4.   Role for Private Sector:
     Encourage private Sector in River Transport for Passengers
     Privatize Government Shipping Companies
     Determine Role of Guyana Airways Corporation
     Encourage Private Sector Development of Ogle Aerodrome
     Improve Competition in Quarry Development
     Create a Contractors' Association

5.   Increase Transport User Charges:
     Prepare a plan for Increased Road User Fees

6.   Hinterland Development:
     Defer further expense on Guyana/Brazil Road
     Investigate Options for Hinterland access

7.   Longer Term Initiatives:
     Guyana/Brazil Road
     New Port Facilities
     Extension of Terminal Building and Runway at Timehri
     Introduction of New Marine Technologies

11.165   In the longer term future, a modern river front general/cargo container terminal that consolidates Georgetown's four obsolete terminals may be needed. A broad mix of riverine, coastal, coasting and deep sea vessels would have to be handled at such a facility. Linkages with trucking, river vessels and commercial wheeled and amphibious aircraft would be required to facilitate multi-modal transfers.

11.166   Improved marine cargo handling, inter-modal and vessel technologies should be introduced on a pilot basis to select the most appropriate approach. The internal transport of bulk materials such as aggregates, sugar, and rice could be made less expensive. Greater use of technologies such as: RORO (roll on, roll off) coastal and river vessels, floating wharves, floating ramps, bulk materials handling coupled with improved navigation services have the potential to reduce costs and increase vessel and vehicle productivity. Better navigation services and specialized private commercial river vessels can reduce the cost of re-supplying interior communities and of bringing out exportable products. As in other countries with wilderness hinterlands, complementary marine and air services offer the means to access Guyana's interior at lower cost to government than by costly efforts to maintain secondary roads. Electronic and satellite navigation systems may be worthwhile subjects for study as the means to overcome chronic difficulties in maintaining short range navigation aids (eg. buoys, beacons and range lights) and to encourage night navigation.

G. ACTION PLAN

1. Review of Present Budget

11.167   Current allocations for new ferries and for completion of the Guyana/Brazil road should be reconsidered. The IDA IRP program should be expanded to provide emergency T&N as well as CFR assistance to make Timehri International Airport safe. In addition, the proposed IDA study of the creation of a Port Authority should expand its scope to investigate the option of creating a private sector consortium enterprise.

2. Seek Support for Unfinanced Priorities

11.168   Government should seek funding for the following strategic projects in the Transport Sector:

> Technical Assistance for Introduction of Airport Authority
> Timehri Airport Maintenance Management
> Telecommunications and Navigational Aids (air)
> Improvement of Hinterland Airstrips
> Buoy Tender and River Navigation
> Dredging and Navigation Study
> Feeder Roads Rehabilitation
> Georgetown Urban Road Rehabilitation

3. Optimizing the Impact of Funded Priorities

11.169   The proposed PSIP includes many significant investments which already have secured funding. The Government can optimize the impact of these investments by taking parallel action in the following areas:

- The Government should submit to parliament enabling legislation for the recentralization of the Operation and Maintenance for the road network.

- The Government should encourage the strengthening of the CTPU as effective transport planning agency and an intrinsic part of the budgeting process.

- The Government should prepare an updated National Transportation Plan.

- The Government should submit to parliament enabling legislation for the establishment of an Airports Authority and Civil Aviation Authority.

- The CARICOM should investigate the feasibility of establishing a Regional Airworthiness Authority.

- The CARICOM should investigate the feasibility of establishing a Regional Aviation and Maritime Training Institute.

- The Government should support study into the establishment of a Port and River Traffic Authority.

- A preliminary port/development strategy plan (not detailed) is needed as soon as possible to ensure that the acquisition of cargo and container storage lands by Georgetown terminals does not compromise more comprehensive port development in the future. Such a study should not unduly delay the acquisition of off port lands needed by terminal operators.

- The Government should encourage private sector participation in government owned shipping, construction, and quarrying companies, as well as in the operation of ferries and Guyana Airways Corporation.

- The Government should promote reconstruction of the contractors' industry.

- The Government should improve donor coordination in general, and specifically regarding various related infrastructure projects; this would include the review of scheduling of sea wall and road reconstruction so as to avoid possible flooding of newly reconstructed roads.

- The Government should develop a plan for increasing user charges for the transportation system and for increasing current account allotments for operation and maintenance.

H.   PROPOSED INVESTMENT PROGRAM

11.170   The proposed 1993-96 investment program for the transport sector is presented in Table 11.10.   Of the proposed total expenditures of US$123 million for 1993-96, US$90 million have already been financed.   Part of the remaining US$33 million could be financed by deferring the planned expenditure on the Guyana/Brazil road.

11.171   In terms of sustainability and strategic impact, the most important initiative for the Government of Guyana is to rebuild institutional capacity through the Central Transport Planning Unit, and to prepare a new National Transport Plan to guide development and attract donor confidence.

Table 11.10: PROPOSED PUBLIC SECTOR INVESTMENT PROGRAM - TRANSPORT 1993-96
(Current US$ 1000)a/

Project	Budgeted 1993	1994	1995	1996	Agency
Ongoing Projects	4767.3	6499.9	7941.0	7693.2	
Ferries (reconditioning)	1091.6	1649.8	663.7	0.0	EC
Demerara Harbor Bridge	1115.5	1651.8	3850.2	4838.2	EC
Navigational Aids	27.9	598.4	598.4	110.8	EC
Mabura/Lethem Road b/	23.9	0.0	0.0	0.0	Brazil
Urban Roads	203.2	219.9	229.5	243.0	Other
Equipment Civil Aviation	219.1	239.0	280.5	282.9	Local/PAP
Land and Water Transport	278.1	0.0	0.0	0.0	Local/PAP
Timehri Airport (incl. Firehall)	565.7	796.8	796.8	796.8	Local
Roads (Regions)	478.1	521.9	599.2	637.5	Local
Reconditioning of Ships	199.2	159.4	200.0	19.9	Local
Stellings & Wharves	95.6	214.3	230.3	246.2	Local
Ferry Services	8.0	17.5	18.3	19.9	Local
Bridges	143.4	100.4	105.2	110.8	Local
Bridges (Region)	110.8	0.0	0.0	0.0	Local
Guyana/Suriname Ferry	8.0	79.7	105.2	110.8	Local
Hinterland Airstrips	199.2	251.0	263.7	276.5	Local
New Projects (identified) c/	2711.2	9600.1	14239.5	18811.4	
Rehab W. Berbice Rd	358.6	1200.0	2400.0	4200.8	IDB
Rehab G/T Soesdyke Rd	358.8	1200.0	2400.0	4200.8	IDB
Roads - Agri Hybrid Load	330.0	770.0	1320.0	2750.0	IDB
Rehab G/T Mahaica Rd	0.0	2390.0	3120.0	2390.0	IDB
Road Design and Maintenance	553.8	0.0	0.0	1320.0	IDB
Reseal Soesdyke-Linden Rd	260.6	1099.9	1559.6	1300.4	IDA
Rehab E.Essequibo Coast Rd	429.5	1720.3	2580.1	2149.8	IDA
Road Maintenance	380.1	719.5	360.2	0.0	IDA
Fire equip CAD	0.0	500.4	499.6	499.6	IDA d/
Transport Study	39.8	0.0	0.0	0.0	Local
TOTAL (Identified)	7478.4	16100.0	22180.5	26238.6	
New Projects (Unidentified)	0.0	0.0	5275.0	8649.4	
Urban Roads Project	0.0	0.0	275.0	549.8	
Demerara River Navigation (Buoy Tender and equip)	0.0	0.0	1000.0	1000.0	
Hinterland Airstrips	0.0	0.0	1000.0	2000.0	
Air Navigational Aids	0.0	0.0	1000.0	1099.6	
Timehri Airport Rehab	0.0	0.0	1000.0	2000.0	
Feeder Roads Rehab	0.0	0.0	1000.0	2000.0	
TOTAL	7478.4	16100.0	27455.5	35154.0	
Memorandum Item:e/					
Port Authority (T.A.)	0.0	0.0	100.0	200.0	IDA
Roads Department (T.A.)	300.0	300.0	200.0	200.0	IDA
Central Planning CTPU (T.A.)	100.0	100.0	100.0	0.0	IDA
Harbors THD (T.A.)	0.0	100.0	170.0	0.0	EC
Airport Authority (T.A.)	0.0	800.0	200.0	0.0	Uniden.
GRAND TOTAL	7878.4	17400.0	28225.5	35554.0	

a/ Excludes GAC, Guyana Shipping and Guyana Engineering (shipping) Companies.
b/ Recommended that the completion of this project be deferred.
c/ Includes construction supervision, physical and price contingencies.
d/ Fire equipment is urgently needed; should be provided earliest 1993.
e/ PSIP does not include Technical Assistance.

Source: Mission Estimates

CHAPTER XII. WATER SUPPLY AND SANITATION

A. INTRODUCTION

12.1   While the access to potable water through house connections and public standpipes is quite high, the water and sanitation sector suffers from grave deficiencies with practically the entire network in incipient or actual failure. Back siphonage of polluted water due to low pressure, faulty joints etc., poses a significant health risk. Preventative maintenance is non existent and there is chronic shortage of spare parts and supplies. Cost recovery is extremely weak, sector institutions have limited capabilities due to human resource constraints and are financially bankrupt. Budgetary practices are inappropriate. This chapter reviews the situation in the water and sanitation sector and identifies some of the main sector issues. The expenditure program being proposed is modest, but entirely adequate given the sector's limited absorptive capacity to meet sector needs. It is proposed that major capital investments in the sector over the next three years be linked to two donor-financed projects: the Georgetown Water Supply and Sewerage project in the city of Georgetown being financed by the Inter-American Development Bank and the Water Supply Technical Assistance and Rehabilitation project for the Regions, including New Amsterdam being financed by the World Bank.

B. SECTOR OVERVIEW

1. Water Resources and Uses

12.2   Guyana's water resources are abundant due to high and well distributed seasonal rainfall, many rivers and a comparatively low demand. The total catchment of rivers flowing through Guyana to the coast is over 170,000 sq. km. A small amount of the copious supplies of surface water which run off this area is trapped by long low earth embankment to form large shallow dams known locally as conservancies. Groundwater sources along the coastal strip is saline and in some areas suffer from contamination; however, there exists a system of three aquifers recharged primarily from the rolling white sand region inland. The "Upper" sand is the shallowest of the three aquifers and occurs at depths varying from 100 to 200 feet, with thickness ranging from 50-400 feet. It is not used as a source for water because of its high iron content (>5mg/l) and salinity (up to 1200 mg/l). Most potable water is obtained from the two deep aquifers. The "A" sand is typically encountered between 200 and 300 meters below the surface with thickness ranging from 50 to 200 feet. Water from the "A" aquifer requires treatment for the removal of iron. The "B" sand are found at about 300 to 400 meters with thickness of between 1,200 to 2,600 feet. Water from this aquifer has a high temperature (105oF) and a trace of hydrogen sulphate which can be treated with aeration. The water contains very little iron.

12.3   Water is demanded for irrigation purposes, domestic consumption, commercial and industrial uses. Irrigation has the highest demand for water. The seasonal variability of rainfall makes irrigation an important prerequisite for large scale agricultural production. Rice and sugarcane are extensively cultivated under surface irrigation which is supplied by gravity from the conservancies. Practically all the potable water to the rural population and about 50 % of the Georgetown supply are from the aquifers of the "A" and "B" sands. Nationwide, water supply facilities include about 178 groundwater wells and 8 surface water sources. There are three major water treatment facilities: the Shelter Belt treatment plant in Georgetown; the New Amsterdam treatment plant; and the GUYMINE treatment plant in the Linden/Wismar area. The remaining water supply and sanitation facilities are concentrated in the peri-urban strip along the north-eastern coast covering an area estimated at about 20 km wide and 400 km long.

2. Water Supply and Sanitation System

12.4   It is estimated that nearly 95% of the urban population (representing about 32% of the total population) and 93% of the rural population (68% of the total) have access to potable water through house connections and standpipes. The Georgetown area sewage collection systems serves a limited area of about 7,500 connections containing 50,000 population. Waste water sanitation facilities, mostly septic tanks, pit privies etc., are available to about 90% of the urban population and 80% of the rural population. However, while there is high coverage, the quality of these services (water pressure, quality and hours of service, etc.) is very poor.

12.5   The water supply and sanitation systems have suffered from inadequate planning, design and construction. In addition, erratic commercial electric power supply, lack of effective standby capacity,water storage, spare parts, and equipment, transportation, communication,and security have all contributed to the deterioration of service. Inadequate operating budgets have resulted in a lack of sufficient diesel fuel purchase and insufficient purchase of water treatment chemicals and chlorine. It is estimated that leakage of water from the distribution systems in the regions may exceed 50%. This high rate due to improper design and installation, vandalism and shortage of packing and pipes for repair of broken pipes. Vandalism occurs as people breach water mains to obtain water during service interruptions. As a result , when water pressure is restored, excessive leakage occurs and flows do not reach outlying customers. The inability to attract and retain an adequate number of competent staff at all levels due to poor remuneration, the lack of sufficient budgetary resources, effective organization, tariffs, cost recovery policies have also contributed to the continuing decline of the publicly owned water facilities in Guyana.

12.6   As a result, the water and sanitation sector suffers from grave deficiencies in all critical areas. It is characterized by the general inability of the public water potable water systems to provide service meeting minimal international standards of quality and quantity. With the exception of Linden/Wismar, the potable water systems in Guyana are in a state of incipient or actual failure. Presently, parts of Linden/Wismar area and the portions of the New Amsterdam system capable of being served by the recently completed water treatment plant are the only locations in the ten regions where there is effective disinfection through the use of chlorine. In Georgetown and other urban areas, the contamination of potable water supplies by raw sewage and a poorly maintained physical infrastructure (back-siphonage of polluted water due to low pressure, cross connections to non-potable supplies, faulty joints etc.) poses a significant health risk. There has been a nationwide sharp increase in the incidence of waterborne diseases such as typhoid, gastro-enteritis, hepatitis, and malaria. It is estimated that waterborne diseases increased from 140 cases per 100,000 in 1980 to 670 per 100,000 in 1988, with the largest increases in amoebiasis and typhoid.

C. INSTITUTIONAL AND REGULATORY FRAMEWORK

1. Overview

12.7   The current legislative framework, establishing the institutions in the water sector in Guyana has evolved in an ad hoc fashion over the years. As a result many institutions were established some with overlapping or potentially conflicting roles and responsibilities. The Georgetown Sewerage and Water Commissioners (GS&WC) operates the potable water system in the city of Georgetown. The Guyana Water Authority (GUYWA) assists the Region with the operation and maintenance of their potable water systems. In addition, GUYWA engages in well drilling, equipment repairs and rentals. The Town Council of New Amsterdam operates the systems in New Amsterdam. The Regional Democratic Councils (RDCs) operate the potable water systems in their respective Regions. The Sugar Industry Labor Welfare Committee (SILWFC) operates the systems in the Sugar Estates. The Guyana Bauxite Mining Company (GUYMINE) operates the water systems in the Bauxite producing areas.

12.8   In addition to GS&WC, GUYWA, New Amsterdam Town Council, the 10 regions, SILWFC, and GUYMINE, the other Government institutions that are involved in the Water sector are: (i) the hydro-meteorological service in the Ministry of Agriculture, which has the responsibility for the monitoring and assessment of the quantity of Guyana's surface water and ground water resources and for providing basic information for a variety of meteorological applications: (ii) the Hydraulics Division, also in the Ministry of Agriculture, which advises the governing bodies of the regions (the Regional Democratic Councils) on sea defence, drainage, and irrigation; (iii) the Hydropower Unit in the Guyana Water Resources Agency which is responsible for investigating hydropower sites throughout Guyana. Furthermore, three organizations appear to have responsibility for water quality in Guyana--the Government Analysts laboratory, the recently established Guyana Agency for Health, Science, Environment and Food Policy and the Institute of Applied Science and Technology of the University of Guyana. None of the agencies is fully capable of carrying out its mandate of assessing the quality because of lack of equipment or personnel.

2. Water Supply

12.9   GS&WC. The Water Supply system in Georgetown is operated by the Georgetown Sewerage and Water Commissioners (GS&WC). About 50% of Georgetown's Water Supply is drawn from 10 wells. Three of the wells are located in the Shelter Belt Treatment plant area while the other 7 wells are located in various sites around the city. The remaining 50% of the city's Water Supply is provided by surface water obtained from the East Demarara Conservancy via the 12 km long Lamaha Canal. About one half of the length of the canal is through highly populated areas, so that the surface water is highly contaminated when it reaches the treatment plant. Total water production of the Georgetown systems is estimated at 17 million Imperial gallons per day (MIGD) in 1987 compared with an estimated demand of 25 MIGD. The Shelter Belt Treatment Plan has a nominal capacity of 10 MIGD and is presently incapable of producing water of acceptable health standard. It is currently being operated at 13 MIGD, i.e., 3 MIGD beyond its rated capacity.

12.10   As of August 1992 GS&WC had 351 employees including 16
Administrative staff, 278 technical and professional staff and 57 unskilled
and informal workers. The main executive officer is the chief engineer who is
responsible for the day-to-day operations. There are 11 departments. Many of
them are supposed to be filled by a superintendents or Department heads.
However, because of the low levels of salaries, many positions go unfilled or
are occupied by acting staff who lack the knowledge or the experience to
perform the required duties.

12.11   GUYWA. In 1972, the Government established the Guyana Water
Authority (GUYWA) under the Ministry of Public Works, Communications and
Regional Development, to provide water and sewerage services in the country.
At its establishment it was expected that GUYWA would take over all the water
supply assets of the institutions operating in the sector. Indeed, the Sugar
Industry Labor Welfare Committee (SILWFC) transferred 13 wells in the East
Demarara to GUYWA; however, because of lack of adequate funding and foreign
exchange, the quality of service in the areas that had been taken over by
GUYWA declined considerably. As a result of pressure from SILWFC, it was
decided that the remaining assets of SILWFC and those of the other
institutions operating in the sector such as GUYMINE, the city of New
Amsterdam would not be transferred to GUYWA. GUYWA thus assumed
responsibility for the water and sewerage services in all ten regions, except
for Georgetown, New Amsterdam, Linden/Wismar, and most of the sugar estates.
However, the authority of GUYWA to operate the water supply systems in the
Regions was rescinded in 1984 when the Government decided to adopt a policy of
administrative decentralization. After the decentralization GUYWA found a
niche for itself performing maintenance services, equipment repair and rental,
and specialized services such as well drilling for sector agencies and the
private sector.

12.12   GUYWA had total of 87 employees in 1991 including 7 administrative
staff, 10 senior technical staff, 39 technical and craftsmen, 21 clerical and
office staff and 14 unskilled and semi-skilled. The administrative staff
include the General Manager, the Chief Accountant, 3 engineers and the Chief
Administrative Officer. Many departments have vacancies and the turnover rate
is very high because of the low salaries and relatively isolated location of
GUYWA head office which entails relatively high commuting costs for GUYWA
working level staff.

12.13   The New Amsterdam Town Council is responsible for providing
potable water services to the city. Water supply facilities consist of 2
wells and relatively modern treatment plant which was completed in 1992 with
EC financing. The population of New Amsterdam is estimated at around 30,000
in about 4,000 households all of which have individual house connections.
Data on the staffing situation of the water department in New Amsterdam is
presently not available. It is being collected as part of the World Bank-
financed project.

12.14   RDCs. The provision of water and sewerage services in the regions
was first delegated to the Regional Democratic Councils (RDCs) in 1984. This
mandate was strengthened by the delegation of Functions Order of 1991 which
was intended to establish more clearly, the respective roles of GUYWA, the
regions and other agencies responsible for the provision of water and sewerage
services in Guyana. It delegated to the regions, the responsibility for
operation and maintenance of water and sewerage systems within their

jurisdiction, except where such functions are currently being provided by other agencies. GUYWA is supposed to control and monitor the activities of the regions, while the regions in turn were to collect water tariffs and be accountable to GUYWA for carrying out an agreed operations and maintenance plan. Thus, with the 1991 order, the regions collectively took responsibility for operation and maintenance of about 165 wells and 7 surface water supply systems within their respective jurisdictions. Unfortunately, the order was unclear about the legal ownership of the assets that were transferred. The resulting uncertainty has resulted in the accounting anomaly whereby, GUYWA continues to carry the depreciation charges of the transferred assets but the benefits derived for operating the assets accrue to the regions. Also, the regions have been known to refer customers to GUYWA during system breakdowns; GUYWA, in turn, re-direct the customers to the regions, thereby causing ill-will and frustrations to all the parties involved.

12.15   The regional water systems are varied with each tailored to meet local conditions. For instance, the system at Bartica has two pumps to lift water from the Essequibo River. The water is treated at a plant that was installed in 1982 and which although in apparent good condition, is not being used because of lack of chemicals. At Matthew's Ridge, the small system developed by a mining company now serves a farming community of about 2,000. Hand pumps are installed in 61 communities and windmills in 32 communities, primarily in the livestock regions of the southern Savannah.

12.16   SILWFC. The water supply systems in the sugar estates comprising 22 wells with 12,611 connections and serving about 70,000 people is operated by SILWFC. Most borehole pumps are provided with two alternative drive units, either electric or diesel. Most of the wells have dual angle drives so that drive units are always in place, and standby can be brought into operation immediately when the electricity fails. However SILWFC facilities are very old, some are over 30 years of age; and the many years of poor maintenance due to shortage of spare parts during periods of stringent exchange control have taken their toll. There are daily breakdowns.

12.17   GUYMINE. The water systems in Linden/Wismar in Region 10 are operated by the National Bauxite Company (GUYMINE). It comprises four river intakes and treatment plants in Linden, with a borehole and treatment plant at Amelia's Ward, and an in-take, treatment plant and tank at Ituni. Even though GUYMINE's facilities were modernized with external assistance in the 1980's, they are beginning to show signs of deterioration due to lack of adequate maintenance. This has become more apparent with the decline in the price of bauxite.

3. Sewerage

12.18   Georgetown is the only area with a substantial and functioning sewer services. The main sewerage system covers about 1,160 acres (about 470 ha.) in central Georgetown and serves about one-third of the city's population. The sewerage system has not been extended since it was originally constructed over 60 years ago. There are 24 pumping stations on the ring main, which have recently been refurbished with EC funds; however, they cannot function properly because of frequent power outages. Few of the pumps feeding the ring main are in good working order. The remainder of the city is served by septic tanks without leaching beds and pit latrines which discharge to adjacent ditches and storm drainage channels. Collected sewage is discharged, untreated into Demarara lower estuary.

12.19   There are three other small sewerage systems in Guyana, in addition to the Georgetown system. There is one at the University of Guyana, but the treatment plant was stripped soon after its installation some 20 years ago. Another small system, without any treatment plant serves several thousand people in the Tucville area. A third system serves the Timehri airport and its environs. Again, the system is in disrepair, having blocked sewers and overflowing manholes.

4.   The Role of the Private Sector

12.20   Private sector participation in the operation of water facilities has so far been limited (except for the facilities being run by SILWFC and GUYMINE which are parastatals although their status might soon change). The private sector is sometimes engaged by the regions to undertake minor repairs to pumps and engines, and private truck operators are used to deliver fuel to pumping stations. Public transport (and farm tractors) is sometimes used to transport repair crews. An interesting exception is the operations of the Eccles well and treatment facility by the Georgetown Seafood Company. It is interesting because it presents a successful model that could be adopted for meeting the needs of industrial and commercial customers with heavy water demands. The Eccles facility was one of seven water production facilities installed with USAID financing in the early 1970s, but it is the only one of the seven that has remained fully functional.

D.   SECTOR FINANCES

1.   Overview

12.21   Presently the tariff levels in the country are too varied and too low to provide adequate cost recovery in the sector. This situation is further exacerbated by the failure to adjust tariff levels in line with inflation and changes in the exchange rate, as the value of the Guyana dollar depreciated over the last several years. There are at least seven tariff regimes (ranging from flat rate charges to size service connection to metered charges) operating in the country, based on different charging principles. Collection practices are poor and the billing system is only partially operational, with bills not being prepared and delivered to customers. The financial situation of GUYWA and GS&WC, the two main sector institutions, is very poor. Arrears are high and the financial statements of both institutions have not been audited since the mid-1980's. The situation in regions is worse, since no separate records exist of the expenditures of the regional water divisions. Water is provided to SILWFC customers free of charge. GUYMINE customers are charged a nominal tariff without expectations that the revenue collected will fully cover the cost of providing the services.

2.   Tariff Levels and Cost of Supply

12.22   GS&WC. Water and sewerage changes in the city of Georgetown are based on property values. Each year the city council estimates the amount it will take to operate and maintain the water supply and sewerage system, including sinking fund payments on loans for capital investments. This amount is then expressed as a proportion of the total assessed ratable values (RV) of all connected properties. The water rate was set at 18.5% of RV in 1989 resulting in an average water charge of G$1,073. Properties having both water supply and sewerage connections pay slightly higher, at 26.6% of the RV, the annual charge was G$3,186. There were about 16,920 properties liable to pay water rates and 7,500 liable to pay both. In addition, there were 279 metered properties charged at a rate of G$12/1000 gallons. Connections are made at cost. Charges are collected by the City Council which usually retains about 15% of the amounts collected to help meet the cost of collection.

12.23   GUYWA. Since decentralization of the provision of water services to the regions in 1984, GUYWA's main sources of revenues have been derived from: (i) maintenance work and equipment repair performed on water facilities in the regions and for the private sector; (ii) well drilling, rehabilitation and maintenance; (iii) equipment rental (mostly of well drilling equipment to entities with appropriate personnel willing to undertake the work by themselves); and (iv) consultancy services such as well testing, supervision and certification of well drilling activities, etc.

12.24   New Amsterdam. Water charges in New Amsterdam is based on the size of service connection. Domestic consumers with service pipe of ¾" diameter are charged $200/year. The rate rises by G$240 for each additional ½" or less. (Thus a one-inch pipe will result in a charge of G$440). The cost for shops and offices for a ¾" connection is G$260 with G$240 connection. The tariff schedule identifies 25 different categories. Tariff for gasoline stations, sawmills, factories start at G$1,900/year for ¾" connection and G$400 per ½" increment. Documentation by the number of customer category is unavailable. As indicated earlier, the number of household connection is estimated at 4,000.

12.25   The Regions. The tariff charged in the regions was inherited from GUYWA during the decentralization of 1984 and is based on a flat rate charge which varies according to the customer category (Table 12.1). Connection charge for water supply is G$50 and reconnection charge is also G$50. Data on the number of connections in the regions is being prepared as part of the World Bank-financed project under preparation.

Table 12.1: REGIONAL TARIFFS a/

Customer Category	G$/year	US$ Equivalent
Domestic	75	$0.60
Commercial	300	$2.40
Industrial	450	$3.60

a/   Rates in effect since 1972.

Source: Government of Guyana

12.26   The Sugar Estates. SILWFC provides water to workers and their families in the sugar estates free of charge. The SILWFC funded systems also supply water to non-sugar estate workers whose properties lie adjacent to the estates. They are charged a nominal sum of G$6.60/year. SILWFC serve 17,000 households and per capita consumption is estimated at 35 gallons/day.

12.27   GUYMINE. Until 1988 water was supplied to Linden residents free of charge. As of September 1988, GUYMINE instituted a flat rate fee G$192/year to GUYMINE employees and pensioners, G$240 for non-employees, and G$400/year for commercial entities. Collection in the first three months of the tariff was only 10% of billing indicating stiff resistance to paying for a hitherto free service.

12.28   Cost of Supply. In a consultant report financed by the IDB on the water sector, it was estimated that actual cost of water supply to households in 1988 differ widely (Table 12.2). Even though the estimates are very preliminary, they nonetheless confirm that fact that current tariffs are extremely low relative to both the cost of operating and maintaining the systems and to consumer incomes.

Table 12.2:   COST OF WATER SUPPLY TO HOUSEHOLDS, 1988

System	Tariff/year	Cost per 1000 gallon
	--------------G$----------------	
Regions	75	178-860
SILWFC	0-6.6	147
GUYMINE	192	985
New Amsterdam	200	575
Georgetown	1,100	881

Source: Baptie Shaw and Morton, Consulting Engineers

12.29   The extent to which current tariff levels are insufficient to cover operating and maintenance is also illustrated by a preliminary revenue and expenditure analysis of the Bartica system in Region 7, undertaken by an IDA-financed consultant, which indicated that tariff revenues cover only about 1.4% of operating and maintenance costs (Table 12.3). Comparable analysis undertaken for Regions 5 and 6 indicate that potential tariff revenues are sufficient to cover 3% and 5.8% respectively. Assuming that the existing ratio is maintained between domestic and commercial tariffs, annual domestic tariffs would need to be increased to G$1,295 in Region 5, G$5,170 in Region 6, and G$21,660 in Bartica to fully cover operations and maintenance costs.

12.30   These estimates are preliminary. A tariff study would be prepared as part of the world Bank-financed Water Supply Technical Assistance and Rehabilitation project. The study will establish a uniform tariff policy to be applied in all regions as well as an appropriate tariff structure or structures and specific tariff levels over a five year period. The Terms of Reference of the study has been approved by World Bank and the Government is in the process of reviewing proposals. The study will require about 3 staffmonths and will be undertaken by May 1993. In preparation for the study, the regions commenced the updating of their customer ledgers in November 1992.

In addition, GUYWA has begun to update the assets inventory in the regions. The Inter-American Bank will finance a parallel tariff review for the city of Georgetown, under its Georgetown Water and Sewerage project. The World Bank and IDB will coordinate the two studies to minimize conflicting and contradictory recommendations.

Table 12.3: POTENTIAL REVENUES AND ESTIMATED OPERATING AND MAINTENANCE EXPENSE--BARTICA WATER SYSTEM 1992
(G$1000)

Total Potential Tariff Revenue	73
Total Expenditure:	5,280
Labor	1,117
Fuel	1,500
Electricity	170
Chemicals	1,150
Other Operating and Maintenance	1,343
Net Balance	-5,207
Cost Recovery	1.4%

Source: Stanley Associates Engineering Limited

12.31   The World Bank-financed tariff study would systematically investigate the relative merits of the various charging principles that are presently being employed: flat rate charges; volumetric (or metered) charges; charges based on ratable values; and size of service connections. A revised uniform tariff structure will be proposed. The objectives of the tariff structure to be recommended would be that it: (i) is consistent with the principles of (eventual) full cost recovery; (ii) encourages water conservation and favors customers using small quantities of water; (iii) enables low income residential customers to obtain an adequate supply of water at an affordable price; and (iv) can be implemented by the water entities at an acceptable cost and is easily understood by consumers.

3. Billings and Collections

12.32   GS&WC. Metered customers are charged monthly for water but on different basis and payments are recorded on a Property Record Card (sometimes known as customer ledgers). Combined bills for local taxation and water charges are prepared annually and billings take up to three months to be prepared. Bills are collected by the City Council which assesses a retention fee of about 15% to cover the cost of collection. Property owners have the option of paying in four equal installments. Payment can be made at the town hall or at one permanent outstation. Payments at the Town Hall at peak periods take considerable time partly because of the practice to recalculate each bill presented before payment is accepted. Payment is recorded on the Property Record Cards, although they have not been reconciled to arrears reported in the financial statements. Payments are transferred to GS&WC with delay. Delinquent customers are referred to the supreme court, which usually results in payment being made. Failure to make payment after court action can result in the premises being sold to settle the debt; however, this drastic action is seldom taken. Metered customers are disconnected for non payment. Arrears for metered and non-metered customers amount to about six months billing.

12.33   GUYWA. GUYWA usually submits its bills promptly after service is provided and its income statements provides details of its accounts receivable, including the number of reminders that have been sent to the customer in question. Despite GUYWA's efforts, its financial statements covering the period 1988 to 1992 indicate a collection performance that is extremely poor. Total receivables increased from G$4.6 million in 1988 to over G$21.2 million equivalent to between 900-1,000 days. As of the end of 1991, the regions and G$&WC accounted for 23% of the receivables each, and the remainder 54% is distributed among various Government ministries and parastatals.

12.34   GUYWA's poor collections performance is due more to the government's policies than to poor financial management by GUYWA. The regional water divisions and GS&WC cannot operate on a full cost recovery basis and must therefore, depend on Government grants for operations maintenance and capital works. Since the Government allocations are not sufficient to cover the cost of the service that GUYWA provides to the regions and GS&WC, and since GUYWA is prohibited by the Government from requiring cash payment in advance of services rendered, GUYWA has no choice but accumulate high arrears for these services. Since GUYWA's receivables are owed mostly by public sector agencies, improvement in GUYWA's collection performance is tied to a general overhaul of the sector finances.

12.35   New Amsterdam. The billing and collection system is based on a manual card system. Customers are billed annually and payments can be made in four equal installments. Disconnections are made for non-payments, but the extent is not known.

12.36   The Regions. The billing system is based on a manual card system. The Property Record Card is the basic record. Ordinarily, bills are prepared and delivered by hand to the consumer. Payment can be made at the regional GUYWA office or at various locations visited occasionally by collection staff. Consumers are informed by a town crier a day or two before collections take place. Due to transportation problems scheduled collections are cancelled without warning or substantially delayed. Sometimes problems occur because collectors are not supplied with a change float and thus cannot accept payment because they are unable to change monies offered in settlement of the accounts. Receipts are given to customers when cash is collected and a record is made in the Property Record Card. Copies of the receipts are provided to the regional council financed department at a 2 weekly intervals.

12.37   A recent review of the billing system of the Regions indicated that it is only partially operational. Bills are not being delivered to customers and collections are made only from those customers who voluntarily make payments at the regional GUYWA office. Those customers who voluntarily make payment are also expected to produce past receipts to prove that their accounts are current. Since the Property Record Card is not reconciled with cash collections, there is no basis for determining individual arrears and thus, not surprisingly delinquent customers are hardly ever disconnected as required. Arrears are estimated to be over 50% region wide. Preliminary estimates for arrears in Region 6 was 45% between January-July 1992 and ranged from 76% to 58% in Region 5 between 1989-92.

12.38   The poor collection performance is due to a number of factors: (i) the Property Records Cards are not reconciled with cash payments recorded. Often they are poorly organized, incomplete, out of date and probably inaccurate. Consequently, they cannot form the basis of any rigorous billing and collection system even if the regions wanted to have one and besides they are presently not capable of maintaining one; (ii) there is very little incentive to properly undertake billings and maximize collections since the Regions are required to remit all tariff revenues to the Government's consolidated account; there is widely held perception that Government services, including water should be provided free of charge; (iii) tariff levels have eroded over the years to such a point that even if all tariffs revenue were collected, they would generate funds that are minuscule compared to the true cost of operating and maintaining the systems; and (iv) staff in the water divisions in the regions, like most staff employed in the public sector in Guyana are poorly paid, trained and motivated.

12.39   SILWFC and GUYMINE. Billings and collection data for SILWFC and GUYMINE are not available. Since water is provided to workers in the sugar estates free-of-charge while other SILWFC customers pay only a nominal charge, such data for SILWFC are not expected to be significant. However, in the case of GUYMINE, it is understood that there exists resistance to pay the tariff charges that were instituted in 1988, but the extent of the resistance in recent years is unknown. It is expected that such data would be collected under the World Bank-financed project under preparation.

4. Affordability

12.40   Given the extremely low levels of current tariffs, it would appear that significant increases in tariffs will be needed in order to move the sector toward financial self-sustainability. However, even if very conservative ability-to-pay criteria are employed, relatively large increases in the annual charges should be affordable. Given the rule of thumb that 3%-6% of gross household income could reasonably be expected to be expended on water and sewerage services, an affordable tariff should start at about G$875 per annum. This amount is equivalent to about 3% of the income of a household with one worker earning the minimum wage in Guyana of G$117 per day or about G$29,250 per annum. A water charge at that level is already almost 12 times the current water charge for domestic customers in the regions. Whether or not increases in this magnitude in the tariff structure can be implemented remains to be seen. However, the obstacle to tariff increases is more likely to be due to a lack of willingness to pay rather than due to affordability constraints. As the resistance to the GUYMINE tariff increases clearly attests, there is a widely held perception in Guyana that government services, including water should be provided free of charge. Also, willingness to pay has been adversely affected by the generally low level of service provided in the sector. This aspect will also be investigated in the IDA-financed tariff study being carried out under the World Bank-financed project.

5. Financial Management of Sector Institutions

12.41   GS&WC. GS&WC is financially administered by the City Council of Georgetown which sets the financial policies relating to tariffs, collection policies and approves all major expenditures. GS&WC has been operating at loss over the last several years because of the low tariffs and poor collection efficiency. The company is operated on a cash accounting basis. The accounting department is understaffed and has been unable to produce a balance sheet since 1985 and GS&WC accounts have not been audited ever since. Because of the low salaries and limited resources, GS&WC lacks the qualified personnel and facilities necessary for proper accounting, planning and control its finances.

12.42   GUYWA. GUYWA's financial statements are produced on an accrual basis each month and submitted to the GUYWA Board for Approval. The statements consist of an income statement, a detailed statement of receivables, statement of work in progress and a cash flow statement. GUYWA's accounting department is understaffed with staff turnover estimated at around 50%. GUYWA's financial performance has steadily deteriorated over the 1988-91 period. GUYWA generated an operating profit of G$0.646 million in 1989 and incurred a loss (before subsidy) of G$0.858 million in 1990. The operating loss before subsidy was G$4.6 million in 1991. Following a Government subsidy of G$1.1 million, the loss was reduced to G$3.5 million. The increase was due to the civil service pay increases of 25% and 20% which were approved by the Government in the mid and late 1991, but applied reactively to January 1, 1991. It is important to note that GUYWA's financial performance is being adversely affected by the very high level of arrears which amount to between 900-1,000 days of revenues. GUYWA's financial statements have not been audited since 1986. Arrangements are underway to audit the 1990 and 1991 accounts. The audit will be financed under a Project Preparation Facility (PPF) Advance provided by the World Bank. In addition, the PPF Advance would finance an Accounting and Financial Management Study which will assist GUYWA and the Regional Water Division to develop, with the help of consultants, a practical and implementable accounting, management information and billing and collection systems.

12.43   New Amsterdam. Information on the financial situation of the water system operated by the New Amsterdam Town Council is not presently available. It would be prepared under the World Bank-financed project.

12.44   The Region. The financial management and reporting systems employed in the regions is practically non-existent. Each Regional Democratic Council (RDC) prepares a monthly consolidated record of cash expenditures for all regional services. There is no separate record of expenditures for the Regional Water Division. The RDCs do not prepare regular reports of water tariff revenues billed and collected. This information can only be derived by examining detailed billing records. No accounts receivable data is maintained. Measures are currently underway to strengthen the financial management of the Regions. GUYWA and consultants financed under the PPF are assisting the Regions to prepare financial statements and to develop a management information on water operations, tariffs, arrears and staffing. The data being developed would serve as inputs to the accounting and Financial Management Study that will help establish an accounting and management information system for GUYWA and the Regional Water Divisions.

12.45   SILWFC and GUYMINE. The SILWFC and GUYMINE systems are operated primarily as a benefit to employees and thus separate financial records beyond the direct cost of providing the service are not being kept.

6. Sector Financial Flows

12.46   Annual capital expenditures for the rehabilitation of water facilities in Georgetown, New Amsterdam and the Regions both from the Government own resources and from foreign sources is contained in the capital budget of the Government and channelled through GUYWA. Capital expenditures were G$67.5 million in 1989, G$82.6 million in 1990, G$267.3 million in 1991 and estimated at G$159 million in 1992. Overall, these levels are deplorably low with respect to the investment and rehabilitation needs of the sector. Usually capital improvements for water facilities in the Regions, including New Amsterdam are typically grouped in a general category of Rural Water Supply. Capital expenditures for GS&WC are shown separately. Expenditures relating to GUYWA's equipment is shown under Force Account and Institutional Development related expenditures are shown under Water Improvement.

Table 12.4:   CURRENT WATER AND SANITATION EXPENDITURE
(G$ million)

	1989	1990	1991	1992
Recurrent Expenditure (all Regions)	32.6	36.0	56.2	108.7
Total Capital Expenditures:	67.5	82.6	267.3	159.0
Water Supply (Force Acc.)	0.0	0.5	0.0	5.0
Georgetown Sew. & Water PHII	8.2	1.5	30.0	43.0
Rural Water Supply	41.5	74.0	185.5	80.0
Water Improvement	14.8	3.7	48.4	25.2
Regional Water Divisions	3.0	2.9	3.4	5.8

Source: Government of Guyana

12.47   The Government does not provide funding to the regions specifically for the coverage of operating and maintenance costs incurred for water-related services. Instead, the Government provides a block grant to the Regional Democratic Councils for the provision of all municipal services, including water. Regional recurrent expenditures for Water Services in all ten Regions were estimated at G$32.6 million in 1989, G$36 million in 1990, G$56.2 million in 1991 and G$108.7 million in 1992. Furthermore, recurrent expenditures for water and sewerage services are not shown separately in the recurrent budget. Since tariff revenues are transferred to the Government, the link between internally generated revenues and expenditures is broken. This practice is inimical to financial self sustainability in the sector and inconsistent with cost recovery principles.

12.48   Recent major involvement of external agencies include construction of the 2.0 MIGD New Amsterdam treatment plant, estimated to cost about US$3.6 million financed by the EC under Lomé III. Earlier EC provided US$400,000 for the rehabilitation of Georgetown sewerage pumps. IDB is preparing a Remedial Maintenance Program for Georgetown under the Georgetown Water and Sewerage project to repair service connections and distribution mains and provision of borehole pumps for which US$2.8 million will be provided. The IDB financed an institutional study of the sector by Baptie Shaw and Morton in 1988-89. The report was finalized in 1991. IDB is also financing the preparation of a master plan for the water and sewerage in Georgetown. In September 1992, IDA approved a Project Preparation Advance of US$958,000 to help prepare a Water Supply Technical Assistance and Rehabilitation project which aims at strengthening the sector, rehabilitating or replacing dilapidated water facilities and putting in place an improved operations and maintenance program for water facilities outside of Georgetown. CIDA has just financed a rehabilitation study for 8 water treatment plants, five along the East Bank of the Demarara River, and 3 along the East Coast. It has been estimated that it would require about US$2.8 million to return the 8 plants to full operational capabilities. Minor works have been implemented by UNICEF and under the Social Impact Amelioration Program.

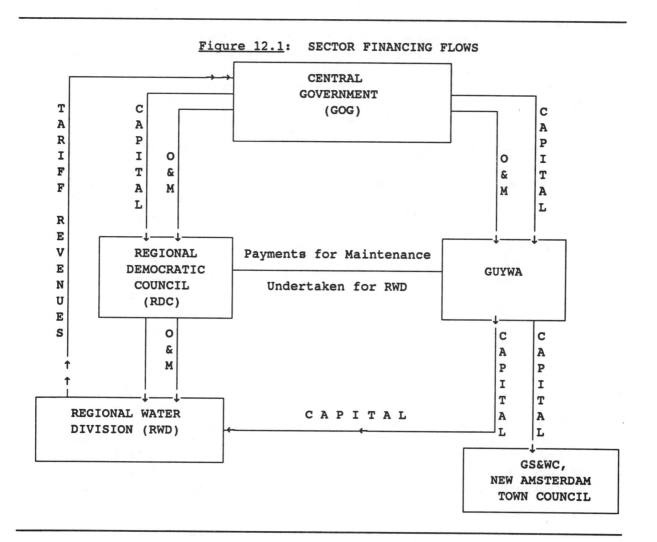

Figure 12.1: SECTOR FINANCING FLOWS

E. MAIN SECTORAL ISSUES

12.49   Future Structure of the Water Sector. At present GUYWA's key responsibility is to provide strategic planning and monitoring of the water sector. Operational functions and service delivery have devolved to the regional level under the administration of the Regional Democratic Councils (RDCs). This decentralization arrangement has not, however, been effective due to the competing priorities and responsibilities of the RDCs for other sectors, lack of qualified professionals to manage the facilities and a serious lack of budgetary allocations to meet capital and recurrent expenditures. This situation has been further compounded by an inadequate tariff structure and dismal revenue collection performance. Currently, the sector is fragmented and suffers from confused lines of accountability and responsibility between GUYWA and the Regions. The World Bank is in the process of financing legal and institutional studies whose principal objectives are to: (a) review the existing laws and regulation of the water sector; (b) review the root causes for the lack of performance of sector agencies; and (c) recommend remedial measures for its restructuring. The studies are estimated at 3 man months to be undertaken between January-April 1993. It proposed that the Government delay taking any action affecting the structure of the sector until after the studies have been completed. Furthermore, it is expected that the studies will address the complete range of water-related activities from monitoring and assessment to development and management of water resources to ensure an environmentally sound and sustainable development of the country's water resources. To this end, the studies will explore the merits and demerits of a National Water Commission to coordinate potable, agricultural, energy-related and recreational water.

12.50   Groundwater Resources. Groundwater is the main source of domestic and industrial water supply on the coastland and is obtained from 3 major aquifer systems: the "upper" sand, the "A" sand and the "B" sand. So far only the lower "A" and "B" sands are being exploited because the "upper" sand has been found to be brackish. As noted in a recent UNDP study[1], there has been a steady decline in piezometric levels (i.e., artisan pressure) in both aquifer systems, pointing to a future possible increases in pumping costs possible long-term unreliability of supply, and increased risk of sea water intrusion and land subsidence. It is important that the government support a possible UNDP project to prepare a detailed study for a phased investigation and assessment of ground water resources of the coastal basin. Since the "Upper" sand aquifer is known to be recharged, its exploitation holds huge potential cost savings in drilling and pumping costs, if the boundary of the brackish water could be properly delineated.

12.51   Human Resource Constraints. As with other sectors in Guyana, the development of the water supply/sanitation sector has been considerably affected due to the lack of human resources. In the past decade, the low wages associated with the economic crisis in Guyana caused a massive migration of qualified professionals to other countries. The level of salaries still remains very low and it is extremely difficult to attract the necessary qualified workers to fill the existing vacancies in the sector. The total

---

1/   "A Programme for Enhancing Climate, Weather and Water Resources Monitoring Capability for Sustainable Economic Development in Guyana". WMO August 1992 by Mr. J.L. Bassier.

staff turnover has been estimated at 20% in the last three to four years. The situation continues to decline as can be seen most clearly in the weakened managerial and technical abilities of GS&WC and GUYWA at present. A recent consultant study (by David Horsefield, November 1991) financed by IDB summarized the human resource needs as follows: (i) low levels of staffing and skills; (ii) lack of adequate tools, supplies and equipment to accomplish tasks; (iii) lack of an organized program to upgrade skills; and (iv) extremely poor working conditions leading to low morale.

12.52   Operations and Maintenance. Due to the dilapidated nature of water and sanitation systems, it is very important that an effective preventive maintenance program is put in place as systems are rehabilitated and/or replaced. This will ensure that equipment and facilities are utilized for their full useful life. A good O&M program will also limit the level of unaccounted-for water and thus help reduce the amount of capital investments needed for each level of service. In addition, it will ensure a consistent level of service thereby helping check vandalism as pipes are breached to obtain water during frequent service interruptions. This issue is being addressed under the World Bank-financed project, one of whose objectives is to set up an operations and maintenance program for facilities in the Regions to be rehabilitated under the project. However, successful implementation of an operations and maintenance program assumes that concurrent efforts would be made to address the other sectorial problems, especially those related to cost recovery without which rehabilitation facilities will merely slip again into a state of disrepair.

12.53   Metering. It is essential that bulk meters for water sources and treatment works are installed as soon as practicable. This will provide useful information on water production and estimated losses. As in the case of Georgetown, industrial and commercial metering should be extended to other towns (such as New Amsterdam) and regions as soon as possible. While metering would be the best charging mechanism for domestic consumption, the special circumstances of Guyana would warrant a careful consideration of its application, including the heavy capital cost involved, need for training of technicians, need for meter testing facilities and the need for periodic replacement of meters, etc. Furthermore, the current low pressures of the system would not enable the effective use of meters at the present time. It is proposed that, after system has been improved and the constancy of good quality water supply is ensured, a pilot project on the use of domestic consumption meters should be initiated in selected areas (parts of Georgetown, New Amsterdam, Region IV, etc.) to assess the economic benefits of the metering scheme. Until the introduction of system-wide domestic metering in the long run, the Government should consider other feasible options to service as the uniform basis of charge across the country. The proposed tariff study will evaluate the most feasible options for consideration by the Government.

12.54   Budgetary Levels and Allocation Practices. The current budgetary allocations for capital and recurrent expenditures are grossly inadequate to provide adequate potable and sanitation service levels to the population. (capital expenditures for the entire sector in 1992 were budgeted at G$153.2 million or less than US$1.5 million). The recurrent budget for water is provided to the Region as part of block grants to the Regional Democratic Councils (RDC's) for the provision of all municipal services (including water). All tariff revenues collected by the Regions are turned over to the Government. This practice breaks the link between internally generated

revenues and expenditure and is therefore incompatible with cost recovery and
financial self-sustainability principles. Besides the RDC's, like the central
Government, face competing priorities and responsibilities under very severe
resource constraints. The end result is that the actual expenditures for
water service do not reflect their priority. Furthermore, the recurrent
expenditures for water are not shown as a separate line items on the
Government's recurrent Budget, whereas expenditures on items such as postage,
telexes, janitorial and cleaning services etc., are shown as separate items.
Given the priority of water in the country's development program, steps should
be taken to improve the Government's budgetary practices in the sector.

12.55   Tariff. Presently at G$75 per year for rural domestic customers
in the Regions and about G$200 for Linden and New Amsterdam customers, and
G$1,100 for Georgetown customers (on the average basis), the tariff levels are
too varied and too low to provide adequate cost recovery. This situation was
aggravated by the failure to adjust the tariff levels in line with inflation
and as the value of the Guyanese dollar depreciated over the last several
years. There are at least seven tariff regimes (ranging from flat range
charges to the size of the service connection to rateable values of property
to volumetric charges etc.) operating in the country based on different
charging principles. The Project Preparation Facility (PPF) Advance provided
by the World Bank for the preparation of the Water Supply Technical Assistance
and Rehabilitation project will finance a water supply Tariff study to help
establish a uniform tariff policy to be applied in all Regions, including New
Amsterdam as well as appropriate tariff structure (or structures). The study
will contain specific proposals for tariff levels covering a five year period.
The World Bank-financed tariff study should be closely coordinated with the
IDB-financed tariff study to be undertaken as part of the IDB-supported
project in Georgetown. The implementation of the findings of the two studies
should also be closely coordinated.

12.56   Cost Recovery. The tariff levels are very low and are grossly
inadequate to ensure financial sustainability of the sector. It is estimated
by a Bank-financed consultant that if all customers receiving water actually
paid their annual water charge, total tariff revenues would be sufficient to
cover only about 3% of operation and maintenance costs in Region 5 and about
6% in Region 6. A similar review of the system in Bartica showed a recovery
rate of only 1.4%. A realistic target for achieving full cost recovery will
be addressed in the tariff study alluded to above. In this regard, the
Minister of Finance indicated his strong support for the commercialization of
the provision of water supply services, within a framework of appropriate cost
recovery policies, in order to assure the eventual financial sustainability
and viability of sector institutions. He stressed the fact that the adequate
pricing of water should initially be kept separate from affordability
considerations which should be handled by the appropriate agencies in a
systematic and transparent manner. Financial sustainability is necessary to
assure that sector facilities will be properly maintained and the qualified
personnel will be attracted to sector institutions.

12.57   Billings and Collections. The billing system is only partially
operational, with bills not being prepared and delivered to customers. The
situation is particularly bad in the regions where collections are made only
from those customers who voluntarily make payments at the Regional Water
Department collection offices or local authority office during designated
collection periods. Spot-checks have indicated that no records of overdue

accounts exist in the Regions. Information on overdue payments can be obtained only by reviewing the customer ledgers which are poorly organized, out-of-date and incomplete. Proposals for improving billing and collections will be made in an Accounting and Financial Management Study to be financed under the PPF. The study will establish a simple accounting and management information system which can be applied to the Regions. The billing and collection system to be developed will be consistent to the recommendation of the tariff study.

12.58   Legal Status of GUYWA's Assets. Presently GUYWA's assets have been assigned to the regions for operation and maintenance, with the legal transfer of their ownership to the RDCs. This issue would need to be addressed in the Institutional/Legal studies as this affects GUYWA's financial statements and its other legal obligations. Often customers needing their facilities to be repaired are given the run around by both the regional water departments and GUYWA, with neither entity wishing to assume the responsibility for the repairs.

12.59   Financial Statements. The financial statements for most sector institutions are non-existent. The financial statements of GUYWA are incomplete. Only income statements have been prepared since 1986. These show a very high level of accounts receivable in the order of G$19-20 million equivalent to 900 to 1,000 days in 1990 and 1991. GUYWA has agreed to bring its financial statements up-to-date. The reconstituted statements for 1990 and 1991 will be audited by external independent auditors acceptable to IDA. GUYWA and the mission agreed to a short-list of domestic firms that will be invited to submit proposals for the audits. GUYWA's statements for 1993 and beyond will be prepared in accordance with the recommendations of the Accounting and Financial Management Study. Presently, the regions, including New Amsterdam do not prepare any financial statements covering their water-related activities. GUYWA, with the assistance of consultants is helping the regions prepare their financial statements covering 1989-92. These statements would be used as input by the consultants for the accounting and Financial Management Study being financed under the PPF. GS&WC would be assisted in improving its finance reporting under the IDB-financed project.

12.60   Role of the Private Sector. The highly successful operation of the Eccles Plant facilities seem to point to the potentially crucial role that the private sector could play in the provision of water supply and sewerage services in Guyana. The assessment of private sector interest and capabilities in the water sector in Guyana are among the activities to be supported under the PPF. If sufficient interest and capabilities are identified, pilot operations would be devised to help identify problems and fully evaluate the potential of private sector participation in sector activities. Private sector involvement would be explored for areas such as billing and collections, longer-term operations and maintenance of facilities, leasing and facilities management.

F.   PROPOSED STRATEGY

12.61   The proposed strategy for the development of water and sanitation sector in Guyana would call for: (a) rehabilitating and/or replacing the existing facilities to bring service levels in the sector over the medium- and long-term to minimum internationally acceptable standards; (b) restructuring of the regulatory framework of the sector and strengthening of the sector institutions so that they are able to operate and maintain sector facilities to meet adequately the potable water and sanitation needs of the population; and (c) improving the sector finances and financial management practices to enable the sector eventually to attain self-sufficiency. In the short-term (1993-1995) the strategy should focus on: (i) rehabilitating dilapidated infrastructure to begin the process of progressively improving service levels; (ii) strengthening sector institutions; and (iii) improving budgetary practices and implementing an efficient cost recovery system. For the longer-term, the focus of the strategy for the water/sewerage sector should be on improving and maintaining adequate service levels, achieving financial self-sufficiency, and on increasing the level of private sector participation in the sector in order to enhance its efficiency.

G.   ACTION PLAN

12.62   The Government should plan to attain its short-term objectives within the context of the proposed IDB-financed Water and Sewerage projects (which will address sectoral issues and would begin to address the water supply and sanitation issues and rehabilitation within Georgetown) and the proposed World Bank-financed Water Supply Technical Assistance and Rehabilitation project (which will address several key sectoral issues relating to institutional strengthening, human resource development, facilities rehabilitation and operation and maintenance improvement in the regions and in New Amsterdam). The key actions proposed are as follows:

- implement the rehabilitation, replacement and maintenance of facilities based on a prioritization of the facilities to be rehabilitated in line with absorptive capacity constraints and availability of financial resources;

- assist the Government with the reorganization of the water sector (with emphasis on legal, financial and managerial autonomy of the water agencies), and strengthen sector planning, management and monitoring;

- improve operation and maintenance activities in the sector in accordance with a preventive maintenance program and link to monitorable targets for the reduction of unaccounted-for water and improvement of water quality (to meet WHO standards);

- initiate an intensive program of recruiting and training qualified personnel for sector institutions to operate and maintain the system facilities;

- introduce more efficient cost-recovery policies to reduce the level of subsidies with a view toward their eventual elimination, in conjunction with improved collection procedures and financial and budgetary practices;

- improve sector service levels with less interruptions and avoidance of contamination of water supplies;

- introduce and foster the participation of the private sector in the operation and maintenance of water/sewerage facilities;

- coordinate the activities of the international donors to minimize duplication of effort and facilitate a coordinated approach to the resolution of sector problems.

H. PROPOSED INVESTMENT PROGRAM

12.63   Currently, there are five ongoing projects in the water sector: (i) the IDB financed Georgetown Water Improvement (Master Plan) project and four local projects for Georgetown and the regions. Given the limited financial resources of the Government and the limited absorptive capacity of sector institutions, only two sets of new projects are being proposed for the period 1993-96: three IDB financed projects which focus on Georgetown, and the Water Supply Technical Assistance and Rehabilitation project financed by the World Bank which focuses on the regions (Table 12.5).

Table 12.5: PROPOSED INVESTMENT PROGRAM, 1993-96
(US$ 1000)

Project	Budgeted 1993	1994	1995	1996	Agency
Ongoing Projects	1628.7	718.8	918.8	5308.4	
Water Improvement (Master Plan)	360.2	360.2	360.2	4800.0	IDB
Rural Water Supply	539.4	358.6	558.6	508.4	Local
Georgetown Water & Sewerage Project	398.4	0.0	0.0	0.0	Local
Water Supply (Regions)	12.0	0.0	0.0	0.0	Local
New A'dam Water Project	318.7	0.0	0.0	0.0	Local
New Projects (Identified)	1271.7	3049.4	5630.3	3796.8	
TA & Water Supply/Sewerage	557.8	1849.4	2629.5	3155.4	IDA
G/T Water Supply Emergency	533.9	1200.0	3000.8	641.4	IDB
Technical Cooperation	68.5	0.0	0.0	0.0	IDB
Water Improvement Project	111.6	0.0	0.0	0.0	IDB
TOTAL	2900.4	3768.2	6549.1	9105.2	

Source: Mission Estimates

CHAPTER XIII. <u>THE SOCIAL SECTORS</u>

A. INTRODUCTION

13.1   Since independence, the Guyanese Government has repeatedly stressed its commitment to ensuring broad access by the population to social services. In the 1960s, Guyana's achievements in the education and health sectors were considerable; the illiteracy rate was among the lowest in the Caribbean and Latin American region and favorable health indicators reflected a well-designed health care system emphasizing preventive and primary health care. In the late 1960s, the Government, seeking to ensure equal access by all the population to education and health, undertook to fully subsidize education and health care. Private facilities in both sectors were absorbed into the public system and all services were provided free of charge. Fees and other forms of cost-recovery were prohibited in all educational institutions, primary through university, as well as in all health care facilities.

13.2   The country's economic difficulties and the declining budget shares allocated to the sectors in the 1980s, however, meant that the Government was unable to maintain quality levels while fully subsidizing use of these services. The reluctance to institute cost-recovery, even as resource constraints became increasingly severe in the late 1980s, has thus led to sharp declines in the quality of services provided. Infrastructure has deteriorated to the point where it is severely dilapidated and books and equipment are either not available, broken, or obsolete. These poor working conditions, coupled with low salaries, have encouraged skilled and qualified personnel to move out of the sectors or seek work abroad. By 1990, Guyana's education and health indicators were among the lowest in the Caribbean.

13.3   Improvements in the education and health sectors are urgently needed. While it is clear that some of the needed improvements can be financed through savings achieved by the more efficient use of existing resources, additional resources must be found to support more substantial improvements. As the Treasury cannot support these increases, the introduction of fees and other cost-recovery measures will have to be considered. A re-evaluation of the potential role the private sector might play in service delivery -- an issue the Government has already paid some attention to -- should also be pursued.

13.4   This chapter reviews the efficiency and effectiveness of service delivery in Guyana's education and health sectors and outlines an action plan for upgrading quality in each sector. Particular concern is paid to resource issues and the chapter focuses on the two fundamental sector expenditure issues: (i) the size of the budget envelope in each sector and how it may be increased; and (ii) the need to reallocate spending within each sector so as to achieve maximum efficiency in the use of resources.

13.5   Any social sector review should include a discussion of poverty which considers its nature and extent and which also discusses poverty reduction efforts in the country. In Guyana, however, the lack of data prevents a review of this type. Census data is available only from 1980 and, given the significant economic and demographic changes that have occurred over the past decade, this data cannot provide a useful measure of the extent of poverty. Household surveys have not been collected for over two decades. For these reasons, only a brief discussion of poverty is included in this Chapter. A better assessment will be possible once the results of a Household Survey and Living Standards Measurement Survey (LSMS) become available later in 1993.

B. TRENDS IN SOCIAL SECTOR SPENDING

1. Planning and Budgeting under the Decentralized System

13.6   In 1985 the Government decentralized the health and education systems, passing responsibility for all service delivery, except that in the central Georgetown area, to the ten Regional Administrations. The ministries have continued to be responsible for service delivery in the Georgetown area. Under the terms of the decentralization policies, however, the ministries' principal functions are to establish broad sector policy frameworks to guide policy and implementation at the regional level and to act as monitoring and quality control units to ensure that service quality does not differ unduly between regions. In addition to these functions, the ministries have retained responsibilities for a few key activities, the Ministry of Education and Culture (MEC) for funding, procuring and distributing textbooks to all schools and the Ministry of Health (MOH) for funding, procuring and distributing drugs and medical supplies and for providing dental care.

13.7   The decentralized system grants the Regional Administrations considerable autonomy from the central Ministry. There is no mechanism or requirement that the regions consult with the ministries in preparing their budgets and their full budget is funded by unconditional block grants from the Treasury. No monies are transferred in the form of conditional grants between the Ministry of Education and Culture and the Regional Administrations. The system does not allow for any transfer of funds between the ministries and the Regional Administrations. The regions also determine their staffing requirements and pay staff salaries from their own budgets.

13.8   Coordination between the two Government levels is intended to be achieved through one person, the Regional Education/Health Officer, who is a Ministry employee but works directly in the Regional Administrations. This individual is meant to inform the regions about central policy, relay information about the region's performance relative to others, and provide guidance on day-to-day management issues. Staff appointed by the Regional Administrations, principally the District Health/Education Officers, are responsible for supervising and monitoring the operation of facilities in the region. In practice, coordination between the two levels of Government is very limited for two reasons: first, the ministries have not been able to fill the Regional Education/Health Officer positions in several regions[2] and, second, communications (mail and telephone) and travel between the regions and Georgetown are extremely unreliable and often not available.

---

[2]   In 1992, for instance, the Regional Health Officer positions were vacant in Regions 1, 3, 5 and 9.

13.9   A lack of accountability mechanisms in the decentralized system
have also had an impact on service delivery and quality. Accountability is
limited in several respects:

- The Regional Administrations levy no taxes and are fully funded by
  the Central Treasury. They thus have little incentive to heed or
  respond to local concerns. Local responsiveness is further
  weakened by the fact that key positions in the Regional
  Administrations are filled by political appointees rather than
  locally elected officials.

- There is no incentive for Regional Administrations to feel
  accountable to the ministries in following national policy
  objectives; the ministries have no capacity to make conditional
  grants to the regions or to provide fiscal incentives to encourage
  regions to implement central policies. It is not surprising,
  then, that several regions fail to provide the ministries with
  basic information (school enrollment and attendance rates and
  hospital occupancy rates, for example) necessary for setting
  policy and evaluating service efficiency.

- The only mechanism making Regional Administrations accountable to
  the Central Government, central auditing, has largely broken down
  and is currently more than five years behind schedule. Indeed,
  there is evidence that some regions treat monies in their budget
  as fungible across sectors, moving funds from one sector
  (education, for example) to cover expenses in another sector
  (agriculture, for example). The extent to which this does, or
  does not, occur seems to be determined by the negotiating strength
  of the Regional Education/Health Officer. Where these positions
  are unfilled, the likelihood that funds may be transferred appears
  to be greater.

13.10   The institutional weakness of the social sector ministries and the
Regional Administrations means that planning and budgeting processes are
limited and almost completely divorced from each other. Planning is
particularly weak; neither Ministry has developed a formal medium- or long-
term strategy plan outlining and prioritizing key objectives. There is no
means, therefore, by which budgets can be structured to reflect sector
objectives. Line ministries and Regional Administrations are also unprepared
to invest resources in developing new budget proposals because they believe
they have little capacity to influence the amount of funds allocated to their
sector. Annual budget submissions by the health and education sectors thus
tend to mirror the previous year's budget with an increment to cover
inflation. Little attention is therefore paid to the future implications of
budget decisions made in the current year.

2. Sector Finances

Trends in Recurrent Spending on the Social Sectors

13.11   As economic conditions have worsened, public sector spending on
the social sectors has declined sharply. The proportion of resources
allocated to education, for instance, has halved since 1986, declining from
15.1 percent of total government recurrent spending to just over 7 percent in

1991. Allocations to the health sector show similar declines, falling from 11
percent of total recurrent spending in 1986 to less than 7 percent in 1991.
The limited allocations made under the labor/human services category (which
funds old age homes, job counseling and placement services, etc.) were also
halved and accounted for 1 percent of recurrent funding in 1991.

13.12   The extent of the reduction in public spending on the social
sectors is made very clear by the drop in public spending on health and
education as a proportion of GDP (Table 13.1).

TABLE 13.1:   RECURRENT PUBLIC EXPENDITURES IN THE SOCIAL SECTORS, 1986-1992a/
(Percent of GDP)

	1986	1987	1988	1989	1990	1991	1992b/
Education	5.2	4.8	5.8	4.3	2.0	2.3	2.0
Health	3.9	4.1	4.7	3.6	2.8	2.1	2.9
Labor/Human Services	0.7	0.8	0.5	0.6	0.5	0.3	0.4
TOTAL	9.8	9.7	11.0	8.5	5.3	4.7	5.3

a/   These figures reflect total (central and regional) public spending.
b/   1992 figures are budgeted, not actual.

Source: Ministry of Finance

13.13   The impact of reduced public spending in the sectors is especially
severe given that it accounts for the bulk of spending in the sectors; no
additional resources enter the systems by way of user fees or cost-recovery
measures and private sector participation is very limited having been
prohibited until recent years.   Some additional contributions to the health
sector come from two public enterprises, GUYSUCO and GUYMINE, which support
health facilities for employees and from six private hospitals and several
small private clinics.   In the education sector only one private facility (a
pre-school) has been established.   Public spending thus essentially accounts
for all spending in the education sector.

Trends in Capital Expenditures

13.14   Investments in health and education infrastructure were extremely
limited until 1990.   This was especially true in the health sector, which
accounted for 0.4 percent of total capital expenditures in 1986 and 1.0
percent of total capital expenditures in 1988 (Table 13.2).3/   Just over 2
percent of total capital expenditures were made in the education sector.   The
sharp increases in capital expenditures in both sectors in the 1990s reflect
investments made under one large project in each sector, the Health Care II
project in the health sector and the Primary Education Project in the

3/   These estimates do not include expenditures by the Regional
Administrations, which are negligible.

education sector, both funded by IDB loans. While these additional investments are sorely needed, investment in infrastructure rehabilitation and construction under the Health Care II project is to occur in the Georgetown area where facilities are already considerably better than elsewhere. Improving facilities in the Georgetown area without undertaking concurrent improvements in other areas may serve to further break down the referral system (see Section E).

13.15   Some additional capital expenditures on the social sectors are also being funded under the SIMAP project. The Public Sector Investment Plan (PSIP) estimates that these will amount to about 4 percent of Central Government capital spending between 1993 and 1996.

TABLE 13.2: CAPITAL EXPENDITURES IN HEALTH AND EDUCATION 1986-1992a/

	1986	1988	1990	1991	1992
EDUCATION SECTOR					
Real Capital Expenditures (1986 G$1000)	13,620	13,365	5,749	11,393	33,751
Share of External Financed (%)	n.a.	n.a.	51.2	51.2	77.9
Share in Total Capital Expenditures (%)	2.0	2.5	1.1	1.6	7.2
HEALTH SECTOR					
Real Capital Expenditures (1986 G$1000)	2,713	5,006	9,901	34,342	42,481
Share of External Financed (%)	n.a.	n.a.	71.8	62.1	86.5
Share in Total Capital Expenditures (%)	0.4	1.0	2.0	4.7	9.1

a/ Capital expenditures by Regional Administrations are not included.

Source: Ministry of Finance and State Planning Secretariat

A Cross-Country Comparison

13.16   Recurrent public spending on education in Guyana is low relative to other Caribbean countries (Table 13.3). In 1990, 7 percent of public recurrent expenditures were allocated to education, well below the 17 percent and 18 percent allocated in Jamaica and Trinidad and Tobago, respectively. Recurrent spending as a share of GDP was 2 percent in 1990, less than half the 5 percent in Barbados and 6 percent in Trinidad and Tobago.

TABLE 13.3: RECURRENT EXPENDITURES IN THE SOCIAL SECTORS IN THE CARIBBEANa/

	Education	Health	Education	Health
	--- % of Gov. Rec. Exp. ---		------- % of GDP -------	
Caribbean Countries				
Barbados	19.3	14.9	5.4	4.2
The Bahamas	24.1	15.7	47.4	3.1
Dominican Republic	9.5	11.3	1.5	0.6
Jamaica	16.7	8.5	4.1	2.1
Trinidad & Tobago	18.3	8.0	5.6	3.1
GUYANAb/	6.8	9.7	2.0	2.8

a/ Data are for most recent year available, generally 1988 or 1990.
b/ Data for Guyana are for 1990. For Guyana, total recurrent expenditures allocated to health and education are estimated excluding public debt.

Source: World Bank and Pan American Health Organization

13.17   Recurrent spending in the health sector in Guyana is not substantially below that in other Caribbean and middle-income Latin American countries. Approximately 10 percent of government recurrent expenditures were allocated to the sector, slightly more than in Jamaica and Trinidad and Tobago, but below allocations in The Bahamas. As a percentage of GDP, spending in the health sector compared favorably with levels in the other countries.

13.18   Guyana has committed a substantially smaller proportion of total capital spending to the social sectors than have other Caribbean countries (Table 13.4). In 1988 and 1989, approximately 2 percent of total capital expenditures were allocated to the health sector as compared to an average 13 percent in Barbados and 8 percent in Trinidad and Tobago. A comparison of capital expenditures in the education sector shows similar findings; allocations of just over 1 percent in Guyana in 1989 compared with allocations of 9 percent in Trinidad and Tobago and almost 19 percent in Barbados.

TABLE 13.4: CAPITAL EXPENDITURES IN THE SOCIAL SECTORS
GUYANA, BARBADOS AND TRINIDAD AND TOBAGO
(% OF TOTAL CAPITAL EXPENDITURES)

	1989	1990	1991
Guyana			
Health	2.5	2.0	4.7
Education	1.0	1.1	1.6
Barbados			
Health	12.8	13.6	12.6
Education	10.5	18.9	20.9
Trinidad and Tobago			
Health	8.0	7.5	7.1
Education	12.8	9.3	8.9

Source: Ministry of Finance and State Planning Secretariat

C. POVERTY REDUCTION EFFORTS

13.19   The information necessary to obtain a clear picture of the nature and extent of poverty is not available in Guyana. The most recent surveys available that could be used to examine poverty include the 1980 National Census and a survey conducted by the Guyana Agency for Health Sciences Education, Environment and Food Policy (GAHEF) in 1986. The very significant demographic and economic changes that have taken place in the country over the past 7 years clearly precludes the use of these data in any useful analysis. More reliable information should, however, become available in mid-1993 as data become available from the 1990 National Census as well as from an Incomes and Expenditure and Living Standards Measurement Survey.

13.20   Until more accurate data are available, some idea of the extent of poverty can only be obtained through the analysis of indirect indicators. Malnutrition, for example, is commonly associated with poverty. The available data on the incidence of malnutrition among children aged 0-5 years does indicate that malnutrition has increased significantly since 1986, with 23 percent of all children surveyed in 1992 being classified as mild/moderately malnourished (see Section E). The incidence of severe malnutrition appears to be highest in regions 8 and 5.

13.21   Human capital endowments, and particularly educational attainment, are strongly associated with an individual's employment prospects and earnings ability. In Guyana, no measure of workers' or household heads' educational attainment is available. However, an examination of schooling achievement by region indicates that there are very marked regional differences in average educational attainment (Para. 13.48). The education indicators are considerably lower in regions 9, 8 and 5 than in other regions.

13.22   The data available also suggest that there may be substantial differences in poverty levels between ethnic groups. Where data are available, it shows that Amerindians have poorer access to key medical services and higher mortality rates from diseases that are, in general, easily averted by preventive health care.

13.23   Although accurate data is not available on the extent of poverty, the Government sought to reduce the impact of the on-going structural adjustment loan on the most vulnerable groups. Its efforts have focused on the Social Impact Amelioration Program, a donor supported project of more than US$15 million, which finances small-scale sub-projects initiated and implemented at the community level. Financing is provided to the communities for a variety of project activities, including the rehabilitation and equipping of primary health care facilities, food distribution and nutritional surveillance activities targeted at children and pregnant and lactating mothers in primary health care facilities, the construction and rehabilitation and equipping of day-care centers, and the installation and rehabilitation of basic water supply facilities and sanitation systems. Community and non-government agencies (NGOs) may submit proposals for funding within these categories. Project selection criteria, however, also place considerable importance on the ability of the project to assist vulnerable groups, defined as the unemployed, persons with low fixed incomes (retirees, pensioners, etc.), children of school age and under, female heads of households lacking in skills or living in conditions which limit their ability to work for wages, and residents of remote and depressed rural/hinterland communities.

13.24   A better assessment of poverty and a determination of how to better target resources to the disadvantaged will be possible when better data becomes available. For the time being, the existing efforts to alleviate poverty under the SIMAP and Basic Needs projects continue to be the best mechanisms to ease the burdens of poverty (Table 13.5).

TABLE 13.5: POVERTY ALLEVIATION - SUGGESTED PUBLIC SECTOR INVESTMENT PROGRAM
(US$ 1000)

PROJECT	Budgeted 1993	1994	1995	1996	Agency
Ongoing Projects	3635.1	2900.4	2400.0	1101.2	
SIMAP	3635.1	2900.4	2400.0	1101.2	IDA
New Projects	3027.1	4916.3	5354.6	3656.6	
SIMAP	2421.5	4000.0	4000.0	1385.7	IDB
Basic Needs	605.6	916.3	1354.6	2270.9	CDB
TOTAL	6662.2	7816.7	7754.6	4757.8	

Source: Mission Estimates

D. THE EDUCATION SECTOR

1. Sector Overview

13.25   In the 1960s, Guyana's educational system was considered one of
the best in the Caribbean. Today, it is very probably the weakest. Learning
in the schools, as measured by national and Caribbean-wide examinations, is
extremely low, a large proportion of the teaching force is unqualified and
untrained, and textbooks and other teaching aids are seldom available.
Guyana's success in achieving universal access to primary school in the early
1970s appears to be eroding and is accompanied by rising repetition and
dropout rates. The sector's problems are further exacerbated by educational
subsidies which tend to be regressive, favoring wealthy rather than poor
children and tertiary rather than primary education.

13.26   The decline of the educational system reflects, to a large extent,
the decreasing resources available in the sector. The proportion of GDP
allocated to education has declined sharply over the past decade and is now
well below that in other Caribbean countries. However, while additional
resources will be essential if significant improvements are to be made, this
alone will not remedy the situation. There is also a need to improve
efficiencies in resource use and develop institutional capacity to identify
priority areas of concern, develop medium- and longer-range plans, improve
budgeting procedures, and develop more effective monitoring and evaluation
systems.

13.27   The challenges facing the sector are significant. Reforming the
way resources are currently allocated and used will be central in meeting
these challenges effectively.

2. Institutional and Regulatory Framework

Sector Organization

13.28   Under Guyana's decentralized system, the ten Regional
Administration Councils hold much of the responsibility for educational
provision. They construct and maintain schools in their jurisdictions,
allocate resources to different school sites and levels, recruit and pay
teachers, and ensure that schools operate in accordance with regional and
national objectives. The Ministry of Education and Culture's principal
functions are to monitor educational indicators across the regions and ensure

that large differences in educational quality do not arise between regions, to procure and deliver textbooks to all schools, to coordinate and administer key primary and secondary school examinations, and to control the operation of schools in the central Georgetown area. Most of the institutions of higher education also fall under the Ministry, including the post-school technical and agricultural institutes and the Teacher Training Institute. Although the Ministry provides some financial support to the University, it receives a substantial portion of its funding from the Ministry of Finance and operates autonomously.

13.29   Guyana's education system closely resembles those of other Caribbean countries and includes preschool, six years of primary school, four to six years of secondary school, and between three and four years of higher academic or practical education. Schooling is mandatory up to fourteen and a half years, meaning that all children should complete primary school and at least two years of secondary school. Secondary education is divided into two tracks, a general academic track and a vocational track, entrance to one or the other being determined by a student's score on the Secondary School Entrance Examination (SSEE) taken in the final year of primary school. Entrance to higher education is determined by two factors, the particular secondary track the student has attended and their score on national or Caribbean-wide examinations. With adequate examination scores, graduates of vocational track schools may gain entrance to one of several technical training institutes or pursue a teacher training program in agricultural or vocational subjects. General academic graduates may enter the Cyril Potter Teacher Training College or the University. A very limited number of short-term adult education courses are provided through a University extension program.

13.30   In 1976, a decision was made to transfer all responsibility for education provision to the public sector. Existing private schools were absorbed into the public system which undertook to fully subsidize education at all levels, primary through university. The introduction of student fees or other cost-recovery measures was prohibited at all institutional levels. As resource constraints became increasingly severe in the 1980s, and the public sector found it increasingly difficult to fully subsidize education, the Government began to re-evaluate the role of private providers in the sector. In 1992, restrictions on the private sector were lifted. To date, however, only one private school, a pre-school, has applied for licensing. All formal education thus continues to be funded by the Central Treasury. The actual provision of educational services under the decentralized system, however, is the responsibility of the Regional Administrations in the ten regions and of the Ministry in the Georgetown area.

Planning and Budgeting

13.31   Planning and budgeting functions in the sector are extremely weak. There are three reasons why this is so. First, the institutional capacity of the Ministry, the institution responsible for setting national policy, is very limited. Over the past decade low salaries and poor working conditions have meant that a large proportion of higher level staff have left the sector. The remaining staff have generally had little training in the policy, management and evaluation skills necessary to develop longer-term policy. The Ministry has not developed a medium- or longer-term policy framework for some time and budgeting and educational provision in the regions occurs without reference to broader national education objectives. Second, the poor communications and flow of information between the Regional Administrations and the Ministry means that the latter has only limited information with which to develop a national policy framework (see Section A). And, third, the Ministry's inability to provide incentives to the regions to follow national policy directives raises questions within the Ministry itself about the value gained from developing a national policy framework.

13.32   Clearly, strengthening of the planning and budgeting functions will be fundamental to any efforts to address educational efficiency and equity issues.

3.   Sector Finances

Sources of Revenue

13.33   Education in Guyana is funded exclusively from Central Treasury funds. Policy directives introduced in 1976 prohibited the introduction of student fees or other cost-recovery measures at any educational level, primary through university. All education is thus _de jure_ free. The public sector also undertook to fully subsidize textbooks, exercise books and writing materials.

13.34   Although the Government has been unwilling to consider the introduction of fees and cost-recovery, even when confronted with extremely limited resources for the sector, there is clearly a willingness to pay for education among parents. The poor education offered in schools has meant that parents have been increasingly willing to pay for after-school tuition. A very high proportion of students now receive private coaching. Parents have also become accustomed to purchasing their children's exercise books and writing materials which have not been provided by the public sector because of funding constraints.

13.35   If significant improvements in the provision of education are to be achieved, additional resources must be found. It is clear that the Central Treasury is unable to provide these resources. Carefully structured fee schedules plus some additional cost-recovery is the most feasible way of generating the needed resources. If the system is well-conceived, and the bulk of funds retained by the Regional Administrations, this could also help to ensure that the Regional Administrations and schools become more responsive to the concerns of parents and the local community. The introduction of any fee or cost-recovery schedule must, however, be taken concurrently with efforts to improve the quality of education offered. Without such a step the public's willingness to pay will be lost.

Trends in Recurrent Education Spending

13.36   Although the Government has widely acknowledged and stressed the important role of education in Guyana's economic development, resource allocations to the sector have declined sharply over the past decade. Spending on education accounted for only about 7.4 percent of total recurrent expenditures in 1991, whereas in 1984 they had accounted for 17.6 percent of total recurrent spending.

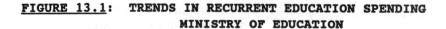

FIGURE 13.1: TRENDS IN RECURRENT EDUCATION SPENDING MINISTRY OF EDUCATION

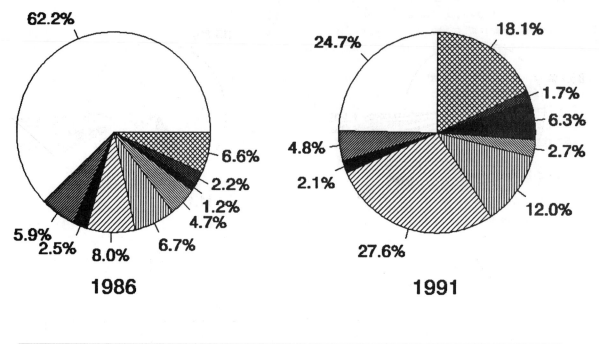

1986

1991

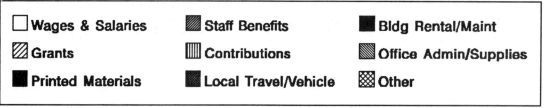

☐ Wages & Salaries   ▨ Staff Benefits   ■ Bldg Rental/Maint

▨ Grants   ▥ Contributions   ▨ Office Admin/Supplies

■ Printed Materials   ■ Local Travel/Vehicle   ▨ Other

13.37   The structure of spending within the sector has altered significantly over the past decade. The magnitude of these changes is shown in Figures 13.1 and 13.2 which show spending on nursery, primary and secondary education levels by the Ministry and the Regional Administrations.

13.38   The most notable change has been the <u>sharp decline in spending on teachers' salaries</u> both by the Ministry and the Regional Administrations between 1986 and 1991 (Figures 13.1 and 13.2). Over this period, spending on salaries by the Ministry dropped from 62 percent of total recurrent spending to 25 percent. The Regional Administrations reduced spending on salaries from 86 percent to 66 percent of their budgets over the same time period.

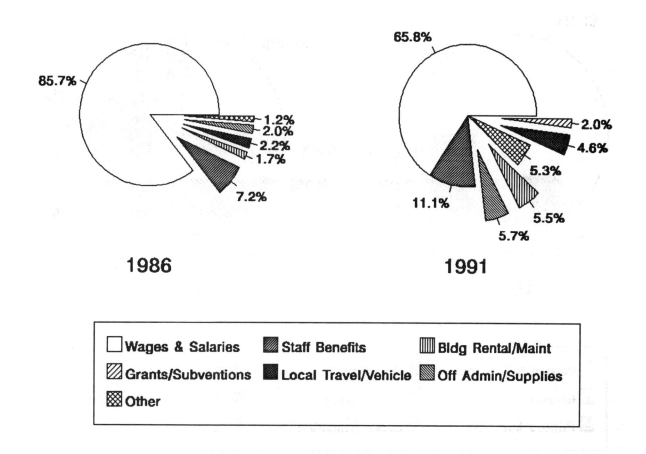

**FIGURE 13.2:   TRENDS IN RECURRENT EDUCATION SPENDING
REGIONAL ADMINISTRATIONS**

85.7%

1.2%
2.0%
2.2%
1.7%

7.2%

1986

65.8%

2.0%
4.6%

5.3%

11.1%

5.5%

5.7%

1991

☐ Wages & Salaries   ▨ Staff Benefits   ▥ Bldg Rental/Maint

▨ Grants/Subventions   ■ Local Travel/Vehicle   ▧ Off Admin/Supplies

▨ Other

13.39   While a high level of spending on teachers' salaries does not
necessarily ensure the provision of high quality education, it is almost
always true that when very limited resources are allocated for teachers'
salaries -- as is the case in Guyana -- the quality of education provided is
low.   Teachers are, after all, the key element in the learning process.   Two
factors explain the reduction in the proportion of total resources allocated
to teacher salaries: (i) teacher vacancy rates have increased as qualified
teachers have left the sector for higher paying employment in the private
sector and abroad and, (ii) the total wage bill has been reduced because of
the schools' increased reliance on lower paid unqualified teachers.

13.40   The sector has been unable to stem the outflow of qualified and
trained teachers because teacher salary scales are determined centrally by the
Public Sector Commission, not by the sector itself.   The size of the decline
in real salaries between 1985 and 1990 was substantial (Table 13.6).   A
graduate teacher's maximum salary in 1985, for example, was more than two and
a half times the real value of the maximum salary in 1990.   Although salaries
were substantially increased in 1992, their real value remains below 1985
salary levels.

TABLE 13.6: TRENDS IN TEACHER SALARIES, 1985-1992
(in 1985 G$)

Categories	1985 Minimum	1985 Maximum	1990 Minimum	1990 Maximum	1992 Minimum	1992 Maximum
Headmaster/Mistress						
Graduate	1756	1979	653	733	1581	1708
Non Graduate	1488	1709	575	658	1258	1360
Teacher						
Graduate	1225	1447	480	561	1262	1354
Non Graduate	1002	1225	398	480	1046	1138
Other Categories						
Acting Teacher	382	382	170	170	477	477

Source: Ministry of Education and Culture

13.41   Both the Ministry and the Regional Administrations have sought to increase teachers' emoluments by providing supplementary benefits in the form of meal expenses and local travel costs. This is reflected in the large spending increases recorded under the "other" category in Figures 13.1 and 13.2. Expenditures under this category increased from 7 percent to 18 percent of the Ministry's budget between 1986 and 1991, and from 1 percent to 5 percent of Regional Administration spending over the same period. These supplementary benefits have, however, been insufficient to check the outflow of better qualified teachers and, because they are provided to all teachers regardless of qualification and training, have effectively reduced incentives for teachers to pursue additional qualifications.

13.42   Spending on educational aids for the classroom has been consistently low. In 1991, the Ministry allocated 6 percent of recurrent spending for these supplies. Much of this money has been used to purchase student exercise books; simple, but effective, learning materials such as classroom posters, cardboard and pencils and crayons are seldom supplied and rarely seen in schools. The Ministry is responsible for financing, procuring and distributing textbooks. Funding shortages, however, have meant that it has been unable to meet these obligations and the resources allocated for these expenditures have been extremely low. This has meant that the Regional Administrations and, in the case of Georgetown, the Ministry, have tried to purchase textbooks by using discretionary funds. These costs are typically subsumed under the "Office Administration/Supplies" category. The decline in spending under this category serves to emphasize the severe shortage of textbooks; visits to primary schools revealed that students frequently had no access to textbooks.

13.43   Interestingly, as economic conditions have worsened and poverty become more severe, the schools have extended their mandate and sought to provide some form of assistance to poor and disadvantaged students. In 1991, the Regional Administrations spent 2 percent of their total recurrent budget on such assistance (shown under the "Grants/Subventions" category). These funds reportedly provide students with uniforms and, occasionally, spectacles or medical treatment. It is freely acknowledged, however, that, in the absence of means-testing, these funds subsidize students from families in a broad range of income levels.

13.44   Note should also be made of the increasing proportion of resources being spent on <u>school security</u>. Schools, which generally lack fences and seldom have secure windows or shutters, have become targets of theft and water faucets, furniture and other equipment are routinely stolen. This theft is causing scarce resources to be diverted from educational spending for security services. In 1992, for instance, the Ministry budgeted over 9 percent of recurrent spending for security.

<u>Educational Expenditures and Equity Issues</u>

13.45   The present allocation of subsidies in the education system appears to be regressive, favoring students from wealthier families and students attending higher education levels. This is shown most clearly by comparing unit cost estimates across education levels. Subsidies to secondary and tertiary level students are substantially higher than those to primary students (Table 13.7). On average, nursery and primary schooling costs US$24 per student, secondary US$37 and tertiary US$146. Calculating the unit cost ratios of secondary and tertiary (university) education relative to primary schooling shows that secondary is more than twice, and tertiary more than 33 times, as costly as primary education. Stating the position more starkly, the annual subsidy provided to one university student could provide 33 children with one year of primary schooling. The equity effects of this are severe, given the very small percentage of students that attend tertiary level education; the total subsidy received by individuals who only complete primary school is very low relative to the total subsidy received by a student who has completed higher education.

TABLE 13.7: UNIT COST ESTIMATES AND UNIT COST RATIOS BY EDUCATION LEVEL

EDUCATION LEVEL	UNIT COST<u>a</u>/ G$	UNIT COST US$ equivalent	UNIT COST RATIO (per student year)
Nursery	985.8	24.9	..
Primary	961.9	24.3	1.0
Secondary	1474.6	37.3	2.1
Tertiary	5771.4	146.0	33.0

<u>a</u>/ These are gross estimates only, derived by dividing total education spending at each education level by total student enrollments in 1991.

<u>Source</u>: Ministry of Education

13.46   It is important to note, however, that while education is fully subsidized by the public sector, public expenditures actually do not reflect the full investment in a child's education. This is because a burgeoning private tuition industry has developed as formal education quality has declined. Although information has not been collected on the extent of this sector, it is clearly well-developed and a high proportion of students at all levels receive after-school tuition. Costs for this tuition appear to range from as much as US$200 per month for individual classes to US$5 per month for large group coaching. At the cheapest rate, this tuition would amount to approximately 13 percent of a lower-level Grade 5 civil servant's monthly salary. Students from poor families who are unable to afford private tuition are, therefore, severely disadvantaged because investments in their education are considerably lower than for other groups.

13.47   Although, as Table 13.8 shows, there has been some effort to reallocate public education resources to lower levels of education, these efforts have focused on nursery/pre-school education (where attendance is not compulsory) and not on primary education. Indeed, allocations to primary education have continued to fall as spending on post-school technical training institutes and teachers' Resource Centers has increased.[4] Allocations to Teacher Training Institutes, however, have declined.

TABLE 13.8:   **RECURRENT EXPENDITURES BY EDUCATION LEVEL, 1986 and 1991**
MINISTRY OF EDUCATION AND CULTURE
(in percent)

EDUCATION LEVEL	1986	1991	CHANGE
Nursery	1.0	8.5	+7.5
Primary	32.3	24.8	−7.5
Secondary/Multilateral	43.3	30.4	−12.9
Technical/Pre-Vocational	11.8	19.2	+7.4
Teacher Training	7.4	2.6	−4.8
Resource Centers	4.2	14.6	+10.4

Source: Ministry of Finance.

13.48   Inequities in public education subsidies are further illustrated by the existence of President's College, a residential secondary school which accepts students scoring in the top 2 percent on the Secondary School Entrance Examination. This school has considerably better facilities and more highly trained teaching staff than other schools. Attendance at the school is fully subsidized, including lodging and food. Considerably higher student pass rates on the CXC examination (Table 13.9) attest to the higher quality of education offered by this institution.

4/   Resource Centers provide teachers with a room in which to meet to discuss teaching methods and prepare teaching materials. The Centers provide them with access to equipment not available in the schools.

TABLE 13.9:   **CXC EXAMINATION PASS RATES BY REGION, 1992a/**
(in percent)

Region	English	Mathematics	Social Science
1	8.1	4.1	1.2
2	1.7	0.0	0.0
3	1.4	13.0	2.0
4	4.3	12.5	3.9
Georgetown	16.3	24.5	5.4
5	3.2	13.7	6.6
6	8.8	13.3	20.5
10	9.6	10.1	0.0
President's College	65.5	79.3	68.4

a/   No candidates sat for the examinations in regions 7, 8 and 9.

Source: National Examinations Board, Guyana

13.49   It is not possible to estimate unit costs by education level at the regional level because of a lack of data. The significant regional differences in student pass rates on the Caribbean Examination Council (CXC) examinations taken at secondary school (Table 13.9) and substantial regional differences in the proportion of the teaching force which is qualified and trained (Table 13.11), however, suggest that educational quality differs markedly across regions. Student pass rates in core subjects such as English and Mathematics, for example, are almost twice as high in Georgetown as in any of the regions. Pass rates in these core subjects in regions 1 and 2 are especially low. Indeed, in region 2, not one of the students writing the examinations in Mathematics or Social Science passed. These regional disparities strongly suggest the need for a more equitable distribution of educational resources across regions as well as the need to target special resources to regions where student achievement is lowest.

13.50   Students attending general secondary schools receive an additional form of subsidy if they write the CXC or British-based GCE "O" or "A" level examination. In both cases, the examination councils charge a fee to students writing the examination. This fee is largely subsidized by the Ministry, although the actual size of the subsidy is determined by a means test. However, the fact that (i) only students attending general academic schools (33 percent of all secondary enrollments) have the opportunity to write the examination and, (ii) that only a small proportion of these secondary students get approval from their teachers to write the examinations, means that this subsidy benefits very few students. These subsidies accounted for over 2 percent of the Ministry's total educational spending in 1992.

4. Main Sectoral Issues

13.51   Educational efficiency in Guyana is low and the range of problems to be addressed are vast. Learning is low, teacher quality poor and resource constraints severe. Guyana also faces special difficulties in ensuring that educational subsidies are made more equitable. There are currently large regional differences in the educational system, both in terms of the availability and condition of physical infrastructure and in terms of the quality of educational inputs.

Efficiency of the Education System

13.52   By the 1970s, Guyana had achieved one of the highest primary school enrollment rates in the Latin American and Caribbean Region and reported very low dropout and repetition rates at this level. While Guyana has been successful in keeping primary enrollment rates high, at around 94 percent, the efficiency of the education system has declined sharply. While data is often scanty and not representative of conditions in the country at large, the available data show that examination test scores and school attendance rates have fallen sharply while dropout rates have risen.

13.53   Student scores on national and Caribbean-wide examinations provide the clearest measure of student learning and educational efficiency. Three key examinations provide this information, the nationally administered Secondary School Entrance Examination (SSEE) taken by students in their final year of primary school, the Secondary Schools Proficiency Examination (SSPE II) written by secondary students in community/vocational schools in their final year, and the Caribbean-wide Caribbean Examination Council (CXC) examinations written by students in their fifth year of general academic secondary school. Student learning, as measured by these examinations is unacceptably low.

13.54   The percentage of primary students passing the SSEE is exceedingly low; in 1990, only 19 percent passed English, 18 percent Mathematics and 19 percent Social Studies. If scores on this multiple choice test are adjusted for guessing, almost half of the students scored less than one sixth of the marks available. Inefficiency and the failure to learn basic skills at the primary level translates into poor student preparation for secondary school and, ultimately, very low pass rates on the secondary level examinations. As Table 13.10 shows, in 1992, of students writing the CXC examination, only 9 percent passed English, 5 percent Social Studies, and 18 percent Mathematics. These rates compare poorly with CXC pass rates in other Caribbean countries. In Barbados, for example, 41 percent of students passed English and 42 percent Mathematics. In Jamaica 27 percent of students passed English and 22 percent Mathematics. It is also very clear that learning in the schools has dropped sharply over the past decade, particularly in subjects requiring basic writing skills. In English, for example, the pass rate dropped from 23 percent in 1984 to 9 percent in 1992. It should be noted that a relatively small proportion of general secondary school students -- the highest achievers -- sit the CXC examinations.[5] The pass rate on this examination thus reflects learning among the better prepared students; learning by the average secondary student is likely to be considerably lower.

5/   Rough estimates indicate that less than 15 percent of all secondary level enrollees sit this examination.

TABLE 13.10: CXC EXAMINATION STUDENT PASS RATE, SELECTED SUBJECTS
(in percent)

Subject	1984	1985	1988	1989	1990	1991	1992
English	23	20	11	12	13	7	9
Mathematics	20	16	16	13	15	19	18
Social Studies	n.a.	25	18	10	12	11	5
Business Studies	n.a.	n.a.	20	15	22	38	27

Source: National Examinations Board, Guyana

13.55   Student pass rates on the SSPE II are just as discouraging. The results in 1986, for instance, showed that mathematics students, on average, scored 12.7 out of a possible 40 points, only 2.7 points above the score that could be achieved by random guessing. In Science the average student scored 15 out of a possible 40 points, 6.3 points above the chance score.

13.56   School enrollment, attendance and dropout rates also provide information about educational efficiency. Where education quality is poor and the possibility of student achievement low, parents may decide that the returns on investments in education are insufficient to warrant the child's continued attendance at school. Because an increasing number of schools are failing to submit data on enrollment, attendance and repetition rates, estimates of dropout and repetition rates are imprecise. However, the available data suggests that this is not an especially severe problem at the primary level. Approximately 11 percent of first grade enrollments are repeaters and dropout rates range from 3.2 percent in the first grade to 7.8 percent in the final grade. The primary cohort survival rate is around 80 percent. The secondary enrollment ratio is very low, however, and has dropped from 59 percent in 1980 to an estimated 43 percent in 1991, well below levels in other Caribbean countries. Daily secondary school attendance rates are also low, with wide variations occurring across regions; in region 1 the rate is 30 percent while in Georgetown general academic schools it is 78 percent.

Teacher Quality Issues

13.57   The quality of the teaching force in Guyana is extremely low, both at primary and secondary levels. Data for 1990 show that 38 percent of teachers in primary schools and 42 percent of teachers in secondary schools were either untrained or unqualified (Table 13.11). The situation is considerably worse in poorer and more rural regions; 76 percent of primary teachers in region 8 and 90 percent of secondary teachers in region 7 are unqualified and untrained.

TABLE 13.11: REGIONAL DISTRIBUTION OF UNTRAINED AND UNQUALIFIED TEACHERS,
1989 and 1990a/
(percent of total)

Region	Primary School Level		Secondary School Level	
	1989	1990	1989	1990
1	69	64	44	..b/
2	36	41	39	31
3	22	33	36	38
4	21	31	11	36
4 G/T	19	32	25	37
5	41	43	30	33
6	25	34	30	57
7	67	77	..	90
8	74	76	..	..
9	69	67	..	..
10	31	40	34	46
Average	30	38	31	42

a/ Some schools did not submit data.
b/ .. means not applicable.

Source: Ministry of Education and Culture

13.58   The increased reliance on unqualified and untrained teachers over the past decade can be largely attributed to the low salaries paid in the sector. Salaries of graduate teachers, for example, fell by more than 50 percent in real terms between 1985 and 1990 (Table 13.6 above). It is clear that the sector will not be able to attract or retain qualified teachers until salaries become more competitive with alternative sources of employment.

13.59   However, low teacher quality also reflects the need for improved pre- and in-service training. Teacher training is mainly provided by the Cyril Potter College of Education. Teaching practices taught here are outdated and emphasize the need to teach students routine skills and memorization of prescribed facts without application to practical situations. Training has also suffered from high faculty turnover in the teachers' training college and inadequate resources such as library books, science laboratories and audio-visual equipment.

Non-Teacher Inputs

13.60   Spending on non-teacher inputs such as textbooks and other educational aids fell sharply over the past decade as resource allocations to the education sector declined. Provision of textbooks is the responsibility of two agencies falling under the Ministry, the National Center for Educational Resource Development (NCERD) and the Book Distribution Unit (BDU). While the NCERD has produced some curriculum guides and primary school language textbooks, most teaching materials used in the schools are imported and have consequently become more scarce as the value of the Guyana dollar has declined. Few students have textbooks at any school level and school libraries are uncommon. But, even when some textbooks and teaching aids are available, the limited resources and institutional capacity of the BDU means that delivery to the regions is problematic. These problems will be partly redressed beginning in 1993 through projects supported by CIDA and the UNDP which will assist the Ministry in developing local capacity to print texts for the first three primary grades.

Infrastructure

13.61   Limited capital investment in the sector has meant that very few schools have been constructed during the past two decades. Much of the capital stock is extremely old and dilapidated; Ministry records show that approximately 35 percent of schools in use were constructed before 1920. In addition, facilities are often severely overcrowded. Visits to schools revealed, for instance, that facilities built to accommodate 150 students may house as many as 420. Learning is probably seriously impeded in these crowded conditions, especially since most schools consist of one large room divided into classes only by blackboards. Limited investment in infrastructure maintenance means most structures are severely dilapidated. A limited survey of infrastructure in the sector in 1991 showed only 10 percent of schools to be in satisfactory condition. Forty percent need significant repairs and the remaining 60 percent require substantial rehabilitation. Many schools lack doors and windows and have inadequate sanitation facilities without running water. Steps and floors are often shaky and have large holes.

5.   Proposed Strategy

13.62   Every effort should be made to improve the quality of education and learning in Guyana. If these issues are not addressed the low level of human capital is likely to profoundly affect future economic growth and development. Shortages of semi-skilled and skilled manpower, already acute, will greatly hinder private sector activity at a time when it should be expanding and increasing economic output.

13.63   A set of clearly defined policy objectives will be one of the most important building blocks in any effort to upgrade education quality. The sector needs to identify and prioritize medium- and longer-term objectives and determine what can be achieved realistically given projected resource flows and staffing capacity. This process should be a collaborative one in which the Ministry and the Regional Administrations participate. The medium-term objectives should be itemized in a formal document which also assigns responsibility to agencies for the implementation of specific objectives, and which clearly states what procedures are to be followed in achieving these objectives. Monitoring and evaluation activities should be strengthened so that data is available with which to set policy and measure progress.

13.64   Given the need to increase resources available to the sector, it will be necessary to institute user fees and other cost-recovery measures. Student fees should be introduced at secondary and higher education levels where public subsidies are currently highest. Some limited cost-recovery for publicly provided textbooks should also be introduced. These revenues could be used to improve capacity in the country to produce and distribute primary school texts. The capacity of schools to purchase teaching aids and educational equipment should also be increased. Resources in the sector could also be increased by reducing subsidies to the University which has the capacity to introduce fees and provide student loans.

13.65   If student fees and other cost-recovery measures are to be introduced, it is necessary to concurrently improve the quality of services provided. Improving teacher salaries will be important in attracting and retaining better qualified staff. The current system of providing a package of emoluments should be eliminated in favor of a basic salary scale in which increases are linked to the acquisition of additional training and qualifications. Efforts should be made also to improve pre- and in-service teacher training. Staff in the Ministry and the Regional Administrations should be provided with additional training in basic management, planning, monitoring and budgeting skills so as to improve their capacity to implement and sustain improvements in the sector.

13.66   The current system of subsidies favors higher and vocationally-oriented education which typically have the lowest social rates of return. Resources should be reallocated to favor primary education where social returns are highest.

13.67   The Ministry should be given the capacity to provide fiscal incentives to the regions to pursue national policy objectives and submit timely and accurate data on the student population. The Ministry should also have the capacity to target additional resources and funds to regions where educational indicators are lowest. This capacity could be developed by ensuring that some proportion of the revenues collected from fees are transferred to the Ministry for such purposes.

6. Action Plan

13.68   Although capital investments in infrastructure are sorely needed, the most far-reaching reforms in the sector will be achieved by reallocating resources under the recurrent budget to priority areas identified in a well-formulated policy document.

13.69   Given existing resource constraints and the limited institutional capacity of the sector, it is important that priorities for action be established and that they be tackled systematically in stages. In Stage 1, it is recommended that efforts focus on:

- developing a comprehensive strategy plan for the sector which develops medium-term objectives, prioritizes the activities to be undertaken, and assesses what can be achieved given anticipated revenue flows;

- increasing resources available to the sector through the introduction of user fees; and

- strengthening the planning and management capacities of key personnel in the Ministry and the Regional Administrations.

13.70   In Stage 2 sector reform would focus on:

- reallocating resources where social returns are highest and more equitably distributed, i.e., on primary education;

- strengthening teacher training and restructuring the salary schedule; and

- improving teacher and student access to textbooks and teaching aids.

13.71   Recommended strategies to increase revenues and achieve these objectives are outlined in the following matrix.

EDUCATION SECTOR – POLICY MATRIX

ISSUE	POLICY DIRECTION	RECOMMENDED ACTIONS
STAGE 1		
(i) Planning is weak. Medium-term objectives have not been identified or determined.	Develop a medium-term Education sector policy.	- MEC to draft and approve medium-term education sector policies, strategies and priorities with cooperation of Regional Administrations.
(ii) Insufficient resources are available in the sector.	Introduce user fees and pursue other cost-recovery options.	- Prepare a strategy for introducing user fees at higher education institutions and secondary schools, determine appropriate fee levels, and detail collection mechanisms. - Reduce MEC support to the University. - Introduce limited cost-recovery for textbooks in secondary schools.
(iii) Limited institutional capacity of MEC and Regional Administrations	Improve management practices, especially planning, monitoring and budgeting functions.	- Provide training in key management areas - Improve programming and budgeting procedures - Improve expenditure control and auditing - Improve inventory management - Improve data collection, analysis and evaluation - Improve flow of information between regions and MEC
STAGE 2		
(i) The way resources are currently allocated, they: (a) favor higher education levels where social rates of return are typically lowest and, (b) provide the lowest subsidies to the most needy students.	Reduce inequities inherent in public subsidies. Reduce subsidies at higher education levels. Reallocate funds to primary and nursery education.	- Examine the distribution of benefits delivered under the present subsidy system. - Reduce subsidies to higher education levels and reallocate funds to primary and nursery levels. - Determine regional disparities in resource bases and establish systems for targeting additional resources from the center to regions with fewer resources.
(ii) Low quality of teachers	Improve pre- and in-service teacher training. Improve conditions of service so as to retain qualified teachers.	- Establish salary and career incentives to attract and retain qualified teachers. Eliminate supplementary emoluments funded by schools. - Improve quality of pre-service and in-service teacher training. - Develop and enforce examinations as accreditation vehicle for teachers.
(iii) Lack of textbooks and teaching aids.	Improve production, acquisition and distribution of textbooks. Introduce cost-recovery.	- Improve local capacity to design and produce primary texts locally. - Improve availability of secondary level texts. - Provide individual schools with the capacity to purchase necessary teaching aids. - Introduce selective cost-recovery for textbooks.

7. Proposed Investment Program

13.72   Given that the Government's commitment to the Primary Education
Project accounts for over 78 percent of the projected education sector
investment program through 1996 and, given the possibility that the Government
may have some difficulties in meeting its counterpart funding obligations for
this project, there is little room to manoeuver for additional capital
investments in the education sector.   There is some room, however, to adjust
investment levels in other project categories so as to favor education levels
where social returns will be highest.   The recommended capital investment
program is shown in Table 13.12.

TABLE 13.12: EDUCATION SECTOR - SUGGESTED PUBLIC SECTOR INVESTMENT PROGRAM
(US$ 1000)

PROJECTS	Budgeted 1993	1994	1995	1996	Agency
Ongoing Projects	5166.8	5598.5	7612.0	902.4	
Primary Education Project	3597.8	5094.0	7094.00	8492.4	IDB
Human Resource Development	1004.8	0.0	0.0	0.0	IDB
Development of Textbooks	88.4	0.0	0.0	0.0	IDB
Resource Development Center	0.0	5.6	5.6	5.6	Local
Carnegie School of Home Economics	0.0	4.0	0.0	0.0	Local
Building - National Library	47.8	23.9	23.9	26.3	Local
School Furniture (MEC)	0.0	31.9	34.3	36.7	Local
Nursery, Primary & Secondary Schools	79.7	47.8	51.8	57.4	Local
Critchlow Labor College	8.0	12.0	12.0	13.5	Local
School Buildings (Regions)	308.4	335.5	344.2	344.3	Local
School Furniture (Regions)	31.9	43.8	46.2	47.8	Local
New Projects (Identified)	768.9	0.0	0.0	0.0	
Rehab. Education Facilities	796.8	0.0	0.0	0.0	Local
TOTAL (Identified)	5963.6	5598.5	7612.0	9023.9	
New Projects (Unidentified)	0.0	0.0	1500.4	2500.4	
Rehabilitation of Technical and Vocational Schools	0.0	0.0	1500.4	2500.4	
TOTAL	5963.6	5598.5	9112.4	11524.3	

Source: Mission Estimates

E. THE HEALTH SECTOR

1. Sector Overview

13.73   The quality of health care provided in Guyana has declined
markedly over the past decade. Although Government allocations to the sector
dropped sharply over this period high levels of inefficiency, the fragmented
organization of the sector, an inability to identify and prioritize
objectives, and the limited coordination between the relevant agencies has
greatly contributed to this decline.   The deterioration in care has been most
severe in smaller urban and rural areas where health facilities are severely
understaffed and lack even the most basic drugs and diagnostic equipment.

13.74   The health referral system in Guyana was designed to include five
different levels of facility.   However, the extremely poor quality of care

offered at lower levels of the referral system has caused patients to bypass these services and seek care directly from Georgetown Public Hospital, the highest referral level. The breakdown of the referral system has greatly increased inequities; it is the poor and rural population who have access to the poorest quality facilities and who are least able to afford the costs of travel to Georgetown to obtain better care. The consequences of these inequalities are reflected in the low health indicators reported in poorer and more rural regions such as regions 9, 8, and 5.

13.75   The sector faces considerable challenges in its efforts to improve the efficiency and quality of health services. The most immediate need is to identify sector priorities and objectives and formulate a sector strategy plan. Once this is in place, efforts should focus on increasing efficiency in the sector. Longer-run and more substantial improvements in service delivery, however, will require additional resources.

2.   Institutional and Regulatory Framework

Sector Organization

13.76   From the late 1960s, Government has provided fully subsidized public health care to all citizens. In an effort to equalize access to health care across all groups, the Government severely restricted the development of the private sector and prohibited public employees from working outside public facilities. Resource constraints, however, have meant that the Government has been unable to fulfill its objective of providing high quality, free health care to all its citizens. Funding and manpower shortages have led to sharp declines in the quality of service offered and the Government has been forced to relax constraints on private sector activity. Health care is now provided through several avenues, although the public sector remains the principal provider. The private sector has grown rapidly in recent years and six private hospitals (four for-profit and two non-profit institutions) now operate in Georgetown along with several diagnostic facilities and clinics in larger urban areas. Individual private practice is also becoming increasingly common. A further source of medical care has been provided by the larger public enterprises, GUYSUCO and GUYMINE. These services, which consist of two GUYMINE hospitals in region 10, and 19 GUYSUCO dispensaries and clinics with diagnostic facilities, are considered to offer better quality care than the public hospitals.

13.77   Following moves to decentralize the delivery of public services in 1985, responsibility for health care delivery was largely devolved to the ten Regional Administrations. Although they continue to be totally funded by the Central Treasury, the Regional Administrations have responsibility for establishing regional health policy, constructing and maintaining medical facilities, administering the operation of facilities in their jurisdiction, determining staffing requirements, and paying personnel. At the Central Government level, two executing agencies share the responsibility for health service provision, the Ministry of Health and the Guyana Agency for Health Sciences Education, Environment and Food Policy (GAHEF). The Ministry is meant to monitor health indicators in the country at large and act to ensure that health quality does not differ markedly across the regions. In addition, the Ministry has retained responsibility for (i) the provision of specialized curative/hospital care offered through the Georgetown Public Hospital, (ii) the procurement and distribution of pharmaceuticals in all regions and, (iii) dental care in the country at large. GAHEF has responsibility for developing and implementing policies on environmental health and food quality/nutrition issues and running the Health Sciences Education Unit which provides training courses for most health care professions. It also has responsibility for inspecting and monitoring waste water and sewerage removal activities and disposal of hazardous waste.

13.78   The design of the health care delivery system is particularly well-suited to Guyana's geographic and demographic characteristics. The design emphasizes primary health care and consists of five different levels of service, each providing successively more sophisticated services and having a staff composition suited to the level of service provided.

13.79   At the base of the system is the Community Health Post located in rural and hinterland areas. These are staffed by Community Health Workers and ideally provide preventive health care and simple treatment for selected common diseases. Cases that cannot be treated here are referred to the Health Care Centers, the second level of service. The Centers are located in more populous areas and, being ideally staffed by a MEDEX (who has one year of specialized medical training) or a public health nurse, plus a nursing assistant, dental nurse and midwife, are able to provide a wider range of services than the Health Posts. At the third level of the referral system are the District Hospitals which should serve a geographically defined area with a population of 10,000 or more. Although these hospitals principally provide out-patient services, they are meant to have some limited capacity to provide in-patient treatment including basic surgery and obstetric and gynecological care. They should also be equipped for simple radiological and laboratory services and be able to provide preventive and curative dental care. At the fourth level of referral are the Regional Hospitals which should provide emergency services, routine surgery and gynecological care, and dental services. These Hospitals were designed to include the laboratory, x-ray, pharmacy and dietetic services necessary to perform this level of medical care. The fifth, and highest, referral level consists of several specialized facilities, the foremost of which is the Public Hospital in Georgetown. Among the other specialized facilities are a geriatric hospital, a chest clinic and a paediatric hospital.

13.80   The basic infrastructure necessary for the operation of this referral system was established in the 1960s and covers much of the country. Its operation, however, is problematic given that the facilities are very dilapidated and in need of urgent rehabilitation, are severely understaffed, and do not receive regular consignments of basic drugs and supplies. These operational problems mean that a fairly large number of facilities, especially those at the lower levels, are no longer functional. This has led to the almost complete breakdown of the referral system with the result that: (i) most people no longer seek preventive care and attend health facilities only for curative care and, (ii) the sick tend to bypass the first four referral levels to seek treatment directly from Georgetown Public Hospital. For those who can afford it, treatment from a private facility is the preferred option. The number of operational facilities in each region in 1991 are shown in Table 13.13.

TABLE 13.13: DISTRIBUTION OF HEALTH CARE FACILITIES BY TYPE AND REGION, 1991

REGION	AREA IN SQUARE MILES	ESTIMATED POPULATION	REGIONAL HOSPITAL	DISTRICT HOSPITAL	HEALTH CENTER	HEALTH POSTa/	OTHER
1	7,853	18,615	0	3	6	13	
2	2,392	41,966	1	1	9	2	
3	1,450	102,760	1	3	15	0	
4	862	310,758	0	0	18	0	
5	1,610	55,556	0	2	14	0	
6	13,998	148,967	1	3	21	0	1b/
7	18,229	17,941	0	1	3	12	
8	7,742	5,672	0	0	2	14	
9	22,313	15,338	0	2	3	20	
10c/	6,595	38,596	1	1	6	4	
Georgetown			..	0	7	0	6d/

a/ The number of health posts per region are approximate.
b/ Psychiatric
c/ Both hospitals in region 10 are supported by GUYMINE.
d/ Public Hospitals; Palms; Ptolemy Reid Center; Convalescent Home; Chest Clinic; Immunization Center.
.. means not applicable.

Source: Ministry of Health

Planning and Budgeting

13.81   Low salaries and poor working conditions have meant that the agencies responsible for the administration and delivery of health care services have been unable to retain qualified, higher level staff. As a result, the institutional capacity of these agencies to identify sector priorities, formulate medium-term policies and allocate their budgets accordingly is extremely weak. Indeed, budgeting currently appears to be undertaken without reference to broader sector policy. The Ministry, which is meant to oversee national health policy, itself does not have consistent, well-formulated medium-term policy plans. The Regional Administrations, where institutional capacity is even weaker, are thus left to develop regional policy without reference to a set of national policy objectives. In practice, most regions have not attempted to develop a regional health policy.

13.82   The usefulness of planning at the regional level has, however, been greatly reduced by the collapse of standard auditing procedures. Faced with severe resource constraints and no systematic auditing[6] by the Central Treasury, Regional Administrators have increasingly treated funds as fungible across sectors. Hence, a crisis in one sector (agriculture, for example) may be resolved by transferring funds from another sector (health, for example). This crisis management approach clearly precludes effective planning. The fact that key health care planning positions have remained unfilled in several regions (regions 1, 3, 5 and 9) has very probably led to reduced spending on health care services in these regions (see Para. 13.8)

13.83   Planning and budgeting problems are especially severe at the service delivery level. The problems are a result of:

[6]   Auditing of the Regional Administrations is now more than five years behind schedule.

- the infrequency with which funding is received from the Regional Administrations;

- the almost complete lack of personnel trained in bookkeeping and accounting; and

- the use of obsolete budgeting methods and procedures.

3. Sector Finances

Revenue Sources

13.84   Since the 1960s, health care in Guyana has been almost completely subsidized by the Central Treasury. Neither the public facilities nor the Regional Administrations have been permitted to introduce any form of cost-recovery, be it for in- or out-patient services. During the 1980s some of the larger public enterprises (GUYSUCO and GUYMINE), in response to the declining quality of public health care, began to provide medical care for their employees in their own clinics and hospitals. Although the enterprises were permitted to provide health care, they too were prohibited from introducing cost-recovery measures.

13.85   As the economic crisis in Guyana became more severe in the late 1980s, however, it became clear that the Government would not be able to continue to fully subsidize health care. Indeed, increasingly severe resource constraints in the 1980s had led to a severe decline in health care coverage and quality. The Government was forced to relax some of the restrictions on the private sector and a number of private hospitals and clinics were established. In 1991 the Government also removed restrictions on public sector health workers which prevented them from opening private practices.

13.86   Although a wider range of providers now contribute to health care provision, the public sector continues to account for the bulk of spending in the sector (Table 13.14).

TABLE 13.14: HEALTH CARE EXPENDITURE BY PROVIDER, 1989
(percent of GDP)

SERVICE PROVIDER	Expenditure
Ministry of Health	4.9
GUYMINE	0.3
GUYSUCO	0.3
Georgetown Municipality	0.4
Regional Administrations	1.1
Private Hospitals	0.9
Private Practice	3.0

Source: State Planning Secretariat

13.87   Public health care is _de jure_ free, but in practice patients do contribute towards the costs of the treatment. Resource constraints have meant that the Ministry has been unable to supply health facilities with adequate quantities of pharmaceuticals and medical supplies. As a result, patients typically purchase the drugs and supplies needed from private providers. Treatment from a public facility would thus typically involve: (i) a visit to the facility the for a diagnosis, (ii) a trip to a pharmacy to purchase required prescriptions, injections and other supplies and possibly a trip to a private radiographer or diagnostic facility and, (iii) a return visit to the hospital for treatment with the supplies purchased. Despite this evidence that patients are willing to pay for services, the sector continues to be reluctant to introduce fees for services.

13.88   Several partly autonomous insurance agencies provide some medical coverage, the largest of which is the National Insurance Agency. All formal sector employers and employees have been required to contribute to an insurance scheme which includes medical coverage even though medical care was, until recently, fully subsidized. With the growth of the private health sector the insurance agencies have begun to receive more claims. They have not, however, developed an efficient system for processing these claims and many claimants report that they are never reimbursed. Conversations with private health facilities revealed that they, too, considered the agencies unreliable and would not favor direct reimbursement systems between the hospitals and the insurance agencies. Without substantial organizational reforms, it appears unlikely that the insurance agencies can be looked to as a potential revenue source for the health sector.

Trends in Public Sector Health Expenditures

13.89   Government allocations to the health sector have declined sharply over the past decade, having accounted for 11.3 percent of total recurrent spending in 1984 but only 7.3 percent in 1991. In terms of the percentage of GDP allocated to the health sector, Guyana's allocation of 2.1 percent is below that of Caribbean countries such as Trinidad and Tobago and the Bahamas, but equivalent to that of Jamaica (Para. 13.18).

13.90   The pattern of spending within the sector has altered significantly since 1986, as Figures 13.3 and 13.4 illustrate.[7] Most significant has been the sharp drop in spending on salaries which, in the Ministry, declined from 38 percent of total spending in 1986 to only 11 percent in 1991. Regional Administration spending on salaries shows similar declines, falling from 50 percent to 26 percent of total spending over the same time period. The reduced spending on salaries reflects the severe manpower shortages experienced by the sector over the past decade. Data for 1990, for instance, show a 40 percent vacancy rate among health care personnel positions. The principal reason for manpower shortages is the low salaries paid in the sector, although the extremely poor working conditions have undoubtedly contributed as well. The salary schedules of all medical personnel are determined by the Public Service Commission and, being linked to

---

7/   It should be noted that spending by the Ministry of Health includes spending both on medical care and general administration. It was not possible to further separate allocations by category of activity.

the general civil service pay scale, have suffered the same decline in real values as other civil service salaries.

FIGURE 13.3: TRENDS IN RECURRENT HEALTH SPENDING
MINISTRY OF HEALTH

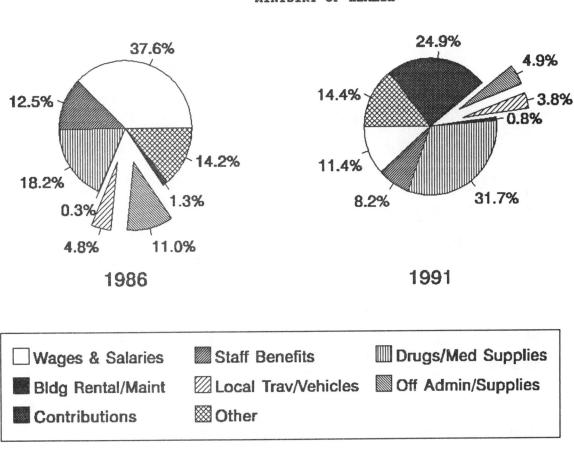

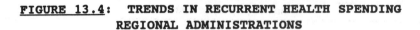

FIGURE 13.4: TRENDS IN RECURRENT HEALTH SPENDING REGIONAL ADMINISTRATIONS

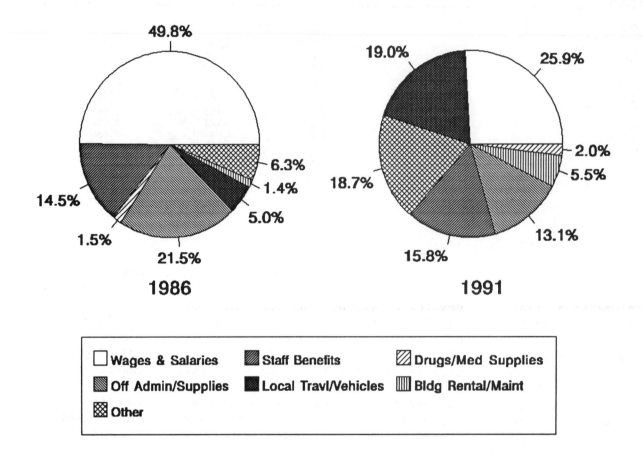

13.91   In real terms, physicians' salaries dropped by almost a half for fully qualified physicians and by one third for newly qualified physicians between 1985 and 1991 (Table 13.15). As salaries declined, physicians either entered the higher paying private sector or emigrated to other Caribbean countries and North America. The incentive to immigrate is strong given the substantially higher salaries and better working conditions in other countries; in 1991 a medical registrar's basic monthly salary, for example, was equivalent to only US$107. While nurses' salaries also declined sharply, the real value of salaries was maintained at around the 1985 level. Nurses' salaries are still low, however, relative to earnings in the growing private health sector and other Caribbean countries. The large number of nurses trained in the fully subsidized public training facilities thus flow out of the public system after their internship and into private hospitals, after which they seek employment in other Caribbean countries. By not charging fees to students attending nursing school, Guyana is thus effectively subsidizing training for surrounding Caribbean countries.

TABLE 13.15: TRENDS IN HEALTH SECTOR WAGES, 1985-1992
(monthly salary in 1985 G$)

Category	1985	1991	mid-1992
Physicians			
Medical Consultant	4,200	2,251	..
Medical Registrar	3,250	1,810	4,924
Medical Officer	2,266	1,715	4,570
Medical Intern	1,910	1,498	3,847
Nursing Staff			
Ward Sister	1,052	831	1,212
Staff Nurse/Midwife	819	775	1,037
Staff Nurse	790	753	1,037
Nursing Assistant	560	441	6,939
Nurse Aide	462	383	6,086
Other Medical Personnel			
Medex	1,062	786	..
Medical Technologist	..	..	1,192
Environmental Health Officer	..	..	1,192

.. means not available.

Source: Ministry of Health

13.92   The Government responded to the acute shortage of manpower by substantially increasing wages in the sector in 1992. The package of tax free emoluments available to physicians was also greatly extended and now makes up a significant proportion of physicians' earnings. Medical registrars in their first two years of practice, for instance, qualify for an institutional allowance of G$800 - G$1,500 per month, a night duty allowance of G$350 per month, an overtime allowance of G$60 per hour, and an on-call allowance of G$400 per month. Additional tax free emoluments have also been provided to nurses, including a cash allowance for meals. Although these emoluments significantly increase earnings in the sector, they work to reduce incentives among staff to pursue higher qualifications by equalizing benefits across all staff level. The value of the emoluments is not linked to either good performance or level of qualifications.

13.93   The provision of pharmaceuticals and medical supplies is the responsibility of the Ministry which procures and distributes them to all Regional Hospitals and clinics. As Figure 13.3 shows, spending on drugs has increased sharply, accounting for 18 percent of total spending in 1986 and 32 percent in 1991. This increased allocation has not, however, translated into improved availability of drugs and medical supplies in hospitals and clinics. Indeed, shortages of drugs and supplies are chronic and availability is far more limited now than in 1985 with few of the major hospitals having basics such as syringes, drip bags and basic painkillers in stock. What the increased allocations really reflect is the rising cost of purchasing these imported goods as the value of the Guyana dollar has fallen relative to other currencies.

13.94   Another significant change in the Ministry's spending patterns concerns the increased percentage of funds allocated under the "contributions" category. This category includes subscriptions and contributions to international health organizations which, because they must be paid in foreign exchange, have absorbed greater proportions of the budget as the value of the Guyana dollar has fallen. Contributions accounted for almost 25 percent of recurrent spending in 1991. No evaluation of the benefits derived from these memberships appears to have been undertaken by Ministry. While membership in some organizations is necessary because they provide diagnostic services not available in the country, it is clear that spending in this category accounts for an unreasonably large proportion of the budget. Every effort should be made to reduce these expenditures and reallocate the funds to more productive activities.

13.95   Spending by the Regional Administrations has increased very markedly under the "local travel/vehicles" and "other" categories. The very substantial growth in the travel category is explained partly by the rising cost of imported goods such as vehicles, spare parts and fuel, but it is also the result of increased travel by medical personnel providing day clinics at understaffed outlying facilities. Funding allocations to this category rose from 5 percent to 19 percent between 1986 and 1991. Growth in spending under the "other" category largely reflects efforts by the regions to supplement staff salaries by providing additional emoluments in the form of meals and travel expenses. The expectation that these benefits will be provided has become institutionalized and draws heavily on operational budgets.

4.   Main Sectoral Issues

Data Quality

13.96   Demographic and health indicators in Guyana are limited, often dated, and of dubious quality. The most reliable data comes from a limited national survey of health conditions conducted by GAHEF in 1986. More recent data on maternal and infant health is available from (i) another GAHEF survey of approximately 3,800 children and 6,000 mothers conducted in nine regions and Georgetown in 1992, and (ii) from some Health Centers following a maternal and child health care (MCH) initiative supported by UNICEF. More general information on morbidity and mortality can be gleaned from birth and death records processed by the Statistical Bureau. While these sources yield valuable information not available elsewhere, it is widely recognized that a large percentage of births and deaths go unrecorded, particularly in the rural and hinterland areas.

Mortality

13.97   Although the data is limited and sometimes inconsistent, it strongly suggests that mortality rates are high and increasing, especially among young children. The epidemiological profile derived from death records lodged with the General Registry Office shows the principal causes of death to be those common to both developed countries (ischemic and other heart diseases and hypertension) and developing countries (enteritis/diarrhea). Cerebrovascular and heart disease accounts for over 37 percent of recorded deaths in the population at large.

13.98   The information available indicates that the principal causes of death differ significantly by ethnic group. Deaths among persons of African origin were overwhelmingly the result of cerebrovascular and heart disease. While these were also important causes of death among those of East Indian origin, diabetes is also a principal cause of death. Amerindians appear to die principally from disorders that are preventable or easily treated with good medical care -- enteritis and other diarrheal disorders and nutritional deficiencies. These data reflect differences in access to health care by the various ethnic groups and point to the need to target different preventive and educational programs to the different population groups.

13.99   A crude estimate of the infant mortality rate can be obtained from the registry of infant births and deaths. Data for 1990 yields an infant mortality rate of 37 per 1,000, well above rates reported by Suriname (30/1,000), Trinidad and Tobago (20/1,000) and Jamaica (18/1,000).[9/] Although the data are incomplete, it is clear that there are striking differences in infant mortality rates across regions. The rates appear to be particularly high in regions 10 and 8 (Table 13.16).

TABLE 13.16:   INFANT MORTALITY RATES PER 1,000 LIVE BIRTHS, 1990[a/]

REGION	RATE
1. Barima/Waini	40.0
2. Pomeroon/Supernaam	53.3
3. W. Demerara/Essequibo Islands	17.6
4. Demerara/Mahaica	48.3
5. Mahaica/Rosignol/Berbice	52.5
6. E. Berbice/Corentyne	21.4
7. Cuyuni/Mazaruni	13.3
8. Potaro/Siparuni	57.1
9. Upper Takatu/Upper Essequibo	..
10. Upper Demerara	65.0
Country Average	37.0

a/   These estimates only reflect infant births and deaths registered with the General Registry Office.

Source: Statistical Bureau

13.100   Mortality among young children (aged 0 to 5 years) appears to result principally from nutritional deficiencies and intestinal infections, conditions which can frequently be averted through effective preventive care. Nutritional deficiencies and intestinal infections accounted for over 44 percent of infant deaths and just over 30 percent of deaths among children five years or less. The prevalence of deaths from these disorders indicates that water and sanitation conditions are poor and that the coverage and effectiveness of pre- and post-natal services needs strengthening.

13.101   No national data on maternal mortality rates are available after 1984 when it was estimated to be 0.6 per 1,000 births. However, data collected at Georgetown Hospital in 1987 suggests that the rate is

8/   This estimate of Guyana's infant mortality rate is obtained by comparing the number of infant deaths reported per 1,000 live births recorded. In 1990, the General Registry Office recorded 14,484 live births and 534 infant deaths, yielding a mortality rate of 37 per 1,000.

substantially higher, possibly around 1.8 per 1,000 births. Toxemia in pregnancy and hemorrhage and sepsis during childbirth were reported to be the principal causes of maternal mortality.

<u>Morbidity Profile</u>

13.102   Guyana's morbidity profile is characterized by disorders that could be substantially reduced by improved preventive health care, educational campaigns and improved access to good quality basic health care. The most prevalent disorders are Acute Respiratory Infection, Hypertension, Diabetes Mellitus, Enteritis/Diarrhea, worm infestation and parasitism, and Malaria.

13.103   Over the past five years there have been occasional upsurges of immuno-preventable diseases such as measles and whooping cough, reflecting the difficulties experienced by the Ministry in conducting nation-wide vaccination campaigns because of the problems faced in maintaining the cold chain and in transporting the vaccines. The situation has been considerably improved in 1991 following the introduction of the Expanded Immunization Program in 1990 which has been supported by donors. Immunization rates against Measles, for example, jumped from 36 percent to nearly 81 percent of the target group of infants between 1985 and 1991. Polio immunization rates increased from 77 percent to 84 percent of the target group over the same period. Immunization rates, however, continue to differ sharply across regions, being generally lower in regions 8, 5 and 1.

13.104   Vector transmitted diseases such as Malaria, Filaria and Dengue have never been fully controlled in Guyana and have always posed a significant health risk. The breakdown of systematic vector control measures in the mid-1980s and, in the case of Malaria, increased migration between hinterland and coastal areas, has led to a resurgence of these diseases. Reported cases of Malaria, for instance, rose from 3,600 in 1984 to 20,822 in 1989 and to 42,204 cases in 1991. Indiscriminate and intermittent use of antimalarial drugs in the endemic areas has served to increase drug-resistant strains of Malaria. The incidence of Filaria and Dengue is not known, but hospitals report an increased number of patients suffering from these diseases.

13.105   Patterns of morbidity are also being affected by the breakdown in basic services, particularly the delivery of potable water, the removal of waste, and the provision of adequate sanitation services. Water services have been drastically reduced or completely cut in some areas and the sewerage system is severely overloaded. As a result, residents in poorly served areas draw water from roadside canals which are also used to remove household waste. The incidence of diseases such as typhoid, hepatitis and gastroenteritis has consequently increased, as Table 13.17 shows.

**TABLE 13.17:   INCREASED INCIDENCE OF DISEASES ASSOCIATED
WITH POOR ENVIRONMENTAL HEALTH**

DISEASE	1983	1986	1988
Infectious Hepatitis	181	310	241
Typhoid Fever	51	119	154
Gastroenteritis	2,142	3,895	4,396
Malaria	n.a.	16,388	35,451

Source: Ministry of Health

Fertility and Contraception

13.106   Guyana's total fertility rate was estimated to be 2.9 in 1989, a
rate similar to that of Jamaica.   The accuracy of this estimate is doubtful,
however, given the unreliability of total population estimates.[9]   Recent
estimates from the United Nations Family Planning service put the prevalence
of contraceptive use at 45 percent, a level similar to those in other
Caribbean countries.   Contraceptives are distributed free of charge in most
health centers throughout the country.   The Guyana Responsible Parenthood
Association, a non-profit organization, also provides approximately US$120,000
per year for the distribution of contraceptives and educational literature.

Pre- and Post-Natal Care

13.107   In 1990 the Ministry, with support from UNICEF and the Pan
American Health Organization, embarked on an effort to improve pre- and post-
natal care by strengthening these functions in the Regional Health Centers.
Insufficient data is available to assess the effectiveness of this program,
but the provision of nutritional supplements to pregnant and lactating women
has reportedly led to increased clinic attendance.

13.108   The proportion of births occurring in institutions, however, is
not especially high, being around 72 percent.   This may partly account for the
fairly high maternal mortality rate.   The percentage of births occurring in
the home are considerably higher in regions 8 and 9 and information gleaned
from birth records shows great regional differences in terms of the medical
support received during birth.   Qualified midwives or nurse/midwives attended
a high proportion (over 70 percent) of births in regions 4 and 6.   Only about
1 percent of births were attended by unqualified assistants.   In contrast,
more than half of all recorded births in region 1 were attended by unqualified
assistants.   While the regional differences in maternal care are great, these
differences are even more striking for women of different ethnic groups.   As
Table 13.18 shows, Amerindian women are much more likely to give birth without
the help of a qualified assistant.   When they do get assistance from a trained

---

9/   Census data collected in 1990 has not yet been released.   Population
estimates are currently drawn from a 1987 survey although emigration
rates have been extremely high in recent years.

birth attendant, it is more likely to be from a lesser qualified Birth Attendant or Nurse/Midwife.

TABLE 13.18: **BIRTHS BY TYPE OF BIRTH ATTENDANT AND ETHNIC GROUPa/, 1990**
(in percent)

TYPE OF ATTENDANT	AFRICAN	AMERINDIAN	CHINESE	EAST INDIAN	OTHER
Not Stated	20.1	12.4	24.2	20.5	15.7
Physician	4.3	1.5	15.1	4.4	5.5
Midwife	55.2	21.2	51.5	57.2	51.8
Nurse/Midwife	15.6	17.6	3.0	14.4	20.7
Nurse	0.1	0.3	..	0.1	0.1
Birth Attendant	0.2	8.8	..	0.5	0.1
Other Unqualified	4.5	37.9	6.0	2.7	5.6

a/ Totals may not sum to 100 because of rounding.
.. means not applicable.

Source: Ministry of Health

Nutritional Status

13.109   Currency devaluation and the removal of generous public subsidies have greatly increased the cost of basic foods. The price of some foodstuffs increased by as much as 200 percent in 1990 following the removal of subsidies. Estimates of the price of a basic foodbasket show increases of 96 percent in 1989, 49 percent in 1990, and 84 percent in 1991. Although remittances from family members abroad have reportedly helped many families to cope with rising food prices, the available data indicates that malnutrition has increased among the poor.

13.110   Data from the Georgetown Hospital pediatric clinic showed a significant increase in the number of young children (under 5 years) suffering from malnutrition; 3,506 cases were treated in 1990 compared to 931 cases in 1989. More recent data on the nutritional status of young children is available from a small-scale survey conducted by GAHEF in 1991.[10] Although this data is not fully representative of nutritional conditions in the country, it does suggest that the nutritional status of young children has declined since survey findings in 1987. While the incidence of severe malnutrition appears to have risen only slightly, mild/moderate malnutrition has increased quite substantially (Table 13.19).

10/   GAHEF, Health and Nutrition Survey.

TABLE 13.19: NUTRITIONAL STATUS OF CHILDREN UNDER 5 YEARS, 1987 and 1991
(in percent)

NUTRITIONAL STATUS	1987	1991
Severely malnourished	2.7	3.0
Mild-Moderate Malnutrition	20.7	23.6
Well-Nourished	71.9	68.5
Obese	5.4	5.0

Source: GAHEF

13.111   Data from the 1991 survey suggests that there is considerable variation across regions in the incidence of malnutrition. It appears to be most severe in regions 5, 6 and 8 where between 4 percent and 5 percent of children surveyed suffered from severe malnutrition. The lowest rates recorded were in regions 2 (0.3 percent) and 10 (0.7 percent). Moderate malnutrition rates are shown to be relatively high in all regions, with over 23 percent of children surveyed being in this category (Table 13.20). The survey showed malnutrition to be most prevalent among Amerindian children.

13.112   Birth weight is generally a good indicator of the mother's nutritional status. The 1991 GAHEF survey data suggests that the incidence of low birth weight has increased since the last national survey in 1987, with the incidence of low weight increasing from 16.3 percent to almost 24 percent of births. This seems to have occurred despite programs to provide pregnant and lactating women with mineral and vitamin supplements and fortified milk. Again, the incidence of low birth weight shows marked variation across regions, with regions 9, 8 and 4 showing the highest incidence.

TABLE 13.20: NUTRITIONAL STATUS OF CHILDREN UNDER 5 YEARS BY REGION, 1991
(in percent)

REGION	SEVERE	MILD-MODERATE	NORMAL	OBESE
1	3.0	18.6	73.0	6.4
2	0.3	22.2	73.1	4.4
3	3.1	21.9	70.3	4.8
4	2.1	22.2	70.0	5.8
5	5.4	25.4	72.3	6.8
6	4.2	27.3	64.2	4.4
7	3.4	28.4	65.9	2.4
8	4.8	33.9	58.4	2.8
9	4.1	24.0	68.2	3.7
10	0.7	13.4	79.0	6.9

Source: GAHEF

Health Care Coverage

13.113   While health facilities are reasonably well distributed throughout
Guyana (see Para. 13.80), the level of service provided to the population is
very poor because of severe staffing shortages, very limited supplies of
drugs, and the poor condition of equipment and facilities.

13.114   Perhaps the most immediate concern is the shortage of trained
staff, particularly physicians. The ratio of physicians per regional resident
is very high, in some cases being 1:27,778 (region 5) and 1:18,615 (region 1)
(Table 13.21). This situation is generally not alleviated by higher
concentrations of MEDEX in these areas.

TABLE 13.21: RATIO OF HEALTH CARE PERSONNEL PER POPULATION
(by Region)

REGION	POPULATION/PHYSICIAN	POPULATION/MEDEX
1	18,615	3,102
2	8,393	8,393
3	12,845	11,417
4	4,932	10,715
5	27,778	7,936
6	14,896	16,551
7	11,806	2,990
8	11,806	2,836
9	15,338	5,112
10	9,298	5,513

Source: Ministry of Health

13.115   This situation has arisen largely because low salaries and poor
working conditions have encouraged the emigration of qualified medical
personnel. The severity of the situation is shown most starkly by the high
number of vacancies reported in the sector (Table 13.22). Until salaries and
working conditions are substantially improved it is unlikely that the coverage
and quality of medical care provided will be significantly improved.

TABLE 13.22: VACANCY RATE FOR KEY MEDICAL POSITIONS BY REGION, 1992a/

(in percent)

REGION	1	2	3	4	5	6	7	8	9	10
Administrative:										
Hospital Admin	100	100	100	..	..	100	..	..	..	..
Dental:										
Dentists/Dental Nurses	..	50	0	75	33	0	50	..	100	100
Senior Medical:										
Med. Health Officers	100	75	27	63	33	40	50	100	100	100
Paramedics:										
Env. Health Officers	100	70	70	58	0	64	67	100	100	..
Health Visitors	100	100	45	25	72	86	100	..	100	0
MEDEX	25	20	0	44	50	31	50	60	43	13
Nursing:										
Nurses and Midwives	74	49	54	5	49	11	66	60	79	49
Technicians:										
Pharmacists	67	75	25	..	100	38	100	..	100	..
Radiographers/X-ray Technicians	..	34	77	..	100	75	..	..	..	..
Medical Technologists	..	80	60	..	100	86	34	..	100	..
AVERAGE VACANCY RATE	66	55	44	57	50	35	62	70	81	47

a/ Estimates include positions above Grade 3.
.. means no positions established in that region.

Source: Mission Estimates

5. Proposed Strategy

13.116   As resource constraints have become more severe, the ability of the sector to provide fully subsidized, high quality health care to all has diminished. The institutional capacity of the sector has also been greatly weakened as personnel have left the sector for more attractive and higher paid positions elsewhere. The challenges confronting the sector are daunting. However, considerable improvements in the sector can be achieved if a number of important policy steps are carefully and systematically followed.

13.117   Most importantly, the sector needs to identify and prioritize its medium- and longer-term objectives and determine what can be realistically achieved. This process should be a collaborative one in which the Ministry, GAHEF and the Regional Administrations participate. A detailed document should prioritize the objectives to be achieved, assign responsibility for implementation of the steps needed to achieve these objectives, and state clearly what procedures should be followed. Progress toward these objectives should be evaluated each year.

13.118   There is clearly potential to substantially increase revenues through the introduction of cost-recovery measures; the fact that the private facilities are well utilized and able to recover 100 percent of operating costs through fees illustrates this quite clearly. A willingness to pay is also evidenced by the fact that patients attending public facilities routinely purchase drugs and supplies from private pharmacists because they are unavailable in public facilities.

13.119   The introduction of cost-recovery measures must, however, be accompanied by <u>immediate improvements in the quality of care provided</u>. This could best be achieved by <u>increasing salaries of health sector workers</u> and by providing additional financial incentives to those willing to work in smaller and more rural facilities. Ensuring that salary levels do not fall below those offered in private facilities will stem the flow of personnel to this sector. The existing emolument system, which blurs the salary scale and reduces incentives to staff to pursue higher qualifications should be eliminated and replaced by a standard salary package. It is also essential that the salaries and working conditions of administrative personnel be improved. Training in key management and budgeting areas should be provided so as to develop institutional capacity to implement improvement programs and monitor progress towards medium-term objectives.

13.120   The large regional differences in health indicators in part reflect the breakdown of the referral system and the growing emphasis on curative health care rather than on primary and preventive care. This situation may be addressed in part by increasing available resources at the lower levels. This could be achieved to a degree by <u>reallocating funds to lower level regional health care services</u>. Some proportion of receipts from user charges introduced at Georgetown Hospital, for example, could be targeted to primary care facilities in regions with the poorest health indicators. This, plus increased financial incentives to attract staff to work in those areas would help to improve the quality of care provided. Strengthening mobile health services serving hinterland areas would also help to improve service delivery in outlying areas.

6. Action Plan

13.121   Although investments in capital infrastructure are badly needed, substantial improvements in health service delivery are possible if recurrent funds are utilized more efficiently and resources augmented through introducing cost-recovery measures. Given that the sector currently lacks a medium-term policy plan and that its institutional and managerial capacity is very weak, progress towards these objectives should be undertaken systematically in clearly identified stages. It is recommended that initial steps be taken to (i) identify priorities and establish a coherent set of medium-term objectives; (ii) move to increase resources available to the sector through the introduction of a carefully structured fee schedule; and, (iii) work to strengthen the management and budgeting capacity of administrative staff in the Ministry, the Regional Administrations and the hospitals.

13.122   It is proposed that the second stage of the sector reform program focus on (i) redirecting resources from curative to primary health care; (ii) strengthening preventive health care services; and, (iii) improving the availability of pharmaceuticals and medical supplies, particularly in the regions.

13.123   The steps to achieve these recommended objectives are shown in the following matrix.

HEALTH SECTOR - POLICY MATRIX

ISSUE	POLICY DIRECTION	RECOMMENDED ACTION
STAGE 1		
(i) Planning is weak. Medium-term objectives have not been identified or determined.	Identify priorities and develop medium-term policy framework.	- MOH to draft and approve medium-term sector policy identifying strategies and priorities with cooperation of Regional Administrations.
(ii) Insufficient resources available in the sector.	Introduce user charges and increase revenues collected from insurance schemes.	- Establish system of user charges by health care level. - Identify fee collection and auditing mechanism. - Develop ability to charge insurers for full cost of services. - Make salaries competitive with those offered by private facilities. Eliminate emolument system.
(iii) Limited institutional capacity of MOH, Regional Administrators and Hospital Administrators.	Improve management practices, especially planning, monitoring and budgeting functions.	- Provide training in key management areas. - Strengthen programming and budgeting functions. - Strengthen expenditure control and auditing activities. - Improve inventory management at all levels. - Improve data collection, analysis, evaluation and dissemination.
STAGE 2		
(i) Resources are currently directed to curative rather than primary health care.	Reallocate funds to regional health care services.	- Reallocate a proportion of user fee receipts from the Georgetown area to Regional hospitals and primary health care facilities. - Provide incentives to attract qualified health care personnel to regional facilities. - Support mobile services to smaller outlying communities.
(ii) Preventive health care systems function poorly.	Strengthen the administration of preventive health care programs and increase funding.	- Invest some proportion of user fee receipts to this function. - Provide additional training to staff.
(iii) Poor procurement, management and distribution of pharmaceuticals and medical supplies.	Eliminate chronic shortages of basic pharmaceuticals and medical supplies.	- Decentralize the procurement of drugs to the regional level. - Permit regional hospitals to apply for drug import licenses or to collaborate with private facilities in drug procurement. - Introduce cost-recovery in the hospitals and clinics for drugs. - Strengthen management and budgeting capacity at hospital level to facilitate management of the system.

7. Proposed Capital Investment Program

13.124   The bulk of capital investments through 1996 are committed to the ongoing IDB supported Health Care II project which focuses principally on the construction and rehabilitation of facilities at the Georgetown public hospital. It would be desirable to channel additional capital investments to the regional hospitals and health care centers but, given the sector's heavy commitment to the Health Care II project, this would have to be done by transferring funds from another sector. Given the central role which human capital development plays in the development process, this should be given serious consideration. The identification of funding sources for the rehabilitation of community and regional hospitals should also be given priority in order to strengthen the primary health care system. The Government's proposed public sector investment program is shown in Table 13.23.

TABLE 13.23: HEALTH SECTOR INVESTMENT PROGRAM, 1993-1996
(US$ 1000)

PROJECTS	Budgeted 1993	1994	1995	1996	Agency
Ongoing Projects	8530.6	6699.6	6992.7	7685.2	
Health Care II (Georgetown Hospital)	7789.6	5500.4	5749.8	6400.8	IDB
Land and Water Transport (Regions)	195.2	0.0	0.0	0.0	Local/PAP
Equipment	56.6	83.7	87.6	89.2	Local/PAP
Hospital (Regions)	489.2	1075.7	1115.5	1155.4	Local
Palms	0.0	39.8	39.8	39.8	Local
New Projects (Identified)	796.8	0.0	0.0	0.0	
Community Health Services	796.8	0.0	0.0	0.0	Local
TOTAL (Identified)	9327.4	6699.6	6992.7	7685.2	
New Projects (Unidentified)	0.0	0.0	4400.0	5500.4	
Rehabilitation of Community Hospitals	0.0	0.0	2200.0	3000.0	
Rehabilitation of District Hospitals	0.0	0.0	2200.0	2500.4	
TOTAL	9327.4	6699.6	11392.7	13185.6	

Source: Mission Estimates

ANNEX A

SEA AND RIVER DEFENSES: TECHNICAL NOTES

1. BREACHES AND OVERTOPPING
2. PROJECT EXECUTION UNIT

A.1. BREACHES AND OVERTOPPING

Breaches and Overtopping

1.   Breaches in the sea defenses and overtopping have been common phenomena in Guyana over the last decades. Unfortunately, no systematic records are available detailing the physical conditions extant during breaches, the reasons for failure, or the extent of the damage in financial or economic terms. A comprehensive overview of the available breach history was reported recently as part of the morphological study by DHV. Table A.1 lists major (recorded) breaches since 1933.

Table A.1: MAJOR BREACHES SINCE 1933

Year	Location	Region	Year	Location	Region
1933	Nog Eens	4	1985	De Willem	3
1957/58	En More	4		37 breaches (5km)	6
1959/61	Buxton	4	1986	River View	3
1961	Hampton Court	2		De Kinderen	3
1961	Blade en Hall	2		Tuschen	3
1977	Hampton Court	2	1988	Lichfield	5
	Dartmouth	2	1989	Clonbrook	4
	G'town East	4		Zeeburg	3
1979	Hampton Court	2		Farm	3
	Devonshire C.	2	1990	Craig	4
	Windsor C.	2		Skeldon	6
1984	Phoenix	3		2 breaches	3
	Louisiana	3		Mon Repos	3

Source: Various

2.   The most important causes for failure of the sea defenses are deterioration of the sea defense structures, such as cracks in degraded concrete slabs and copings; erosion of the foreshore; and erosion of the dike crest and land side slope due to overtopping and heavy rainfall.

Sea Level Rise

3.   Sea level rise is often mentioned as a reason for breaches in the sea defenses. While it has not been a major factor in the past, it may become nevertheless a significant factor in the future. It cannot be determined whether Guyana has experienced a rise in sea level because no water levels have been recorded since 1988. Nevertheless, it is safe to assume that sea level rise must be taken into account in long term planning. Various publications on the subject quote a sea-level-rise between 3 and 10 millimeters per annum for the near future. Over the next 30 years a sea level rise on the order of 0.1 to 0.3m would have to be foreseen.

Hydraulic Design Parameters

4.   The rehabilitation of the old sea defenses will be very costly.
For much of their length, the materials protecting the dikes against erosion
(mainly concrete slabs), have degraded and any rehabilitation would almost
require reconstruction. A more cost efficient design for sea defenses would
be possible when a number of design parameters are better known. In
particular the lack of hydraulic data forces designers to make estimates.
Because such estimates are usually made on the safe side, better information
can result in savings in the cost of the works. In this respect two site
investigation activities are recommended:

    (1)   Recording of waterlevels in different areas, close to the sea
           defenses.

    (2)   Measurement of the dominant wave heights close to the sea
           defenses.

Obviously, these efforts should be started as soon as possible so that more
sea defense rehabilitation projects can benefit from the information obtained.

The Most Economical Type of Design

5.   While the full-scale rehabilitation of the sea defense is
economically justified,[1] the associated costs are beyond Guyana's current
financial abilities. Table A.2 highlights a number of basic options for sea
defense rehabilitation policies. The optimal choice differs for each area.
Some sea defenses may well be abolished as the land immediately behind them is
of little value. On the other hand, near villages and cities the sea defenses
will have to be maintained at a high standard of safety. The optimal solution
also depends on the cost in question. Designs with high investment costs are
more attractive when funds can be easily obtained from donors (grant and loans
with discount rates below 10 percent). Otherwise (in the case of budget
constraints and discount rates over 10%) low-cost solutions are more
attractive. It is clear that budget constraints preclude the most desirable
solution of upgrading the full length of the sea defense. Immediate
consequences of this situation are higher maintenance costs at degraded sea
defenses; more damage due to overtopping and breaches; and more dependence on
the maintenance capabilities of the currently weak Hydraulics Division. More
indirect consequences are greater difficulty with the implementation
(marketing) of sea defense levies (i.e. cost recovery) and a negative impact
on investments as the situation will be perceived as 'less safe.

6.   The need for the Government of Guyana to decide on the type of
design to be adopted for rehabilitation projects is becoming urgent. Such a
decision could also stop the habitual repetition of design works used for
similar conditions in the past.

1/   DHV Environment and infrastructure, funded by EDF under either Lomé III
      or Lomé IV Convention.

Table A.2:   **BASIC OPTIONS FOR SEA DEFENSE POLICIES**

Type of Intervention	Consequences
None	Rapid deterioration of the sea defense and the loss of infrastructure, residential and farm lands.
Continue as in 1992	Slow deterioration of the SQ. An increasing number of breaches per year
Retreat behind the coastal road	The need to protect the road against high water and wave attack and reconstruct a number of drainage sluices. The loss of residential and farm lands.
Low-Cost Rehabilitation	High maintenance, recurrent damage due to overtopping and incidental breaches
Medium-Cost Rehabilitation	Low maintenance, limited overtopping. Further investments required after some 10 years.
High-Cost Rehabilitation	High standard safety and low maintenance costs.

Notes: The net costs of low-cost rehabilitation works if executed by the Hydraulics Division (force account) are in the order of US$600 to 800 per linear meter (m'), depending also on the part of the sea wall to be rehabilitated. Similar works executed with ICB are estimated around US$/m'1000 to 1400

Medium-cost rehabilitation of the SQ (for a 10 year period) would cost between US$/m'1500 to 2200

Full scale construction and upgrading are estimated around US$/m'2300 to 3000 (30 to 50 years lifetime)

The indicated cost ranges are indicative only. They are sensitive to a number of factors. For example between 50 and 70 percent of the costs is decided by the price of quarry rock.

Source: DHV

Mudbanks

7.   The morphology of the mudbanks at the foreshore was investigated by Nedeco in 1972 and by DHV in December 1992 (EDF). These studies concluded that some 40 km long mudbanks move at a speed of around 1.3 km along the coasts from east to west. The (economic) effect of mudbank migration for sea defense is bad. Coastal area becomes more exposed when mudbanks move away and sea defenses have to be built or reinforced. The accretion process in (scarce) other areas does not provide any comparable saving. No benefit exists from sea defenses that have become redundant due to mangrove growth, except perhaps reduced maintenance. The study also concluded that:

- The phenomena involved are of a large scale. The mangrove erosion is a consequence more than a cause of foreshore erosion. Thereby the potential of sea defense through artificial mangrove growth is limited.

- Mudbank migration does not occur everywhere. For example at the recessed coast of Region 3 there is no recognizable migration of the mudbanks.

- Where it occurs, the migration of the mudbanks must be expected to continue. The average increase in exposed coastal zone is estimated around one km per year.

- The foreshore is in general eroding. The average recession of the coastline is estimated at 5 meters per year (with substantial local variations). There are some indications that this recession is part of a long-term cyclic pattern, but data over the last 50 years indicate that over the coming decades erosion will dominate the coastal morphology.

8.   The value of understanding mudbank morphology is only of limited value for the short and medium term prediction of the maintenance works on a particular section of the sea defense. Less predictable (random) factors appear to disturb the general pattern too much for accurate predictions. Simple, visual inspection of mangrove recession is a much more adequate and accurate predictor of short term erosion than mudbank morphology.

9.   The World Bank had planned a Coastal Area Study, concerning the morphology of mudbanks. IDB and UNDP also have indicated plans to make studies of this kind and an EDF funded study of the same phenomena has just been completed. The report is due in January 1993 and will be shared with other donors. In light of the above, donor initiatives to fund further studies in coastal morphology will be reconsidered to prevent duplication of efforts and determine the potential benefit and urgency of such studies. In the present emergency situation, it is advised that priority be given to the short term requirements for the sea defense rehabilitation and maintenance.

Coastal Zone Management

10.   Coastal Zone Management will eventually be required. Some considerations regarding long term planning are added in the next section. The development of a general strategy for the maintenance and rehabilitation of the sea and river defenses in Guyana can make use of the results from a number of earlier studies, in particular the 1972 Nedeco study and the recent morphological study by DHV.

11.   DHV's morphological study included:

- economic feasibility of sea defense rehabilitation;
- morphology;
- potential use of air-photography and satellite images;
- set-up of a sea defense inventory/database, including survey works
- evaluation of existing repair methods;

- estimation of maintenance costs;
- evaluation of designs for future rehabilitation works; and
- evaluations considering the institution of a PEU.

Information is lacking in the following areas:

- the inventory of the sea defense has to be completed;
- water level information for the design of sea defenses;
- wave height information for the design of sea defenses;
- the inventory of drainage structures in the sea defense has to be completed; and
- detailed economic study of the present and the potential value of different costal zones.

12.   The EC has indicated willingness to fund the completion of the sea defense inventory in an extension of the Lomé III Technical Assistance project. Funding for the measurement of waterlevels and waves has not yet been identified. These studies would allow for an optimization of the designs for the upcoming sea defense rehabilitation works. The potential savings are considerable. Draft terms of reference for such undertakings (estimated at 0.5 US$ million) are available at the Hydro-metrological Department of the Ministry of Agriculture (Hydromet). An inventory of an estimated 300 drainage sluices in the sea defense is required to assess the safety factor these structures provide against breaches. In addition, a large number of the sluices are no longer operational and may be abolished. Clearly, such schemes must be coordinated with D&I programs.

13.   Based mainly on their 'engineering judgements', guided by the general (country-wide) conclusions from the economic feasibility report, the various consultants for the donor financed rehabilitation projects have selected the sections of sea wall that are to be protected. A more detailed economic study of the present and potential economic value of various agricultural, residential and industrial areas would contribute to:

- the detailed assessment of the priorities in the rehabilitation of particular sections of the sea defense;
- the weighing of different protection options (retreat, patch-work, low-cost, high-cost designs etc.);
- the prioritizing of drainage, irrigation and road rehabilitation works; and
- assessing the viability of cost recovery schemes.

Such a study would have at least as much value for policy making regarding drainage and irrigation works, as it would have for sea defense works. The study should therefore be undertaken by the Ministry of Agriculture rather than by the Hydraulics Division.

A.2.   PROJECT EXECUTION UNIT[2]

Existing Sea Defense Maintenance Organization

14.   The care of the sea defense involves the following activities:

- regular inspection of the (360 km long) sea defense;
- site investigations (surveys, hydrometeorlogical data acquisition, etc.);
- maintenance of the sea defense;
- emergency response;
- rehabilitation works; and
- collection and development of related engineering expertise.

15.   Apart from the sea defense works, the Hydraulics Division is also responsible for infrastructure for:

- irrigation;
- drainage;
- sluices; and
- other hydraulics related matters including water management.

16.   Responsibility and control for the sea defense will be concentrated in the PEU. While the PEU will already have a considerable autonomy, it will be made more autonomous during the transition period of three to four years, depending on the outcome of intermediate evaluations and further increased insight in the most suitable and sustainable organization.

Coordination

17.   Figure A.1 shows the proposed framework of institutional relations. A regular coordination meeting is an essential part of this framework. The Chief Hydraulics Officer (CHO) will fulfil a central role in the daily liaison, between Government, donors and the operational sections PEU, D&I and Sluices. In particular, the CHO should be concerned with budget control and policy matters.

---

[2]   This technical note contains an abstract from the design of the Project Execution Unit (PEU) as presented in a draft report by DHV from the Netherlands, as part of a study funded by the EDF.

FIGURE A.1:   INSTITUTIONAL RELATIONS

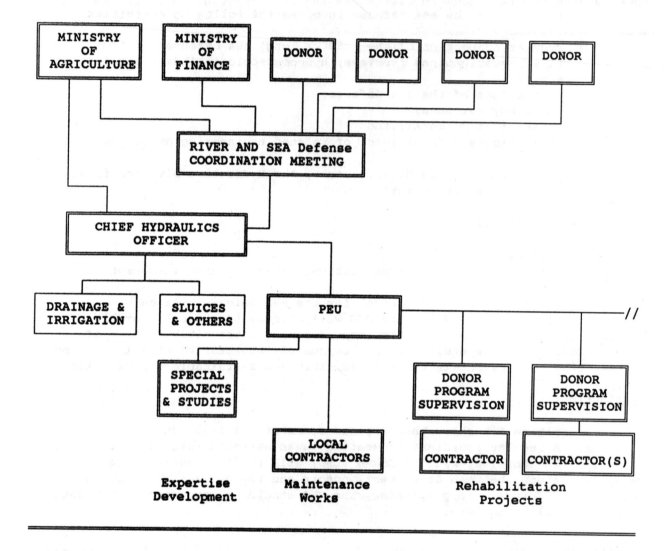

PEU Organization

18.   In the initial period, the PEU will require substantial technical assistance from experienced consultants. Figure A.2 shows the proposed organization. The performance of the PEU as an institution and the employees as individuals will be monitored and evaluated on an annual basis. Based on the evaluations, changes in the PEU organization and institution can be proposed to the regular meeting for sea defense coordination.

PEU Staff

19.   In each region, a 'Regional Engineer' (acting as 'Supervisors Representative' or 'Resident Engineer') and a 'Regional Ranger' will be stationed. Their principal tasks will be the regular inspection (monthly and

after each storm) of the entire sea defense in the region and the daily
supervision of maintenance and repair and possibly emergency works.
In addition, the Regional Engineers will take care of contractual matters, the
contacts with the main office in Georgetown and the reporting requirements.

FIGURE A.2: PEU ORGANIZATION

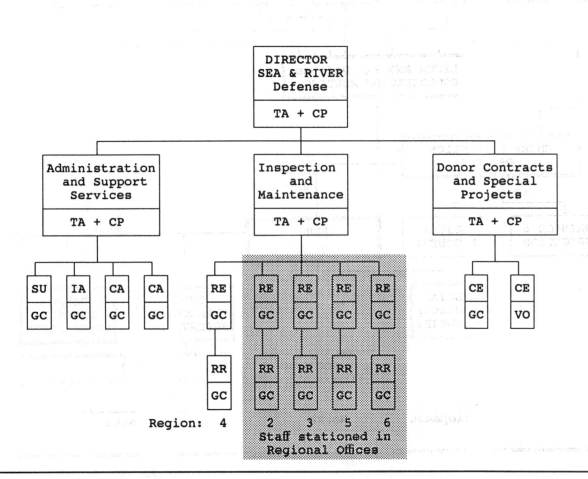

RE: Regional Engineer   SU: Support Services
IA: Internal Administrator   CA: Contract Administrator
CE: Civil Engineer/Survey Expert   RR: Regional Ranger
TA: Technical Assistant   GC: Guyana Citizen
CP: Counter Part (Guyanese)   VO: Volunteers (UNV, VSO)

20.   The Manager of the Inspection and Maintenance section will mainly
be occupied with:

- the contractual aspects of the maintenance works (acting as
  Supervisor);
- the guidance of and coordination between Regional Engineers;

- contractual matters (disputes with local contractors);
- optimization of fund utilization; and
- assistance and coordination in case of sea wall breaches etc.

21.   The manager of the Donor Contracts and Special Projects section
will:

- act as Contracting Authority for donor supported projects
  (coordination, endorsement, contract management, project
  evaluations, reporting etc.);
- preserve and develop engineering expertise (sea defense data base,
  optimization, standardization);
- coordinate and identify special projects;
- coordinate volunteer services;
- coordinate with HYDROMET (Hydrometeorlogical Services Department);
- training of Guyanese PEU staff; and
- oversee divestment of the Hydraulics Division's redundant stores,
  work shops, equipment, tools and spare parts, in coordination with
  the CHO.

22.   The manager of the Administrative and Support Services Section
will take care of the following tasks and the coordination between them:

- general affairs;
- administrative matters such as personnel remunerations, office
  running costs etc. that have to be accounted for, in addition to
  the management of the support staff (secretaries, drivers, office
  helpers etc.).
- local contracts including smaller maintenance contracts with local
  contractors, although much of the bookkeeping should be done on
  simple forms by the Regional Engineers; and
- donor projects--although much of the book keeping should be done
  by the consultant for each particular project, the Contracting
  Authority will have to verify the invoices that are to be
  endorsed.

Three administrators will be appointed for the daily works involved with each
of these three tasks.

23.   To keep the running budget to a minimum, the PEU shall not embark
on special studies. Such undertakings can be contracted to local and foreign
consultancy firms. Until sufficient staff is available, volunteers shall be
welcomed to participate in the PEU organization. For long term sustainability
more permanent arrangements are envisaged.

24.   It has been assumed in the organization of the PEU, that all
donors should contract consultants for the supervision of each particular
donor program. These consultants should have their own responsibilities (as
"Engineer" or "Supervisor"), but work in close cooperation with the PEU
organization. Consultancy services will continue to be required in relation
to the maintenance of the sea defense for such things as topographic and
hydrographic survey works, mud-bank and sea level rise studies, development of
long term coastal zone management programs, etc., but such services are not
included in this program. Such works can be executed by separate

(local/foreign) consultants and (VSO/UNV) volunteers. The collection of hydrometeorlogical data has been assigned to HYDROMET (a separate division under the Ministry of Agriculture). The Manager for special projects and donor contracts should coordinate with HYDROMET for activities in this field.

Legal Reforms

25.   The Government of Guyana will have to provide the following legal arrangements and governmental procedures:

- legal formalization of the role of the PEU with respect to sea defense;
- annual budget allocation for the PEU of about ECU1.4 million (G$230 million for PEU running costs and local maintenance contracts);
- authority for the PEU to disburse funds for its own running and salary costs;
- authority for the PEU to hire and discharge staff in accordance with its own policies;
- authority for the PEU to prepare and award tenders up to an amount of at least ECU100,000 (G$15 million) without prior permissions from the tender board;
- authority for the Hydraulics Division to sell inefficient or redundant workshops, stores, equipment, spare parts and tools; and
- authority for the Hydraulics Division to lay off its redundant staff concerned with the maintenance of equipment and execution of works.

Private Sector

26.   At the moment, the private construction industry in Guyana is not sufficiently developed to cope with the necessary sea defense maintenance works, but a few contractors do have enough experience to make a start and other contractors can be encouraged to undertake small jobs, while the PEU becomes more organized and experienced. This change in approach from force-account to contracting will take a few years, and much initial attention and flexibility from the PEU staff. In the long term this is expected to be the more efficient and economical approach.

27.   Equipment, workshops, stores, spare-parts and tools from the Hydraulics Division, that become redundant as a result of the privatization program should be divested. These facilities should be transferred first to contractors active in the sea defense maintenance works. Selling conditions may have to be customized to the financial abilities of these contractors, e.g. through hire-purchase contracts.

Lean Expert Staff

28.   In view of the financial constraints of the Government of Guyana, the PEU will be staffed with a minimum of engineers and support staff. Even with the recommended small organization, the PEU running costs (ECU450,000 (US$550,000) per year from 2011 onwards) will consume about 30 percent of the annual maintenance budget. The relatively high ratio between PEU costs and total maintenance costs is caused on the one hand by the low annual budget for

locally contracted regular maintenance works, and can be otherwise explained by the fact that PEU costs also include management of the donor financed rehabilitation programs. Higher PEU costs will be unacceptable until the financial position of the Government of Guyana has improved.

29.   The salary levels that have been set, are considered the minimal requirement to hire qualified engineers. The salary level within the PEU will be higher than for staff at comparable positions within the Government of Guyana, but their work attitude should also be very different with regard to their working hours and the flexibility with which they view their duties. Staff should initially be hired on a contract basis so that if performance is lacking, the contract may be terminated. Growth in the number of staff should be tied to the actual requirements which will in turn depend on the success in contracting maintenance and repair works to local contractors.

Contractualization of the Establishment of the PEU

30.   In theory, the Hydraulics Division could organize the PEU by itself, but at the moment it does not have the capacity and expertise to do so. Furthermore, such an approach is expected to be very time consuming and less controllable. Therefore the institutionalization of the PEU, should be contracted out to a consultancy firm. In the present situation it is considered unavoidable to start with an experienced consultant in a leading role, in order to give the necessary impetus at the PEU and to cope with the variety of problems that may come with the changes that are envisaged.

Institutional and Human Resources Development

31.   The establishment of the PEU should be preceded by a review (update) of the existing organization and the preparation of a detailed plan for salaries, fringe benefits and social security, career patterns, and short term training requirements. Continuous monitoring and adjustment of the institutional development is an integral part of the recommended approach. A mixed team of experienced engineers and institutional development experts should initiate the program and make interim evaluation reports (including SWOT analyses and recommendations for institutional changes).

32.   During the program period, the Guyanese staff recruited should be trained to supplement and gradually replace the consultancy team over a three and a half year period. Training should include class room training, on the job training, short courses and workshops, seminars and conferences. The actual progress/development of human resources should be systematically evaluated and the human resources development plan should be regularly updated during the project period.

Finances

33.   The cost of the described PEU has been estimated at ECU5.9 million (US$7.2 million) over three and a half years. The annual costs should be reduced to about US$0.6 million when the expatriate involvement is concluded. The DHV study proposes that US$1.6 million of the initial costs be funded locally.

34.   While, the costs of the institution of this PEU are high in
comparison to the overall expenditures for the public sector in Guyana, the
costs are not high when it is considered that a new maintenance organization
needs to be established and trained and that major rehabilitation programs
will be undertaken. A significant reduction in the costs will only be
possible when salary costs are reduced, which will imply either reduction of
the quality of the staff, or the reduction of the tasks covered by the PEU.

ANNEX B

PUBLIC SECTOR INVESTMENT PROGRAM

GUYANA – PUBLIC SECTOR INVESTMENT PROGRAM, 1993–96
(US 1000)

		ESTIMATED EXPENDITURE 1993			ESTIMATED EXPENDITURE 1994			ESTIMATED EXPENDITURE 1995			ESTIMATED EXPENDITURE 1996		
		Total	External	Local	Total	External	Local	Total	External	Local	Total	External	Local
TOTAL ONGOING PROJECTS		49110.0	34474.9	14635.1	43766.1	28940.6	14825.5	45105.2	29913.1	15192.0	42572.9	26396.0	16176.9
ECONOMIC SECTORS		11550.6	9306.8	2243.8	10180.1	6458.2	3721.9	7274.1	3816.7	3457.4	3334.7	0.0	3334.7
A. AGRICULTURE		11550.6	9306.8	2243.8	10180.1	6458.2	3721.9	7274.1	3816.7	3457.4	3334.7	0.0	3334.7
Agriculture Rehab I **	idb	5143.4	5000.0	143.4	6639.8	6458.2	181.7	3908.4	3816.7	91.8	0.0	0.0	0.0
Fishery Equipment Facility */**	cida	1686.1	1635.9	50.2	0.0	0.0	0.0	0.0	0.0	0.0	0.0	0.0	0.0
National Agri. Research Institute (NARI)*	undp	1039.0	800.0	239.0	916.3	0.0	916.3	996.0	996.0	0.0	996.0	996.0	0.0
East Bank Essequibo Dev. Project*	ifad	1521.9	1155.4	366.5	0.0	0.0	0.0	0.0	0.0	0.0	0.0	0.0	0.0
East Bank Berbice Irrigation Works	other	494.0	462.2	31.9	0.0	0.0	0.0	0.0	0.0	0.0	0.0	0.0	0.0
Artificial Insemination Program	local/PAP	39.8	15.9	23.9	31.9	0.0	31.9	33.5	0.0	33.5	35.1	0.0	35.1
Extension Services, Agricultural	local/PAP	159.4	159.4	0.0	358.6	358.6	0.0	517.9	0.0	517.9	557.8	0.0	557.8
Agriculture Equipment	local/PAP	14.3	14.3	0.0	0.0	0.0	0.0	0.0	0.0	0.0	0.0	0.0	0.0
Land Registration	local/PAP	49.4	41.4	8.0	39.8	0.0	39.8	42.2	0.0	42.2	43.8	0.0	43.8
Geodetic Survey	local/PAP	26.3	22.3	4.0	14.3	0.0	14.3	15.1	0.0	15.1	16.7	0.0	16.7
Drainage and Irrigation (Regions)	local	195.2	0.0	195.2	557.8	0.0	557.8	637.5	0.0	637.5	717.1	0.0	717.1
Black Bush Polder Rehab.	local	318.7	0.0	318.7	637.5	0.0	637.5	239.0	0.0	239.0	278.9	0.0	278.9
Mahaica–Mahaicony–Abary Project (MMA)	local	310.8	0.0	310.8	438.2	0.0	438.2	517.9	0.0	517.9	557.8	0.0	557.8
Forestry Studies **	local	159.4	0.0	159.4	255.0	0.0	255.0	239.0	0.0	239.0	0.0	0.0	0.0
Rehab. of Drainage & Irrigation Areas	local	286.9	0.0	286.9	159.4	0.0	159.4	0.0	0.0	0.0	0.0	0.0	0.0
Hydrometological Services	local	39.8	0.0	39.8	119.5	0.0	119.5	119.5	0.0	119.5	119.5	0.0	119.5
Plant and Animal Quarantine	local	15.9	0.0	15.9	12.0	0.0	12.0	8.0	0.0	8.0	12.0	0.0	12.0
Agriculture Development (Regions)	local	19.1	0.0	19.1	0.0	0.0	0.0	0.0	0.0	0.0	0.0	0.0	0.0
Land and Agriculture Development	local	31.1	0.0	31.1	0.0	0.0	0.0	0.0	0.0	0.0	0.0	0.0	0.0
INFRASTRUCTURE		13675.7	7529.1	6146.6	15350.2	10798.8	4551.4	17941.8	12902.0	5039.8	18467.7	13200.0	5267.7
A. POWER		5295.6	4430.3	865.3	5506.0	5000.0	506.0	5506.0	5000.0	506.0	0.0	0.0	0.0
Rehab, Power Stations	idb	4800.0	4000.0	800.0	5506.0	5000.0	506.0	5506.0	5000.0	506.0	0.0	0.0	0.0
Hydropower Study	other	495.6	430.3	65.3	0.0	0.0	0.0	0.0	0.0	0.0	0.0	0.0	0.0
B. TRANSPORT		4767.3	1216.7	3550.6	6500.0	3498.4	3001.6	7941.0	4601.6	3339.4	7693.2	4400.0	3293.2
Ferries (reconditioning)*	eec	1091.6	956.2	135.5	1649.8	1500.0	149.8	663.7	604.0	59.8	0.0	0.0	0.0
Demerara Harbor Bridge*	eec	1115.5	0.0	1115.5	1651.8	1500.4	151.4	3850.2	3499.6	350.6	4838.2	4400.0	438.2
Navigational Aids*	eec	27.9	0.0	27.9	598.4	498.0	100.4	598.4	498.0	100.4	110.8	0.0	110.8
Mabura/Lethem Road	brazil	23.9	0.0	23.9	0.0	0.0	0.0	0.0	0.0	0.0	0.0	0.0	0.0
Urban Roads	other	203.2	4.0	199.2	219.9	0.0	219.9	229.5	0.0	229.5	243.0	0.0	243.0
Equipment – Civil Aviation	local/PAP	219.1	113.9	105.2	239.0	239.0	0.0	280.5	0.0	280.5	282.9	0.0	282.9
Land and Water Transport	local/PAP	278.1	142.6	135.5	0.0	0.0	0.0	0.0	0.0	0.0	0.0	0.0	0.0
Timehri Airport (incl. Firehall)	local	565.7	0.0	565.7	796.8	0.0	796.8	796.8	0.0	796.8	796.8	0.0	796.8
Roads (Regions)	local	478.1	0.0	478.1	521.9	0.0	521.9	599.2	0.0	599.2	637.5	0.0	637.5
Reconditioning of Ships	local	199.2	0.0	199.2	159.4	0.0	159.4	200.0	0.0	200.0	19.9	0.0	19.9
Stellings & Wharves	local	95.6	0.0	95.6	214.3	0.0	214.3	230.3	0.0	230.3	246.2	0.0	246.2
Ferry Services	local	8.0	0.0	8.0	17.5	0.0	17.5	18.3	0.0	18.3	19.9	0.0	19.9
Bridges	local	143.4	0.0	143.4	100.4	0.0	100.4	105.2	0.0	105.2	110.8	0.0	110.8
Bridges (Region)	local	110.8	0.0	110.8	0.0	0.0	0.0	0.0	0.0	0.0	0.0	0.0	0.0
Guyana/Suriname Ferry	local	8.0	0.0	8.0	79.7	0.0	79.7	105.2	0.0	105.2	110.8	0.0	110.8
Hinterland Airstrips	local	199.2	0.0	199.2	251.0	0.0	251.0	263.7	0.0	263.7	276.5	0.0	276.5

GUYANA – PUBLIC SECTOR INVESTMENT PROGRAM, 1993-96
(US 1000)

		ESTIMATED EXPENDITURE 1993			ESTIMATED EXPENDITURE 1994			ESTIMATED EXPENDITURE 1995			ESTIMATED EXPENDITURE 1996		
		Total	External	Local	Total	External	Local	Total	External	Local	Total	External	Local
C. WATER & SANITATION		1628.7	300.4	1328.3	718.7	300.4	418.3	918.7	300.4	618.3	5308.4	4000.0	1308.4
Water Improvement (Master Plan)	idb	360.2	300.4	59.8	360.2	300.4	59.8	360.2	300.4	59.8	4800.0	4000.0	800.0
Rural Water Supply	local	539.4	0.0	539.4	358.6	0.0	358.6	558.6	0.0	558.6	508.4	0.0	508.4
New A'dam Water Project	local	318.7	0.0	318.7	0.0	0.0	0.0	0.0	0.0	0.0	0.0	0.0	0.0
G/T Water & Sewerage Phase II	local	398.4	0.0	398.4	0.0	0.0	0.0	0.0	0.0	0.0	0.0	0.0	0.0
Water Supply (Regions)	local	12.0	0.0	12.0	0.0	0.0	0.0	0.0	0.0	0.0	0.0	0.0	0.0
D. SEA DEFENSES		200.0	200.0	0.0	2000.0	2000.0	0.0	3000.0	3000.0	0.0	4800.0	4800.0	0.0
Sea Defenses IRP – EEC/EDF*	eec	200.0	200.0	0.0	2000.0	2000.0	0.0	3000.0	3000.0	0.0	4800.0	4800.0	0.0
E. URBAN & HOUSING		1784.1	1381.7	402.4	625.5	0.0	625.5	576.1	0.0	576.1	666.1	0.0	666.1
Urban Rehabilitation	other	1461.4	1381.7	79.7	322.7	0.0	322.7	325.1	0.0	325.1	326.7	0.0	326.7
Central Housing	local	227.1	0.0	227.1	0.0	0.0	0.0	0.0	0.0	0.0	0.0	0.0	0.0
Youth & Sports	local	95.6	0.0	95.6	223.1	0.0	223.1	243.0	0.0	243.0	259.8	0.0	259.8
Cultural Center	local	0.0	0.0	0.0	79.7	0.0	79.7	8.0	0.0	8.0	79.7	0.0	79.7
SOCIAL SECTORS		17332.3	13804.0	3528.3	15198.4	11300.4	3898.0	17004.8	13000.0	4004.8	17810.4	13001.6	4808.8
A. POVERTY		3635.1	3396.0	239.0	2900.4	2800.0	100.4	2400.0	2299.6	100.4	1101.2	1000.8	100.4
SIMAP	ida	3635.1	3396.0	239.0	2900.4	2800.0	100.4	2400.0	2299.6	100.4	1101.2	1000.8	100.4
B. EDUCATION		5166.5	3845.4	1321.1	5598.4	3500.4	2098.0	7612.0	5500.4	2111.6	9023.9	6500.4	2523.5
Rehab Primary Education	idb	3597.6	3000.0	597.6	5094.0	3500.4	1593.6	7094.0	5500.4	1593.6	8492.4	6500.4	1992.0
Human Resource Development	idb	1004.8	823.1	181.7	0.0	0.0	0.0	0.0	0.0	0.0	0.0	0.0	0.0
Development of Textbooks	idb	88.4	22.3	66.1	0.0	0.0	0.0	0.0	0.0	0.0	0.0	0.0	0.0
Resource Dev. Centre	local	0.0	0.0	0.0	5.6	0.0	5.6	5.6	0.0	5.6	5.6	0.0	5.6
Carnegie School of Home Economics	local	0.0	0.0	0.0	4.0	0.0	4.0	0.0	0.0	0.0	0.0	0.0	0.0
Buildings National Library	local	47.8	0.0	47.8	23.9	0.0	23.9	23.9	0.0	23.9	26.3	0.0	26.3
School Furniture (Education)	local	0.0	0.0	0.0	31.9	0.0	31.9	34.3	0.0	34.3	36.7	0.0	36.7
Nursery, Primary & Secondary Schools	local	79.7	0.0	79.7	47.8	0.0	47.8	51.8	0.0	51.8	57.4	0.0	57.4
Critchlow Labor College	local	8.0	0.0	8.0	12.0	0.0	12.0	12.0	0.0	12.0	13.5	0.0	13.5
School Buildings (Regions)	local	308.4	0.0	308.4	335.5	0.0	335.5	344.2	0.0	344.2	344.2	0.0	344.2
School Furniture (Regions)	local	31.9	0.0	31.9	43.8	0.0	43.8	46.2	0.0	46.2	47.8	0.0	47.8
C. HEALTH		8530.7	6562.5	1968.1	6699.6	5000.0	1699.6	6992.8	5200.0	1792.8	7685.3	5500.4	2184.9
Health Care II (Georgetown Hospital)	idb	7789.6	6334.7	1455.0	5500.4	5000.0	500.4	5749.8	5200.0	549.8	6400.8	5500.4	900.4
Land and Water Transport (Regions)	local/PAP	195.2	191.2	4.0	0.0	0.0	0.0	0.0	0.0	0.0	0.0	0.0	0.0
Equipment	local/PAP	56.6	36.7	19.9	83.7	0.0	83.7	87.6	0.0	87.6	89.2	0.0	89.2
Hospital (Regions)	local	489.2	0.0	489.2	1075.7	0.0	1075.7	1115.5	0.0	1115.5	1155.4	0.0	1155.4
Palms	local	0.0	0.0	0.0	39.8	0.0	39.8	39.8	0.0	39.8	39.8	0.0	39.8

GUYANA – PUBLIC SECTOR INVESTMENT PROGRAM, 1993–96
(US$ 1000)

	Source	ESTIMATED EXPENDITURE 1993			ESTIMATED EXPENDITURE 1994			ESTIMATED EXPENDITURE 1995			ESTIMATED EXPENDITURE 1996		
		Total	External	Local	Total	External	Local	Total	External	Local	Total	External	Local
OTHER		6551.4	3835.1	2716.3	3037.5	383.3	2654.2	2884.5	194.4	2690.0	2960.2	194.4	2765.7
Statistical Bureau*	undp	239.8	28.7	211.2	374.5	194.4	180.1	374.5	194.4	180.1	374.5	194.4	180.1
GUYMIDA*	undp	2182.5	2158.6	23.9	0.0	0.0	0.0	0.0	0.0	0.0	0.0	0.0	0.0
Institutional Strengthening	idb	450.2	418.3	31.9	0.0	0.0	0.0	0.0	0.0	0.0	0.0	0.0	0.0
SPS/National Planning Project*	idb	424.7	382.5	42.2	225.5	188.8	36.7	0.0	0.0	0.0	0.0	0.0	0.0
Step Fund	cdb	235.1	227.1	8.0	0.0	0.0	0.0	0.0	0.0	0.0	0.0	0.0	0.0
Equipment and Furniture	local/PAP	862.2	588.0	274.1	72.5	0.0	72.5	75.7	0.0	75.7	78.9	0.0	78.9
General Register Office	local/PAP	31.9	31.9	0.0	39.8	0.0	39.8	40.6	0.0	40.6	43.8	0.0	43.8
Contributions International Agencies	local	718.7	0.0	718.7	830.3	0.0	830.3	830.3	0.0	830.3	830.3	0.0	830.3
Buildings (Various)	local	903.6	0.0	903.6	1129.9	0.0	1129.9	1185.7	0.0	1185.7	1243.8	0.0	1243.8
Minor Works	local	103.6	0.0	103.6	153.0	0.0	153.0	161.0	0.0	161.0	168.9	0.0	168.9
Agencies (Various)	local	164.9	0.0	164.9	161.0	0.0	161.0	163.3	0.0	163.3	164.9	0.0	164.9
Guyana Defense Force	local	87.8	0.0	87.8	0.0	0.0	0.0	0.0	0.0	0.0	0.0	0.0	0.0
Guyana National Service (GNS)	local	47.8	0.0	47.8	21.5	0.0	21.5	23.1	0.0	23.1	23.9	0.0	23.9
Equipment/Transport (Police/Prisons/Fire)	local	98.0	0.0	98.0	29.5	0.0	29.5	30.3	0.0	30.3	31.1	0.0	31.1
Acquisition of Property	local	0.8	0.0	0.8	0.0	0.0	0.0	0.0	0.0	0.0	0.0	0.0	0.0

GUYANA – PUBLIC SECTOR INVESTMENT PROGRAM, 1993-96
(US$ 1000)

		ESTIMATED EXPENDITURE 1993			ESTIMATED EXPENDITURE 1994			ESTIMATED EXPENDITURE 1995			ESTIMATED EXPENDITURE 1996		
		Total	External	Local	Total	External	Local	Total	External	Local	Total	External	Local
TOTAL NEW & UNIDENTIFIED		12124.7	7662.5	4462.1	29110.9	24757.8	4353.0	54722.1	48912.6	5809.4	66378.7	59806.5	6572.3
ECONOMIC SECTORS		651.8	500.4	151.4	1171.3	1065.3	106.0	3513.9	3193.8	320.3	5625.5	5100.4	525.1
A. AGRICULTURE		651.8	500.4	151.4	1171.3	1065.3	106.0	3513.9	3193.8	320.3	5625.5	5100.4	525.1
Agriculture Hybrid Loan (TCC 877)	idb	651.8	500.4	151.4	1171.3	1065.3	106.0	0.0	0.0	0.0	0.0	0.0	0.0
Hydromet. Services	unidentified	0.0	0.0	0.0	0.0	0.0	0.0	215.1	193.6	21.5	111.6	100.4	11.2
Drainage and Irrigation	unidentified	0.0	0.0	0.0	0.0	0.0	0.0	2199.2	2000.0	199.2	4414.3	4000.0	414.3
Land Reform – Long Lease/Freehold	unidentified	0.0	0.0	0.0	0.0	0.0	0.0	1099.6	1000.0	99.6	1099.6	1000.0	99.6
INFRASTRUCTURE		6670.5	4212.4	2458.1	22023.2	18295.7	3727.5	38953.1	34623.4	4329.7	48095.9	43027.2	5068.7
A. POWER		0.0	0.0	0.0	3296.8	3000.0	298.8	5498.0	5000.0	498.0	5498.0	5000.0	498.0
Power Transmission	idb	0.0	0.0	0.0	3296.8	3000.0	298.8	5498.0	5000.0	498.0	5498.0	5000.0	498.0
B. TRANSPORT		2711.1	2393.2	317.9	9600.1	8539.5	1060.6	19514.5	17422.2	2092.3	27460.8	24296.5	3164.3
Rehab W. Berbice Rd.	idb	358.6	298.8	59.8	1200.0	1000.0	200.0	2400.0	2000.0	400.0	4200.8	3500.4	700.4
Rehab. G/T-Soesdyke	idb	358.8	298.8	60.0	1200.0	1000.0	200.0	2400.0	2000.0	400.0	4200.8	3500.4	700.4
Roads–Agriculture Hybrid Load	idb	330.0	300.0	30.0	770.0	700.0	70.0	1320.0	1200.0	120.0	2750.0	2500.0	250.0
Rehab G/T Mahaica Rd	idb	0.0	0.0	0.0	2390.0	2120.0	270.0	3120.0	2820.0	300.0	2390.0	2120.0	270.0
Road Design and Maintenance	idb	553.8	520.3	33.5	0.0	0.0	0.0	0.0	0.0	0.0	1320.0	1200.0	120.0
Reseal Soesdyke–Linden	ida	260.6	230.3	30.3	1099.9	929.9	170.0	1559.6	1389.6	170.0	1300.4	1160.2	140.2
Rehab East Essequibo	ida	429.5	404.8	24.7	1720.3	1619.9	100.4	2580.1	2430.3	149.8	2149.8	2024.7	125.1
Road Maintenance	ida	380.1	340.2	39.8	719.5	679.7	39.8	360.2	340.2	19.9	0.0	0.0	0.0
Fire Equipment CAD	ida	0.0	0.0	0.0	500.4	490.0	10.4	499.8	490.0	9.8	499.8	490.0	9.8
Transport Study	local	39.8	0.0	39.8	0.0	0.0	0.0	0.0	0.0	0.0	0.0	0.0	0.0
Urban Roads	unidentified	0.0	0.0	0.0	0.0	0.0	0.0	275.0	250.0	25.0	549.8	500.4	49.4
Demerara River Navigation	unidentified	0.0	0.0	0.0	0.0	0.0	0.0	1000.0	900.4	99.6	1000.0	900.4	99.6
Hinterland Airstrips	unidentified	0.0	0.0	0.0	0.0	0.0	0.0	1000.0	900.4	99.6	2000.0	1800.0	200.0
Air Nav. Aids	unidentified	0.0	0.0	0.0	0.0	0.0	0.0	1000.0	900.4	99.6	1099.6	1000.0	99.6
Timehri Airport Rehabilitation	unidentified	0.0	0.0	0.0	0.0	0.0	0.0	1000.0	900.4	99.6	2000.0	1800.0	200.0
Feeder Roads Rehabilitation	unidentified	0.0	0.0	0.0	0.0	0.0	0.0	1000.0	900.4	99.6	2000.0	1800.0	200.0
C. WATER & SANITATION		1271.7	1126.7	145.0	3049.4	2881.3	368.1	5630.3	4890.8	739.4	3795.8	3390.4	405.4
TA & Water Supply/Sewerage	ida	557.8	478.1	79.7	1849.4	1681.3	168.1	2629.5	2390.4	239.0	3155.4	2866.5	286.9
G/T Water Supply Emergency	ida	533.9	478.1	55.8	1200.0	1000.0	200.0	3000.8	2500.4	500.4	641.4	521.9	119.5
Technical Cooperation	idb	66.5	60.6	6.0	0.0	0.0	0.0	0.0	0.0	0.0	0.0	0.0	0.0
Water Improvement Project	idb	111.6	110.0	1.6	0.0	0.0	0.0	0.0	0.0	0.0	0.0	0.0	0.0
D. SEA DEFENSES		2687.6	692.4	1995.2	6074.9	4074.9	2000.0	8310.4	7310.4	1000.0	11340.2	10340.2	1000.0
IRP–Sea Defenses (capital works)	idb	422.3	422.3	0.0	2000.0	2000.0	0.0	4000.0	4000.0	0.0	7000.0	7000.0	0.0
IRP–Sea Defenses (capital works)	cdb	0.0	0.0	0.0	1000.0	1000.0	0.0	1700.0	1700.0	0.0	2000.0	2000.0	0.0
IRP–Sea Defenses (capital works)	ida	285.3	270.1	15.1	1140.2	1074.9	65.3	1710.0	1610.4	99.6	1425.5	1340.2	85.3
IRP–Sea Defenses (counterpart funds)	local	1980.1	0.0	1980.1	1934.7	0.0	1934.7	900.4	0.0	900.4	914.7	0.0	914.7

GUYANA – PUBLIC SECTOR INVESTMENT PROGRAM, 1993–96
(US $000)

		ESTIMATED EXPENDITURE 1993			ESTIMATED EXPENDITURE 1994			ESTIMATED EXPENDITURE 1995			ESTIMATED EXPENDITURE 1996		
		Total	External	Local	Total	External	Local	Total	External	Local	Total	External	Local
SOCIAL SECTORS		4620.7	2780.1	1840.6	4916.3	4396.8	519.5	11255.0	10095.6	1159.4	11657.4	10678.9	978.5
A. POVERTY		3027.1	2780.1	247.0	4916.3	4396.8	519.5	5354.6	4795.2	559.4	3656.6	3377.7	278.9
SIMAP Basic Needs*	idb	2421.5	2286.1	135.5	4000.0	3600.0	400.0	4000.0	3600.0	400.0	1385.7	1385.7	0.0
	odb	605.6	494.0	111.6	916.3	796.8	119.5	1354.6	1195.2	159.4	2270.9	1992.0	278.9
B. EDUCATION		796.8	0.0	796.8	0.0	0.0	0.0	1500.4	1300.4	200.0	2500.4	2300.4	200.0
Rehab. Education Facilities	local	796.8	0.0	796.8	0.0	0.0	0.0	1500.4	1300.4	200.0	2500.4	2300.4	200.0
Rehab. of Schools	unidentified	0.0	0.0	0.0	0.0	0.0	0.0	0.0	0.0	0.0	0.0	0.0	0.0
C. HEALTH		796.8	0.0	796.8	0.0	0.0	0.0	4400.0	4000.0	400.0	5500.4	5000.8	499.6
Community Health Services	local	796.8	0.0	796.8	0.0	0.0	0.0	0.0	0.0	0.0	0.0	0.0	0.0
Rehabilitation of Community Hospitals	unidentified	0.0	0.0	0.0	0.0	0.0	0.0	2200.0	2000.0	200.0	3000.0	2700.4	299.6
Rehabilitation of District Hospitals	unidentified	0.0	0.0	0.0	0.0	0.0	0.0	2200.0	2000.0	200.0	2500.4	2300.4	200.0
OTHER		181.7	169.7	12.0	1000.0	1000.0	0.0	1000.0	1000.0	0.0	1000.0	1000.0	0.0
Public Administration Project	ida	0.0	0.0	0.0	1000.0	1000.0	0.0	1000.0	1000.0	0.0	1000.0	1000.0	0.0
Land Transport (Fire/Prison)	local/PAP	181.7	169.7	12.0	0.0	0.0	0.0	0.0	0.0	0.0	0.0	0.0	0.0
TOTAL GROSS PSIP (Incl. Transfers)		61234.6	42157.5	19097.2	72877.0	53699.5	19176.5	99827.2	78825.8	21001.5	108951.6	86202.5	22749.2
TRANSFERS (PRIVATE SECTOR)		6988.8	6635.9	353.0	6894.8	6458.2	436.7	4147.4	3816.7	330.7	0.0	0.0	0.0
TOTAL NET PSIP		54245.8	35501.6	18744.2	65982.2	47240.3	18741.9	95679.8	75009.0	20670.8	108951.6	86202.5	22749.2

* grants
** transfers

Source: World Bank Staff Estimates.

STATISTICAL APPENDIX

1. **HISTORICAL TABLES**
2. **PROJECTION TABLES**

STATISTICAL APPENDIX

1. HISTORICAL TABLES

TABLE OF CONTENTS

Table 1.1: GUYANA - POPULATION TRENDS, 1980-90

	1980	1981	1982	1983	1984	1985	1986	1987	1988	1989	1990
Total Population (beginning of year)a/	756960	757173	757386	757600	757300	756900	756500	756100	755700	755300	754900
Total births b/	23000	23000	23000	22500	23000	20900	18600	18300	19568	20521	17522
Total deaths c/	5575	6000	6500	6500	9000	11500	5400	5800	5967	5605	6134
Natural population increase	17425	17000	16500	16000	14000	9400	13200	12500	13601	14916	11388
Apparent net migration d/ (Reported net migration)	-17212 (-11000)	-16787 (-10000)	-16286 (-11010)	-10772 (-10000)	-14400 (-8113)	-9800 (-8000)	-13600 (..)	-12900 (..)	-14001 (..)	-15316 (..)	-11788 (..)
Net population increase	213	213	214	-300	-400	-400	-400	-400	-400	-400	-400
Crude birth rate (per 1000)	30.4	30.4	30.4	29.7	30.4	27.6	24.6	24.2	25.9	27.2	23.2
Crude death rate (per 1000)	7.4	7.9	8.6	8.6	11.9	15.2	7.1	7.7	7.9	7.4	8.1
Rate of natural increase(%)	2.3	2.2	2.2	2.1	1.8	1.2	1.7	1.7	1.8	2.0	1.5

a/ April 7, 1970 census showed population of 669,848 excluding persons in institutions, and May 12, 1990 population census showe
b/ Estimated from 1977 onwards.
c/ Estimated from 1979 onwards.
d/ Equals net population increase less natural population increase

Source: Statistical Bureau.

Table 1.2: GUYANA - EMPLOYMENT IN THE PUBLIC SECTOR, 1987-92

	December				March	
	1987	1988	1989	1990	1991	Prel. 1992
Total employment	72,300	68,304	66,892	67,511	65,650	65,239
Central government	25,384	24,391	22,034	18,656	17,821	18,006
Rest of the public sector	46,916	43,913	44,858	48,855	47,829	47,233
Guyana State Corporations (GUYSTAC group)	13,361	11,542	10,911	9,993	9,706	7,249
Guyana Rice Board (GRB)	1,860	1,460	1,299	1,050	1,189	214
Guyana Nat'l. Eng'g Corp. (GNEC)	1,172	1,037	976	997	904	923
Guyana Stores Ltd. (GLT)	1,436	1,457	1,291	1,306	1,348	1,327
Guyana Electricity Corp. (GEC)	1,494	1,482	1,582	2,324	2,402	2,514
Guyana Pharmaceutical Corp. (GPC)	577	532	468	446	427	312
Guyana Transport Corp. (GTC)	733	265	236	75	24	18
Other corporations	6,089	5,309	5,059	3,795	3,412	1,941
Guyana Sugar Corp. (GUYSUCO)	23,926	23,133	25,502	30,963	31,056	32,167
Guyana Mining Enterprises Ltd. (GUYMINE)	5,693	5,780	5,051	4,507	3,635	3,803
Other independent Corporation	2,001	1,371	1,287	1,282	1,309	895
Financial Institutions	1,935	2,087	2,107	2,110	2,123	3,119

(as percent of total public sector employment)

Central government	35.1	35.7	32.9	27.6	27.1	27.6
Rest of public sector	64.9	64.3	67.1	72.4	72.9	72.4
GUYSTAC group	18.5	16.9	16.3	14.8	14.8	11.1
GUYSUCO	33.1	33.9	38.1	45.9	47.3	49.3
GUYMINE	7.9	8.5	7.6	6.7	5.5	5.8
Other	5.4	5.1	5.1	5.0	5.2	6.2

Source: State Planning Secretariat.

Table 1.3: Sectoral Distribution of Public Service Employees
Ministries and Regional Administrations Only

Grades	1-5	6-9	10-14	15-Spec	Total
POSITIONS APPROVED	**13397**	**3223**	**1377**	**239**	**18236**
Management of Policy Making	15	233	87	23	358
Office of the President	15	233	87	23	358
Economic & Fiscal Mgt/Revenue	114	679	293	61	1147
Ministry of Finance	114	679	293	61	1147
Production	1537	182	119	20	1858
Ministry of Agriculture	385	79	44	16	524
Regional Administration (Agriculture)	1109	90	46	0	1245
Ministry of Trade, Tourism & Industry	43	13	29	4	89
Social Well Being	4611	1466	708	49	6834
Ministry Health	1789	632	265	26	2712
Regional Administration (Health)	1226	563	95	0	1884
Ministry Education	812	93	256	9	1170
Regional Administration (Education)	407	43	56	0	506
Min. of Labor, Human Serv. & Social Security	123	87	20	3	233
Ministry of Public Works, Comm. & Reg. Dev.	254	48	16	11	329
Law and Order	5149	356	98	64	5667
Ministry of Legal Affairs	341	40	8	53	442
Ministry of Home Affairs	4808	316	90	11	5225
External Affairs	137	112	51	22	322
Ministry of Foreign Affairs	137	112	51	22	322
Regional Administration (Administration)	1834	195	21	0	2050
POSITIONS FILLED	**8718**	**1853**	**796**	**165**	**11532**
Management of Policy Making	8	149	61	18	236
Office of the President	8	149	61	18	236
Economic & Fiscal Mgt/Revenue	73	418	188	39	718
Ministry of Finance	73	418	188	39	718
Production	972	74	79	17	1142
Ministry of Agriculture	284	40	37	14	375
Regional Administration (Agriculture)	663	29	16	0	708
Ministry of Trade, Tourism & Industry	25	5	26	3	59
Social Well Being	3079	788	331	28	4226
Ministry Health	1210	326	107	14	1657
Regional Administration (Health)	838	309	37	0	1184
Ministry Education	491	44	136	6	677
Regional Administration (Education)	265	20	28	0	313
Min. of Labor, Human Serv. & Social Security	101	60	19	3	183
Ministry of Public Works, Comm. & Reg. Dev.	174	29	4	5	212
Law and Order	3378	287	87	41	3793
Ministry of Legal Affairs	208	23	3	33	267
Ministry of Home Affairs	3170	264	84	8	3526
External Affairs	31	62	42	22	157
Ministry of Foreign Affairs	31	62	42	22	157
Regional Administration (Administration)	1177	75	8	0	1260

Source: Government of Guyana, Office of the President, Public Service Management.

Table 1.3: Sectoral Distribution of Public Service Employees
Ministries and Regional Administrations Only

Grades	1–5	6–9	10–14	15–Spec	Total
TOTAL VACANCIES	**4679**	**1370**	**581**	**74**	**6704**
Management of Policy Making	7	84	26	5	122
Office of the President	7	84	26	5	122
Economic & Fiscal Mgt/Revenue	41	261	105	22	429
Ministry of Finance	41	261	105	22	429
Production	565	108	40	3	716
Ministry of Agriculture	101	39	7	2	149
Regional Administration (Agriculture)	446	61	30	0	537
Ministry of Trade, Tourism & Industry	18	8	3	1	30
Social Well Being	1532	678	377	21	2608
Ministry Health	579	306	158	12	1055
Regional Administration (Health)	388	254	58	0	700
Ministry Education	321	49	120	3	493
Regional Administration (Education)	142	23	28	0	193
Min. of Labor, Human Serv. & Social Security	22	27	1	0	50
Ministry of Public Works, Comm. & Reg. Dev.	80	19	12	6	117
Law and Order	1771	69	11	23	1874
Ministry of Legal Affairs	133	17	5	20	175
Ministry of Home Affairs	1638	52	6	3	1699
External Affairs	106	50	9	0	165
Ministry of Foreign Affairs	106	50	9	0	165
Regional Administration (Administration)	657	120	13	0	790
VACANCIES AS % OF APPROVED	**35**	**43**	**42**	**31**	**37**
Management of Policy Making	47	36	30	22	34
Office of the President	47	36	30	22	34
Economic & Fiscal Mgt/Revenue	36	38	36	36	37
Ministry of Finance	36	38	36	36	37
Production	37	59	34	15	39
Ministry of Agriculture	26	49	16	13	28
Regional Administration (Agriculture)	40	68	65	0	43
Ministry of Trade, Tourism & Industry	42	62	10	25	34
Social Well Being	33	46	53	43	38
Ministry Health	32	48	60	46	39
Regional Administration (Health)	32	45	61	0	37
Ministry Education	40	53	47	33	42
Regional Administration (Education)	35	53	50	0	38
Min. of Labor, Human Serv. & Social Security	18	31	5	0	21
Ministry of Public Works, Comm. & Reg. Dev.	31	40	75	55	36
Law and Order	34	19	11	36	33
Ministry of Legal Affairs	39	43	63	38	40
Ministry of Home Affairs	34	16	7	27	33
External Affairs	77	45	18	0	51
Ministry of Foreign Affairs	77	45	18	0	51
Regional Administration (Administration)	36	62	62	0	39

Source: Government of Guyana, Office of the President, Public Service Management.

Table 1.4: Share of Benefits and Allowances in Total Employment Costs
(G$ thousands)

	Budget 1992			Revised 1991		
	Benefits/ Allowances	Total Employm.Costs	Percent	Benefits/ Allowances	Total Employm.Costs	Percent
Office of the President	21,144	83,182	25	12,364	31,114	40
Guyana Defence Force	51,756	263,964	20	36,533	101,694	36
Guyana National Service	10,500	59,947	18	7,896	25,766	31
Public Service Ministry	0	0	0	195	1,851	11
Office of Prime Minister	0	0	0	319	2,272	14
Parliament Office	156	1,540	10	93	650	14
Office of Auditor General	1,289	21,134	6	1,898	11,741	16
Office of Ombudsman	4	222	2	2	92	2
Public & Police Service Commissions	396	2,752	14	272	1,286	21
Teaching Service Commission	24	1,408	2	18	576	3
Public Prosecutions	444	3,313	13	408	1,556	26
Public Service Appellate Tribunal	4	336	1	3	173	2
Elections Commission	72	1,070	7	4	245	2
Public Utilities Commission	120	3,174	4	86	342	25
Ministry of Legal Affairs – Head Office	252	1,688	15	83	286	29
Supreme Court of Judicature	900	8,036	11	657	3,790	17
Magistrates	2,004	6,048	33	1,330	4,972	27
Attorney General	732	7,617	10	695	2,761	25
Official Receiver	156	1,682	9	128	639	20
Deeds Registry	204	2,316	9	134	1,056	13
Ministry of Foreign Affairs	390,103	585,726	67	130,162	518,042	25
Ministry of Home Affairs – Head Office	420	4,865	9	275	1,920	14
Police	172,440	406,726	42	104,284	179,140	58
Prisons	9,840	30,166	33	5,952	13,286	45
Police Complaints Authority	36	657	5	13	203	6
Fire Protection Services	7,740	20,636	38	6,117	10,684	57
National Registration Centre	12	2,078	1	2	910	0
General Register Office	120	2,180	6	84	1,044	8
Ministry of Agriculture – Head Office	396	6,426	6	371	3,072	12
Crops and Livestock Division	1,800	14,405	12	1,323	6,016	22
Lands and Surveys Division	1,044	8,407	12	716	4,640	15
Hydraulics Division	456	6,009	8	154	974	16
Fisheries Division	168	1,770	9	90	832	11
Ministry of Health – Head Office	3,096	17,778	17	572	5,154	11
Nat'l Hospitals	44,688	114,815	39	22,021	53,073	41
Other Health Programmes	11,220	37,544	30	2,554	17,151	15
Ministry of Education/Cultural Dev.	2,580	30,618	8	1,576	13,665	12
Nursery Schools	372	19,876	2	20	6,721	0
Primary Schools	192	52,422	0	153	19,694	1
Secondary/Multilateral/Comm. High	1,182	60,104	2	250	22,948	1
Technical and Vocational Schools	300	17,163	2	20	6,479	0
Practical Instruction Centres	0	3,999	0	0	1,182	0
Teacher Training Institutions	288	12,436	2	137	4,268	3
Resource Centre	566	3,317	17	538	2,540	21
Min. Labour/Human Serv./Social Scty.	2,736	17,027	16	1,474	6,684	22
Ministry of Finance	2,352	85,900	3	1,921	753,429	0
Accountant General Department	2,076	47,712	4	971	22,045	4
Customs and Excise Department	8,438	39,528	21	3,251	20,682	16
Inland Revenue Department	994	31,036	3	993	15,951	6
Min. of Trade, Tourism & Industry	1,752	10,072	17	1,194	3,257	37
Ministry of Public Utilities a/	n.a.	n.a.	n.a.	54	341	16
Min. of Public Works/Comm./Reg.Dev.	1,152	16,550	7	1,630	10,226	16
Plant Maintenance and Hire Division	0	0	0	0	0	0
Civil Aviation Department	2,400	15,951	15	2,978	10,905	27
Ministry of Housing	0	0	0	0	0	0

Table 1.4: Share of Benefits and Allowances in Total Employment Costs
(G$ thousands)

	Budget 1992			Revised 1991		
	Benefits/ Allowances	Total Employm.Costs	Percent	Benefits/ Allowances	Total Employm.Costs	Percent
Region 1 – Administration	612	8,423	7	503	5,081	10
Region 1 – Agriculture	48	1,250	4	57	547	10
Region 1 – Education	1,020	12,003	8	870	4,834	18
Region 1 – Health	216	5,498	4	335	2,239	15
Region 2 – Administration	1,140	13,539	8	558	6,662	8
Region 2 – Agriculture	540	4,272	13	323	2,038	16
Region 2 – Education	1,980	43,763	5	858	16,804	5
Region 2 – Health	4,320	20,847	21	995	6,649	15
Region 3 – Administration	304	12,229	2	296	4,469	7
Region 3 – Agriculture	516	5,846	9	418	3,967	11
Region 3 – Education	1,512	73,141	2	575	25,553	2
Region 3 – Health	4,842	27,127	18	3,354	12,749	26
Region 4 – Administration	1,260	15,052	8	833	6,007	14
Region 4 – Agriculture	2,136	15,183	14	817	6,018	14
Region 4 – Education	1,308	98,934	1	718	33,545	2
Region 4 – Health	2,480	27,415	9	1,674	8,559	20
Region 5 – Administration	480	8,052	6	356	2,877	12
Region 5 – Agriculture	240	1,912	13	201	798	25
Region 5 – Education	58	40,351	0	15	16,101	0
Region 5 – Health	2,685	15,484	17	1,269	5,604	23
Region 6 – Administration	816	9,539	9	733	5,082	14
Region 6 – Agriculture	972	12,257	8	769	4,164	18
Region 6 – Education	252	101,073	0	232	36,833	1
Region 6 – Health	22,574	82,742	27	8,504	31,089	27
Region 7 – Administration	744	4,695	16	229	2,033	11
Region 7 – Agriculture	36	1,059	3	28	469	6
Region 7 – Education	996	10,650	9	769	4,274	18
Region 7 – Health	672	7,039	10	519	2,936	18
Region 8 – Administration	106	1,960	5	111	1,124	10
Region 8 – Agriculture	12	229	5	11	92	12
Region 8 – Education	415	2,918	14	343	1,853	19
Region 8 – Health	394	1,532	26	56	521	11
Region 9 – Administration	180	3,493	5	187	1,733	11
Region 9 – Agriculture	156	1,627	10	112	731	15
Region 9 – Education	1,416	12,284	12	1,085	5,030	22
Region 9 – Health	1,221	5,643	22	316	1,860	17
Region 10 – Administration	192	3,326	6	147	1,273	12
Region 10 – Agriculture	198	1,474	13	140	590	24
Region 10 – Education	2,160	31,627	7	2,085	12,692	16
Region 10 – Health	1,301	5,456	24	821	2,126	39
Total	823,626	2,944,272	28	387,190	2,217,626	17
Ministries/Departments Total	696,351	1,834,468	38	307,436	1,783,627	17
Regional Administrations Total	62,510	750,944	8	32,222	287,606	11
Constitutional Agencies Total	2,389	31,775	8	2,698	16,319	17
Other b/	62,376	327,085	19	44,515	127,802	35

a/ Ministry abolished.
b/ Includes the Guyana Defence Force, the Guyana National Service, and the Public Utilities Commission.

Source: Current & Capital Revenue and Expenditure, Ministry of Finance, Government of Guyana.

Table 1.5: GUYANA - WORK STOPPAGES IN THE PUBLIC SECTOR, 1980-91

	1980	1981	1982	1983	1984	1985	1986	1987	1988	1989	1990	Prel. 1991
Number of Strikes	333	621	653	731	493	718	453	497	349	138	329	307
Sugar Industry	276	585	639	704	480	712	447	489	345	134	315	257
Other	57	36	14	27	13	6	6	8	4	4	14	50
Workers Involved	40,652	87,697	81,564	103,519	60,300	93,718	47,550	57,757	39,358	113,320	61,474	..
Sugar Industry	35,475	84,100	80,373	94,818	58,779	93,304	46,957	57,052	38,856	107,875	60,905	..
Other	5,177	3,597	1,191	8,701	1,521	414	593	705	502	5,445	569	..
Man-days Lost	67,620	125,582	140,744	290,296	152,000	208,888	138,364	131,449	232,595	686,356	244,498	..
Sugar Industry	60,593	110,118	127,987	164,309	144,157	208,443	135,109	128,986	231,089	594,339	229,291	110,871
Other	7,027	15,464	12,757	125,987	7,843	445	3,255	2,463	1,506	92,017	15,207	..
Wages Lost (G$ million)	1.20	2.60	3.30	5.10	3.40	4.36	3.40	4.50	8.50	35.90	..	..
Sugar Industry	1.10	2.30	3.10	3.00	3.30	4.35	2.90	3.80	8.10	29.30	16.90	21.51
Other	0.10	0.30	0.20	2.10	0.10	0.01	0.50	0.70	0.40	6.60	..	..

Source : Ministry of Labor; State Planning Secretariat; and GUYSUCO.

Table 2.1: GUYANA - SECTOR ORIGIN OF GROSS DOMESTIC PRODUCT AT CURRENT FACTOR COST, 1987-91
---------   (G$ million)

	1987	1988	1989	1990	1991
Agric., Forestry & Fishing	899	942	2,164	2,901	6,724
Sugar	540	400	1,203	1,503	4,452
Rice	51	58	166	148	360
Other crops	120	187	295	537	802
Livestock	60	95	140	150	195
Forestry	69	122	196	342	572
Fishing	59	80	164	221	343
Mining and Quarrying	344	363	1,094	1,729	4,500
Bauxite & Alumina a/	293	303	997	1,008	2,997
Other	51	60	97	721	1,503
Manufacturing & Processing	418	463	1,224	1,207	2,683
Sugar milling	189	127	331	422	1,415
Rice milling	17	23	69	62	104
Other b/ c/	212	313	824	723	1,164
Construction	142	248	449	687	1,311
Services	1,199	1,609	2,365	3,995	7,278
Distribution d/	169	292	434	803	1,577
Transport & communications e/	192	301	490	766	1,435
Rent of dwellings	40	66	99	175	327
Financial services	136	186	257	445	842
Government	543	638	881	1,533	2,562
Other	119	126	204	273	535
Total GDP at Factor Cost	3,002	3,625	7,296	10,519	22,496

a/ For 1989, includes G$849 million of devaluation losses of GUYMINE.
b/ Includes electricity, gas and water.
c/ For 1989, includes G$250 million and G$ 12 million of devaluation losses of GEC and GPC,
    respectively.
d/ For 1989, includes G$10 million of devaluation losses of GNTC.
e/ For 1989, includes G$84 million of devaluation losses of GTC.

Source: Statistical Bureau of Guyana.

Table 2.2: GUYANA-SECTORAL ORIGIN OF GROSS DOMESTIC PRODUCT-CONSTANT FACTOR COST, 1987-91
(1988 G$ million)

	1987	1988	1989	1990	1991
Agric., Forestry & Fishing	1,023	942	926	801	889
Sugar	478	400	409	326	378
Rice	60	58	62	41	67
Other crops	183	187	187	196	200
Livestock	95	95	94	65	57
Forestry	88	80	71	70	73
Fishing	119	122	103	103	115
Mining and Quarrying	370	363	322	386	453
Bauxite	316	303	260	257	266
Other	54	60	62	129	187
Manufacturing & Processing	478	463	423	371	410
Sugar milling	159	127	125	98	129
Rice milling	23	23	20	17	20
Other a/	296	313	278	256	261
Construction	245	248	235	240	243
Services	1,579	1,609	1,600	1,620	1,611
Distribution	275	292	280	287	301
Transport & communications	289	301	298	303	302
Rent of dwellings	65	66	65	66	68
Financial services	184	186	193	197	196
Government	644	638	637	637	609
Other	122	126	127	130	135
Total GDP at Factor Cost	3,695	3,625	3,506	3,418	3,606

a/ Includes electricity, gas and water.

Source: Statistical Bureau of Guyana.

Table 2.3: GUYANA - IMPLICIT DEFLATORS, 1987-91
--------- (1988 = 100)

	1987	1988	1989	1990	1991
Agric., Forestry & Fishing	87.9	100.0	233.7	362.2	756.4
Mining and Quarrying	93.0	100.0	339.8	447.9	993.8
Manufacturing & Processing	87.4	100.0	289.4	325.3	654.5
Construction	58.0	100.0	191.1	286.3	538.8
Services	75.9	100.0	147.8	246.6	451.7
Total GDP at Factor Cost	81.2	100.0	208.1	307.8	623.8

Source: Tables 2.1 and 2.2.

Table 2.4: GUYANA - EXPENDITURES ON GROSS DOMESTIC PRODUCT AT CURRENT PRICES, 1987-91
--------- (G$ million)

	1987	1988	1989	1990	1991
Total Consumption	2,783	3,488	6,023	9,330	20,149
Public	952	1,163	1,742	2,301	4,641
Private	1,831	2,325	4,281	7,029	15,508
Gross Domestic Investment	1,081	875	2,297	4,877	10,983
Fixed Capital Formation	966	746	1,949	4,341	6,289
Public	495	406	846	2,081	2,239
Private	471	340	1,103	2,260	4,050
Change in inventories	115	129	348	536	4,694
Gross Domestic Expenditure	3,864	4,363	8,320	14,207	31,132
Resource Balance	(389)	(178)	(739)	(2,472)	(4,749)
Exports of goods & NFS	2,765	2,633	6,855	9,805	32,302
Imports of goods & NFS	3,154	2,811	7,594	12,277	37,051
GDP at current m.p.	3,475	4,185	7,581	11,735	26,383
Net factor income from abroad	(1,091)	(1,135)	(4,287)	(6,246)	(16,738)
GNP at current m.p.	2,384	3,050	3,294	5,489	9,645
Gross Domestic Savings	692	697	1,558	2,405	6,234
Net transfers from abroad	109	128	462	585	1,659
Gross National Savings a/	(290)	(310)	(2,267)	(3,256)	(8,845)

a/ Domestic savings plus net factor income plus net current transfers.

Source: Statistical Bureau of Guyana.

Table 3.1: GUYANA - BALANCE OF PAYMENTS, 1987-91
(US$ million)

	1987	1988	1989	1990	1991
Exports of Goods & NFS	283	264	252	251	292
Merchandise Exports	241	215	205	204	239
Sugar	90	75	83	75	82
Bauxite	86	80	73	75	79
Rice	16	15	12	14	17
Other	48	45	37	40	60
Nonfactor Services	43	49	47	47	53
Imports of Goods & NFS	304	264	255	289	295
Merchandise Imports, c.i.f.	262	216	212	250	245
Nonfactor Services	42	48	43	39	50
Resource Balance	-21	-0	-3	-37	-4
Net Factor Income	-109	-113	-130	-139	-137
Net Current Transfers (Private)	11	13	14	13	14
Current Account Balance	-119	-101	-119	-163	-127
Official Transfers	10	7	7	15	8
Medium and Long-Term Debt	-23	-28	237	522	86
Gross Disbursements	39	29	68	225	79
Amortization	134	130	175	121	43
Rescheduling	72	73	344	419	50
Other Capital (net) a/	-1	5	-7	9	73
Capital Account Balance	-14	-16	237	547	167
Errors and Ommissions	-4	11	1	1	1
Overall Balance	-137	-106	119	385	41
Financing	137	106	-119	-385	-41
BOG Net Foreign Assets (incl IMF)	77	32	29	-18	-41
Private Sector Commercial Arrears	4	4	10	-101	0
Non-Financial Public Sector Arrears	56	70	-157	-265	-0

a/ Residual: Includes direct investment, private capital, short-term capital, SDR
   allocation, debt reduction/deferment and other.   deferment and other.

Source: Statistical Bureau of Guyana, Bank of Guyana and IMF.

Table 3.2: GUYANA - VALUE AND VOLUME OF MERCHANDISE EXPORTS (FOB), 1977-91
(US$ million)

	1977	1978	1979	1980	1981	1982	1983	1984	1985	1986	1987	1988	1989	1990	1991
Total Exports	259.3	295.5	292.5	389.1	322.8	251.5	193.3	200.3	219.4	228.2	240.5	214.6	204.7	203.9	238.6
Re-Exports	3.6	5.5	3.6	6.2	6.9	8.8	6.7	4.8	6.6	5.6	8.3	5.7	4.6	4.5	5.2
Domestic Exports	255.6	290.0	288.9	382.9	315.9	242.7	186.7	195.5	212.8	222.7	232.2	208.9	200.1	199.4	233.4
Sugar	72.8	92.0	90.4	120.6	102.0	87.9	71.5	65.4	68.0	85.8	90.4	74.8	83.4	74.9	82.2
Rice	26.2	37.6	31.7	34.3	36.7	20.2	21.6	19.7	13.6	13.8	16.1	15.4	12.0	13.6	17.1
Calcined bauxite	82.9	79.1	85.6	119.8	86.5	68.6	47.4	65.3	75.0	63.0	66.7	57.9	49.1	47.6	52.9
Dried bauxite & alumina cement	16.2	19.0	21.5	24.5	26.0	23.8	23.2	19.3	26.6	22.3	19.4	21.6	23.4	27.4	26.2
Gold	0.4	0.1	0.0	0.0	0.0	1.3	1.7	4.0	4.1	5.8	9.4	.8	5.7	13.2	19.4
Other Manufactured	10.8	11.4	13.4	15.2	14.3	16.2	6.6	10.4	8.8	10.4	.6	11.8	7.5	5.1	.7
Other	46.4	50.8	46.2	68.5	50.5	24.7	14.6	11.4	16.6	21.6	24.2	19.4	19.0	17.6	28.6
AS PERCENT OF DOMESTIC EXPORTS															
Bauxite	38.8	33.8	37.1	37.7	35.6	38.1	37.8	43.2	47.7	38.3	37.1	38.1	36.2	37.6	33.9
Sugar	28.5	31.7	31.3	31.5	32.3	36.2	38.3	33.5	32.0	38.5	38.9	35.8	41.7	37.6	35.2
Rice	10.2	13.0	11.0	9.0	11.6	8.3	11.6	10.1	6.4	6.2	6.9	7.4	6.0	6.8	7.3
Gold	0.1	0.0	0.0	0.0	0.0	0.5	0.9	2.0	1.9	2.6	4.0	3.8	2.8	6.6	8.3
Other manufactures	4.2	3.9	4.6	4.0	4.5	6.7	3.6	5.3	4.1	4.7	2.6	5.6	3.7	2.6	3.0
Other	18.1	17.5	16.0	17.9	16.0	10.2	7.8	5.9	7.8	9.7	10.4	9.3	9.5	8.8	12.3

Source: Statistical Bureau.

Table 3.3: GUYANA - MERCHANDISE IMPORTS (CIF) BY END-USE CATEGORY, 1987-91
(US$ million)

	1987	1988	1989	1990	1991
Consumer Goods	26.2	21.6	21.3	25.1	26.5
Fuels and Lubricants	76.9	73.8	70.3	87.2	77.8
Other Intermediate Goods	101.2	74.9	42.9	39.9	19.5
Capital Goods	55.0	43.1	75.7	94.3	121.3
Miscellaneous	2.6	2.2	2.2	3.1	-0.1
Total Merchandise Imports	261.9	215.6	212.4	249.6	245.0

Source: Statistical Bureau.

Table 3.4: GUYANA - VALUE, VOLUME AND UNIT VALUE OF PRINCIPAL FUEL IMPORTS, 1987-91

(Value in millions of US dollars; volume in millions of imperial
gallons and unit value in US dollars per imperial gallon) a/

	1987	1988	1989	1990	1991
Total value of fuel					
imports (cif)	76.9	73.8	70.3	87.2	77.8
Gasoline					
Value	10.0	10.6	11.8	14.0	12.1
Volume	14.1	14.2	16.3	15.5	13.7
Unit value	0.71	0.75	0.72	0.90	0.88
Kerosene					
Value	5.2	5.3	5.8	7.3	5.9
Volume	7.2	7.7	7.4	7.2	6.7
Unit value	0.72	0.69	0.78	1.01	0.88
Gas oil/diesel oil					
Value	18.6	19.0	18.7	27.9	24.3
Volume	26.2	30.3	25.4	30.3	29.0
Unit value	0.71	0.63	0.74	0.92	0.84
Butane and propane					
Value	1.9	2.2	1.9	2.1	1.4
Volume b/	10.9	..	..	10.0	7.1
Unit value	0.17	..	..	0.21	0.20
Aviation fuel					
Value	0.6	0.8	0.6	0.4	0.4
Volume	0.5	0.6	0.5	0.3	0.3
Unit value	1.20	1.33	1.20	1.33	1.33
Bunker "C"					
Value	34.2	22.9	18.6	24.6	21.0
Volume	51.6	54.0	37.3	42.2	43.0
Unit value	0.66	0.42	0.50	0.58	0.49
Other					
Value c/	6.4	13.0	12.9	10.9	12.7

a/ One barrel of petroleum is equal to 34.973 imperial gallons.
b/ In millions of pounds.
c/ Inclues lubricating grease and oils, and white spirit.

Source: Guyana National Energy Authority and IMF.

Table 3.5: GUYANA - DIRECTION OF FOREIGN TRADE, 1987-90
--------- (US$ million)

	1987	1988	1989	1990
Total Exports (F.O.B.) a/	240.5	214.6	204.7	203.9
United States	54.4	48.5	51.0	41.6
Canada	22.8	12.0	14.1	16.1
Japan	7.2	6.0	11.7	12.6
EC Countries	121.9	107.3	93.1	97.5
United Kingdom	82.0	66.1	57.3	65.5
Germany	12.0	11.2	16.2	12.4
Other	27.9	30.0	19.7	19.4
CARICOM	11.8	15.2	15.4	13.9
Trinidad and Tobago	2.2	3.6	7.8	8.8
Jamaica	4.6	5.6	3.3	0.4
Barbados	1.9	2.4	2.7	2.9
Other	3.1	3.6	1.6	1.8
CMEA Countries	2.4	3.2	5.7	5.7
Rest of the World	20.0	22.3	13.7	16.5
	(percent of total exports)			
Total Exports (F.O.B.) a/	100.0	100.0	100.0	100.0
United States	22.6	22.6	24.9	20.4
Canada	9.5	5.6	6.9	7.9
Japan	3.0	2.8	5.7	6.2
EC countries	50.7	50.0	45.5	47.8
United Kingdom	34.1	30.8	28.0	32.1
Germany	5.0	5.2	7.9	6.1
Other	11.6	14.0	9.6	9.5
CARICOM	4.9	7.1	7.5	6.8
Trinidad and Tobago	0.9	1.7	3.8	4.3
Jamaica	1.9	2.6	1.6	0.2
Barbados	0.8	1.1	1.3	1.4
Other	1.3	1.7	0.8	0.9
CMEA Countries	1.0	1.5	2.8	2.8
Rest of the World	8.3	10.4	6.7	8.1

a/ Inlcudes re-exports.

Source: IMF, Direction of Trade.

Table 3.5: GUYANA - DIRECTION OF FOREIGN TRADE, 1987-90 (con't)
(US$ million)

	1987	1988	1989	1990
Total Imports, C.I.F.	261.9	215.6	212.4	249.6
United States	80.7	71.6	85.2	87.1
Canada	5.8	5.0	4.2	10.7
Japan	12.3	11.6	10.6	14.7
Venezuela	..	..	0.8	1.0
EC Countries	55.8	35.6	40.8	65.9
United Kingdom	34.0	20.1	23.8	31.2
Germany	7.3	5.4	4.2	6.2
Other	14.4	10.1	12.7	28.2
CARICOM	21.2	21.8	35.9	38.9
Trinidad and Tobago	34.0	20.1	23.8	31.2
Jamaica	7.3	5.4	4.2	6.2
Barbados	14.4	10.1	12.7	28.2
Other	4.7	4.3	1.7	1.7
CMEA Countries	3.1	2.8	7.6	9.2
Rest of the World	83.0	67.3	27.2	22.0

(percent of total imports, c.i.f.)

	1987	1988	1989	1990
Total Imports, C.I.F.	100.0	100.0	100.0	100.0
United States	30.8	33.2	40.1	34.9
Canada	2.2	2.3	2	4.3
Japan	4.7	5.4	5	5.9
Venezuela	..	..	0.4	0.4
EC Countries	21.3	16.5	19.2	26.4
United Kingdom	13	9.3	11.2	12.5
Germany	2.8	2.5	2	2.5
Other	5.5	4.7	6	11.3
CARICOM	8.1	10.1	16.9	15.6
Trinidad and Tobago	13	9.3	11.2	12.5
Jamaica	2.8	2.5	2	2.5
Barbados	5.5	4.7	6	11.3
Other	1.8	2	0.8	0.7
CMEA Countries	1.2	1.3	3.6	3.7
Rest of the World	31.7	31.2	12.8	8.8

Source: IMF, Direction of Trade.

Table 4.1: GUYANA - EXTERNAL PUBLIC DEBT, 1987-91
(US$ million)

	1987	1988	1989	1990	Prel. 1991
Total Public Sector Debt	1,722	1,760	1,851	1,940	1,853
Public and publicly-guaranteed debt	1009	1017	1099	1193	1060
of which: Multilateral agencies	375	374	396	429	491
Bank of Guyana debt	637	660	704	702	753
of which: IMF	124	122	128	112	146
Non-guaranteed public debt	18	22	26	45	40
Public sector commercial arrears	58	61	22	..	..
Public Debt Service					
Scheduled Debt Service Payments	215	215	269	222	141
Principal (FROM BOP)	134	130	175	121	43
Interest	81	85	94	101	98
Actual debt service payments	32	41	44	58	96
Principal a/	11	21	23	32	50
Interest	21	20	21	26	46
Rescheduled Debt	..	..	754	997	1082
(percent of exports of goods and non-factor services)					
Total external public debt	607.8	667.4	735.4	772.3	635.5
Scheduled debt service payments	75.9	81.4	106.8	88.5	48.4
Actual debt service payments	11.3	15.5	17.5	23.1	32.9

a/ Includes US$12 million of repayment of loans obtained in 1990 for clearance of arrears.

Source: IBRD Debt Reporting System, Ministry of Finance and Bank of Guyana.

Table 4.2: GUYANA - SELECTED MEDIUM-TERM EXTERNAL DEBT INDICATORS, 1987-91

	1987	1988	1989	1990	1991
IN PERCENTAGE					
DOD/XGNFS	607.8	667.4	735.4	772.3	635.5
DOD/GDP	495.5	420.5	805.7	743.9	856.9
Actual					
TDS/XGNFS	11.3	15.5	17.5	23.1	32.9
TDS/GDP	9.2	9.8	19.2	22.2	44.4
INT/XGNFS	7.4	7.6	8.3	10.4	15.8
INT/GDP	6.0	4.8	9.1	10.0	21.3
Scheduled					
TDS/XGNFS	75.9	81.4	106.8	88.5	48.4
TDS/GDP	61.8	51.3	117.1	85.2	65.2
INT/XGNFS	28.6	32.2	37.3	40.2	33.6
INT/GDP	23.3	20.3	40.9	38.7	45.3
IN US$ MILLION					
DOD	1722.0	1760.0	1851.0	1940.0	1853.0
GDP	347.5	418.5	229.7	260.8	216.3
XGNFS	283.3	263.7	251.7	251.2	291.6
MGNFS	304.2	264.0	255.1	288.5	295.3
TDS(scheduled)	214.9	214.6	268.9	222.3	141.0
INT(scheduled)	81.0	85.0	94.0	101.0	98.0
PRI(scheduled)	133.9	129.6	174.9	121.3	43.0
TDS(actual)	32.0	41.0	44.0	58.0	96.0
INT(actual)	21.0	20.0	21.0	26.0	46.0
PRI(actual)	11.0	21.0	23.0	32.0	50.0
Memo item:					
Average Exchange Rate (G$/US$)	10.0	10.0	33.0	45.0	122.0

Note:

DOD = Disbursed and Outstanding Debt (end-year).
TDS = Public Debt Service Payments (interest and amortization).
INT = Public Debt Interest Payments.
GDP = Gross Domestic Product.
XGNFS = Exports of Goods and Non-factor Services.

Source: Table 3.1 and 4.1.

Table 5.1: GUYANA - PUBLIC SECTOR OPERATIONS, 1987-91

(G$ Million)

	1987	1988	1989	1990	Prel. 1991
Current Account Balance	-294.5	-654.5	-1943.8	-3353.5	-5481.2
Central Government a/	-1255.5	-1129.5	-2791.8	-4069.5	-6305.2
Revenue	1138.8	1660.7	2935.0	4779.9	10595.7
Expenditure	2394.3	2790.2	5726.8	8849.4	16900.9
Rest of public sector b/	953.0	462.0	1518.0	289.0	-25.0
Consolidated current transfers	8.0	13.0	-670.0	427.0	849.0
Capital revenue (net of transfers)	0.8	1.7	36.3	292.4	2082.0
Grants	101.4	59.2	215.8	551.0	1055.0
Capital Expenditure	977.0	760.0	1942.0	4300.0	6310.0
Overall Balance	-1169.3	-1353.6	-3633.7	-6810.1	-8654.2
Financing	1169.3	1353.6	3633.7	6810.1	8654.2
Net External Borrowing	1246.9	680.0	3023.0	5361.2	14052.4
Net Flows	-884.8	-1112.0	-127.4	7323.2	7108.0
Rescheduling	702.4	731.0	438.9	8035.2	6757.9
Change in Arrears	1429.3	1061.0	2662.0	-10102.5	332.6
Short-term	0.0	0.0	49.5	105.3	-146.1
Change in Commercial Arrears	..	..	..	518.7	-207.4
Change in BOG reserves (-increase)	-2.9	47.0	-320.9	-537.0	-12142.6
Domestic Financing	-74.7	626.6	931.6	1467.2	6951.8

(percent of GDP)

	1987	1988	1989	1990	Prel. 1991
Current Account Balance	-8.5	-15.6	-25.6	-28.6	-20.8
Central Government a/	-36.1	-27.0	-36.8	-34.7	-23.9
Revenue	32.8	39.7	38.7	40.7	40.2
Expenditure	68.9	66.7	75.5	75.4	64.1
Rest of public sector b/	27.4	11.0	20.0	2.5	-0.1
Consolidated current transfers	0.2	0.3	-8.8	3.6	3.2
Capital revenue (net of transfers)	0.0	0.0	0.5	2.5	7.9
Grants	2.9	1.4	2.8	4.7	4.0
Capital Expenditure	28.1	18.2	25.6	36.6	23.9
Overall Balance	-33.6	-32.3	-47.9	-58.0	-32.8
Financing	33.6	32.3	47.9	58.0	32.8
Net External Borrowing	35.9	16.2	39.9	45.7	53.3
Net Flows	-25.5	-26.6	-1.7	62.4	26.9
Rescheduling	20.2	17.5	5.8	68.5	25.6
Change in Arrears	41.1	25.4	35.1	-86.1	1.3
Short-term	0.0	0.0	0.7	0.9	-0.6
Change in Commercial Arrears	0.0	0.0	0.0	4.4	-0.8
Change in BOG reserves (-increase)	-0.1	1.1	-4.2	-4.6	-46.0
Domestic Financing	-2.1	15.0	12.3	12.5	26.3

a/ Includes transactions with public enterprises.
b/ Includes Bank of Guyana.

Source: Ministry of Finance and IMF.

Table 5.2: GUYANA - SUMMARY OF CENTRAL GOVERNMENT OPERATIONS, 1987-91
(G$ Million)

	1987	1988	1989	1990	Prel. 1991
Total Revenue and Grants	1241.0	1721.6	3187.1	5620.9	13075.2
Current Revenue	1138.8	1660.7	2935.0	4779.9	10595.7
Capital Revenue	0.8	1.7	36.3	292.4	2175.2
	101.4	59.2	215.8	548.6	304.3
Total Expenditure	2969.9	3263.9	6820.3	11027.3	19651.5
Current Expenditure	2394.3	2790.2	5726.8	8849.4	16900.9
Capital Expenditure	575.6	473.7	1093.5	2177.9	2750.6
Primary Current Account Balance	-47.7	184.0	428.4	1309.0	3766.0
Current Account Balance	-1255.5	-1129.5	-2791.8	-4069.5	-6305.2
Primary Overall Balance	-521.1	-228.8	-413.0	-27.9	3494.9
Overall Balance	-1728.9	-1542.3	-3633.2	-5406.4	-6576.3

Source: Tables 5.3 and 5.4.

Table 5.3: GUYANA - CENTRAL GOVERNMENT REVENUES, 1987-91
(G$ Million)

	1987	1988	1989	1990	Prel. 1991
TOTAL REVENUE	1241.0	1721.6	3187.1	5620.9	13075.2
CURRENT REVENUES	1138.8	1660.7	2935.0	4779.9	10595.7
Tax Revenue	1029.3	1525.7	2608.3	4511.9	9679.2
Income tax	422.9	608.4	1053.6	1710.6	3442.4
Personal	157.8	178.4	185.0	305.3	492.6
Companies	238.7	396.1	815.6	1314.6	2444.1
Withholding tax	13.7	17.9	35.0	61.9	457.2
Self-employed	12.2	13.9	18.0	26.8	48.5
Other	0.5	2.1	0.0	2.0	0.0
Property tax	18.3	22.1	42.9	88.5	121.7
Production and Consumption taxes	395.1	439.6	832.4	1416.2	3459.5
Consumption tax	324.8	351.0	715.7	1300.1	3271.6
On imports a/	208.6	217.2	430.2	897.4	2460.3
On local goods	116.2	133.8	285.5	402.7	811.3
Other b/	70.3	88.6	116.7	116.1	187.9
Taxes on International Trade	148.8	158.9	403.6	732.5	1586.3
Import duties	81.3	92.0	296.4	559.3	1167.5
Export duties	20.3	18.2	50.2	94.0	179.5
Travel tax	47.2	48.7	57.0	79.2	239.3
Other	44.2	296.7	275.8	564.1	1069.3
Sugar levy (net of remittances)	..	240.0	225.0	478.7	962.1
Other	44.2	56.7	50.8	85.4	107.2
Nontax Current Revenue c/	109.5	135.0	326.7	268.0	916.5
GRANTS	101.4	59.2	215.8	548.6	304.3
CAPITAL REVENUE	0.8	1.7	36.3	292.4	2175.2

a/ Includes revenue from nonfinancial public corporations.
b/ Includes excise tax and purchase tax on cars.
c/ Includes dividends from state-owned financial enterprises.

Source: Ministry of Finance and IMF.

Table 5.4: GUYANA - CENTRAL GOVERNMENT EXPENDITURE, 1987-91
--------- (G$ million)

	1987	1988	1989	1990	Prel. 1991
Total expenditures a/	2969.9	3263.9	6820.3	11027.3	19651.5
Current expenditures b/	2394.3	2790.2	5726.8	8849.4	16900.9
Goods and services	951.9	1165.3	1741.8	2302.5	4641.7
Personal emoluments c/	535.2	602.5	754.8	1191.1	2192.3
Wages and Salaries	422.6	439.8	511.9	696.1	1473.7
Allowances and Contributions	112.6	162.7	242.9	495.0	718.6
Other goods and services	416.7	562.8	987.0	1111.4	2449.4
Interest d/	1207.8	1313.5	3220.2	5378.5	10071.2
External	244.2	293.8	945.7	1970.4	6416.6
Domestic	963.6	1019.7	2274.5	3408.1	3654.6
Transfers	219.1	300.1	759.0	1161.9	2164.3
Public Corporations	57.4	58.0	334.4	412.9	823.0
Local and international organizatio	88.8	117.8	223.6	505.4	895.6
Other private e/	41.9	86.5	152.8	189.6	329.1
Other	31.0	37.8	48.2	54.0	116.6
Refund of revenues	15.5	11.3	5.8	6.5	23.7
Capital expenditure	575.6	473.7	1093.5	2177.9	2750.6
Capital formation	494.6	405.8	799.8	1982.0	2153.2
Acquisition of financial assets	11.6	14.5	39.8	58.6	106.0
Transfers (grants & loans)	69.4	53.4	253.9	137.3	491.4
Public corporations	48.6	50.4	189.2	70.3	398.5
Financial institutions	20.8	3.0	64.7	67.0	92.9

a/ Excludes equity contributions and loans to replace overdrafts of some public corporations
b/ For 1990, includes estimated arrears payments relating to obligation of the Ministry of
   Foreign Affairs and transfers to interational organizations estimated at G$390 million.
c/ Includes payments to the NIS.
d/ Scheduled interest payments.
e/ For 1989 and 1990 inclues SIMAP transfers.

Source: Ministry of Finance and IMF.

Table 6.1: GUYANA - SUMMARY ACCOUNTS OF THE BANKING SYSTEM, 1987-92
--------- (G$ million)

	December 31					June 30	
	1987	1988	1989	1990	1991	1991	1992
Net Foreign Assets a/	-6200.2	-6515.9	-22137.9	-28658.2	-76004.0	-77877.3	-76312.6
Net International Reserves a/	-6107.2	-6312.5	-21193.1	-27891.1	-74035.3	-75815.4	-74522.0
Medium-Term Liabilities	-93.0	-203.4	-944.8	-767.1	-1968.7	-2061.9	-1790.6
Net domestic assets	9201.0	10636.0	28330.0	38073.0	92270.0	89598.0	96566.0
Net domestic assets (net of valuation)	9201.0	10636.0	13345.0	15271.0	20484.0	17812.0	24870.4
Credit to public sector	6351.0	7681.0	9162.0	9034.0	5736.0	7421.0	6710.0
Central Government (net) b/ c/	6515.0	7777.0	9848.0	10020.0	9889.0	8888.0	11399.0
Public enterprises (net) b/	-96.0	-50.0	-501.0	-684.0	-2187.0	-750.0	-2578.0
Other public sector	-68.0	-46.0	-185.0	-302.0	-1966.0	-717.0	-2111.0
Credit to private sector	987.0	1591.0	2566.0	4160.0	6672.0	5029.0	7893.0
Credit to rest of the financial system	-350.0	-671.0	-968.0	-1435.0	-2778.0	-2143.0	-3310.0
External payments deposits	-679.0	-789.0	-958.0	-916.0	-746.0	-766.0	-512.0
Capital reserve and other d/	2892.0	2822.0	16612.5	25398.0	81894.0	78525.0	84762.0
Liabilities to private sector	3001.0	4120.0	6192.0	9414.0	16266.0	11720.0	20253.0
Monetary liabilities	1141.0	1657.0	2383.0	3432.0	6099.0	4217.0	6101.0
Currency	726.0	1058.0	1506.0	2211.0	3712.0	2670.0	3564.0
Demand deposits & cashier's checks	415.0	599.0	877.0	1221.0	2387.0	1547.0	2537.0
Time and savings deposits	1860.0	2463.0	3809.0	5982.0	10167.0	7503.0	14152.0

a/ Includes short-term liabilities of the Bank of Guyana that are in arrears.
b/ Excludes special interest-free debenture contributions from the Treasury to the Bank of Guyana to
   cover exchange rate losses.
c/ Reflects Central Government equity contributions to certain public enterprises to cover
   their commercial bank overdrafts.
d/ Includes private capital and surplus and exchange rate losses.

Source: Bank of Guyana.

Table 6.2: GUYANA - ACCOUNTS OF THE BANKING SYSTEM, 1987-92

(G$ million)

	December 31					June 30	
	1987	1988	1989	1990	1991	1991	1992

I. CONSOLIDATED ACCOUNTS OF THE BANKING SYSTEM

	1987	1988	1989	1990	1991	1991	1992
Net International Reserves a/	-6107.2	-6312.5	-21193.1	-27891.1	-74035.3	-75815.4	-74522.0
Assets	249.5	204.6	1262.5	3597.2	17533.7	10661.1	19887.2
Liabilities a/	-6356.7	-6517.1	-22455.6	-31488.3	-91569.0	-86476.5	-94409.2
Net Domestic Credit	6576.7	8612.5	11609.3	14191.4	27174.1	20161.7	59130.8
Public Sector (net)	6350.7	7680.6	9161.5	9034.2	5736.1	7421.3	6709.5
Central Government b/	6515.3	7777.1	9847.6	10020.5	9889.2	8887.9	11398.8
Treasury Bills	4020.9	4020.5	5430.0	5468.5	2584.9	5758.7	6046.5
Debentures c/	839.7	991.9	948.9	728.2	4825.9	3551.5	4815.1
Advances	1753.8	2888.3	3688.3	4184.9	3346.4	170.0	1716.7
Deposits	-99.1	-123.6	-219.6	-361.1	-868.0	-592.3	-1179.5
Special Funds	-6.5	-6.5	-6.5	-6.5	-6.5	-6.5	-6.5
Social Security & Pension Funds	-62.5	-41.1	-184.3	-279.8	-1931.3	-671.0	2079.9
Other b/	-95.6	-48.9	-495.3	-700.0	-2215.3	-789.1	-6762.7
Contingency reserve (gross)	-4256.4	-4494.4	-17540.0	-25926.3	-52092.1	-56202.9	-54977.8
Other d/	1105.0	1751.9	3155.7	4600.7	7508.5	6369.6	8614.2
Unclassified (net)	3377.4	3674.4	16832.1	26482.8	66021.6	62573.7	98784.9
Counterpart unrequited foreign exchang	-3822.2	-3715.9	-19034.0	-27029.5	-70670.0	-73984.4	-44092.2
Liabilities to rest of financial syste	350.3	670.9	967.7	1435.3	2778.2	2143.1	3309.6
External payments deposits	678.8	7888.9	957.5	916.2	745.8	765.7	511.8
Medium-term liabilities	93.0	203.4	944.8	767.1	1968.7	2061.9	1790.6
Liabilities to the private sector	3170.2	4353.7	6580.2	10211.2	18316.1	13360.1	23089.0
Monetary liabilities	1140.7	1657.2	2382.7	3431.5	6008.6	4216.9	6100.6
Currency in circulation	726.3	1057.8	1506.0	2211.4	3711.5	2669.7	3569.3
Demand deposits	352.5	468.1	652.1	1059.8	1903.6	1373.8	2242.5
Cashiers checks and bank acceptan	61.9	131.3	224.6	160.3	393.5	173.4	288.8
Time and savings deposits	1859.9	2462.6	3809.3	5982.9	10256.9	7503.5	14152.7
Private capital and surplus	169.6	233.9	388.2	796.8	2050.6	1639.7	2835.7

a/ Includes short-term liabilities of the Bank of Guyana that are in arrears.
b/ Includes Central Government equity contributions to certain public enterprises to cover their
commercial bank overdrafts.
c/ Excludes special interest-free debenture contributions from the Treasury to the Bank of
Guyana to cover exchange rate losses.

Source: Bank of Guyana and IMF.

Table 6.2: GUYANA - ACCOUNTS OF THE BANKING SYSTEM, 1987-92 (con't)
(G$ million)

| | December 31 | | | | | June 30 | |
	1987	1988	1989	1990	1991	1991	1992
II. MONETARY AUTHORITIES							
Net International Reserves a/	-6124.0	-6334.2	-21764.1	-29403.5	-75526.5	-78148.8	-75885.3
Assets	89.0	40.4	501.6	1195.3	15125.2	7303.2	17324.7
Liabilities a/	-6213.0	-6374.6	-22265.7	-30598.8	-90651.7	-85452.0	-93210.0
Net Domestic Credit	5491.2	6304.0	6097.3	6349.5	15124.4	9151.1	43052.9
Public Sector (net)	6288.4	7241.2	7326.9	6137.0	1788.7	3025.2	37.0
Central Government b/	6262.9	7169.8	7381.5	6270.2	3531.9	3531.8	1890.5
Treasury Bills	3806.9	3591.6	3047.3	1662.4	5.5	3082.1	8.4
Debentures c/	750.9	714.2	672.1	458.5	221.2	303.9	211.2
Advances	1705.1	2864.1	3662.1	4149.3	3305.2	145.8	1670.9
Deposits	..	..	..	..	..	..	..
Special Funds	-6.5	-6.5	-6.5	-6.5	-6.5	-6.5	-6.5
Social Security & Pension Funds	32.1	77.8	-48.1	-126.3	-1736.8	-500.0	-1847.0
Contingency reserve (gross)	-4256.4	-4494.4	-17540.0	-25926.3	-52092.1	-56202.9	-54977.8
Other d/	38.6	20.2	314.9	467.8	-2022.0	1000.9	304.7
Unclassified (net)	3420.6	3537.0	15995.5	25671.0	67449.8	61327.9	97689.0
Counterpart unrequited foreign exchang	-3822.2	-3715.9	-19034.0	-27029.5	-70670.0	-73984.4	-44092.2
SDR allocation account	206.1	188.9	623.4	930.2	2497.3	2341.2	2492.2
Valuation adjust. fund accounts	-807.0	-715.2	-2860.0	-3607.9	-7557.2	-11128.8	-7646.6
Valuation adjust. gold and foreign	-3221.3	-3189.6	-16797.4	-24351.8	-65610.1	-65196.8	-38937.8
Liabilities to commercial banks	2369.8	2627.9	1861.1	1764.1	6556.4	2317.1	7695.5
Currency in circulation	726.3	1057.8	1506.0	2211.4	3711.5	2669.7	3564.3
Currency issue	753.7	1095.2	1585.1	2407.5	4008.2	2833.0	3808.6
Holdings of commercial banks	-27.4	-37.4	-79.1	-196.1	-296.7	-163.3	-244.3

a/ Includes short-term liabilities of the Bank of Guyana that are in arrears.
b/ Includes Central Government equity contributions to certain public enterprises to cover their
commercial bank overdrafts.
c/ Excludes special interest-free debenture contributions from the Treasury to the Bank of
Guyana to cover exchange rate losses.

Source: Bank of Guyana and IMF.

Table 6.2: GUYANA - ACCOUNTS OF THE BANKING SYSTEM, 1987-92 (con't)
(G$ million)

| | December 31 | | | | | June 30 | |
	1987	1988	1989	1990	1991	1991	1992
III. COMMERCIAL BANKS							
Net International Reserves	16.8	22.8	571.0	1512.5	1491.2	2333.4	1363.1
Assets	160.5	164.2	760.9	2402.0	2408.5	3357.9	2562.4
Liabilities a/	-143.7	-141.4	-189.9	-889.5	-917.3	-1024.5	-1199.3
Claims on the Bank of Guyana (net)	2414.7	2712.0	2115.2	1764.2	6688.9	2499.2	7861.2
Currency	27.4	37.4	79.2	196.0	296.7	163.2	244.3
Deposits (net of advances)	1708.5	1895.6	1079.6	653.0	5646.4	1570.3	7105.1
External payments arrears	678.8	779.0	956.4	915.2	745.8	765.7	511.8
Net Domestic Credit	1040.7	2020.9	4313.2	7074.6	9948.5	8766.6	14121.7
Public Sector (net)	62.3	439.5	1834.7	2896.8	3947.4	4396.0	6672.5
Central Government b/	252.5	607.2	2466.0	3750.2	6357.2	5356.2	9508.0
Treasury Bills	214.0	428.9	2382.6	3806.0	2579.4	2676.7	6038.1
Debentures c/	88.8	277.7	276.8	269.6	4604.7	3247.6	4603.9
Advances	48.7	24.2	26.2	35.6	41.1	24.2	45.8
Deposits	-99.0	-123.6	-219.6	-361.0	-868.0	-592.3	-1179.8
Social Security & Pension Funds	-94.6	-118.9	-136.1	-153.5	-194.5	-171.0	-233.0
Other b/	-95.6	-48.8	-495.2	-699.9	-2215.3	-789.2	-2602.5
Credit to private sector	986.7	1590.9	2566.1	4159.6	6672.4	5028.8	7892.9
Interbank float	27.2	50.4	35.0	44.1	90.4	101.6	165.3
Unclassified (net)	-35.5	-59.9	-122.6	-25.9	-761.7	-759.8	-609.0
Liabilities to rest of financial syste	350.3	670.9	967.7	1435.3	2778.2	2143.1	3309.6
Deposits on external payments arrears	678.8	788.9	957.5	916.2	745.8	765.7	511.8
Liabilities to private sector	2444.0	3295.9	5074.2	7999.8	14604.6	10690.3	19524.7
Monetary liabilities	414.4	599.4	876.7	1220.1	2297.1	1547.1	2536.2
Demand deposits	352.5	468.1	652.1	1059.8	1903.6	1373.8	2242.5
Cashiers' checks and bank acceptanc	61.9	131.3	224.6	160.3	393.5	173.3	293.7
Time and savings deposits	1859.9	2462.6	3809.3	5982.9	10256.9	7503.5	14152.7
Private capital and surplus	169.7	233.9	388.2	796.8	2050.6	1639.7	2835.8

a/ Includes short-term liabilities of the Bank of Guyana that are in arrears.
b/ Includes Central Government equity contributions to certain public enterprises to cover their commercial bank overdrafts.
c/ Excludes special interest-free debenture contributions from the Treasury to the Bank of Guyana to cover exchange rate losses.

Source: Bank of Guyana and IMF.

Table 7.1: GUYANA - PRICE MOVEMENTS a/
-------- (annual percentage change)

	1987	1988	1989	1990	1991
Urban Consumer Price index (end of period)	34.6	51.5	104.7	75.9	81.5
Food	36.9	61.0	..	..	..
Clothing	62.8	45.1	..	..	..
Housing	15.6	6.5	..	..	..
Other	26.5	37.2	..	..	..
Urban Consumer Price index (period average)	28.7	39.9	89.7	63.6	105.9
Food	30.0	47.0	..	..	..
Clothing	51.4	39.8	..	..	..
Housing	14.8	4.4	..	..	..
Other	24.4	28.5	..	..	..

a/ Since 1989, no official data have been compiled and estimates are based
   on IMF estimates.

Source: IMF Staff estimates.

STATISTICAL APPENDIX

2. PROJECTION TABLES

TABLE OF CONTENTS

TABLE P.1.1: GUYANA KEY INDICATORS

	1992	1993	1994	1995	1996	1997	1998	1999	2000	2001
Real Growth Rates:										
Gross Domestic Product (GDP)	7.9%	5.5%	5.0%	4.5%	4.5%	4.5%	4.0%	4.0%	4.0%	4.0%
Gross Domestic Income (GDY)	12.5%	-5.3%	8.5%	5.6%	3.4%	3.2%	2.6%	1.7%	1.8%	1.8%
Real Per Capita Growth Rates:										
Gross Domestic Product (GDP)	7.4%	5.0%	4.5%	4.0%	4.0%	4.0%	3.5%	3.5%	3.5%	3.5%
Total Consumption	-0.4%	9.7%	2.6%	1.5%	1.4%	1.7%	1.6%	1.5%	1.2%	1.4%
Private Consumption	-0.7%	11.9%	2.7%	1.5%	1.5%	1.9%	1.8%	1.7%	1.3%	1.6%
Debt and Debt Service (LT+ST+IMF):										
Total DOD (US$M)	1793	1883	1990	2068	2111	2146	2174	2226	2330	2434
DOD / GDP	675.5%	648.3%	640.4%	620.4%	585.7%	550.3%	518.0%	492.8%	479.1%	464.9%
Debt Service (US$M)	135	117	114	102	105	100	99	121	173	177
Debt Service / Exports	36.1%	29.6%	26.2%	21.4%	20.1%	17.5%	16.0%	18.2%	24.0%	22.6%
Debt Service / GDP	50.9%	40.2%	36.7%	30.7%	29.1%	25.6%	23.5%	26.9%	35.6%	33.8%
Interest Burden (LT+ST+IMF):										
Interest Paid (US$M)	66	65	72	71	73	73	72	70	69	67
Interest / Exports	17.6%	16.4%	16.5%	14.8%	13.9%	12.8%	11.7%	10.5%	9.5%	8.5%
Interest / GDP	24.7%	22.3%	23.2%	21.2%	20.1%	18.7%	17.1%	15.5%	14.1%	12.7%
Gross Investment / GDP	34.5%	35.5%	34.8%	34.1%	33.1%	32.0%	31.2%	30.5%	29.8%	29.0%
ICOR	5.1	6.5	7.4	8.1	7.9	7.7	8.4	8.1	7.9	7.8
Domestic Savings / GDP	37.1%	24.6%	28.8%	31.1%	31.6%	31.7%	31.5%	30.6%	30.0%	29.3%
BOP Resource Balance / GDP	2.6%	-10.9%	-6.1%	-2.9%	-1.5%	-0.3%	0.3%	0.2%	0.2%	0.3%
National Savings / GDP	4.8%	-5.4%	0.8%	5.1%	8.4%	9.8%	11.0%	11.7%	12.4%	12.8%
BOP Current Account Balance / GDP	-29.8%	-40.9%	-34.1%	-29.0%	-24.7%	-22.3%	-20.2%	-18.8%	-17.4%	-16.2%
Government Investment / GDP /1	9.9%	13.5%	13.5%	13.3%	12.8%	12.2%	11.8%	11.3%	10.8%	10.3%
Government Savings / GDP	-11.4%	-7.2%	-4.6%	0.2%	1.1%	0.5%	0.6%	1.6%	2.3%	3.7%
Private Investment / GDP /2	24.7%	22.0%	21.3%	20.8%	20.3%	19.8%	19.4%	19.2%	19.1%	18.8%
Private Savings / GDP /2	16.2%	1.8%	5.3%	4.8%	7.3%	9.3%	10.4%	10.0%	10.2%	9.1%

/1 excludes social sector et al. PSIP expenditures
/2 includes public enterprises

TABLE P.1.1. GUYANA KEY INDICATORS (cont.)

	1992	1993	1994	1995	1996	1997	1998	1999	2000	2001
Government Current Revenue / GDP	52.4%	48.4%	47.3%	46.3%	45.6%	43.1%	41.7%	41.2%	40.3%	40.3%
Government Current Expenditure / GDP	63.8%	55.6%	51.8%	46.1%	44.5%	42.6%	41.0%	39.5%	38.0%	36.6%
Government Current Account Balance / GDP	-11.4%	-7.2%	-4.6%	0.2%	1.1%	0.5%	0.6%	1.6%	2.3%	3.7%
Government Overall Revenue / GDP	56.3%	50.1%	47.9%	48.1%	48.3%	45.9%	44.5%	44.0%	43.2%	43.2%
Government Overall Expenditure / GDP	73.7%	76.0%	74.6%	74.6%	72.2%	67.0%	62.5%	59.4%	56.5%	53.8%
Government Overall Balance / GDP	-17.4%	-26.0%	-26.7%	-26.5%	-23.9%	-21.1%	-18.0%	-15.4%	-13.4%	-10.6%
Primary Deficit (-) or Surplus / GDP	17.9%	3.3%	0.5%	-4.0%	-2.5%	-1.0%	0.8%	2.0%	2.8%	4.3%
Urban CPI (% growth rate)	14.2%	12.0%	10.0%	8.0%	7.4%	7.7%	7.8%	8.9%	8.8%	8.7%
GDP Deflator (% growth rate)	17.0%	10.0%	8.0%	6.5%	5.5%	5.5%	5.5%	5.5%	5.5%	5.5%
Real Exchange Rate (1991=100)	100.1	100.1	100.1	100.1	100.1	100.1	100.1	100.1	100.1	100.1
Terms of Trade Index (1991=100)	99.3	93.6	93.0	92.7	91.3	90.0	88.9	87.9	87.1	86.4
Exports (G&NFS) Volume Growth Rate	28.0%	8.5%	9.5%	7.3%	6.5%	6.8%	5.3%	5.4%	5.2%	5.2%
Exports (G&NFS) / GDP	132.1%	126.0%	130.0%	133.4%	135.1%	137.3%	138.1%	139.2%	140.4%	141.6%
Imports (G&NFS) Volume Growth Rate	18.4%	11.4%	8.0%	5.6%	4.7%	5.1%	3.9%	4.2%	4.0%	3.9%
Imports (G&NFS) / GDP	129.5%	136.9%	136.0%	136.4%	136.6%	137.6%	137.8%	139.1%	140.3%	141.3%
BOP Curr Acct (US$M) (before grants)	-79	-119	-106	-97	-89	-87	-85	-85	-85	-85
Gross Reserves Central Bank (US$M)	186	197	203	212	217	223	229	234	239	244
Gross Reserves (US$M)	217	222	230	241	248	257	265	273	282	291
Net Reserves	-175	-180	-150	-116	-83	-46	-12	22	55	87
Net Reserves (months imports)	-6.1	-5.4	-4.3	-3.1	-2.0	-1.0	-0.2	0.4	1.0	1.4
Money & Quasimoney / GDP	74.6%	74.1%	75.5%	76.9%	76.9%	78.4%	80.0%	81.6%	83.3%	84.7%
Velocity of Money	1.4	1.4	1.3	1.3	1.3	1.3	1.3	1.2	1.2	1.2
Total Credit / M	50.2%	49.3%	44.5%	41.3%	39.4%	35.6%	32.5%	30.7%	30.2%	30.4%
Total Credit / GDP	39.3%	38.0%	34.7%	32.6%	31.2%	28.7%	26.7%	25.7%	25.9%	26.5%
Government Credit / GDP	25.9%	20.9%	14.6%	11.4%	9.4%	6.5%	3.3%	1.3%	0.6%	0.5%
Private Credit / GDP /1	13.5%	17.1%	20.1%	21.2%	21.8%	22.2%	23.3%	24.4%	25.2%	26.0%

/1 includes public enterprises

TABLE P.2.1: GUYANA NATIONAL ACCOUNTS
CURRENT PRICES (G$ MILLION)

	1992	1993	1994	1995	1996	1997	1998	1999	2000	2001
Gross Domestic Product	33307	38652	43832	48782	53780	59292	65055	71378	78316	85928
Net Indirect Taxes	8157	8046	9208	10195	10901	11336	12310	13713	15262	16971
GDP at Factor Cost	25149	30607	34624	38587	42880	47955	52744	57665	63054	68958
Imports (GNFS)	43140	52918	59630	66524	73455	81582	89635	99258	109842	121426
Exports (GNFS)	44005	48691	56973	65089	72659	81391	89829	99374	109971	121662
Resource Balance	865	-4227	-2657	-1436	-795	-191	194	115	129	236
Total Expenditures	32442	42880	46489	50217	54576	59483	64861	71263	78187	85693
Total Consumption:	20938	29158	31224	33602	36774	40483	44575	49519	54819	60737
Government	6889	6889	7365	7925	8643	9447	10337	11423	12619	13920
Private	14049	22270	23858	25677	28131	31036	34238	38096	42200	46817
Gross Domestic Investment:	11504	13721	15266	16615	17802	19000	20285	21743	23368	24955
Government	3292	5218	5935	6488	6884	7254	7644	8030	8419	8808
Private \1	8212	8503	9331	10127	10918	11746	12641	13713	14949	16148
Domestic Saving	12369	9494	12608	15179	17006	18809	20479	21859	23497	25191
Net Factor Income	-12542	-13509	-14389	-15124	-15603	-16932	-17951	-18872	-19835	-21003
Net Current Transfers	1758	1926	2110	2419	3116	3931	4620	5335	6075	6842
National Saving	1585	-2090	329	2474	4519	5807	7149	8321	9737	11030
Optional details for RMSM-X:										
Net Indirect Taxes	8157	8046	9208	10195	10901	11336	12310	13713	15262	16971
Indirect Taxes	10661	11209	12492	13659	14521	15119	16264	17845	19579	21482
Subsidies	2504	3164	3284	3464	3620	3783	3953	4131	4317	4511

TABLE P.2.2: GUYANA NATIONAL ACCOUNTS
CONSTANT PRICES (1991 G$ MILLION)

	1992	1993	1994	1995	1996	1997	1998	1999	2000	2001
Gross Domestic Product	28467	30033	31535	32954	34437	35986	37426	38923	40480	42099
Net Indirect Taxes	7262	5938	6463	6762	6770	6579	6671	6891	7114	7340
GDP at Factor Cost	21495	23782	24910	26067	27457	29106	30344	31445	32591	33784
Imports (GNFS)	39735	44281	47815	50503	52866	55579	57762	60198	62589	65033
Exports (GNFS)	39322	42667	46719	50147	53409	57045	60041	63312	66626	70071
Resource Balance	-413	-1615	-1097	-356	543	1466	2279	3114	4037	5038
Total Expenditures	28881	31648	32631	33310	33894	34521	35147	35809	36443	37061
Total Consumption:	18632	20536	21184	21611	22013	22501	22983	23451	23854	24318
Government	4687	4851	4997	5097	5173	5251	5330	5410	5491	5573
Private	13945	15684	16187	16514	16839	17250	17653	18041	18363	18745
Gross Domestic Investment:	10248	11112	11447	11699	11881	12019	12163	12358	12589	12743
Government	2933	4226	4450	4568	4594	4589	4583	4564	4536	4498
Private /1	7315	6886	6997	7130	7286	7431	7580	7794	8054	8246
Terms of Trade (TT) Effect	1210	-1922	-1034	-733	-1115	-1596	-2154	-3044	-3963	-4912
Gross Domestic Income	29677	28111	30500	32220	33321	34390	35272	35879	36516	37187
Domestic Savings (TT adjusted)	11045	7575	9316	10609	11308	11889	12288	12428	12663	12869

1/ Includes Public Enterprises

TABLE P.2.3: GUYANA NATIONAL ACCOUNTS
VALUE ADDED BY SECTOR

	1992	1993	1994	1995	1996	1997	1998	1999	2000	2001
Agriculture	35.7%	33.7%	33.3%	32.8%	32.0%	31.0%	30.3%	29.8%	29.4%	28.9%
Industry, of which:	31.7%	31.3%	32.1%	31.8%	31.4%	30.8%	30.6%	30.6%	30.6%	30.6%
Mining	18.6%	19.1%	20.1%	19.9%	19.5%	19.0%	18.9%	18.9%	18.9%	18.8%
Manufacturing	13.1%	12.2%	12.0%	12.0%	11.9%	11.7%	11.7%	11.7%	11.8%	11.8%
Services	32.6%	35.0%	34.6%	35.4%	36.6%	38.3%	39.1%	39.6%	40.0%	40.5%

TABLE P.2.4: GUYANA NATIONAL ACCOUNTS
LONG TERM GROWTH RATES

	1992	1993	1994	1995	1996	1997	1998	1999	2000	2001
Gross Domestic Product at Market Prices:	7.9%	5.5%	5.0%	4.5%	4.5%	4.5%	4.0%	4.0%	4.0%	4.0%
Agriculture	14.0%	4.5%	3.5%	3.0%	3.0%	2.5%	2.0%	2.0%	2.0%	2.0%
Industry, of which	-5.0%	9.2%	7.3%	3.9%	3.9%	3.9%	3.7%	3.7%	3.7%	3.7%
Manufacturing	5.0%	3.0%	3.0%	4.5%	4.5%	4.5%	4.0%	4.0%	4.0%	4.0%
Mining	-11.0%	13.5%	10.0%	3.5%	3.5%	3.5%	3.5%	3.5%	3.5%	3.5%
Services	3.9%	18.8%	3.7%	6.9%	8.8%	10.9%	6.5%	4.8%	4.9%	4.9%
Imports (GNFS)	18.4%	11.4%	8.0%	5.6%	4.7%	5.1%	3.9%	4.2%	4.0%	3.9%
Exports (GNFS)	28.0%	8.5%	9.5%	7.3%	6.5%	6.8%	5.3%	5.4%	5.2%	5.2%
Total Expenditures	-1.2%	9.6%	3.1%	2.1%	1.8%	1.9%	1.8%	1.9%	1.8%	1.7%
Total Consumption:	0.1%	10.2%	3.2%	2.0%	1.9%	2.2%	2.1%	2.0%	1.7%	1.9%
Government	1.0%	3.5%	3.0%	2.0%	1.5%	1.5%	1.5%	1.5%	1.5%	1.5%
Private	-0.2%	12.5%	3.2%	2.0%	2.0%	2.4%	2.3%	2.2%	1.8%	2.1%
Gross Domestic Investment:	-3.6%	8.4%	3.0%	2.2%	1.6%	1.2%	1.2%	1.6%	1.9%	1.2%
Government /1	36.2%	44.1%	5.3%	2.6%	0.6%	-0.1%	-0.1%	-0.4%	-0.6%	-0.8%
Private Investment /2	-13.8%	-5.9%	1.6%	1.9%	2.2%	2.0%	2.0%	2.8%	3.3%	2.4%

1/ Excludes social sector et al. PSIP expenditures
2/ Includes Public Enterprises

TABLE P.3.1: GUYANA EXTERNAL TRADE
EXPORTS

	1992	1993	1994	1995	1996	1997	1998	1999	2000	2001
Volume Indices 1991=100										
Merchandise Exports:										
Sugar	160.0	152.0	153.5	162.7	170.9	179.4	187.5	195.9	204.4	213.1
Rice	190.0	190.0	203.3	217.5	231.7	246.7	261.5	277.2	293.2	310.0
Timber	115.0	140.3	164.9	181.3	198.6	218.4	235.9	254.8	274.5	295.5
Calcined Bauxite/a	60.0	81.0	103.3	118.8	134.8	152.3	163.0	174.4	186.2	198.5
Dried Bauxite/a	98.5	97.3	97.3	102.1	107.2	112.6	118.2	124.1	130.0	136.2
Gold	165.0	264.0	297.0	323.7	346.4	370.6	392.9	416.4	440.4	465.3
Shrimp	106.0	111.6	116.6	117.8	117.8	117.8	117.8	117.8	117.8	117.8
Molasses	150.0	195.0	204.8	215.0	225.7	237.0	248.9	261.3	273.7	286.0
Spirits	510.0	561.0	589.1	618.5	649.4	681.9	716.0	751.8	787.5	822.9
Other/b	170.0	189.1	273.3	300.6	327.7	357.2	385.7	416.6	447.8	481.4
Total Merchandise Exports (FOB)	132.0	144.2	159.1	171.7	183.6	196.4	207.3	218.8	230.5	242.8
Value Current Prices (US$ millions)										
Merchandise Exports:										
Sugar	133	110	109	115	122	129	136	144	153	163
Rice	33	33	35	39	43	46	50	54	59	64
Timber	5	6	7	8	10	11	12	14	16	18
Calcined Bauxite/a	30	40	51	63	73	85	93	102	112	123
Dried Bauxite/a	25	24	25	28	30	32	35	38	40	44
Gold	32	51	57	65	73	81	90	100	111	123
Shrimp	16	17	19	19	20	21	21	22	23	24
Molasses	0	0	0	0	0	0	0	0	0	0
Spirits	9	10	11	12	13	15	16	17	19	20
Other/b	24	27	40	45	51	58	65	72	80	89
Re-Exports	6	6	6	6	7	7	7	8	8	8
Total Merchandise Exports (FOB)	312	326	362	401	441	485	526	572	621	675

TABLE P.3.2: GUYANA EXTERNAL TRADE
IMPORTS

	1992	1993	1994	1995	1996	1997	1998	1999	2000	2001
Volume Indices 1991=100										
Merchandise Imports:										
Food	139.5	162.5	178.8	191.6	204.1	218.8	230.2	244.0	256.7	270.1
Other Consumption Goods	139.5	162.7	177.2	187.1	198.7	212.3	222.6	235.2	246.6	260.6
Primary Goods' n.e.i.	127.3	150.4	165.9	177.5	187.6	199.5	208.8	220.2	230.5	239.7
Intermediate goods	127.3	150.4	165.9	177.5	187.6	199.5	208.8	220.2	230.5	239.7
Fuel	127.3	150.4	165.9	177.5	187.6	199.5	208.8	220.2	230.5	239.7
Capital Goods	127.3	150.4	165.9	177.5	187.6	199.5	208.8	220.2	230.5	239.7
Total Merchandise Imports (CIF)	117.1	135.8	143.4	150.9	157.5	165.3	171.9	180.4	189.1	198.0
Value Current Prices (US$ millions)										
Merchandise Imports:										
Food	7	8	9	10	11	13	14	15	17	18
Other Consumption Goods	30	36	40	44	49	54	59	65	70	77
Primary Goods	128	151	168	186	208	233	256	283	311	339
Intermediate goods	32	39	44	48	53	59	64	70	76	83
Fuel	96	112	125	138	155	175	192	213	235	256
Capital Goods	121	126	132	139	145	152	159	168	177	185
Total Merchandise Imports (CIF)	286	338	362	392	428	469	509	556	608	663
US$ Prices Indices 1991=100										
Merchandise Export Prices	0.99	0.95	0.95	0.98	1.01	1.04	1.07	1.10	1.13	1.17
Merchandise Import Prices	1.00	1.02	1.03	1.06	1.11	1.16	1.21	1.26	1.31	1.37
Merchandise Terms of Trade	0.99	0.93	0.93	0.92	0.91	0.89	0.88	0.87	0.86	0.85

TABLE P.3.3: GUYANA EXTERNAL TRADE
GROWTH RATES

	1992	1993	1994	1995	1996	1997	1998	1999	2000	2001
Merchandise Exports (% p.a.):										
Sugar	60.0%	-5.0%	1.0%	6.0%	5.0%	5.0%	4.5%	4.5%	4.4%	4.3%
Rice	90.0%	0.0%	7.0%	7.0%	6.5%	6.5%	6.0%	6.0%	5.8%	5.8%
Timber	15.0%	22.0%	17.5%	10.0%	9.5%	10.0%	8.0%	8.0%	7.8%	7.7%
Calcined Bauxite	-40.0%	35.0%	27.5%	15.0%	13.5%	13.0%	7.0%	7.0%	6.8%	6.7%
Dried Bauxite	-1.5%	-1.3%	0.0%	5.0%	5.0%	5.0%	5.0%	5.0%	4.8%	4.8%
Gold	65.0%	60.0%	12.5%	9.0%	7.0%	7.0%	6.0%	6.0%	5.8%	5.7%
Shrimp	6.0%	5.3%	4.5%	1.0%	0.0%	0.0%	0.0%	0.0%	0.0%	0.0%
Molasses	50.0%	30.0%	5.0%	5.0%	5.0%	5.0%	5.0%	5.0%	4.8%	4.5%
Spirits	410.0%	10.0%	5.0%	5.0%	5.0%	5.0%	5.0%	5.0%	4.8%	4.5%
Other Exports	70.0%	11.3%	44.5%	10.0%	9.0%	9.0%	8.0%	8.0%	7.5%	7.5%
Re-Exports	5.0%	3.0%	1.0%	1.0%	1.0%	1.0%	1.0%	1.0%	0.5%	0.5%
Total Merchandise Exports (FOB)	32.0%	9.3%	10.3%	7.9%	6.9%	7.0%	5.5%	5.6%	5.4%	5.3%
Merchandise Imports (% p.a.):										
Food	39.5%	16.7%	8.9%	5.6%	6.2%	6.9%	4.9%	5.7%	4.9%	5.7%
Other Consumer Goods	39.5%	16.5%	10.0%	7.2%	6.5%	7.2%	5.2%	6.0%	5.2%	5.2%
Primary Goods	27.3%	18.1%	10.4%	7.0%	5.7%	6.3%	4.7%	5.5%	4.7%	4.0%
Intermediate goods	39.5%	16.5%	10.0%	7.2%	6.5%	7.2%	5.2%	6.0%	5.2%	4.8%
Fuel	23.7%	18.6%	10.5%	6.9%	5.4%	6.0%	4.5%	5.3%	4.5%	3.7%
Capital Goods	0.0%	0.0%	3.0%	2.2%	1.2%	1.3%	1.2%	1.6%	1.9%	1.2%
Total Merchandise Imports (CIF)	17.1%	15.9%	5.6%	5.2%	4.3%	5.0%	4.0%	4.9%	4.8%	4.7%

TABLE P.3.4: GUYANA EXTERNAL TRADE
BALANCE OF PAYMENTS
(US$ million at current prices)

	1992	1993	1994	1995	1996	1997	1998	1999	2000	2001
A. Exports of GNFS:	351	366	404	445	487	535	580	629	683	741
1. Merchandise (FOB)	312	326	362	401	441	485	526	572	621	675
2. Nonfactor Services	39	40	42	44	46	50	53	57	62	66
B. Imports of GNFS:	344	398	423	455	492	537	578	628	682	740
1. Merchandise (CIF)	286	338	362	392	428	469	509	556	608	663
2. Nonfactor Services	58	60	61	63	65	67	69	72	74	77
C. Resource Balance	7	-32	-19	-10	-5	-1	1	1	1	1
D. Net Factor Income:	-100	-102	-102	-103	-105	-111	-116	-119	-123	-128
1. Factor Receipts	23	28	32	33	35	36	37	38	40	41
2. Factor Payments	123	130	134	137	139	147	153	158	163	169
a. Total Interest due	66	65	72	71	73	73	72	70	69	67
b. Other Factor Payments	58	65	62	66	67	74	81	88	94	102
E. Net Current Transfers:	14	14	15	17	21	26	30	34	38	42
F. Current Account Balance:	-79	-119	-106	-97	-89	-87	-85	-85	-85	-85
G. M&LT Capital Inflows	113	100	93	109	120	120	116	116	115	114
1.a. Direct Investment (Ongoing)	35	34	17	10	10	8	8	8	8	8
1.b. Direct Investment (New)	0	0	7	13	25	30	35	40	45	50
2. Divestment proceeds	10	5	2	6	10	-11	12	13	14	15
3.a. Grants (Ongoing and New)	4	29	8	10	9	2	0	0	0	0
3.b. Grants (Unidentified)	0	5	26	23	23	30	30	30	30	30
4. Net Long-Term Borrowing	-15	27	33	49	43	40	31	25	18	11
a. Disbursements	54	79	75	80	75	67	58	77	123	123
o.w. (Ongoing and Identified)	54	60	58	66	51	47	39	27	16	7
(not yet identified)	0	19	16	15	24	19	19	49	108	116
b. Repayments	70	53	43	32	33	27	27	52	106	110
H. Adjustment to Scheduled Debt Service	10	15	43	20	0	0	0	0	0	0
1. Interest Not Paid	0	10	30	17	0	0	0	0	0	0
2. Principal Not Paid	0	5	13	3	0	0	0	0	0	0
3. Prepayments of Principal/Interest	10	0	0	0	0	0	0	0	0	0
I. Total Other Items (net):	5	0	0	0	0	0	0	0	0	0
1. Net Short-Term (ST) Capital n.e.i.	0	0	0	0	0	0	0	0	0	0
2. Errors and Omissions	5	0	0	0	0	0	0	0	0	0
J. Change in Net Reserves:	-49	4	-30	-33	-31	-34	-32	-31	-30	-30
[-indicates increase]										
1. Net Credit from the IMF	25	9	-22	-22	-23	-25	-23	-23	-22	-21
2. Reserve Changes n.e.i.	-74	-4	-8	-11	-7	-8	-9	-8	-8	-9

TABLE P.4.1: GUYANA GOVERNMENT BUDGET
(G$ million)

	1992	1993	1994	1995	1996	1997	1998	1999	2000	2001
Direct Taxes	5904	6120	6644	7452	8345	9226	9829	10785	11161	12246
Indirect Taxes	10661	11209	12492	13659	14521	15119	16264	17845	19579	21482
Non-Tax Receipts	885	1396	1583	1485	1637	1212	1005	746	818	898
Total Current Revenues	17450	18725	20718	22596	24503	25558	27098	29375	31559	34626
Interest on External Debt	6801	7208	8614	9263	9900	10185	10433	10533	10582	10529
Interest on Monetary Credit	2198	1293	1010	479	445	402	306	174	73	41
Interest on Domestic Debt	2739	2805	2295	1189	1150	1287	1476	1741	1982	2197
Current Transfers to PE	1440	732	0	0	0	0	0	0	0	0
Subsidies	2504	3164	3284	3464	3620	3783	3953	4131	4317	4511
Consumption	6889	6889	7365	7925	8643	9447	10337	11423	12619	13920
Total Current Expenditures	21255	21494	22716	22477	23924	25280	26690	28198	29779	31414
Current Account Balance	-3804	-2769	-1997	119	579	278	408	1177	1780	3212
Capital Revenues	1309	625	282	878	1492	1673	1860	2054	2255	2462
Capital Transfers	0	0	0	0	0	0	0	0	0	0
Capital Expenditures	3292	2672	4068	7415	8033	7191	6305	6189	6075	5966
Central Government Investment	3292	5218	5935	6488	6884	7254	7644	8030	8419	8808
Total Capital Expenditures	3292	7890	10003	13903	14917	14445	13949	14219	14494	14774
Total Deficit Financing	-5788	-10034	-11718	-12905	-12846	-12495	-11682	-10988	-10459	-9099
External Capital Grants	502	4524	4797	4683	4773	4790	4650	4740	4831	4925
External Borrowing (net)	-943	1850	2785	5369	3368	3593	2362	-3322	-13847	-16474
Banking System Credit (net)	-1270	-543	-1692	-819	-538	-1204	-1656	-1251	-412	-51
Other Domestic Borrowing (net)	6377	-334	-2515	-1468	1712	2354	3323	3010	2679	1880
Memorandum Item:										
Primary Current Account Balance	7933	8537	9922	11050	12075	12153	12623	13626	14417	15978

TABLE P.5.1: GUYANA MONEY AND CREDIT
(G$ million)

	1992	1993	1994	1995	1996	1997	1998	1999	2000	2001
A. Annual Flows:										
Gross International Reserves	9864	3022	2615	2535	1805	2009	2110	2122	2223	2328
Net Domestic Credit	691	1570	533	702	857	238	355	1015	1903	2504
To Government Budget /1	-1270	-543	-1692	-819	-538	-1204	-1656	-1251	-412	-51
To Private Sector /1	1961	2113	2225	1520	1395	1441	2010	2266	2315	2555
Total Assets and Liabilities	10555	4592	3148	3236	2662	2247	2465	3138	4127	4832
Money and Quasimoney	9826	3685	4379	4400	3951	5275	5693	6395	7188	7765
Net Other Liabilities	729	907	-1231	-1164	-1289	-3028	-3228	-3258	-3061	-2933
B. End of Year Stocks:										
Net International Reserves	27398	30420	33035	35570	37375	39384	41494	43616	45840	48168
Net Domestic Credit	13099	14669	15203	15905	16762	16999	17354	18370	20273	22777
To Government Budget	8619	8077	6385	5567	5029	3825	2169	918	507	456
To Private Sector /1	4480	6593	8818	10338	11733	13174	15185	17451	19766	22321
Total Assets and Liabilities	40498	45090	48238	51475	54137	56383	58848	61986	66113	70945
Money and Quasimoney	26092	29777	34156	38556	42507	47782	53475	59870	67058	74823
Net Other Liabilities	14406	15313	14082	12918	11630	8601	5373	2116	-945	-3878
C. Offsets to Expansion of MQM:										
Increase in Money and Quasimoney (in %)	100.0%	100.0%	100.0%	100.0%	100.0%	100.0%	100.0%	100.0%	100.0%	100.0%
Net Foreign Assets	99.9%	59.0%	49.5%	54.3%	48.2%	42.5%	41.3%	37.0%	33.5%	33.0%
Net Domestic Credit	7.0%	42.6%	12.2%	15.9%	21.7%	4.5%	6.2%	15.9%	26.5%	32.2%
To Government Budget	-12.9%	-14.7%	-38.6%	-18.6%	-13.6%	-22.8%	-29.1%	-19.6%	-5.7%	-0.7%
To Other Official Entities	-9.1%	-20.8%	-24.3%	-41.2%	-82.7%	-101.6%	-155.4%	-172.3%	-188.9%	-202.5%
To Private Sector	29.0%	78.1%	75.1%	75.8%	118.0%	128.9%	190.7%	207.7%	221.1%	235.4%
Net Other Liabilities	32.6%	126.8%	16.6%	-16.7%	-38.4%	-5.9%	1.5%	-0.2%	-1.7%	-2.9%
D. Memorandum Items:										
Net International Reserves (in millions of US$)										
Change during the year(increase = [-])	-74	-4	-8	-11	-7	-8	-9	-8	-8	-9
Stock at the end-of-year	217	222	230	241	248	257	265	273	282	291

/1 Includes public enterprises

TABLE P.6.1: GUYANA PRIVATE SECTOR
(G$ million)

	1992	1993	1994	1995	1996	1997	1998	1999	2000	2001
Current Account										
Factor Income	22646	27443	31340	35123	39260	44172	48791	53534	58737	64446
Interest Income	5466	5725	5053	3034	3382	3748	4242	4837	5448	6078
Dividend Income	-507	-927	-573	263	305	272	281	289	154	128
Current Transfers from Central Governme	2504	3164	3284	3464	3620	3783	3953	4131	4317	4511
Current Transfers from ROW	1883	2062	2257	2576	3282	4105	4805	5550	6281	7059
Less Direct Taxes	5904	6120	6644	7452	8345	9226	9829	10785	11161	12246
Less Indirect Taxes	10661	11209	12492	13659	14521	15119	16264	17845	19579	21482
Less Non-Tax Budgetary Receipts	885	1396	1583	1485	1637	1212	1005	746	818	898
Less Interest Expenditures	5592	6495	5932	6041	5929	6696	7301	7924	8408	9184
Less DFI Profits Paid to ROW	171	506	1018	1449	1866	2381	2957	3626	4392	5259
Total Disposable Income	19438	22949	26185	28032	32072	36565	40979	45240	50157	54635
Uses of Disposable Income:										
Private Consumption	14049	22270	23858	25677	28131	31036	34238	38096	42200	46817
Private Savings	5390	679	2327	2355	3940	5529	6741	7144	7957	7818
Capital Account										
Total Capital Sources:	16463	3731	5896	8505	13002	15131	19055	20977	23250	24074
Private Saving	5390	679	2327	2355	3940	5529	6741	7144	7957	7818
Direct Foreign Investment	4393	4524	3386	3293	5221	5778	6665	7583	8535	9521
LT Borrowing from ROW (net)	-1107	-846	-411	-224	-209	-65	-64	-65	-66	-66
Other LT Inflows from ROW (net)	10490	0	0	0	0	0	0	0	0	0
Capital Transfers	0	2672	4068	7415	8033	7191	6305	6189	6075	5966
Monetary System Net Borrowing	1961	2113	2225	1520	1395	1441	2010	2266	2315	2555
Total Capital Uses:	21126	9143	11595	14359	18380	19875	21657	23118	24816	25793
Gross Domestic Investment	8212	8503	9331	10127	10918	11746	12641	13713	14949	16148
Loans to Government	6377	-334	-2515	-1468	1712	2354	3323	3010	2679	1880
Money and Quasimoney	9826	3685	4379	4400	3951	5275	5693	6395	7188	7765

Distributors of World Bank Publications

ARGENTINA
Carlos Hirsch, SRL
Galeria Guemes
Florida 165, 4th Floor-Ofc. 453/465
1333 Buenos Aires

**AUSTRALIA, PAPUA NEW GUINEA,
FIJI, SOLOMON ISLANDS,
VANUATU, AND WESTERN SAMOA**
D.A. Information Services
648 Whitehorse Road
Mitcham 3132
Victoria

AUSTRIA
Gerold and Co.
Graben 31
A-1011 Wien

BANGLADESH
Micro Industries Development
Assistance Society (MIDAS)
House 5, Road 16
Dhanmondi R/Area
Dhaka 1209

   Branch offices:
   Pine View, 1st Floor
   100 Agrabad Commercial Area
   Chittagong 4100

   76, K.D.A. Avenue
   Kulna 9100

BELGIUM
Jean De Lannoy
Av. du Roi 202
1060 Brussels

CANADA
Le Diffuseur
C.P. 85, 1501B rue Ampère
Boucherville, Québec
J4B 5E6

CHILE
Invertec IGT S.A.
Americo Vespucio Norte 1165
Santiago

CHINA
China Financial & Economic
Publishing House
8, Da Fo Si Dong Jie
Beijing

COLOMBIA
Infoenlace Ltda.
Apartado Aereo 34270
Bogota D.E.

COTE D'IVOIRE
Centre d'Edition et de Diffusion
Africaines (CEDA)
04 B.P. 541
Abidjan 04 Plateau

CYPRUS
Center of Applied Research
Cyprus College
6, Diogenes Street, Engomi
P.O. Box 2006
Nicosia

DENMARK
SamfundsLitteratur
Rosenoerns Allé 11
DK-1970 Frederiksberg C

DOMINICAN REPUBLIC
Editora Taller, C. por A.
Restauración e Isabel la Católica 309
Apartado de Correos 2190 Z-1
Santo Domingo

EGYPT, ARAB REPUBLIC OF
Al Ahram
Al Galaa Street
Cairo

The Middle East Observer
41, Sherif Street
Cairo

FINLAND
Akateeminen Kirjakauppa
P.O. Box 128
SF-00101 Helsinki 10

FRANCE
World Bank Publications
66, avenue d'Iéna
75116 Paris

GERMANY
UNO-Verlag
Poppelsdorfer Allee 55
D-5300 Bonn 1

HONG KONG, MACAO
Asia 2000 Ltd.
46-48 Wyndham Street
Winning Centre
2nd Floor
Central Hong Kong

INDIA
Allied Publishers Private Ltd.
751 Mount Road
Madras - 600 002

   Branch offices:
   15 J.N. Heredia Marg
   Ballard Estate
   Bombay - 400 038

   13/14 Asaf Ali Road
   New Delhi - 110 002

   17 Chittaranjan Avenue
   Calcutta - 700 072

   Jayadeva Hostel Building
   5th Main Road, Gandhinagar
   Bangalore - 560 009

   3-5-1129 Kachiguda
   Cross Road
   Hyderabad - 500 027

   Prarthana Flats, 2nd Floor
   Near Thakore Baug, Navrangpura
   Ahmedabad - 380 009

   Patiala House
   16-A Ashok Marg
   Lucknow - 226 001

   Central Bazaar Road
   60 Bajaj Nagar
   Nagpur 440 010

INDONESIA
Pt. Indira Limited
Jalan Borobudur 20
P.O. Box 181
Jakarta 10320

IRELAND
Government Supplies Agency
4-5 Harcourt Road
Dublin 2

ISRAEL
Yozmot Literature Ltd.
P.O. Box 56055
Tel Aviv 61560

ITALY
Licosa Commissionaria Sansoni SPA
Via Duca Di Calabria, 1/1
Casella Postale 552
50125 Firenze

JAPAN
Eastern Book Service
Hongo 3-Chome, Bunkyo-ku 113
Tokyo

KENYA
Africa Book Service (E.A.) Ltd.
Quaran House, Mfangano Stree
P.O. Box 45245
Nairobi

KOREA, REPUBLIC OF
Pan Korea Book Corporation
P.O. Box 101, Kwangwhamun
Seoul

MALAYSIA
University of Malaya Cooperati√e
Bookshop, Limited
P.O. Box 1127, Jalan Pantai Barı
59700 Kuala Lumpur

MEXICO
INFOTEC
Apartado Postal 22-860
14060 Tlalpan, Mexico D.F.

NETHERLANDS
De Lindeboom/InOr-Publikatie s
P.O. Box 202
7480 AE Haaksbergen

NEW ZEALAND
EBSCO NZ Ltd.
Private Mail Bag 99914
New Market
Auckland

NIGERIA
University Press Limited
Three Crowns Building Jericho
Private Mail Bag 5095
Ibadan

NORWAY
Narvesen Information Center
Book Department
P.O. Box 6125 Etterstad
N-0602 Oslo 6

PAKISTAN
Mirza Book Agency
65, Shahrah-e-Quaid-e-Azam
P.O. Box No. 729
Lahore 54000

PERU
Editorial Desarrollo SA
Apartado 3824
Lima 1

PHILIPPINES
International Book Center
Suite 1703, Cityland 10
Condominium Tower 1
Ayala Avenue, H.V. dela
Costa Extension
Makati, Metro Manila

POLAND
International Publishing Service
Ul. Piekna 31/37
00-677 Warzawa

   For subscription orders:
   IPS Journals
   Ul. Okrezna 3
   02-916 Warszawa

PORTUGAL
Livraria Portugal
Rua Do Carmo 70-74
1200 Lisbon

SAUDI ARABIA, QATAR
Jarir Book Store
P.O. Box 3196
Riyadh 11471

**SINGAPORE, TAIWAN,
MYANMAR, BRUNEI**
Information Publications
Private, Ltd.
Golden Wheel Building
41, Kallang Pudding, #04-03
Singapore 1334

SOUTH AFRICA, BOTSWANA
For single titles:
Oxford University Press
Southern Africa
P.O. Box 1141
Cape Town 8000

For subscription orders:
International Subscription Service
P.O. Box 41095
Craighall
Johannesburg 2024

SPAIN
Mundi-Prensa Libros, S.A.
Castello 37
28001 Madrid

Librería Internacional AEDOS
Consell de Cent, 391
08009 Barcelona

SRI LANKA AND THE MALDIVES
Lake House Bookshop
P.O. Box 244
100, Sir Chittampalam A.
Gardiner Mawatha
Colombo 2

SWEDEN
For single titles:
Fritzes Fackboksforetaget
Regeringsgatan 12, Box 16356
S-103 27 Stockholm

For subscription orders:
Wennergren-Williams AB
P. O. Box 1305
S-171 25 Solna

SWITZERLAND
For single titles:
Librairie Payot
Case postale 3212
CH 1002 Lausanne

For subscription orders:
Librairie Payot
Service des Abonnements
Case postale 3312
CH 1002 Lausanne

THAILAND
Central Department Store
306 Silom Road
Bangkok

**TRINIDAD & TOBAGO, ANTIGUA
BARBUDA, BARBADOS,
DOMINICA, GRENADA, GUYANA,
JAMAICA, MONTSERRAT, ST.
KITTS & NEVIS, ST. LUCIA,
ST. VINCENT & GRENADINES**
Systematics Studies Unit
#9 Watts Street
Curepe
Trinidad, West Indies

TURKEY
Infotel
Narlabahçe Sok. No. 15
Cagaloglu
Istanbul

UNITED KINGDOM
Microinfo Ltd.
P.O. Box 3
Alton, Hampshire GU34 2PG
England

VENEZUELA
Libreria del Este
Aptdo. 60.337
Caracas 1060-A

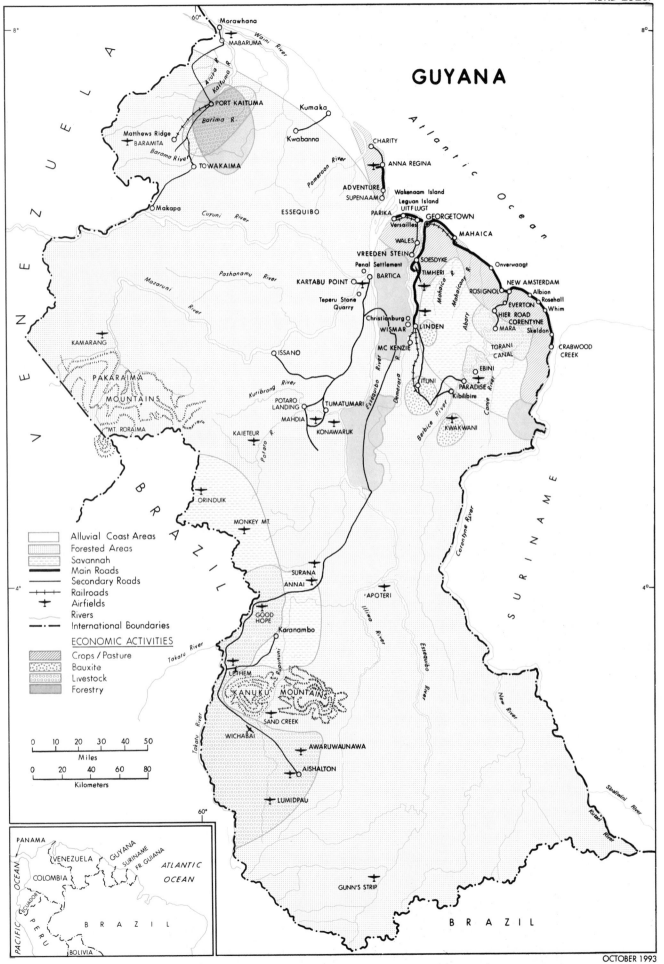

IBRD 25237

GUYANA

Legend:

- Alluvial Coast Areas
- Forested Areas
- Savannah
- Main Roads
- Secondary Roads
- Railroads
- Airfields
- Rivers
- International Boundaries

ECONOMIC ACTIVITIES
- Crops / Pasture
- Bauxite
- Livestock
- Forestry

Miles
0 10 20 30 40 50

Kilometers
0 20 40 60 80

OCTOBER 1993

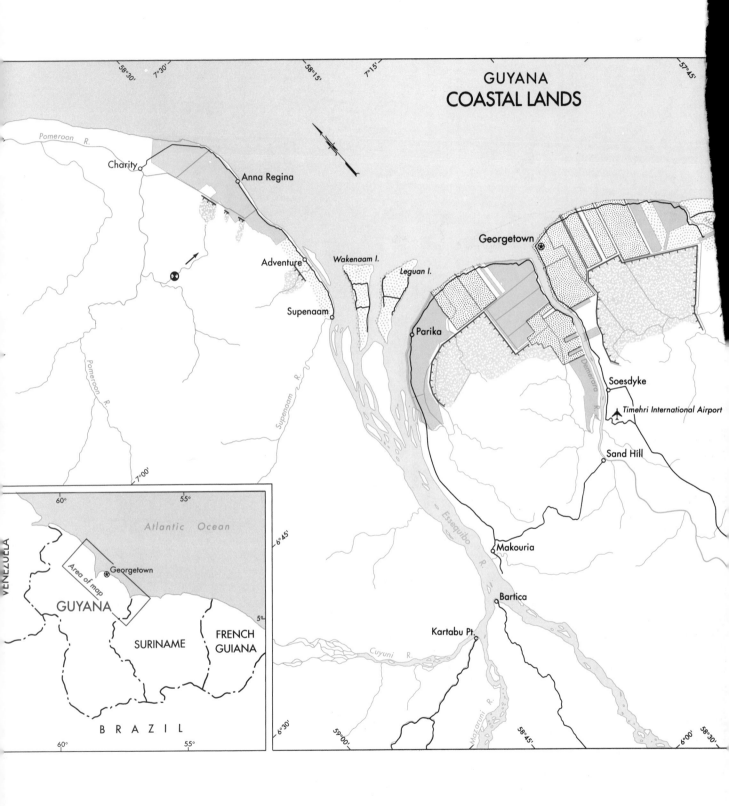

GUYANA
COASTAL LANDS

Charity

Anna Regina

Pomeroon R.

Georgetown

Adventure

Wakenaam I.

Leguan I.

Supenaam

Parika

Soesdyke

Timehri International Airport

Sand Hill

Makouria

Bartica

Kartabu Pt.

Pomeroon R.

Supenaam R.

Essequibo R.

Demerara R.

Cuyuni R.

Mazaruni R.

VENEZUELA

Atlantic Ocean

Area of map

Georgetown

GUYANA

SURINAME

FRENCH GUIANA

B R A Z I L

Atlantic Ocean

SURINAME

Rossignol

New Amsterdam

Skeldon

Mahaicony R.

Abary R.

Berbice R.

Canje R.

Corentyne R.

Mahaica R.

Mara

Berbice R.

SUGAR ESTATES

DECLARED DRAINAGE AND IRRIGATION AREAS

PARTIAL DRAINAGE AND IRRIGATION AREAS

NATIONAL CAPITAL

TOWNS

ROADS

MAIN CANALS

DIKE AND WATER CONSERVANCY:

EXISTING

FUTURE

PUMPING STATIONS:

EXISTING

FUTURE

RIVERS

INTERNATIONAL BOUNDARIES

Demerara R.

Mackenzie

0   10   20   30 MILES

6°45'   57°30'   6°30'   57°15'   6°15'   57°00'   6°00'

5°45'

57°30'

58°15'   58°00'   5°30'

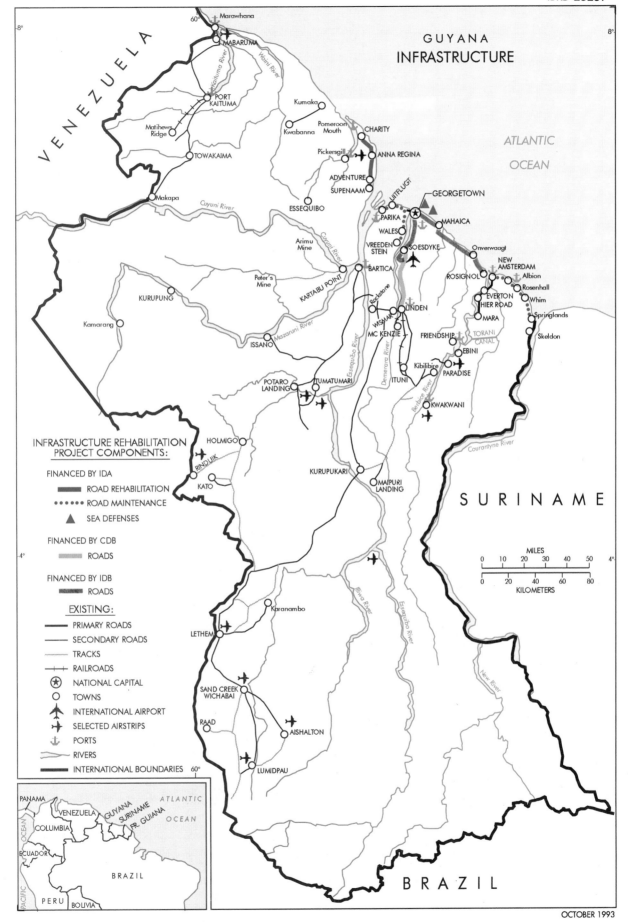

IBRD 25239

GUYANA
INFRASTRUCTURE

ATLANTIC
OCEAN

VENEZUELA

SURINAME

BRAZIL

INFRASTRUCTURE REHABILITATION
PROJECT COMPONENTS:

FINANCED BY IDA
━━━ ROAD REHABILITATION
•••••• ROAD MAINTENANCE
▲ SEA DEFENSES

FINANCED BY CDB
▨▨▨ ROADS

FINANCED BY IDB
▨▨▨ ROADS

EXISTING:
━━━ PRIMARY ROADS
─── SECONDARY ROADS
········ TRACKS
┼┼┼ RAILROADS
✪ NATIONAL CAPITAL
○ TOWNS
✈ INTERNATIONAL AIRPORT
✈ SELECTED AIRSTRIPS
⚓ PORTS
～ RIVERS
━━━ INTERNATIONAL BOUNDARIES

MILES
0 10 20 30 40 50
0 20 40 60 80
KILOMETERS

Marawhana
MABARUMA
PORT KAITUMA
Matthews Ridge
Kumaka
Kwabanna
Pomeroon Mouth
CHARITY
TOWAKAIMA
Pickersgill
ANNA REGINA
ADVENTURE
SUPENAAM
Makapa
Cuyuni River
ESSEQUIBO
UITVLUGT
GEORGETOWN
PARIKA
MAHAICA
WALES
Arimu Mine
VREEDEN STEIN
SOESDYKE
Onverwaagt
NEW AMSTERDAM
Peter's Mine
BARTICA
ROSIGNOL
Albion
Rosenhall
KARTABU POINT
Rockstone
EVERTON
HIER ROAD
Whim
KURUPUNG
Mazaruni River
LINDEN
MARA
Springlands
WISMAR
Skeldon
Kamarang
MC KENZIE
FRIENDSHIP
TORANI CANAL
ISSANO
Demerara River
EBINI
Kibilibire
PARADISE
POTARO LANDING
ITUMATUMARI
ITUNI
HOLMIGO
KWAKWANI
RINDUIK
Berbice River
KATO
KURUPUKARI
MAIPURI LANDING
Courantyne River
Karanambo
Iliwa River
LETHEM
New River
Essequibo River
SAND CREEK
WICHABAI
RAAD
AISHALTON
LUMIDPAU

PANAMA
VENEZUELA
GUYANA
SURINAME
FR. GUIANA
ATLANTIC
OCEAN
COLUMBIA
ECUADOR
BRAZIL
PERU
BOLIVIA

OCTOBER 1993